William Hodgson

Select Historical Memoirs of the Religious Society of Friends,

Commonly Called Quakers

William Hodgson

Select Historical Memoirs of the Religious Society of Friends, Commonly Called Quakers

ISBN/EAN: 9783337408985

Printed in Europe, USA, Canada, Australia, Japan

Cover: Foto ©Lupo / pixelio.de

More available books at **www.hansebooks.com**

SELECT HISTORICAL MEMOIRS

OF THE

RELIGIOUS SOCIETY OF FRIENDS,

COMMONLY CALLED

QUAKERS;

BEING

A SUCCINCT ACCOUNT OF THEIR CHARACTER AND COURSE DURING THE SEVENTEENTH AND EIGHTEENTH CENTURIES.

BY

WILLIAM HODGSON.

"We are nothing; Christ is all."—GEO. FOX.

THIRD EDITION.

PREFATORY REMARKS.

THERE are many thousands of the descendants of Friends in the United States and in Great Britain, who know very little of the true character or history of their forefathers as a church of Christ, and do not by any means realize the value of those pure principles of primitive Christianity, which the "people called Quakers," after a long night of darkness and apostasy, and the dawning of a better day, was raised up to revive in the view of the various denominations of professing Christians, and to testify to ages yet to come. A considerable proportion of these, doubtless, cherish a respect for the memory of their ancestors, and would willingly, if they could readily, know more than it has fallen to their lot to know, of the grounds of their remarkable conscientious position, for which they were made willing to suffer the loss of property, liberty, reputation, and all the usual comforts of life, and even life itself.

The author of the following work has had this class very much in view in preparing a second edition; and should any among them be brought through its means to a deep and heartfelt appreciation of the gospel truths advocated by those servants of the Lord alluded to in its pages, so as not only to assent to the truth of their testimony, but to be made willing to be followers of them as they followed Christ, and thus, through the Lord's mercy in Christ Jesus, obtain the end of their faith, even the salvation of their souls, he would be amply repaid for the little he may have contributed to so happy a result.

CONTENTS.

CHAPTER I.

Introductory remarks on the character of the primitive Christian Church, and subsequent corruptions, — 11

CHAPTER II.

Early life and convincement of George Fox — his call to the ministry — and imprisonment — called a Quaker, ... 21

CHAPTER III.

Account of some of the doctrines and testimonies promulgated by the founders of the Society of Friends, ... 34

CHAPTER IV.

Convincement of William Dewsbury — and Edward Burrough, ... 43

CHAPTER V.

Convincement of Thomas Thompson — and further transactions of George Fox, ... 51

CHAPTER VI.

Convincement of Francis Howgill — George Whitehead — and Judge Fell's family — George Fox still persecuted — first convincements in London, 59

CHAPTER VII.

Rise of the Society in Ireland — William Edmundson, ... 71

CHAPTER VIII.

Convincement of Humphrey Bache, . . . 84

CHAPTER IX.

Account of James Parnell — he dies in prison — George Fox imprisoned in Launceston jail, . . 91

CHAPTER X.

The convincement, ministry, and fall of James Nayler — his repentance, and death, ... 104

CHAPTER XI.

First visits of Friends to America — cruel persecutions in New England, &c., ... 115

CHAPTER XII.

Martyrdom of William Robinson, Marmaduke Stevenson, Mary Dyer, and William Leddra — George Fox imprisoned in Scarborough Castle, . . 129

CHAPTER XIII.

Convincement of Richard Davies, ... 138

CHAPTER XIV.

George Robinson goes to Jerusalem, and Mary Fisher to Turkey, ... 153

CHAPTER XV.

The sufferings of Catharine Evans and Sarah Cheevers in the inquisition at Malta — and of John Philly and William Moore, in Hungary, &c., . 156

CHAPTER XVI.

Edward Burrough and Richard Hubberthorn, being violently seized at the Bull-and-Mouth Meeting, die in prison, ... 164

CHAPTER XVII.

The sufferings of Elizabeth Hooton and others in New England, ... 170

CHAPTER XVIII.

The extravagancies of John Perrot, . . . 175

CHAPTER XIX.

Rise of the Society in Scotland, ... 179

CHAPTER XX.

Account of Thomas Lurting and the Algerine pirates, ... 191

CHAPTER XXI.

Death of Samuel Fisher — account of his convincement, &c., ... 199

CHAPTER XXII.

The sufferings of Richard Seller, for his testimony against war, on board the flag-ship "Royal Prince," 203

CHAPTER XXIII.

William Penn's early life, and convincement, . . 211

CHAPTER XXIV.

Remarkable conversion of a woman imprisoned for murder — death of Francis Howgill in prison, . 218

CHAPTER XXV.

Meetings for discipline instituted in the Society— George Fox goes to America—and returning, is imprisoned at Worcester, ... 223

CHAPTER XXVI.

The trial of William Penn and William Mead at the Old Bailey—destruction of Friends' meeting-houses, ... 235

CHAPTER XXVII.

The separation of Wilkinson and Story—and the heresy of Jeffery Bullock, ... 244

CHAPTER XXVIII.

William Penn's travels in Holland and Germany, . 249

CHAPTER XXIX.

Account of Isaac Penington, ... 258

CHAPTER XXX.

Pennsylvania granted to William Penn—persecution at Bristol, ... 266

CHAPTER XXXI.

The deaths of David and Robert Barclay, and George Fox, ... 274

CHAPTER XXXII.

The persecution of Friends during the civil wars in Ireland, in the reign of James II., . . . 286

CHAPTER XXXIII.

Account of Thomas Story's convincement, . . 299

CHAPTER XXXIV.

The labors of Joseph Pike and others in Ireland, for a reformation from the spirit and habits of the world, ... 305

CHAPTER XXXV.

The apostasy of George Keith, ... 310

CHAPTER XXXVI.

Peter Gardiner's journey to Scotland, and death, . 318

CHAPTER XXXVII.

Samuel Bownas comes forth in the ministry — account of his early life — Friends' peaceable testimony maintained during the Indian wars in New England, ... 326

CHAPTER XXXVIII.

Shipwreck and remarkable preservation of Susanna Morris — examples of zeal and simplicity in Ireland, ... 335

CHAPTER XXXIX.

The trials to which Friends were subjected during the American revolutionary war, ... 340

CHAPTER XL.

Rise and progress of the Society's testimony against Slavery, ... 350

CHAPTER XLI.

Account of John Woolman, ... 359

CHAPTER XLII.

Account of John Churchman, ... 371

CHAPTER XLIII.

The sufferings of Friends in Ireland, during the rebellion of 1798, for their faithful adherence to the principles of peace, ... 377

CHAPTER XLIV.

The separation in Ireland in 1799, &c., . . . 391

CHAPTER XLV.

Thomas Shillitoe's early life and convincement — his remarkable gospel labors in Ireland, &c., . 397

Conclusion, ... 410

HISTORICAL MEMOIRS

OF THE

RELIGIOUS SOCIETY OF FRIENDS.

CHAPTER I.

INTRODUCTORY REMARKS ON THE CHARACTER OF THE PRIMITIVE CHRISTIAN CHURCH, AND SUBSEQUENT CORRUPTIONS.

THE religion instituted by our Lord and Saviour Jesus Christ, and spread abroad in the world by his blessed Spirit accompanying the labors of his inspired apostles, was beautiful for its simplicity and adaptation to man's spiritual need. The preceding Mosaic dispensation, while it enjoined devotion of heart to the Creator, according to the measure of light vouchsafed, was nevertheless characterized by a multitude of outward observances, suited to the state of the people, which did not make the comers thereunto perfect, yet pointed to the substance of that which was to follow. But when our blessed Lord, in his coming, sufferings and death, had fulfilled and abrogated the ceremonial requirements of the law, he introduced the more glorious dispensation of the Gospel, in which life and immortality, and the mysteries of redeeming love, were brought to light. The former dispensation was outward and typical, the latter inward and spiritual; in which, through the regenerating power of divine grace, the heart was to be made the temple of the Holy Ghost. Christ declared himself to be "the way, the truth and the life;" that no man can come to the Father but by Him; and that "except a man be born again, he cannot see the kingdom of God." It was not in outward appearance only, that a change was to be made in the natural man; but the axe was to be laid to the root of the tree, and every tree that bringeth not forth good fruit, was to be hewn down and cast into the fire.

The lives of his followers were to be characterized by holiness, and watchfulness unto prayer; every individual seeking a knowledge of God for himself, instead of depending on a class of men set apart for the purpose of exclusively conducting the affairs of religion, as had prevailed among the heathen, and even in degree among the Jews themselves. This knowledge of God and of the way of life was to be obtained by the repenting sinner, through inward waiting of the soul on the Lord himself in humility and sincerity; through submission to the cleansing operations of the "Word quick and powerful, and sharper than any two-edged sword, piercing to the dividing asunder of soul and spirit;" and through unreserved obedience to the secret manifestations of the Divine Spirit, which was promised "to lead into all truth." The disciples were distinctly informed by the Saviour, that He was "the Light of the world," and that He who was with them in that prepared body, should henceforth be *in* them, by his blessed Spirit. To this Light therefore, even Christ in them the hope of Glory, the primitive Christians looked, as the great Guide of life. This it was that was to "sanctify them wholly;" so that all were to be "kings and priests unto God," and to seek to be made "perfect as the Father who is in Heaven is perfect."

The followers of our crucified Lord, desirous of avoiding every thing that might minister to the natural vanity of the human heart, and thus imperceptibly lead away from that humility which was known to be an essential requisite to the character of a true Christian, renounced the vanities of the world, and set an example of simplicity in life and conduct. Not that they affected singularity, as the ascetics, hermits and monks afterwards did; but remembering the declaration of the Saviour, "whosoever doth not bear his cross, and come after me, cannot be my disciple," they dared not to sanction in their own practice any incentives to a worldly spirit, or the gratification of "the lust of the eye and the pride of life."

Neither dared they, in defiance of the law of universal love taught them by their adorable Redeemer, to cherish in their hearts those dispositions which lead man to destroy his fellow-man, either in revenge or in self-preservation. War they knew to be prohibited by the whole tenor of "the gospel of peace," no less than by the positive injunctions of Him who said, "love your enemies—do good to them that hate you, and pray for them that despitefully use you and persecute you." Many instances of deep suffering proved the hold which this peaceful principle had on the minds of the early believers. We need hardly cite the well known example of the martyr Maximilian, who, even in the third century, nobly declared in the face of death, that "*because he was a Christian*" he could not take arms nor engage in war, even though at the command of the Roman proconsul; for the refusal to fight was generally acknowledged to be a distinguishing feature of the Christian profession.*

Their outward callings were to be such as should not clash with their testimony to purity and holiness and self-denial; nor were they at liberty, like the people of the heathen world around them, to please themselves with frivo-

---

* Tertullian (*De Coronâ militis*) says emphatically, "Will the child of peace engage in battle, to whom it is not becoming even to dispute with his fellow-men at law?"—"Faith admits not the plea of necessity."

lous amusements, calculated to drown serious thought, and call away their attention from the one great business of this life, a preparation for the life to come. Hence the primitive Christians could not join their fellow-men in attending theatrical entertainments; and a modern European author* declares: "It was no uncommon mark, by which a man's conversion to Christianity was ascertained, that he wholly withdrew from the theatre"—where "much took place which violated the moral feelings and decencies of Christians; and even where this was not the case, yet even then the hour-long pursuit of idle and vain objects—the unholy spirit which reigned in these assemblies—the wild uproar of the collected multitude, seemed hardly to suit the holy seriousness of the Christian's priestly character."

All oaths they declined, as positively forbidden by Christ and his apostle James, and confined themselves to a simple affirmation or denial.

Sincerity and Truth were indeed stamped upon their character. Their lives and actions were to be examples of the one, and all their words of the other. Hence they could not address their fellow-man in the plural number, as if he were more than a common man like themselves; a practice which then began to prevail, in flattery towards the emperors, and soon rapidly spread to other men who desired the honor or deference of their supposed dependents.

The church was the community of the faithful disciples of Christ, the world over—and *a church* was a collection of these disciples wherever assembled, under the presidency of Christ their holy head, owning no other, waiting for the help and guidance of His blessed Spirit, and moving only according to the pointings of His heavenly finger. These, being

---

* Neander, of Berlin, author of a "History of the Christian Religion and Church." See also Tertullian, "De Spectaculis;" and Cyprian, Ep. vi. ad Eucratium.

truly gathered in His name, knew Him to be "in the midst of them."

Their worship was to be spiritual—"in spirit and in truth." The preaching of the gospel was to be "not in the words which man's wisdom teacheth, but which the Holy Ghost teacheth," and "in demonstration of the Spirit and of power." As it was to be "freely received" from Him who ascended up on high and "gave gifts unto men," so it was to be freely dispensed to the people, without any pecuniary consideration, and in simple reliance on the openings of the divine gift from time to time. It was not to be dependent on school learning for its qualification, nor on the will of man for its appointment; but the preacher of the gospel was to be "called of God as was Aaron;" and, whether male or female, was to "minister in the ability which God giveth." A state of silent waiting before the Lord was evidently the right posture of mind in which his poor and dependent creatures should appear before Him, and essential to the performance of divine worship. There can be no question that their devotional exercises were of the most simple nature, consisting primarily of this waiting together on the God of their lives, and secondly of prayer and praise to the author of all good, and preaching the gospel of the kingdom, for the edification of the churches or the conversion of men. And that these exercises were extempore— without previous preparation—there never has been a doubt.

Equally certain is it, that those who were exercised among them as pastors, teachers or apostles, claimed no salary or emolument as the price of their services; but generally obtained their temporal subsistence by their own exertions, in common with their brethren; though when actually prevented from attending to their outward affairs, by travelling in the service of the Gospel, they considered themselves at liberty to partake of the hospitality of the churches, freely offered for their accommodation.

For a time, the church continued practically to carry out these principles; and some of them were even for several ages generally acknowledged. But a change came gradually over this pure and simple state. Not that the system of religion instituted by the divine author of Christianity was less calculated in its simple form for an advanced state of civilization than for the condition of the world when the Son of God appeared in the prepared body. A most admirable feature of genuine Christianity is its perfect adaptation to man in every state of mental advancement, and in all possible variety of outward circumstances. But man's natural, unregenerate will is ever seeking an *easier* way to the kingdom of heaven than the way of the cross and of unreserved obedience to the Light of Christ shining in the heart. And as the community of professing Christians became more and more composed in part of individuals who had received their profession by birth, and not by the thorough heart-searching work of conversion, this feature of seeking an easier way, rapidly gained ground; and the life of religion being much lost, form usurped the place of power.

We have no means of ascertaining at the present day, at what time the system of hiring the services of preachers crept into the church; but there is reason to believe that it commenced at an early date after the decease of the apostles, and of those who had enjoyed the privilege of personal association with them. The necessity for *all* to be "kings and priests unto God," in all holiness and spiritual conversation, was gladly forgotten by the seekers after ease; and it was found much more agreeable to the carnal mind and inclinations, to fall back upon the old practice of a priesthood, and depend on the ceremonial exercises and performances which others could do for them, than to "work out their own salvation with fear and trembling."

A class of men was accordingly set apart, whose business

it should be to take the (*cura*) care of souls; and this class soon arrogantly assuming the epithet of *clergy*, (κληρος, inheritance or *lot*,*) as if they only were the "Lord's portion" and the "lot of his inheritance," disdained to obtain their livelihood by labor or common business; but professing that their time must be entirely taken up in caring for those dependent on them for "the means of grace," claimed to be maintained at the expense of the community. Thus did a hireling priesthood supplant both the free unpaid ministry of the gospel, and the individual priestly character of the spiritual Christian; and thus was a wide door opened, both for further corruptions in the profession of Christianity, and for relaxation of the solemn responsibilities resting upon each individual.

When once the hireling ministers had established themselves in the professing Christian church, they were not slow in discovering that their influence over the flock, and consequently their pecuniary interest, would be greatly enhanced by the introduction of one ceremonial performance after another as necessary to salvation or edification. Instead, therefore, of guarding the profession of religion from innovation, they eagerly promoted various corruptions; which gradually changed Christianity (so called) from the character of a pure and spiritual, heart-searching and heart-cleansing religion, to that of a system of lifeless performances, "which could never make the comers thereunto perfect."

* "*Clerus* (a κληρος, *sors, quia clerus sors Dei, vel cleri sors Deus,*) — the clergy or churchmen. *Hæc notio apud Latinos scriptores, S. Hieronymi temporibus paulo antiquior.*" (Beatson & Ellis's Ainsworth.) So also Neander; "The Greek names κληροι and κληρικοι had even in Cyprian's time been applied in an unevangelic sense, &c., — 'οι εισι 'ο κληρος του Θεου, or, 'ων 'ο κληρος 'ο Θεος 'εστι — in imitation of the Levites." History of the Christian Religion and Church, vol. 1, Sect. ii. i. B.

Undoubtedly there were other causes which contributed to this mournful result. Originally, Christians had believed that all days were to be kept alike holy unto the Lord—though the church was wont to come together at stated times—more especially on the first day of the week—for divine worship, religious edification, and mutual encouragement for good. This principle of the necessity of holiness and mental introversion every day of our lives, was manifestly calculated to incite the mind to continual watchfulness as in the presence of the omniscient Lord, and thus to promote the entire purification of man's nature. But gradually, as the institution of a *caste of priests* took place of the maintenance of the doctrine that *all* are called to be "priests unto God," so the doctrine that one day was more holy than another, took the place of keeping all days holy; and the notion consequently gained ground, that on the six working-days of the week, men were not required to be so inward and spiritual in their minds, nor so pure in their lives and conduct, as on the one which was more particularly set apart for religious purposes.

Another source of the corruptions of the church was the desire to make the way easier for *heathens* to embrace nominal Christianity. In pursuance of this object, many heathen ceremonies were engrafted under new names into the system of Christianity, and some even of their idolatrous "holy days" were incorporated into the Christian calendar, under the pretended patronage of "Christian saints," instead of the heathen deities. This made the change from heathenism to the new profession comparatively nominal, and introduced great multitudes into the visible church, who were destitute of the spirit and life of Christianity.

This result, as well as the priestly influence, was greatly increased by the Emperor Constantine's adoption and patronage of the Christian religion; the power of money and worldly rank and authority, being thrown by that event into the hands of its professors, it became thenceforth, with only occasional and temporary exceptions, the religion of the state, and the whole Roman Empire appeared as the protector of the religion of Christ. Men did not perceive how much this religion was changed from the state of purity and simplicity in which it emanated from the Lip of Truth. It is true, the Almighty had not left himself without witnesses for his Truth in all times of the world; many sincere-hearted ones here and there were touched by the power and light of his blessed Spirit, and bore from time to time a faithful testimony against the idolatry and superstition which had usurped the place of Christ. But they were comparatively few, and were not able to stem the torrent of bigotry and corruption which overwhelmed the church.

Rome now became the centre of (so-called) religious influence and power; and these corruptions were, from motives of human policy, amazingly multiplied during a long succession of ages. But the human mind was at length awakened, and public attention was directed to the corrupt state of the profession of Christianity. The reformation from Popery, which took place in the sixteenth century, freed a great part of Europe from many of the most glaring perversions of Christian doctrine and practice; and there can be no doubt that the Divine Hand promoted this great revolution, and guided, to a certain extent, the proceedings of those engaged in the work.

It appears, however, that even the pious and enlightened men who were instruments in bringing about this mighty change, stopped short of arriving at an unclouded view of the nature of primitive Christianity. Excellent as were many of their spirits, and far advanced as they were before their fellow-professors of the name of Christ, and thirsting as they did after a redemption of the world from the gross pollutions of Popery, they were nevertheless trammelled in some degree with the dogmas of their school education, and weakened by their dependence on the arm of flesh for support, and gave not themselves up unreservedly to the thorough operations of that Holy Comforter in the secret of the soul, which, as it is faithfully attended to, guides "into all truth." They nobly stepped forward, and claimed a place in the attention of mankind for the Holy Scriptures, which the Papacy had shut up as a book not fit for general perusal; and this was a great point gained. But it is to be feared that they did not sufficiently regard the all important truth, that these Holy Scriptures themselves point to a higher rule than their own pages, for the direction of the mind of man, even the manifestations of the Spirit of Christ in the soul, by whose Light alone the heavenly mysteries contained in them are to be rightly understood. In considering the Holy Scriptures as the "word of God," and the primary guide of life and rule of faith, they fell into the error of valuing the branch above its parent stem; an error which prevented them from seeing clearly the whole beauty, and excellency, and purity, and spirituality of the gospel dispensation.

They boldly opposed the groundless assumption of the Pope to be the head of the church, and dragged to shame the enormities practised by the priesthood in the name of religion and for the sake of filthy lucre. But they went not down to the root of the evil—to destroy the whole system of hireling ministry—so that what they deemed the gospel, still continued to be bought and sold; and the result was as might have been anticipated, that a priesthood whose temporal subsistence depended on the implicit confidence placed in them by the people, still retained that people more or less in the outward court, in a state of blind reliance on them and their external performances, "ever learning, but never able to come to the knowledge of the Truth."

It was accordingly reserved in the counsels of inscrutable

wisdom, for weak and despised men, in the eye of the world, to be the instruments by whom the attention of mankind should be powerfully directed to the inward principle of religion, the Spirit of Truth, operating in every heart, and the church should be called back to a state of purity and spirituality, such as characterized it in the days of the apostles and primitive believers.

CHAPTER II.

EARLY LIFE AND CONVINCEMENT OF GEORGE FOX—HIS CALL TO THE MINISTRY—AND IMPRISONMENT—CALLED A QUAKER.

IT was about the middle of the seventeenth century, that the Lord was pleased to visit the British nation, and some other portions of professing Christendom, with a more clear and certain sound of the word of life, and proclamation of the way of salvation, than had been known for many ages past.

That nation was still heaving in great unsettlement, from the effects of the awful storm which had uprooted the foundations of its ancient social, religious, and political establishments, deprived Charles the First of his throne and life, and placed Oliver Cromwell at the head of the English commonwealth. As, under Charles, great laxity of morals and neglect of duty had prevailed among the ministers of the "established church," many of whom had given themselves up to idle and licentious practices; so on the other hand, when these were turned out, to give place to the Puritans under the commonwealth, great outward strictness and loud pretensions to sanctity, often unaccompanied by the real life of religion, were the road to preferment, and were consequently in many instances assumed as a mere cloak over a worldly spirit, from ambitious views.

The profession of religion, nevertheless, was certainly held in much higher esteem than before. In the camp, as well as at the fire-side, religion was the absorbing topic. The republican army abounded with preachers; and preaching, praying, and disputing on doctrines, were daily to be heard among both officers and soldiers: though much of this was extremely superficial, and a pharisaical notion of soundness, and contempt for others, too much prevailed.

The spirit of inquiry, however, which had arisen with the reformation of the sixteenth century, had greatly shaken the general confidence in the priesthood; men now considered themselves at liberty to form their own opinions on matters relating to their eternal condition; and the public assemblies for divine worship were continually scenes of religious dispute between the contending parties. The late intestine wars, with the troubles thereby brought on many families throughout the nation, were instrumental in turning the minds of some to an anxious desire after a resting-place for the agitated soul. There were those who had learned in sore adversity, duly to estimate the emptiness and uncertainty of all the gratifications of this world, and to pant after a knowledge of the Source and Centre of happiness and peace. And the Lord left not to themselves these sincere-hearted seekers after a solid foundation for their hopes; but led many of them into greater degrees of spiritual-mindedness; in which they were enabled to perceive and feel the unsatisfactory nature of those forms of religion, which, notwithstanding the partial reformation from Popery, still stood in the place of pure and primitive Christianity. But these were scattered abroad in the country, as sheep having no shepherd nor fold; they were unknown to each other, and not gathered into the enclosure of a visible society professing what their souls yearned after. They knew not but that they were alone in the deep exercise and spiritual travail which they experienced; and consequently they hailed as a most welcome message the testimony borne by George Fox and his fellow-laborers to pure and spiritual religion. They found a life and savor in his ministry very different from the dead and formal discourses to which they had been wont to listen; which was a cordial to their panting spirits, and led them to a more intimate knowledge of that Divine and inspeaking Word whom their souls had sincerely loved and earnestly waited for.

George Fox, the honored instrument of gathering these scattered and retired ones into a visible church, was born at Drayton, in Leicestershire, England, in the year 1624. His father was noted for the justice and honesty of his character, and his mother, who was of the stock of the martyrs, was a woman accomplished above most of her station in the place of their residence. From a child, George displayed a remarkably religious, inward, quiet frame of mind. At the same time he was observing, even beyond his years, frequently to the astonishment of those who heard and conversed with him, especially on religious topics. He was brought up in country business, and was skilful in the tending of sheep; an employment which well suited a mind seeking after solitude and innocency, and was a just emblem of his subsequent ministry and service in the fold of Christ. The restraining and sanctifying operations of Divine Grace were experienced by him whilst very young; and the Lord taught him to be faithful in all things, inwardly to God, and outwardly to man. His own account says that when he was about eleven years of age, he experienced pureness and righteousness; he was taught to keep strictly to the truth in all things, not daring to use the least degree of prevarication: his words were to be few and savory, seasoned with grace; and he was to observe temperance both in eating and drinking, using the creatures of God as servants in their places, to the glory of Him who created them.

When he was about nineteen years of age, being on business at a fair, his mind was greatly distressed, in observing the wantonness of some professors of religion, who scrupled not to indulge themselves in excess of drinking, and what is termed drinking of healths. He bore his testimony against their folly, and went away; but could not rest the following night, which he spent in walking up and down, and in prayer to the Lord. He was answered by this divine intimation: "Thou seest how young people go together into vanity, and old people into the earth; thou must forsake all, both young and old, and keep out of all, and be a stranger unto all." Soon after this, he believed it to be his duty to leave his relations, and for some time he led a solitary life, intimately communing with none but his Maker and Redeemer; and was thus gradually weaned from all dependence on his fellow-man, in matters relating to the safety of the soul. He travelled through various counties of England, avoiding the company of the high but empty professors of religion; and many were the deep exercises and sore temptations which befell him for several months; in which he was led to review his past life, and consider whether his own wrong doings were the cause of his present distress. He knew not at that time that those deep baptisms of spirit were necessary to prepare him for the work whereunto his Master was about to call him. After a while, being fearful that his long absence might grieve his relations, he returned home, and continued there with some intermission, for more than a year, in great sorrows and troubles, often spending the night in walking alone, and in religious meditation.

Some of the priests of the neighborhood sought his acquaintance, and reasoned with him at various times on religious subjects, but could give him no satisfaction. In their carnal wisdom they knew not his condition, and could not understand the nature of his mental conflicts. One bid him take tobacco, and sing psalms. Another, who was accounted an experienced man, he says he found only like an empty hollow cask. A third disgusted him by his unchecked passionate temper, ruffled by the least trifle, showing the possessor to be far from that state of meekness and calmness which would have become his profession. A fourth priest advised medicine and bleeding; so that George found them miserable comforters, and entirely ignorant of his need.

One of his interviews with Nathaniel Stevens, the priest of Drayton, with whom he often conversed, and who frequently made the observations of this enlightened youth serve as embellishments of his own sermons, is worthy of particular notice. This priest asked George, why Christ cried out upon the cross, "My God, my God, why hast thou forsaken me?" and why he said, "If it be possible, let this cup pass from me; yet not my will, but thine be done." George told him, "that at that time the sins of all mankind were upon Him, and their iniquities and transgressions; with which He was wounded, which He was to bear, and to be an offering for as He was man, but he died not as He was God; and so, in that He died for all men, and tasted death for every man, He was an offering for the sins of the whole world." This, he says, he spoke, being then in measure sensible of Christ's sufferings, and what he went through; and the priest remarked that "it was a very good answer, and such as he had not heard." This comprehensive reply to the inquiring priest, who with all his learned preparation for the ministry, could not understand the mysteries of redeeming love, furnishes abundant refutation of the calumny by which George Fox has been maliciously charged in modern times with unsoundness in the very fundamental articles of the Christian faith. It shows, in a manner not to be contradicted, that this heavenly-minded man had a clear and full belief in the Saviour as the eternal Son of God, and yet as having partaken also of the nature of man; in the sacrifice which He made of himself upon the cross for the sins of mankind; and in the atoning virtue and universal efficacy of this sacrifice to the redemption of the souls of men, through living faith and obedience to His Divine Light in the heart. And that this sound belief in these important doctrines was not merely the belief of George Fox's youthful days, is proved by his thus fully recording this transaction in after-life.

During this time of opening manhood, not only was he exercising himself in the duties of Christian benevolence to his destitute fellow-creatures, but his mind was enlarging in experience, and in acquaintance with the doctrines of pure Christianity, as distinguished from the systems taught in the schools and colleges. He was enabled to see that notwithstanding men's high professions, none were true believers but those who " were born of God and passed from death unto life," and that being brought up at the universities or colleges was not enough to qualify a man to be a minister of Christ. Here again he was brought off from a reliance on any but the Lord Jesus Christ, the great Minister of ministers, who would teach his people himself. He was also shown that he was not to apply the word *church* or *temple of God* to any building; the Lord, according to the apostle's testimony, dwelling in the heart of man and making that his temple, and a church of Christ being a collection of living disciples, not the walls within which they or others might assemble.*

Early in the year 1647, he felt an impression of duty to travel into Derbyshire and some parts of the counties of

---

* "Not the place, but the congregation of the elect, I call a church."—*Clement of Alexandria, Stromat. vii.* 715 *B.*

Leicester and Nottingham. He met with some serious friendly people, of tender spirits, among whom he "had some meetings and discourses." But his mental exercises still continued. "I fasted much," says he, "and walked abroad in solitary places many days, and often took my Bible and went and sat in hollow trees and lonesome places till night came on; and frequently, in the night, walked mournfully about by myself; for I was a man of sorrows, in the times of the first workings of the Lord in me." During all this time he kept himself much as a stranger, "seeking heavenly wisdom and getting knowledge from the Lord; and was brought off from outward things, to rely wholly on the Lord alone." He was here instructed that Christ Jesus was he who could speak effectually to his condition. He was made a partaker also, at times, notwithstanding his deep and long-continued provings, of that joy and peace, which is peculiarly the Christian's portion; in which he could exclaim: "Thou killest and makest alive; all honor and glory be to thee, O Lord of glory!" Thus his desires after the Lord grew stronger, and zeal in the pure knowledge and love of God, which surpasses all the knowledge that men have in the natural state, or can obtain by history or books. And being by these deep baptisms weaned from all confidence in his own powers, his mind became more and more divinely enlightened to understand the mysteries of the Holy Scriptures, many deep things therein being clearly opened to him; as well as the dark state of the professors of religion generally, who could talk greatly of Christ and of his blood, and yet knew it not in their own experience, but trampled upon it in their airy notions, and fed upon the words of man's own wisdom, or such as they had stolen out of the Scriptures of Truth.

During this year (1647) his mouth appears to have been first opened of the Lord in gospel ministry. Several persons in the parts where he travelled were convinced of the truth, and united with him in the bonds of the Gospel. And in the year following they began to have great meetings of the people, and a mighty power and work of God there was among them, to the astonishment of both people and priests. At this time he was an example of silence, endeavoring to bring people from self-performances; testifying of, and turning them to the light of Christ within them, and encouraging them to wait in patience, and to feel the power of it to stir in their hearts, that their knowledge and worship of God might stand in the power of an endless life, which was to be found in the light, as it was obeyed in the manifestation of it in man. He was led to see clearly, and to open to those who heard him discourse, these three great practical truths; that all men are called and may be enabled to be perfect, or free from the power as well as guilt of sin—that none can understand the Scriptures aright, without the assistance of the same Spirit by which they were written—and that every man is enlightened by the divine Light of Christ, which would lead all to salvation if its manifestations were humbly and faithfully obeyed. And when he observed drowsiness upon the people when they ought to have been watching unto prayer and looking to the Lord, he told them "they must come to witness death to that sleepy, heavy nature, and a cross to it in the power of God, that their minds and hearts might be on things above.

He now received an intimation from the Lord that he was to go forth more publicly into the world at large, to preach the Word of life, which he had received; and it may be well to hear his own account of the nature of his Christian ministry.

"I was sent," he says, "to turn people from darkness to light, that they might receive Christ Jesus. I was to direct people to the Spirit, that gave forth the Scriptures, by which they might be led into all truth, and so up to Christ and God, as they had been who gave them forth. I was to turn them to the grace of God, and to the truth in the heart, which came by Jesus.—I saw that Christ died for all men, and was a propitiation for all, and enlightened all men and women by his divine and saving light, and that none could be a true believer but who believed in it.—With and by this divine power and Spirit of God, and the light of Jesus, I was to bring people off from all their own ways, to Christ the new and living way; and from their churches, which men had made and gathered, to the church in God, the general assembly written in heaven, which Christ is the head of; and off from the world's teachers, made by men, to learn of Christ, who is the way, the truth, and the life; of whom the Father said, 'This is my beloved Son, hear ye Him;' and off from all the world's worships, to know the Spirit of Truth in the inward parts, and to be led thereby; that in it they might worship the Father of spirits, who seeks such to worship him.—And I was to bring people off from all the world's religions, which are vain; that they might know the pure religion, might visit the fatherless, the widows, and the strangers, and keep themselves from the spots of the world.—I was to bring them off from all the world's fellowships, and prayings, and singings, which stood in forms without power; that their fellowship might be in the Holy Ghost, and in the eternal Spirit of God; that they might pray in the Holy Ghost, and sing in the spirit and with the grace that comes by Jesus; making melody in their hearts to the Lord, who hath sent his beloved Son to be their Saviour, and caused his heavenly sun to shine upon all the world. I was to bring people off from Jewish ceremonies, and from heathenish fables, and from men's inventions and worldly doctrines—with their schools and colleges for making ministers of Christ, who are indeed ministers of their own making, but not of Christ's; and from all their images and crosses, and sprinkling of infants, with all their holy days (so called) and all their vain traditions which they had gotten up since the apostles' days, which the Lord's power was against; in the dread and authority of which, I was moved to declare against them all, and against all that preached and not freely, as being such as had not received freely from Christ.

"Moreover, when the Lord sent me forth into the world, he forbade me to put off my hat to any, high or low; and I was required to *thee* and *thou* all men and women, without any respect to rich or poor, great or small. And as I travelled up and down, I was not to bid people Good morrow, or Good evening; neither might I bow or scrape with my leg to any one. And this made the sects and professors to rage. But the Lord's power carried me over all, to his glory, and many came to be turned to God in a little time; for the heavenly day of the Lord sprung from on high, and broke forth apace, by the light of which, many came to see where they were."

These two last mentioned testimonies against the pride of man could not be tolerated by those who loved to "receive honor one of another, but sought not the honor that cometh from God only." It put the priests, magistrates and other high professing people in a great rage, when they found themselves addressed in the same simple style which was used to those whom they disdained as their inferiors. They considered not that this was consistent with Holy Scripture, and even with the rules of grammar taught in their schools; but they soon proceeded to inflame the passions of the people against George Fox and his uncompromising fellow believers, and subjected them to great sufferings from the violence of unrestrained and wicked men.

He was also led to exhort all men to justice in dealing, and teachers and parents in particular to a religious care to bring up children in the fear of the Lord, and guard them from that which would encourage lightness and vanity. Tavern keepers he cautioned against supplying people with liquor to their hurt; judges were exhorted to just decisions; and all were warned against plays, shows and music, as burdening the pure life and stirring up the mind to vanity and folly.

In the year 1649, when he was about twenty-five years of age, being at Nottingham on a First-day, he felt constrained to go into the public place of worship. The priest took for his text the words of Peter: "We have also a more sure word of prophecy, whereunto ye do well that ye take heed, as unto a light that shineth in a dark place," &c.; and he told the people that this referred to the Scriptures. George felt the power of the Lord contradicting in his mind the carnal reasoning of the priest, and was made to cry out, "Oh, no, it is not the Scriptures," and to inform them that it was the Holy Spirit, by which the holy men of God gave forth the Scriptures, and which would lead into all truth: instancing the case of the deluded Jews, who possessed the Holy Scriptures, yet not coming to the light of the Holy Ghost, but reading them in their own spirits, rejected Christ, the bright and morning star, and persecuted his apostles and followers. The people were greatly enraged at this, and seizing George, they put him into a filthy prison. He was that night taken before the magistrates; and afterwards the sheriff, who sent for him to his own home, was so much reached by the Lord's convincing power, that he went forth into the market-place and preached repentance to the people in the streets. After remaining in prison some time, George Fox was released, and was made instrumental at Mansfield Woodhouse, in calming the mind of a distracted woman, who afterwards received the truth, and continued in it to her death. At the same place, he was moved to enter the public meeting-house, and declare the truth to the priest and people. And though such interruptions and even disputes with the ministers were very common in that day of general excitement, and considered as one part of the liberty claimed by those who protested against the superstitions of the Romish priests, yet the doctrines which George Fox preached were so unpalatable, that they fell upon him in a rage, struck him down, and almost stifled him; and he was cruelly bruised with their hands, their sticks, and even with their Bibles. He was then put into the stocks, kept there some hours, and after being threatened with whipping, was at length set at liberty. Some however were that day convinced of the truth, to the rejoicing of his heart.

The next year, 1650, being at Derby, at a time when there was a great lecture preached, he was led to make some communication to the people at the close. They heard him pretty quietly, but an officer soon came and took him before Justice Bennet, and other magistrates of the town. George Fox spoke boldly for the truth, exhorting them to look unto Christ *within* them, as the great sanctifier, and not to man; and bidding them in the words of Holy Scripture, to tremble at the word of the Lord. Justice Bennet, at this, derided him and his fellow believers, calling them Quakers; a designation which has ever since been used by the world to distinguish us from other professors of religion. These justices were exceedingly puzzled to know what to do with George, but after spending about eight hours in examining him, and disputing among themselves, they committed him to the house of correction or common jail, for six months. Being thus kept in confinement, he did not forget those who had been reached through his ministry, and brought by the convincing power of God to a like precious faith; but addressed several epistles to them to confirm them in faithfulness, and remind them that it was Christ Jesus, inwardly revealed, on whom strength was laid, and to him they must look to enable them to persevere to the end. He also wrote several letters of solemn warning to the magistrates and priests of Derby, who had committed him. The time of his commitment at length being nearly expired, he was brought before a body of soldiers in the market-place, and desired to accept the station of captain in the army of the commonwealth against King Charles. But when it was found that he could not be brought over to their purposes, they remanded him to prison, and kept him nearly six months longer in a filthy dungeon, without any bed, and among about thirty felons. He was preserved, however, in great patience, and many occurrences evinced from time to time the strengthening and enlivening presence of the Lord with his tried servant. After a while he was again strongly urged to join the army, and his continued refusal was the occasion of still closer confinement. His persecutors at length became uneasy among themselves, and set him at liberty after an imprisonment of nearly one year. After his liberation from the dungeon of Derby prison, he continued to travel abroad in the ministry of the gospel, holding numerous meetings, and being instrumental to the gathering of many sincere souls into the fold of Christ. Many of these afterwards became eminent fellow-laborers with him in the cause of pure Christianity, and the process of gradual convincement of some of them evinced in a remarkable manner, the immediate operations of that divine Spirit which was promised by the Saviour of men, to lead into all truth.

CHAPTER III.

AN ACCOUNT OF SOME OF THE DOCTRINES AND TESTIMONIES PROMULGATED BY THE FOUNDERS OF THE SOCIETY OF FRIENDS.

ALTHOUGH it would be foreign to the object of this work, to develop at much length the Christian doctrines held by George Fox and his fellow-laborers, yet a short insight into some important principles most surely believed by them, may be necessary to enable us to pursue their history with a clear conception of their real character as advocates of the Truth in Christ.

They never hesitated to declare their belief in "the three that bear record in Heaven"—that there is one God and Father of all, of whom are all things,—one Lord Jesus Christ, by whom all things were made, who was glorified with the Father before the world began, who is God over all, blessed for ever—and one Holy Spirit, the promise of the Father and the Son, the Leader and sanctifier and comforter of his people—and that these three are One, as the Holy Scriptures declare.

They believed that the one only wise, omnipotent and everlasting God was the Creator of all things, and is the preserver of all that he hath made. And they owned and truly believed that Jesus Christ was his beloved and only-begotten Son, conceived by the Holy Ghost, and born of the virgin Mary—in whom we have redemption through his blood, even the forgiveness of sins—that he is the express image of the invisible God, the first-born of every creature—by and for whom all things in heaven and in earth were created—that he offered himself without spot unto God, a sacrifice for sin, and tasted death for every man, being crucified for us in the flesh, without the gates of Jerusalem—that he rose again the third day for our justification, ascended into Heaven, and now sitteth at the right hand of God; being made the propitiation for our sins, and not for ours only, but also for the sins of the whole world. They rejoicingly believed in Him as their Redeemer and Saviour, the Captain of their salvation, their Mediator with the Father, and the author and finisher of their faith—their wisdom, righteousness, justification and redemption—the Shepherd and Bishop of their souls—and sincerely acknowledged that there is no other name under heaven given among men, whereby we must be saved.

The doctrine of immediate divine revelation, which had been lost sight of in the apostasy, was revived and abundantly preached by them as the glory and life of the gospel dispensation. While other professors, too generally, were resting in a bare belief of what Christ had done for them, without them, and in a literal knowledge of the Holy Scriptures, these converted and regenerated witnesses for the truth as it is in Jesus, were made partakers of that faith which is produced by the testimony of the Spirit of Christ in the heart; by which they not only received Him as their Redeemer and Saviour, in what he graciously did and suffered in the flesh, as the propitiation for sin, and as their mediator and intercessor; but likewise in his inward and spiritual appearance, to baptize and sanctify them; so as to prepare their souls to partake of the fulness of the blessings which the Gospel confers.

Concerning the Holy Scriptures, they believed that they were given forth by the Holy Spirit of God, through the holy men of God, who spake as they were moved by the Holy Ghost. They believed that these blessed writings are to be read, believed, and fulfilled (he that fulfils them is Christ); and that they "are profitable for doctrine, for reproof, for correction, for instruction in righteousness, that the man of God may be perfect, thoroughly furnished unto all good works"—and that they "are able to make wise unto salvation, through faith which is in Christ Jesus."

They believed that the testimony of the Spirit is that alone by which the true knowledge of God, or of the Holy Scriptures, can be revealed—that the revelations of the Spirit in the heart are the great guide of life, by which true Christians are to be immediately led and governed; and that these revelations can never contradict, or lead men to slight or lightly esteem the testimony of Holy Scripture, which proceeded from the same Spirit in holy men of old.

Hence they also believed that faith is not a natural faculty of the human mind, to be exercised according to man's will; and that there can be no effectual faith, but that which is produced by the immediate operation of the Holy Spirit in the heart, inclining and enabling us to believe what it reveals to us there, as well as those things which are recorded in the Scriptures.

They plainly declared their conviction, a conviction amply confirmed by what they knew of their own hearts, that man, who was created in the image of God, fell by transgression from this blessed state, and lost the heavenly image; so that all men are by nature fallen, degenerated and dead to the divine life, and subject to the power of sin; though not punishable for Adam's sin, until they make it their own by actual transgression. But they further declared the all-consoling truth, that God, who of his infinite love sent his Son, the Lord Jesus Christ, into the world, who tasted death for every man, hath given to every man, Jew or Gentile, Barbarian, Scythian, bond or free, of whatsoever nation or place, a certain day or time of visitation by the light of His Holy Spirit in the heart, during which it is possible for him to be saved and to partake of the benefits of Christ's death—that these visitations of divine Grace draw men to God, convict for sin, baptize into a death of the first and carnal nature, and if received and co-operated with, work the salvation of all, even of those who are ignorant of the history of Adam's fall, and of the death and sufferings of Christ.

While they fully believed that remission of sin and reconciliation with God is obtained only through Christ and his most satisfactory offering, they were also convinced that no man was justified while he continued in sin, whatever might be his profession of faith. They preached the indispensable necessity of holiness, without which the Scriptures declare that no man shall see the Lord; and they placed justification where the apostle places it, in connection with being washed and sanctified, but not as preceding sanctification. They believed that this sanctification is produced by the mighty work of Christ within us, whereby the power, nature, and habits of sin are destroyed; that men truly repenting and believing, are, by the propitiatory sacrifice of Christ without us, through the mercy of God, justified from the imputation of sins that are past; and that all this is effected, not by a bare act of faith separate from obedience, but in the *obedience* of faith; Christ being the author of eternal salvation to none but those that obey him.

This brought them to that great doctrine, that all mankind are called to perfection, and offered the attainment, through perfect obedience, of a state of freedom from sin even in this life, though not from a liability to fall again, through unwatchfulness, under the power of temptation. And this doctrine of perfection was a groundwork for their uncompromising integrity, and strict attention to what many termed little things, but which were essential to their character as truly faithful Christians, because required by the manifestations of the divine light of Christ in their consciences.

Christian baptism they held to be, not the washing of the

body with water—"the putting away the filth of the flesh"—but the powerful work of the Holy Spirit in the hearts of all who submit thereto, refining them from the pollution of sin, winnowing away the transgressing nature, and preparing the soul for being gathered into the heavenly garner, as grain separated from the chaff.

In like manner they believed, that the communion of the body and blood of Christ, is not the partaking of outward bread and wine; but is inward and spiritual—a real participation of His divine nature in measure, through faith in Him, and obedience to his Spirit in the heart; by which participation the inward man is daily nourished, strengthened, and kept alive unto God.

Acceptable worship, they often testified, could not be offered, but through the assistance of the Spirit of Christ, our mediator, by whom only we can approach unto God; and that in order to experience this necessary qualification, it is our duty to have the mind withdrawn from all outward objects, and engaged in reverently and humbly waiting upon the Lord in the silence of all flesh; that He may be pleased, through the revelation of his Spirit, to give us a true sense of our needs, and a knowledge of his will, and enable us to offer a sacrifice well pleasing in his sight; whether it be in silent mental adoration, the secret breathing of the soul to him, the ministry of the gospel, or vocal prayer and thanksgiving.

They were brought off, by the spirit of meekness and long-suffering which characterizes true Christianity, from all wars and fightings, and from that mind which promotes the warlike disposition; being enabled to see their entire inconsistency with the gospel of the Prince of peace, and that their origin was, as said the apostle James, in those "lusts which war against the soul." Thus they could never take up arms, even though, like the primitive Christians, they should suffer the loss of liberty, property and life, for their faithful adherence to the injunction of the Saviour, "Love your enemies; do good to them which hate you; and pray for them that despitefully use you and persecute you."

Nor did they dare to reason away the plain prohibition of our Lord:—"Swear not at all, but let your communication be yea, yea, nay, nay; for whatsoever is more than these, cometh of evil." And this testimony was the occasion of abundant suffering from the powers of this world.

These were the fundamental doctrines of the Society which the Lord was now gathering into a visible church, under the instrumentality of George Fox and his fellow-laborers. Other views which sprang from these as a branch from the parent stem, may be gathered in perusing the ensuing pages. But one of these branches, connected as it is with that purity of language which the Gospel was to restore to the believers, it may be well in this place to develope in some degree of detail. It is the heathen origin of the common names of months and days, which crept into use among professing Christians, along with other corruptions, and which Friends saw plainly to be a relic of a false religion, and inconsistent with the Holy Scriptures.

"And in all things that I have said unto you, be circumspect; and make no mention of the names of other gods; neither let it be heard out of thy mouth."—Exodus, xxiii. 13.

"For then will I turn to the people a pure language." Zephaniah, iii. 9.

These heathen names may be thus explained.

January—This name was derived from Janus, an ancient king of Italy, whom heathen superstition had deified; to whom a temple was erected in Rome, and the month so called was dedicated to his image.

February—was so called from Februa, a word denoting purgation by sacrifice; it being usual in this month, for the priests of the heathen idol Pan, to offer sacrifices, and to perform certain rites, supposed to conduce to the cleansing or purgation of the people.

March—was so denominated from Mars, the pretended god of war, whom Romulus, the founder of Rome, assumed to be his father.

April—is said to have derived its name from the Greek appellation of Venus, ('Αφρω,) an imaginary goddess worshipped by the Romans in this month, who was pretended to have sprung from the foam ('αφρος) of the sea.

May—The month so called is said to have derived its name from Maia, the mother of Mercury, another pretended heathen deity, whom the Romans worshipped in this month.

June—So named from Juno, another supposed goddess of the Romans.

July—was so called from the great Roman warrior Julius Cæsar, who gave his own name to this month, instead of its former name of *Quintilis*, or the *fifth*. He was deified by his superstitious admirers.

August—So named in honor of his successor, the Emperor Augustus. This month was previously called *Sextilis*, or the *sixth*. He also was deified, and called "the Divine Augustus."

The remaining four months, called *September*, (meaning Seventh,) *October*, (Eighth,) *November*, (Ninth,) and *December*, (Tenth,) were very properly so called until the alteration of the Calendar adopted in England in the year 1752; by which what is called the New Style came into use, so that those four months have ever since been, not what their Latin names indicate, but the Ninth, Tenth, Eleventh and Twelfth; so that it is no longer consistent with that truth incumbent on all Christians, to designate these months by those names. There can be little doubt that the numerical mode of naming the months is the most ancient, as it is unquestionably the most plain, simple and rational.

The Days of the Week were also called, by our idolatrous Saxon ancestors, after the names of the idols or other objects which they worshipped on the respective days. Thus,

The First day of the week was by them called *Sunday*, from their customary adoration of the Sun on that day.

The Second day they called *Monday*, from their custom of worshipping the Moon on that day.

The Third day, *Tuesday*, in honor of one of their idols called Tuisco.

The Fourth day, *Wednesday*, from Woden, another of their idols.

The Fifth day was called *Thursday*, from the name of an idol called Thor, worshipped on that day.

The Sixth day was called *Friday*, from Friga, an imaginary goddess worshipped by them.

The Seventh day, they styled *Saturday*, from Saturn or Seater, another imaginary deity.

The candid mind, on a consideration of the above, must acknowledge that the continued use of these names involved an acknowledgment or sanction of the gross idolatry of the heathen, contrary to the express command of Scripture, that "the names of the idols should no more be heard."

And these were not all the corruptions introduced in reference to the names of days and times. For when the profession of the Christian religion became national in the Roman empire, multitudes of heathen priests, who saw their present craft in danger, embraced the profession of Christianity from selfish views, and labored with too much success to find employment by imposing on the people a new set of ceremonies and sacrifices, bearing some resemblance to those to which in their state of heathenism they had been accustomed. From this corrupt source sprang the Popish sacrifice of the Mass, the celebration of which at particular times, (some of them in connection with the worship of saints) gave rise to the names of Michaelmas, Martinmas, Christmas, and the like.

Another division of the testimony of Friends to a pure and simple language, resulted from the conviction that strict truth must be invariably maintained by the Christian, and that he is not at liberty to flatter the natural pride of his fellow-men. They perceived that pride and fashion had introduced the practice of addressing a single individual by the word "you," as if he were two or more; and when they could no longer thus depart from the pure language of Holy Scripture, they found to their cost, by the sufferings which they underwent on its account, that this pride of the human heart was greatly roused at the idea of being addressed in the same manner as was customary towards those who were considered as inferiors. This confirmed them in the belief that the custom was corrupt in its origin; and they steadily persevered, through much persecution, in adherence to the Scripture example of "thou" or "thee" to a single individual, however exalted in station or character.

The same fear of fostering the pride of man led them to discard the use of the common modes of salutation, some of which implied what was often absolutely false. Thus, the terms "Master" or "Mister," and "Mistress," they could not conscientiously make use of, towards persons who stood not in that relation to them; nor could they dare to offer the appearance of an approach to man-worship, which was involved in the customary practice of bowing and courtesying, and taking off the hat; though this was a supposed honor which stuck very close to the worldly heart, and for faithfully testifying against which, Friends often endured most grievous sufferings.

CHAPTER IV.

CONVINCEMENT OF WILLIAM DEWSBURY—AND EDWARD BURROUGH.

ONE of the most eminent instruments among those who united with George Fox in 1651, was William Dewsbury. He was born at Allerthorpe in Yorkshire, early in the seventeenth century, of religious parents, who were doubtless instrumental in cherishing that susceptibility of mind, which formed, at an early age, a striking feature in his character. When he was only eight years old, the Lord visited him by his Spirit, clearly intimating to the ear of his mind—" I created thee for my glory—an account thou must give me for all thy words and actions;" and his understanding was enlightened to perceive that he had lived in disobedience to the Lord's will. About this period he lost his father; and while lamenting with tears over this solemn and affecting event, he heard in the secret of his soul what appeared to him a voice, saying: " Weep for *thyself*, for thy father is well." So powerful was the effect produced on his mind by this extraordinary incident, that from that time forward he spent many hours, which in childhood are usually devoted to play, in prayer and fasting, under a sense of his lost and undone condition. As he advanced in years, he became increasingly sensible of the corrupt propensities of his nature. The condemnation which attended him, was that he lived without the true knowledge or fear of the Lord his Maker; though there is no reason to apprehend that he exceeded the ordinary levity of young persons, or went beyond the bounds of what is commonly termed morality. But it was gradually given him to see the indispensable necessity of a thorough change of heart, and of being " born again of incorruptible seed, by the Word of God, which liveth and abideth forever." Under these powerful impressions, between his eighth and thirteenth years, he endeavored to alter the course of his life. He ceased from what he was now led to consider the vain conversation in which he had hitherto lived, and became thoughtful and serious far beyond his years. He began to read the Holy Scriptures and other books on religious subjects from his own choice, and was often engaged in mourning and prayer before the Almighty, although at that time he had received no clear understanding as to how or where the Divine Being was to be found — even in the heart of man himself, which is declared to be "the temple of the Lord." His soul was "athirst for God, for the living God;" and he could exclaim with David, "when shall I come and appear before God?" It was in vain that he diligently availed himself of such opportunities as were afforded, of learning, through the public teachers of religion, and other outward means, what he was thus anxious to know and enjoy in himself. The outward and carnal views of that class of persons were not calculated to satisfy his searching spirit; and he found that such a knowledge of the Father and of the Son, as is life eternal, was not to be attained through those physicians of no value. All his own endeavors also, made in his own strength and will, to render himself acceptable to God, were equally fruitless; and thus was he brought in entire prostration to the foot of the cross, feeling his need of Christ the Saviour, and that without him his soul could not live.

Until the thirteenth year of his age, his chief occupation was that of a shepherd's boy, the retirement of which was very congenial to his feelings. But soon after this, he was placed apprentice to a cloth-weaver near Leeds, wishing to have more frequent opportunities of intimate association with a people, whom he believed to have attained to a more advanced state of religious purity, than that to which he had been accustomed. But though he attended assiduously at their places of worship, and discoursed frequently with them on the subject of his anxiety, yet he found himself greatly disappointed, and met with no rest nor peace to his weary soul, "in that worship of God which the world had set up." He was told by his associates that the bread and wine which they called the Sacrament of the Supper, were the seals of the covenant; but when he received them, he found nothing sealed to his soul therewith. The emptiness of this ceremony was at length shown to him, and he was instructed that "the seal of the covenant was the Spirit of Christ, and no outward element; and that the Supper was the body and blood of Christ, which the world doth not know."

About the time that he attained the age of twenty-one years, the civil wars broke out in England, which resulted in the death of King Charles the First. William, in common with many ardent and well meaning persons, fell into a snare which the enemy of all righteousness, who was a murderer from the beginning, laid for them, through the plausible reasoning of some who professed to be ministers of Christ, and who designated the joining of the army of the Parliament, in what was termed a defence of civil and religious liberty, as "going up to the help of the Lord against the mighty." William Dewsbury was taken with this bait, not at that time seeing the inconsistency of the sword, for the disciples of the Prince of Peace; and entered into the army, supposing he was fighting for the gospel. But in this too he was disappointed. At length he was favored to perceive that in all his efforts hitherto, to "find out the Almighty to perfection," he had been "seeking the living among the dead," and *looking out* for that which was only to be found *within;* and that it was in mercy that he had been baffled in all these attempts made in his own strength and wisdom. "Then," says he, "my mind was *turned within* by the power of the Lord, to wait in his counsel, the light in my conscience, to hear what the Lord would say. And the word of the Lord came to me and said: 'Put up thy sword into the scabbard; if my kingdom were of this world, then would my servants fight.' Which word enlightened my heart, and discovered the mystery of iniquity; it showed *the kingdom of Christ to be within*, and that its enemies being within and spiritual, my weapons against them should also be spiritual,—the power of God."

Favored with this clear intimation of the Lord's will, he put up his weapon into its sheath, left the army, and resumed his former occupation of a weaver; and waiting on the Lord in the way of his judgments, he was brought unreservedly to cast himself upon the mercy of God in Christ Jesus, and to yield to His all-wise disposal. He was favored with clear evidence that free redemption was laid up for him in the Lord Jesus, and that though "the wages of sin is death, yet the gift of God is eternal life, through Jesus Christ our Lord." And having passed through the fiery baptisms of the Holy Ghost in the deep provings which have been described, he was effectually convinced that true religious knowledge is not to be acquired as men obtain knowledge in the things of this world, by the ordinary cultivation of the mental faculties alone; but that we must wait in great self-abasement at the feet of Jesus, to receive such an understanding as the natural man does not possess, and in which alone spiritual things can be rightly comprehended and appreciated.

Having thus tasted of the good word of life and of the powers of the world to come, William Dewsbury began to feel, about the year 1646, a strong engagement of mind, inclining him to declare to others what the Lord had done for his soul, that his fellow-creatures might also be persuaded to seek after a like precious experience. But it is remarkable, that though he was freely given up in mind to undertake the work of a preacher of the gospel, yet the necessary commission for undertaking it had not then been given. He was commanded by the secret intimations of the Holy Spirit, to wait until the year 1652, when, it was prophetically revealed to his understanding, there would be a greater opening in the minds of the people to receive the doctrines of spiritual truth. During the six years which intervened, he continued principally about his own home, and had to pass through various conflicts of mind, intended doubtless for the further trial of his faith, and for his more full preparation for the great work and service to which he was appointed. And by the power of the divine Word, he was armed with patience to wait in the Lord's counsel, through all his trials, until it pleased the Almighty to set him free.

It was in the year 1651 that this spiritually-minded man first met that great instrument in gathering the Society of Friends, George Fox. This occurred near Balby in Yorkshire, where George was holding meetings, after his liberation from the dungeon at Derby. William Dewsbury and his wife (whom he had married about two years before,) attended one of these meetings, held at Lieutenant Roper's, at Synderhill Green; and George Fox relates, that after the meeting (it being moonlight) William and Ann Dewsbury came to him in the field, and confessed to the truth. Doubtless their hearts rejoiced to find that as face answereth to face in a glass, so they could read the lines of their own experience in what George had delivered, and could extend to him the right hand of precious fellowship. And in the eighth month of the following year, he clearly received the commission which had been previously appointed for him, in the following secret intimation from the Lord: 'The leaders of my people cause them to err, in drawing them from the light in their consciences.—Freely thou hast received, freely give and minister; and what I have made known to thee in secret, declare thou openly." The power of which message constrained him to leave his family, and to run to and fro, to declare to souls where their Teacher is, even the Light of Christ in their consciences, as the Lord had made manifest to his own soul. His first journey on this account was into Westmoreland, Cumberland and Lancashire, where he was subjected to severe sufferings for the truth's sake, being beaten almost to death, by a mob, for speaking in one of the public places of worship.

Soon after this, being at Sedberg, in Yorkshire, on a market-day, he was constrained to preach the Gospel at the market cross, and to warn the people to turn from the error of their ways, to the grace of God and the light in their own consciences. He was hereupon again beset by a concourse of rude persons, who endeavored violently to push him down. Setting their backs against the high stone cross, which was in a tottering condition, and their hands against this faithful man, they threw down the cross with the force exerted, and broke it on the ground. It was remarkable that no one was injured by the accident, as the people were thickly collected around him.

He was afterwards imprisoned at York, having been pursued during his peaceful labors in the gospel, twice attacked by a constable with an iron fork, and violently urged along the street of the small town where he was apprehended at night, his captors rudely shouting as they went from one tavern to another. He was now brought to trial, but at the conclusion of the assizes was cleared by proclamation, and set at liberty. He was however, about a month afterwards, again seized, as he was preaching to the inhabitants of Derby, and immured once more within the walls of a prison; and this unchristian treatment became in after-life, his very frequent experience.

Other faithful men were alike prepared, under the Lord's own forming hand, for the reception and right appreciation of the truths preached by George Fox and his friends.

Edward Burrough was born in the barony of Kendal in the county of Westmoreland, England, about the year 1635. His parents had the reputation of honest and upright persons, and brought up their son with as good an education as the neighborhood afforded. He was a boy of very good understanding, and of knowledge far beyond his years. His intimate friend Francis Howgill testifies of him, that "he had the spirit of a man when he was but a child. I may say, gray hairs were upon him when he was but a youth, for he was clothed with wisdom in his infancy. He was inclinable from his youth upwards, to religion—always accompanied the best men, who walked in godliness and honesty—was never known to be addicted to any vice or bad behavior—but feared the Lord, and walked uprightly according to the light and knowledge received. In his natural disposition, he was bold and manly, dexterous and fervent, and what he took in hand, he did with his might; loving, kind and courteous, merciful and flexible, and easy to be entreated. His delight was always among good people, and to be reading the Scriptures, and his very strength was bent towards God."

This was his character among his associates. But he himself, under a sense of his deficiencies, says that he was wanton and light, and lived in pleasure, without the fear of God, or knowledge of Him but by hearsay or tradition. When, however, he grew up towards twelve years of age, something stirred within him, and showed him that there was a higher religion than that which he was exercised in. He then inquired after the Presbyterians, under the idea that they were nearer the truth than what he had known; and would go several miles on a First-day to hear the best of their preachers. As he grew into favor with them, he left off some of his lightness and vanity; but instead of it, spiritual pride crept in, and he became puffed up in some degree with his attainments. It pleased the Lord, however, in mercy, not to let him rest here; but he was struck as with a terror by the convicting power of Divine Grace; and after his exercises in prayer, he often heard this voice speaking to his soul: "Thou art ignorant of God; thou knowest not where he is, nor what he is: to what purpose is thy prayer?" Fear and dread came upon him, and he was made to give up even "to the moles and to the bats" his formal exercises, performed in his own will, and all reliance on his attainments in human learning. He lost also his dependence upon the preachers, in whom he had so much delighted, and was favored with some experience of joy and peace, and of water from the living fountain, to the refreshment of his soul. But even in this state, the enemy of man's happiness was busily intent on spoiling the work, and infused into his mind the poisonous leaven of self-righteousness and self-activity. "Thus," says he, "being ignorant of the Cross of Christ, to keep low in it, I ran before my Guide, and grew up into notions, to talk of high things; for it was my delight to comprehend in my busy mind." This was a very dangerous state, of which, at length, in great mercy, he was made sensible. "The witness," he says, "which lay slain in me, would give me no rest. Something which shined deep in me, showed me ignorance in all profession, and I was put to a stand many times in myself at those things which were come to pass." About this time, which was about the 17th year of his age, he met with George Fox, who had much reasoning with him and others, at the house of one Miles Bateman, at Underbarrow. Edward says, "it pleased the Lord to speak to me by him, that I was in the prodigal's state, and above the cross of Christ; not in the pure fear of the Lord, but full of corruption and the old nature. I saw myself to be in bondage to my own will, and to my own lust, and full of airy notions and imaginations. Then trouble and distress came upon me, such as I had never known; and I separated from all the glory of the world, and from all my acquaintance and kindred, and betook myself to the company of a poor despised people called Quakers. And now am I one in that generation, which is and ever was hated by the world, the chief priests and pharisees." Being thus brought freely to an acquaintance with that which he had long sought in vain among the hireling teachers and high professors of what they themselves knew not, in a short time (even that same year, viz. 1652,) being as George Fox declares, "endued with power from on high," he came forth in the work of the ministry, and approved himself a faithful laborer therein, travelling up and down, and preaching the gospel freely.

CHAPTER V.

CONVINCEMENT OF THOMAS THOMPSON—AND FURTHER TRANSACTIONS OF GEORGE FOX.

WE are not informed who were the parents of this individual, nor of the place of his birth, but this is supposed to have been in the north of England, and probably between the years 1630 and 1640. His own account relates, that even when he was very young, it pleased the Lord to incline his heart to seek after Him, and that when he was about eight years old, he was deeply impressed with this language, which sounded in his mental ear: "Now is the axe laid to the root of the trees; every tree therefore that bringeth not forth good fruit, shall be hewn down and cast into the fire." Strong desires were raised in his youthful mind, that he might become one of the trees bearing good fruit; and listening to the voice of the Lord in his soul, He discovered to him the evil of many things practised generally by such as he then was, excited in his mind an abhorrence of sin, and preserved him from much of the wickedness which prevailed around him. For several years he was earnestly engaged, both by frequent attendance on those who were accounted the most able preachers, and by a diligent perusal of the Holy Scriptures, which he much loved, to obtain an understanding of the things of religion; but his mind nevertheless was too much outward, knowing not the Light of Christ Jesus to guide him, and depending unduly on instrumental helps. But, alas! as he grew up and increased in knowledge, his heart was not kept so near the Lord as formerly, nor was his care so great to walk in holiness of life before Him; for he began to take up with a false rest, apprehending that all was well with him, because he knew much of the Scriptures, and could repeat great part of the sermons and other exercises of the priests. These blind leaders of the blind also increased his danger by flattering him with smooth words, telling him that he was a hopeful boy and needed not to doubt that it would be well with him. The Lord, however, in great mercy, showed him that his soul was still in want, and that all was not right with him, though he could speak so much of God, Christ and faith. Good desires were again raised in his mind towards the Lord; his false rest was broken up; and he hungered for the bread of life to satisfy his longing and weary soul. This was not however to be found among the hirelings and formal professors amongst whom he had been seeking the way of truth. He says, "then I went to some meetings of the people called Independents; but neither there could I find what my soul wanted, viz. the Life of Jesus, which I could not be satisfied without the enjoyment of. So, being tired out with going from one to another, the Lord in his goodness was pleased to make known to me that the man-made ministers were not of Him, but were such as ran, and he never sent them. Therefore they did not profit the people at all, but were Babylonish merchants, which made a prey upon the people. And this word sounded in me: 'Come out from amongst them my people; be not partakers with them in their sins, lest ye also partake of their plagues.' So in a little time I left them, and grew retired in my mind, delighting much to be alone, meditating on the things of God, or reading such books as were published, of the experiences of those that had any openings in the way of life.

"And in the forepart of the year 1652, it pleased the Lord to order his faithful and valiant servant and messenger, dear George Fox, into these parts; but I had not then opportunity to see him, though I greatly desired it. But some of my familiars that were with him, gave me an account of his manner of life, and also of his doctrine. They told me, that in his behavior he was very reserved, not using any needless words or discourses that tended not to edification, and that he used not respect of persons; very temperate in his eating and drinking; his apparel homely, yet decent; and as for his doctrine, he directed people to the light of Christ in their consciences, to guide them to God.

"At the hearing of these things, though at second hand, the Lord was pleased mightily to work upon my mind, and brought me to a wonderful retiredness; and my mind was truly turned inward to wait on him and desire his teachings. So by degrees, the Lord manifesting one thing after another, by the working and power of God, self came to be denied, and I was, in many things humbled to the cross; so that several of my neighbors and acquaintances marvelled to see me so changed, and some said I would be distracted. But their words were little to me; for as I obeyed the Lord,

I found peace and satisfaction, and the return of God's love into my bosom. And as I gave up any thing for truth's sake, I found peace, and more strength was given me; so that I can truly say, it is good to keep in the counsel of God, and to give up wholly to serve him; for he is good to them that trust in him; and they that faithfully serve him shall in nowise lose their reward.

'After I had for some time been thus inwardly exercised in the things of God, and the work of the Lord prospered in my inward parts, this word arose in me: 'Have not the faith of our Lord Jesus Christ with respect of persons.' And it was upon me to bear my testimony for God, in speaking the plain, simple, and I may say, pure language of *Thee* and *Thou* to every particular person, of what degree or quality soever. But the enemy prevailed with me to resist the motion of the Spirit of Life; and so a veil came over my heart, and the pure principle which justified me while I was faithful to God, did now judge and condemn me for my disobedience. Yet I persisting in it, stopped the work of God; and the enemy who had thus prevailed upon me, laid other baits and snares to catch my feet in, and drew me again into some of the pleasures of this fading world, which I had once denied myself of. But great is the mercy and compassion of the Lord, who suffered me not long to rest in that carnal security, but was pleased in his infinite love to discover to me my loss, and raised desires in me to be where I had once been, in my way towards Zion. But the enemy had got such strength through my disobedience, that I found it more difficult again to get into the way, than could well be thought of by any that had never gone out thereof. Let all take warning not to give way to the enemy, nor resist the motion of God's Spirit while it strives, neither 'despise the day of small things,' lest ye fall into temptations, and anguish and sorrow come upon you."

He proceeds to relate that about midsummer of the year 1652, he heard of a people raised up that were called Quakers; which was the first time that he had heard of that name being given to any people. Desires were raised in his mind to be acquainted with some of them, and accordingly in the Eighth month, hearing that William Dewsbury and some other Friends were come to Frodingham, he gladly embraced the opportunity to go and see them. "And I," says he, "being on my master's work, at Brigham, could not go in the day, but determined to go in the night, and would gladly have had some of my acquaintance to have gone with me. But the night being very dark, none would go; so I went alone. And coming into the room where William was, I found him writing; and the rest of his company were sitting in great silence, seeming to be much retired in mind, and fixed towards God. Their countenances, grave and solid withal, preached to me, and confirmed what I had before believed, that they were the people of the Lord. After a little time, William ceased writing, and many of the town's-people coming in, he began in the power and wisdom of God to declare the truth. And oh! how was my soul refreshed, and the witness for God reached in my heart; I cannot express it with pen: I had never heard nor felt the like before; so that if all the world say, nay, I could have given my testimony, that it was the everlasting truth of God. And in the same month, my mouth was livingly opened, to declare the name of the Lord, and preach repentance to the people. I knew a bridle to my tongue, and was greatly afraid lest I should offend the Lord in thought, word, or deed; and the word of the Lord was in me, 'Thou shalt not do thy own works, nor think thy own thoughts, nor speak thy own words, on this my holy day.' And though I suffered and went through many exercises, yet the Lord bore up my spirit and carried me on, while I abode faithful to him, to the praise of his own name."

"My mouth was often opened in the congregations of his people, to praise his infinite and worthy name; and I often accompanied William Dewsbury, John Whitehead, and sometimes James Nayler, and other early ministers, to and fro in the East Riding of Yorkshire; and the glorious presence of the Lord God was richly with us, to the overcoming of our immortal souls, the comfort of his heritage, and praise of his own name."

Among those who were reached by the testimony of George Fox to pure simple Christianity, and to the doctrine of the Light of Christ in the conscience of man as his infallible Director, was Justice Hotham, a man of a tender spirit, who had some experience of God's workings in his heart. He conversed freely with George Fox, taking him into his private room; and told him that he had himself been acquainted with this Divine teacher for ten years, and was glad that the Lord did now publish it abroad to the people. On George Fox coming there a second time shortly afterwards, Justice Hotham, as he entered his house, took him in his arms in an affectionate manner, offered him the free use of his house as if it were his own, expressed his exceeding gladness at the work of the Lord, and that His power was revealed, and in other respects behaved towards him with remarkable friendliness. Another justice also, named Robinson, received his testimony with great openness, and told him it was well that he exercised that gift which God had given him. But this was not the manner in which he was always received where he had occasion to sojourn. Soon after this, being denied any refreshment by a woman at whose inn he stopped, though it was near the end of the Twelfth month, he passed the night in a hay-stack, exposed to the rain and snow. And a few weeks afterwards, coming towards night into a town called Patrington, he warned the priest, who was in the street, and the people also, to repent and turn to the Lord; and after preaching to those who gathered around him, as it grew dark he went to seek a lodging at an inn. This was denied him, and he then desired that he might be allowed a little meat, or milk, and offered to pay them for it; but this also was refused. So he walked out of the town, followed by a company of rude fellows, whom he bade repent and fear the Lord. Coming to two other houses, he was again refused either lodging or food. By this time it grew so dark that he could not see the road; but discovering a ditch, he got a little water and refreshed himself; and being weary with travelling, sat down among the furze bushes until day dawned, and then passed on. At a small town about three miles off, though the sun was scarcely up, yet the people set upon him, seized him, and violently took him back to Patrington; where all the town was in an uproar. At length a man more tender than the rest, called him into his house, and gave him milk and bread, a welcome refreshment, for he had not eaten for some days before. The rude people of the town had him before a justice several miles distant; who, however, could find nothing against him; and being set at liberty he returned to Patrington, and having an opportunity to declare the truth to the people, he was the means of convincing a large number, who joined him in religious fellowship. The person who had here been chiefly instrumental in persecuting him, afterwards came and desired his forgiveness. Soon after this, being at another town, and again refused a lodging, he warned the people to repent, directed them to the Light of Christ, and leaving them, once more passed the night under a hay-stack. Thus was this dedicated man, whilst seeking the everlasting welfare of his fellow-creatures, persecuted and abused, and denied even the necessaries of life. But yet a seed was sown in many places, which grew and prospered, even under the treading down of the oppressive foot of man; and sprang up and bore fruit to the praise of the great Husbandman, who had sent his servant forth.

Passing through Yorkshire into Lincolnshire, George Fox came to Gainsborough, and found the people much excited on account of a Friend having preached in the market-place. A man came into the house into which George had entered, and falsely told the people there assembled that George Fox had declared himself to be Christ. This still further enraged them, and they were scarcely restrained from laying violent hands upon him. But he was moved to get upon a table, and with power and authority from on High to tell them, that "Christ was *in* them, except they were reprobates; and that it was Christ the eternal power of God that spoke in him—not that he was Christ." The people generally were satisfied, except this false accuser and some whom he had brought in. George Fox called him Judas, and prophetically told him that Judas's end would be his: which shortly proved true; for this man, like the betrayer of our Lord, went away and hanged himself, and a stake was driven into his grave, as a legal token of his self-murder.

The holy zeal with which this apostle of primitive Christianity revived, pursued his way, was not to be damped by false accusations, nor his courage by the threats of the priests and magistrates. The Lord had shown him, he says, that "if but one man or woman were raised up by His power, to stand and live in the same Spirit that the prophets and apostles were in, who gave forth the Scriptures, that man or woman should shake all the country in their profession for ten miles round; for people had the Scriptures, but were not in that same light, and power, and spirit, which they were in that gave forth the Scriptures." He exhorted his fellow-men wherever he went, to press after this attainment, instead of leaving them satisfied, as the time-serving priests did, with reaching half-way to the kingdom of purity and peace. He earnestly insisted on the important practical truth, not only that we must *aim at* complete freedom from sin, even in this life, but that it was *possible to attain to it,* through obedience to the manifestations of the Light of Christ in the secret recesses of the heart.

He was often led to point out the difference, between a pretended high value of the Holy Scriptures, and a sincere endeavor to live in the spirit which they inculcate. He declared also, in opposition to the favorite opinion, that the Scriptures were to be interpreted by the humanly cultivated powers of man, "that the Holy Scriptures were given forth by the Spirit of God, and all people must first come to the Spirit of God in themselves, by which they might know God and Christ, of whom the prophets and the apostles learned, and *by the same spirit* know the Holy Scriptures; for as the Spirit of God was in them that gave forth the Scriptures, so the same Spirit of God must be in all them that come to understand the Scriptures."

CHAPTER VI.

CONVINCEMENT OF FRANCIS HOWGILL—GEORGE WHITEHEAD—AND JUDGE FELL'S FAMILY—GEORGE FOX STILL PERSECUTED—FIRST CONVINCEMENTS IN LONDON.

AMONG the most eminent of those who were convinced of the truth during this year, and made to sit together in heavenly places in Christ, were Francis Howgill and George Whitehead, who soon after became able ministers of the gospel, and the former of whom sealed his testimony to the truth by laying down his life in prison, for the faith in which he most surely believed.

Francis Howgill was a tender religious man, who from conscientious motives had left the Episcopalian society, and attached himself to the Independents as being less superstitious. Having been trained up for a minister by a university education, he became a teacher among those whom he joined. Yet the strivings of the Spirit of Christ were still mercifully extended to him, making him dissatisfied with his attainments, and convincing him that notwithstanding all his fasting and praying, and what were esteemed good works, yet the root of sin still remained unsubdued within him. Although the common doctrine was, that Christ had taken the guilt of sin upon himself, yet this could not satisfy him, because his conscience told him, "his servant thou art, whom thou obeyest." But increasing in spiritual understanding, it was shown to him, that the Lord, according to ancient prophecy, would in these latter days teach the people himself; and it seemed also to him that the time when this should be more manifestly the case was near at hand. Some time afterwards, on the same day in which he had himself been preaching in Firbank Chapel, George Fox preached there in the afternoon; and when he heard him call the attention to the Light of Christ in man, as the way to salvation, he believed this to be the word of truth, and that he had been ignorant of the principles of true religion. Submitting to the reproofs of this inward Light, he saw the unfruitfulness of all his former labor, which he had undertaken in his own time and way. Anguish and sorrow seized upon him; and judgment came over all his self-righteousness. And being from this time given up to serve the Lord, he and John Audland, who was convinced at the same time, and who had taken pay for preaching, in Lancashire, having now received the gospel freely, and the word of life from Christ himself, in obedience to the command of the Lord, returned the money to the parish and people from whom they had received it. The

Son of God came to be more and more revealed in him; he began to know His command, and powerfully and freely to preach Him and his word of life; which so enraged the priests and magistrates, that within this same year he was seized and locked up in a filthy jail at Appleby, and kept there a prisoner for some time.

George Whitehead was born about the year 1636, at Sun Bigs, in Westmoreland. He was educated at a grammar school in the neighborhood, and appears to have made such progress in his literary pursuits, as to have been employed for some time as a teacher. His parents had a view of educating him for a minister; but his mind was very early in life visited by the enlightening influence of divine grace: and being drawn into secret inquiries after a knowledge of true religion, he was enabled to see how those among whom he had been partly educated, came short of what they professed and pretended in their worship, preaching and praying; so that he felt restrained from intimately uniting himself to them, or continuing to take part in their ceremonious forms of worship, even before he knew any thing of the people called Quakers. Nevertheless, the good desires which the Lord had raised within him, after repentance unto life, were often quenched, and his mind was led away, through an airy, light disposition, after music, vain mirth, and other follies. Yet the Lord mercifully followed him with judgment and reproof in his very young years, and renewed his longings after the right way. He wanted a true support to his mind, more substantial than what he could obtain from the priests and professors of religion among whom he had walked; not knowing the Light of Christ, which convinced him of sin, and would lead him into the paths of righteousness. He was for a time much at a loss, earnestly seeking after an experience of true religion; and wandering, as one bewildered, looking for this attainment among those whom he supposed to be in possession of some higher and more refined views respecting spiritual gifts. He was then about fourteen years of age.

After a short time, he heard of some people called Quakers, who trembled at the word of God; and observing how they were reviled and reproached by wicked and loose people, he was induced to make further inquiry, and was led by the Lord, on whom he relied for counsel, to believe that they were His people. And he even began to contend for them and their principles, so far as he knew them, before he had attended any of their meetings, or heard them minister.

But finding that they held a meeting at a place in the same county where he was born, he went thither, and was, by the eminent power of the Lord which appeared among them, in contriting their hearts, and bringing them into earnest cravings after true repentance and sanctification of spirit, much confirmed in the belief that he must leave the high professing but worldly-minded priests, and unite with this poor despised people, in sitting down in pure dependence upon the Lord alone, and thus seek ability from Him to worship in spirit and in truth. His convincement took place about the seventeenth year of his age. Some time after this, he had an opportunity of hearing the powerful ministry of George Fox; when he found that it proceeded from life and experience, and tended to bring to an inward feeling and sense of the life and power of Christ, and the sanctifying virtue thereof in the heart. He now saw, that to be made wise in the living knowledge of God, he must become a fool to that wisdom of his own in which he had trusted; and thus retiring to the grace of God, with which he was secretly visited, it pleased the Lord to endue him with a gift in the ministry; and the following year, being between 17 and 18 years old, he went forth on foot in that holy service, to the convincing of many, and the edification of the church.

His first journey, as a minister, was into Yorkshire. Lincolnshire, Norfolk, and some adjacent counties. At Norwich he visited in prison, Richard Hubberthorn, a fellow-laborer in the same glorious gospel, who was then confined in an old decayed stone vault or hole in the castle wall, for his faithful adherence to the truth, and whose testimony and sufferings had been made instrumental to the gathering of others in that city into the same faith.

In this neighborhood, George Whitehead held many meetings, and numbers were convinced. Several priests attempted to oppose him, thinking to take advantage of his youth; but the Lord gave him suitable replies to their sophistry; and in the spirit of meekness he exposed some of their unsound and unscriptural practices. He had also to contend several times against Antinomians and Ranters, who falsely asserted the unavoidable continuance of sin in man as long as he lived, and pleaded for some corrupt liberties. These deluded men were greatly struck with the baptizing power which accompanied the ministry of this youth of eighteen years, in testifying against sin and wickedness, the lust of the flesh, the lust of the eye, the pride of life, and the love of the world; and being brought into great self-abasement and fear, they earnestly desired his counsel, and several of them became reformed in their lives and convinced of the truth.

Though so young in the service of his divine Master, his ministry in the counties of Norfolk and Suffolk was remarkably attended by the convincing baptizing power of the Lord. Great numbers joined the Society of Friends, and many meetings were soon established.

Before he was twenty-one years of age, he performed another journey in Suffolk, accompanied by Richard Clayton and John Harwood. In passing through the town of Bures, Richard Clayton thought it his duty to affix a paper on the door of the public worship-house, containing several Scripture texts, to show the evil fruits, covetousness and corruption of false teachers and leaders. For this, they were all three taken up, and Richard Clayton was whipped and sent out of the town. George Whitehead and John Harwood, though innocent of the infraction of any law, after lying more than two months in prison, were tried as disturbers of the peace. At the trial they were scarcely permitted to speak for themselves, the judge himself acting as their accuser, and were fined twenty nobles each. Refusing to acknowledge any guilt by paying this fine, they were remanded to prison, where they continued twelve months, and endured extreme privations and sufferings. For a considerable time, they, with three other Friends, were immured among felons, in a low dungeon-like place under a market-house, their lodging being on rye-straw on a damp, earthen floor. The jailer was much enraged at the Friends, because they testified against his wickedness, and would not contribute to his habits of extortion from the prisoners, nor encourage the great drunkenness produced by his bar-room in the prison, by purchasing any of his beer. This man, as well as his bar-keeper, often shamefully abused them. The latter once violently hit one of them with a stone, and took up a stool also as a missile, and often beat them on their faces and elsewhere with his fists, for no other cause than their faithfully reproving his wickedness. Some of the other prisoners also, encouraged by the example of this man and the jailer, would frequently take away their food, and several times beat and stoned them, and threatened to kill them, or knock them on the head; and very frequently were they struck so violently by the jailer or his agents, that the blood gushed from their mouths and noses.

Some of their fellow-prisoners who joined with them in drinking nothing but water, participated in this ill usage; and after a time, George Whitehead and two others were let down by a ladder into a dismal noisome dungeon, twelve feet deep under the ground, very dark, and very narrow. At the bottom, was an iron grate with the bars more than twelve inches apart, extending over a pit, they knew not how deep, into which they might have fallen, but for the kind warning of a woman who saw them put down into the dungeon; so that by standing close to the sides they kept themselves from slipping in. They were however preserved through all this cruel usage, in great resignation, and were favored with the sweet sense of the glorious presence of the Lord, so that they could even sing praises to his name in the midst of their sufferings.

Whilst they were in this dungeon, some of their Friends from a distance came to visit them, but were not suffered to come to them; and so wickedly sordid indeed was the jailer, that when their friends, moved by compassion, and a desire to minister to their wants, would approach the prison door or window, he or his company would cast water upon them, and refuse them all access unless they would pay money to be allowed to enter. At length, after fifteen months' imprisonment, they were released by order of Oliver Cromwell, at the instance of their friends in London, particularly of a Friend named Mary Sanders, who lived in the Protector's family.

The next winter George Whitehead visited London, and was instrumental to the convincing of many; and after his return, he found it laid upon him to go to Nayland to hold a meeting with the inhabitants, where his life had been threatened on a former occasion, if he should venture to hold a meeting there. The meeting was held in a small orchard, where, after waiting on the Lord for some time in silence, George Whitehead felt himself constrained to preach the everlasting gospel without fear of man. But after he had preached a considerable time, a person rushed in with a constable and rude company, pulled him down from the stool on which he was standing, and carried him off to the justice's hall. After a pretended examination, the justice informed him that he was to be whipped severely the next day; that if he came thither again, he should be branded on the shoulder as a rogue; and if he came a third time, he should be hanged. George exhorted the justice to repentance, and told him that notwithstanding all their threatenings, if the Lord, whom he served, should require his return, he must obey Him.

The next day the sentence was put in execution. George Whitehead was conveyed into the market-place, and stripped to the waist; and a man employed by the constable laid on so violently with a long, sharp whip, that large stripes and cuts were visible on his back and breast, and the blood flowed freely. Many of the spectators wept to see this cruelty, and some cried out to stop it; but the innocent victim was borne above his sufferings by the power of the Lord, and was enabled to sing praises to His Holy name, in that he had been accounted worthy to suffer for His Truth's sake. After the execution, he was permitted to take his horse, and was conveyed out of the county by constables; and coming into Essex, he had many good meetings, the people being aroused by the accounts of his sufferings, and anxious to meet with the young man who had been so cruelly whipped at Nayland. So that the malice of his enemies was overruled, to the spreading of a knowledge of the Truth in the eastern counties of England.

The year 1652, was also productive of the convincement of the wife and family of Judge Fell, of Swarthmore, in Lancashire. Margaret Fell, a descendant of the martyr, Anne Askew, was a woman of a very superior mind, highly esteemed by men of eminence in the neighborhood, for her natural abilities, and her religious disposition. She and her children and several of their household joined the Society; and though her husband did not entirely leave his former profession, yet he remained ever afterwards very friendly to George Fox and his brethren, and their house was a hospitable resting-place for the ministers of Truth for many years. Some time after the decease of Judge Fell, his widow, who had herself become a minister of the Gospel, and travelled extensively in its service, married George Fox, and was for the remainder of her life eminently useful in the church, as a succorer of many under affliction for the gospel's sake, and a strengthener of the hands of the standard-bearers.

The persecutions of various kinds with which George Fox was assailed, during the year 1652, were indeed enough to discourage any man not supported by a consciousness that he was acting under the immediate authority of the Almighty. A few of them may be briefly recounted before we pass on.

At Tickhill, he went, under religious constraint, to the public worship house, and found the priest and the chief persons of the parish in the chancel. He says, " I went up to them, and began to speak; but they immediately fell upon me; and the clerk up with his Bible as I was speaking, and struck me on the face with it, so that my face gushed out with blood, and I bled exceedingly in the steeplehouse. Then the people cried, 'Let us have him out of the church:' and when they had got me out, they beat me exceedingly, and threw me down, and over a hedge; and afterwards they dragged me through a house into the street, stoning and beating me as they dragged me along, so that I was all over besmeared with blood and dirt. They got my hat from me, which I never got again. Yet when I was got upon my legs again, I declared to them the word of life, and showed them the fruits of their teacher, and how they dishonored Christianity."

Shortly after this, he came at night to a small tavern on a common, and found there a company of rude fellows drinking; and because he refused to drink with them, they struck him with their clubs. He reproved them, and walked out of the house upon the common; but one of these men followed him out, and would have come close up to him, under a pretence of whispering something to him; when George perceived that he had a knife, and therefore kept clear of him, warning him to repent and fear God. The man being thus defeated in his wicked attempt, left George on the common during the night, and returned into the house.

Having visited Friends in Westmoreland, he returned into Lancashire; and at Ulverstone on a lecture-day, he felt it to be his duty to address the people assembled in the public meeting-house, after the priest had finished a blustering harangue. They were quiet, and heard him gladly, until a justice of the peace stirred them up against him, inciting them to break the peace, in tumultuously falling upon this innocent man. They got into a great rage, knocked him down, kicked him and trampled on him in the steeple-house; and so great was the uproar, that some people tumbled over their seats for fear. This justice at length led him out of the house, and bid the constables whip him and put him out of the town. They led him about a quarter of a mile, some holding him by his collar, and some by his arms and shoulders, and thus they shook and dragged him along. Many friendly people who heard him gladly in the meeting-house, were also knocked down, and had their heads broken, so that the blood ran from several of them; and Judge Fell's son running after, to see what they would do with George Fox, they threw him into a ditch, some of them crying out, "knock the teeth out of his head." The officers having got George out of the town, beat him with their rods, and thrust him among the rude rabble; who, having furnished themselves with hedge-stakes, large sticks and holly bushes, fell upon him, and beat him on the head, arms and shoulders, till they deprived him of sense, and he fell down on the wet common, where he lay for some time. About two weeks afterwards, at a place called Cockan, in Walney island, there came a man with a pistol, and snapped it at George Fox; but happily it would not go off; and George solemnly addressing the man on his wickedness, he was so struck by the power of the Lord, that he trembled for fear, and went and hid himself.

The next morning, crossing a part of the sea in a boat, as soon as he came to land, about forty men rushed out with staves, clubs, and fishing-poles, who fell upon him, beating and kicking him, and endeavoring to thrust him backward into the sea. But he went up into the midst of them; when they furiously laid at him again, knocked him down, and stunned him. When he came to himself, he looked up and saw a woman throwing stones at his face, while her husband was lying over him, to ward off the stones and other blows. Some of these people had persuaded this woman that George Fox had "bewitched" her husband, and had promised her that if she would let them know when he came thither, they would be the death of him. But the Lord preserved his faithful servant out of the hands of these wicked men. George having at length been set over the water again, came to the town on the other side, when he was assailed by the rabble with flails, pitchforks, and staves, crying, "Kill him! knock him on the head!" etc.: and after they had grossly abused him, they drove him a considerable distance from the town, and there left him. Margaret Fell, hearing of the circumstance, sent a horse to convey him to her hospitable mansion, where he was well cared for in his bruised and exhausted condition; and the woman who had thrown stones at him, afterwards repented of her wickedness and became convinced of the truth, as did also some others of those bitter persecutors.

He was now summoned to appear before the court at Lancaster; where about forty priests appeared against him; but so well did he defend himself and advocate the principles of truth, that he was fully discharged in open court; some of the priests were publicly rebuked from the bench; Justice Benson and the mayor of Lancaster, with many others, were convinced; and the people cried out, that "the Quakers had got the day, and the priests were fallen."

As he stayed two or three days after this in Lancaster, some of the rude people plotted together to draw him out of the house, and throw him over the bridge into the river; but being defeated in this, they set a madman and another fellow at him with sticks, in order to accomplish their wicked intent. George spoke to them "in the Lord's mighty power," which chained them both down, and made them calm and quiet.

It was not till the year 1654, that any ministers of the people called Quakers appear to have visited the city of London; unless Gervase Benson, who was there in 1653, were in that station, which is somewhat doubtful. Several Friends' books however had been printed in that city during the year last mentioned. In the beginning of 1654 some tender people there were drawn into communion with each other by the power of the Spirit of Truth operating upon their minds, and inclining them to greater spirituality and a closer walk with God: and about the end of the first month in this year, Francis Howgill and John Camm visited Oliver Cromwell on behalf of their suffering brethren, and went to some of the public meeting-houses, declaring the way of the Lord. This spring also, two women from the north, one of whom was Isabel Buttery, came to London, and became acquainted with one of those seeking persons, Simon Dring of Moorfields, and also with Amos Stodart, who from conscientious scruples had recently resigned his commission as captain in the army. These women brought with them for distribution, copies of an epistle from George Fox, "To all that would know the way to the kingdom;" which directed people to turn their minds within, where the voice of God is to be heard; and walking with Amos Stodart and Simon Dring in the suburbs, they met with Ruth Brown, a young woman of about sixteen years of age. This young woman, receiving one of the epistles, was convinced of the truth of the principles therein laid down, and thenceforth joined the small number of congenial minds who then began to meet together to wait upon God. They met at the houses of Robert and Simon Dring; and sometimes Isabel and her companion spoke a few words by way of ministry. In the Fifth month of that year, Francis Howgill, Richard Hubberthorn, Edward Burrough, and Anthony Pearson, were moved to visit the hidden seed in that great metropolis; who having meetings in several places, their ministrations were attended with signal success in gathering into the fold of Christ many that were "waiting for the consolation of Israel." Meetings of Friends were soon settled in various parts of the metropolis—at first in private houses—until the Society there growing too large for these to accommodate, a house known by the name of the "Bull and Mouth," near Aldersgate street, was hired as a public meeting-house. This place subsequently became the scene of bitter persecutions to this unoffending people.

CHAPTER VII.

RISE OF THE SOCIETY IN IRELAND—WILLIAM EDMUNDSON.

THERE is no account of Ireland being visited by any ministers of the Society of Friends, previous to the year 1654. The first person who publicly espoused its principles in that country appears to have been that subsequently eminent minister of the Gospel, William Edmundson.

He was born in the county of Westmoreland, England, in the year 1627, and when about twenty-three years of age, went into the army, during the civil wars, and continued for some time a soldier under the Parliament. He had often, even from his youthful days, experienced the good hand of the Lord, tendering his spirit, and bringing him into serious thoughtfulness respecting the eternal welfare of his soul; and while he was serving in the army in Scotland under Oliver Cromwell, it pleased the Lord to bring matters closer home to him, and to visit him by the strivings of His Spirit, in order to draw him out of the corruptions of the world, into a nearer acquaintance and precious communion with Christ, revealed within as the power of God, and the wisdom of God. In 1651, he returned with the army to England, and being quartered in Derbyshire, he there heard of the people called Quakers; and though they were much spoken against, he found his heart secretly drawn towards them for good. He however marched again into Scotland, and then left the army, and returned back to England. About this time he married; and at the solicitation of his brother, who was a soldier in Ireland, he went over and settled at Antrim, entering into mercantile business. Here the officers of the regiment in which his brother served, kindly offered him the usual pay, without his being obliged to perform actual duty, or neglect his business; but his conscience had been awakened by the Lord's judgments, and he declined this offer. He soon sold off his stock of goods; and going over to England to purchase a fresh supply, he heard of George Fox and James Nayler being in the north; and feeling a great desire to meet with them, he went to a place where James Nayler was, and had an opportunity of hearing him discourse of the things of God's kingdom, and the work of regeneration.

And though James's words were not many, yet they were so powerful, and so fully reached and answered the testimony of the divine witness in his own mind, that his heart was opened to receive the word preached, and to confess that it was indeed the truth. He was now brought into great exercise of spirit; his former ways were "hedged up;" and many things to which he had been accustomed were shown to him in the Light of Christ, to be incompatible with the purity and entire obedience to which he was called. He flinched not however from the hand of the Lord, for his sins were set clearly before him, and he felt that he must be purged from them through judgment. And returning shortly to Ireland, the Lord's hand was mercifully laid upon him, while at sea, producing great wrestlings and conflicts of spirit; under a strong temptation to land his goods clandestinely and avoid paying the duty; but this he was enabled to withstand. He landed at Carrickfergus; and rode twelve miles to his own home. His brother meeting him at the door, offered the usual salutation, probably bowing and using the empty complimentary phrases so ready in the mouths of men of the world. The Lord's power that instant so seized upon William, that he could not join in what he now saw to be vanity; and he was broken into many tears. His wife and brother were amazed at the change, but made no opposition.

He had now to undergo a further trial of faith, in passing his goods at the custom-house. The officers required the usual oath, and would have seized his goods; but he firmly told them that he could not swear, for Christ had forbidden it. This was strange to them, having never known it objected to before; and his serious deportment, his refusal to put off his hat in compliment to them, and his steady adherence to the simple language of *Thou* and *Thee*, were very offensive; but after much difficulty he at length obtained the clearing of his goods, and brought them safely home.

His spiritual conflicts continued, his sleep often departed from him, and deep were the baptisms into which his soul was plunged, for its purification from every defilement. He had no outward adviser to depend upon, and would have gone far for the company of an experienced Friend; but he was thus mercifully taught to depend on the Lord alone for all his fresh springs of life and strength.

After a time there came into the country one Major Bousfield, who professed to be a very knowing man in the things of religion, and spoke plausibly of his unity with George Fox and James Nayler. William Edmundson went to see him, and heard abundance of talk, and was at first glad to think that he had met with one so knowing, and so capable of advising him in his great troubles. But Bousfield advised him to be cheerful and merry, and not to look at these inward troubles, which he represented as the work of the enemy, to bring him into despair. This doctrine was very comfortable to the natural inclinations, and love of ease to the flesh prompted him to take hold of it. It seemed quickly to heal his maladies without the daily cross of Christ, or self-denial. But this false healing lasted only about a week. The Lord in great mercy pursued him, and let him see, in that light which cannot deceive, that something was yet in him that withstood the work of God, and that this must be crucified by the Lord's judgments, and by the daily cross of Christ Jesus. "Then," says he, "I saw there was no physician but the Lord alone; and I also saw where Bousfield was, and all of that spirit; that they took up their rest and satisfaction in a talk and notion of religion, without the true cross of Christ, that should mortify their lusts, wills, and vile affections, and crucify them to the world, and the world unto them; being at ease in a form of godliness, without the real work of the power."

Early in the year 1654, Myles Halhead, James Lancaster, and Miles Bateman visited Ireland, and had some interviews with the rulers and the officers of the army, but soon returned to England. William was then removing from Antrim to Lurgan. His wife and brother soon became convinced of that truth which had so powerfully operated upon himself; and they met together in his house twice a week, to wait on the Lord in silence. After a short time, four more were convinced and joined with them; and this was the first settled meeting of Friends in Ireland. A number of sober people were after a while attracted to them, and the name of Friends, and reputation of the way of Truth was spread abroad.

It was not long before the Great Head of the church saw meet to endow William Edmundson with a gift in the ministry of the gospel among this little company; and though he was under great fear of being deluded by a wrong spirit, yet faithfully obeying the divine call, and waiting on the gift in all humility and watchfulness, he was gradually enlarged in experience of the mysteries of the heavenly kingdom, and fitted for extensive usefulness in the church. Being moved to go to the public worship-house at Lurgan, to declare the truth to the people, he was much beaten and abused; but his testimony reached the consciences of several of the congregation, of whom two individuals followed him out of the house and joined with Friends.

The next Friend who came into Ireland was John Tiffin, who spent some time with the small company at Lurgan, occasionally speaking a few words among them, to their edification and comfort. William Edmundson accompanied him to several places, where they had good service, many beginning to inquire into the truth of those principles which they held forth. But one of their most prominent testimonies being levelled against all hire for preaching the gospel, the priests began to be alarmed, and incensed the magistrates against Friends, as holding "damnable doctrines," and being "led away with the delusions of Satan." Their pride too was wounded, by the refusal of Friends to give them the usual complimentary salutations, or to address them singly in the plural number. This they could not suffer, and accordingly beset Friends with frequent abuse, and sometimes with stones and blows.

William and John went to Belfast, where they could find but one inn that would admit them to lodge. John was very desirous of obtaining an open door for preaching the word of Truth in that town; but the people shut their ears, doors, and hearts against it and them. Being disappointed in all their endeavors to obtain a room in which to hold a meeting, they went to a place near the town, where three lanes met, and there sat down and waited on the Lord. People gathered about them in wonder, and they thus had an opportunity of directing their attention to the Spirit of God in their own hearts, and spreading the sound of the Gospel through the land. John Tiffin soon after returned to England; but the Truth gained ground and prevailed, and Friends increased in number, and were preserved in a lowly watchful state of mind, which made their very countenances preach to their sober neighbors. John Shaw (who with his family was convinced about this time) often afterwards said that William Edmundson's words *and deportment* were a means of convincing him of the truth.

The next messenger of the gospel sent into Ireland was Richard Clayton, whom also William Edmundson accompanied in his journey, both of them travelling on foot. At Coleraine they preached to the people in the streets, but being banished from the town, they went and lodged in a cabin among the mountains. They had two meetings at Londonderry, where a family of five persons were convinced, and the governor being at both meetings acknowledged, with several others, the truth of what was testified. At several other places they were made instrumental to the convincement of many tender seeking individuals, and some meetings were soon settled, particularly near Kilmore, and at the Grange below Antrim, and also at Toberhead. But the priests became more and more enraged, and put William Edmundson in prison at Armagh; where the Lord was his strength, in his own conscious weakness, and His power enabled him to confound the sophistry of the priest and the justice, and the jailer could not bear to look him in the face. It does not appear that he remained long in prison; for at his examination the people were satisfied of his innocence, and the court, ashamed of his commitment, set him at liberty. He went over to England this year, on a visit to George Fox, whom he had not before met with. George was tenderly affected, and heard with gladness of the progress of Truth in Ireland. He took William Edmundson into an orchard, where he kneeled down and prayed; and afterwards sent by him a short epistle to the Friends in Ireland, exhorting them faithfully to wait on that Power which had convinced them, and dwell in the life, love, power and wisdom of God, and in love one with another, and with God. Edward Burrough and Francis Howgill had gone over to Ireland, and George Fox desired William Edmundson to join them on his return. These friends were eminently serviceable in that island, particularly in the province of Munster, many receiving their testimony and adhering to the doctrine they preached. At Bandon, Edward Cook, a man of great parts, who had been a cornet of horse in Oliver Cromwell's own troop, and receiver to Lord Cork, was with his wife convinced, and remained a steadfast and useful member. Several others there also joined the Society. At Limerick, attempting to speak to the people in the public meeting-house, they were run upon by a mob, and put out of the town; but as they rode along, Edward Burrough preached through the streets on horseback, and when outside of the gates, had an opportunity of speaking to a great multitude who assembled there, directing them to Christ Jesus, a measure of whose Spirit was given to every man to profit withal; and several were convinced. Several also were convinced by these Friends at Kinsale, among whom was Susanna Worth, wife of Edward Worth, afterwards Bishop of Killaloe, who suffered much from her husband, but lived and died in unity with Friends.

This year also came over Elizabeth Fletcher and Elizabeth Smith, who were the first Friends who held a settled meeting in Dublin, and the first also who came to Cork, where many were convinced.

About this time a singular exercise fell upon William Edmundson, as he was attending a fair on business at Antrim; by which he was instructed in the benefit of faithfully attending to the secret intimations of the divine Monitor, saying, "this is the way, walk in it," even when he might not see immediately the intention of the Almighty in thus leading him by a way that he knew not. Returning with his brother late from the fair, they proposed to lodge at Glenavy, six miles on their way homeward; but before they arrived there, William was introduced into a great exercise of mind, accompanied with an intimation, the source of which he believed to be the divine Spirit, that his shop was in danger of being robbed that night, but that he was to go back towards Clough; and being much perplexed under the apprehension of danger to his property on the one hand if he went not home, and on the other hand not knowing wherefore he should be required to go back to Clough, he cried earnestly to the Lord, to be preserved from following a delusive spirit, and that he might be directed what course to pursue. On which he received a clear intimation, that the same power which required him to go back, would preserve his property from harm. Lodging at Glenavy, he slept but little; but in the morning, not daring to disobey so clear a command, he let his brother proceed homewards, while he went himself to Clough. Two female ministers from London, Anne Gould and Julian Wastwood, had recently come into Ireland, and after passing through much of the northern part of the island, on foot, wading rivers and dirty miry ways during the cold weather of winter, they came to Clough. Anne being a delicate woman, was much exhausted, and staying there, the enemy of all good persuaded her that God had forsaken her, and that she was there to be destroyed; so that she fell into despair. William Edmundson knew nothing of these women, but his feet were directed to the inn where they were staying. Anne was overwhelmed under mental trouble, but he was made the instrument of her consolation, so that she entirely revived, and rejoiced in the consciousness that she had escaped from a great temptation. He assisted them on their journey with his horse as far as Carrickfergus, whence going home he sent a conveyance for them to his house.

On reaching his home, he found that on the night when the foregoing exercise came upon him, the shop-window was broken down by robbers, and fell with such violence on the counter as to awaken his family, and the thieves being frightened ran away. "So," says he, "I was confirmed that it was the word of the Lord, that said, 'that which drew me back should preserve my shop;' and I was greatly strengthened to obey the Lord in what he required; for I was much afraid, lest at any time my understanding should be betrayed by a wrong spirit; not fearing the loss of goods, nor sufferings for the truth, its testimony being more to me than all other things."

About this year or the next, a number of Friends went to Limerick in the ministry of the gospel, and were instrumental in convincing several. These new converts however being but weak, for a time continued to go to hear one

Robert Wilkinson, a captain in the army, a man much esteemed, but greatly given to religious disputation, and much a stranger to that silent and humble waiting in the divine Light, which would mortify the carnal will, and bring down that disposition which would busily but unprofitably intermeddle in spiritual matters. Him, however, these newly convinced ones went to hear, not seeing through the shallowness of the man; until one Abraham Newbold was moved to come from Waterford thither, who going into the meeting where Captain Wilkinson was preaching, stood up, and with a strong voice, and the liberty much exercised in the congregations of that day, cried out, "Serpent, be silent!" Wilkinson hearing these few but potent words, would have entered into dispute, and inquired by what spirit Abraham spoke; to which the latter merely replied, "Thou knowest not." The preacher attempted to proceed, but was utterly confounded, and carried out of the meeting. The next meeting-day also he was taken out fainting, and from that time ceased preaching any more. These convinced persons afterwards became more enlightened in their understandings, met together in silence, and bore a faithful testimony against the fashions and manners of the world; so that they had to bear their share of reproach and imprisonment, and their neighbors were even prohibited by the magistrates from purchasing anything from them in the way of their trade.

We have now briefly traced the steps of some of those pioneers of the spiritual army, who first proclaimed in word and in life the pure principles of the Society of Friends in Ireland. We have seen that in common with their brethren in England, they had to stem the current of prevailing modes of thought, and boldly oppose the most favorite and cherished practices of the community around them; for they were men who, in the Light of Christ, seeing through the emptiness of mere profession without substance, and having themselves felt the sorrowful effects of living in a dependence on outward rites and ceremonies, could not but cry aloud against the corruptions which successive ages had introduced into the professing church, and which were greatly hindering those "who were entering" with sincere hearts, into the kingdom. This brought them, of course, into suffering at the instigation of the priests, whose influence their principles were so directly calculated to overturn; and many were the days and weeks and months passed by these faithful witnesses in dungeons and noisome prisons, for the word of God and the testimony of Jesus; though it does not appear that in Ireland the attempts to put them down by force were so systematic or so violent as in some other parts. The rabble were guilty of much personal abuse, set on by their priests, and the magistrates inflicted grievous imprisonments; but beyond this they seem to have been restrained by the power of Him whose will had called the Society into existence, and who caused the plant of his right-hand planting to prosper even under the foot of the oppressor. William Edmundson, who had now given up his shop, and taken a farm in the county Cavan, thus describes the state of the little band of Friends in Ireland, about twelve years after he had himself openly espoused its cause:

"Truth," says he, "was much spread, and meetings settled in several places; and many being convinced and brought to the knowledge of God, were added to Friends. But sufferings increased for not paying tithes and priests' maintenance, and towards repairing their worship-houses, for not observing their holy-days, so called, and such like. They fleeced us in taking our goods, and imprisoned some.

"In those days the world and the things of it were not near our hearts; but the love of God, his truth and testimony, lived in our hearts; we were glad of one another's company, though sometimes our outward fare was very mean, and our lodging on straw. We did not mind high things, but were glad one of another's welfare in the Lord; and his love dwelt in us. I was often abroad in Truth's service, visiting Friends, and getting meetings in several places. I was moved to travel into Leinster, and went from place to place, as the Lord's good Spirit guided me."

"I went to Mullingar, and lodged there one night, where was a trooper that was convinced, who rode with me several miles the next day, and continued coming to meetings. I came that night to Finagh; but the inn-keepers refused me lodging, for they knew I was a 'Quaker.' It was winter, and cold weather; so I inquired for the constable, and told him he must provide me lodging, for I was a traveller, had money to pay for what I should have, and had been at the inns, where they refused me lodging. He kept an ale-house, and had also refused me; but after much discourse, he told me I must be content with such lodging as he had for me. I told him to let me have a room with a fire, and hay for my horse, and I would be content. So I alighted, went into the house, and there were troopers drinking. They soon perceived what I was, and began to scoff, and ask me many questions, which I answered in my freedom; but when I '*thee'd*' and '*thou'd*' them in our discourse, they were very angry; and one of them swore, if I '*thou'd*' him again, he would cleave my head. But in our discourse, when it came in its place, I '*thou'd*' him again; and he starting up in anger, drew his sword; but one of his corporals sitting by him stopped him, and commanded him to put up his sword, for there should be no cleaving of heads there; so caused the troopers to go to their quarters; but he stayed with me discoursing late in the night, and was convinced, being tender, received the Truth, and came to meetings.

"About this time we had a meeting at Belturbet, and the Lord's power and presence was with us; but the provost of the town was an envious man, who came with some rude people, broke up our meeting, and took us to prison, both men and women. We were all night in a very cold place, and the women mightily pinched with cold, it being frost and snow. The next morning he set all the other Friends at liberty, but me he put in the stocks in the market-place; and people gathered about me, where I had an opportunity to preach the truth to them; which they heard with soberness, were tender, and reflected much upon the provost for abusing us.

"Robert Wardell then (being but a boy) told the provost, he had set a better man than himself in the stocks, and there was a time when such as he durst not have meddled with me: wherefore the provost took him, and set him in the stocks by me. But his father heard of it, and threatened the provost with the law; so Robert Wardell was soon taken out of the stocks; who being convinced, kept with Friends, and afterwards became a serviceable man for Truth, and a preacher of it.

"The people were much dissatisfied with the provost; so he sent his officer to let me loose; who opened the stocks, and bade me 'take out my leg, for I might go my way.' I told him, 'I had been grossly abused, and made a public spectacle to the people, as though I had done some great offence, but I was not convicted of the breach of any law; so let the provost come himself and take me out, for he put me in.' The provost came and opened the stocks, bidding me 'take out my leg.' I told him, 'No; for he had made me a spectacle to the people, and I knew no law that I had broken; but let him take out my leg, that put it in.' So he opened the stocks with one hand, and took my leg out with the other."

CHAPTER VIII.

CONVINCEMENT OF HUMPHREY BACHE.

THE conversion of Humphrey Bache, about the year 1655, from the maxims and religion of the world, to those pure and undefiled principles of Truth under which many seeking souls were now gathering into a visible church, was a remarkable instance of the efficacy of the Light of Christ, received and cherished in the mind, not only to show forth sin in its true character in a manner widely different from the maxims of human policy, but also, in its cleansing operations on the heart, to constrain the subject of its power to righteous confession and compensation for wrongs or injuries committed.

He was brought up a goldsmith in the city of London; but the civil war breaking out between Charles the First and the Parliament, his business failed to afford him a maintenance, and he applied to the leaders of the popular party for some office. He was accordingly employed as an overseer of workmen engaged in building the fortifications about London. His allowance was three shillings a day, with which, for a time, he was well contented. He frequently observed that some of the other overseers would go with those they employed, and treat them to strong drink. Being told by one of the workmen, that the money so spent did not come out of the salaries of those officers, he inquired how that could be. "Do you not know," said his informant, "they can sometimes set down a man more than they employ; or if that cannot so well be, set down for some, two pence a-day more than they give." This was a new idea to Humphrey, who being off his guard, Satan worked therein with much subtilty to betray him. His honesty of purpose at last gave way, and he began to covet more than his wages; and his heart becoming corrupt in its desires, he soon proved unfaithful to his trust, and acting on the hint he had received, he robbed the commonwealth of its dues. During the time he remained in this employment, the amount he took, more than his wages, was about six pounds.

Of course he had no peace of mind, and was often troubled at the thought of the wrong he was doing. But he had departed from his God, through the inward operations of whose Holy Spirit he might have found preservation from all evil; and he now had no will nor strength to resist the temptation. Encouraging himself in the deceitfulness of his heart, his spiritual eye became, for a time, so far blinded, that he did not see the evil to be so great as it first appeared. His heart was hardened through his continued violation of right, until at length he went on without much conviction or remorse.

When the fortifications around London were completed, Humphrey obtained a situation in the custom-house. Having yet some fear of his Heavenly Father remaining in him, he discharged his duty, for a season, with true fidelity. So long as he retained that fear, he was preserved from joining with those about him in robbing the public treasury. At this time he often felt bitterness of soul for what he had formerly done; and this assisted him, as he firmly resisted all bribes, withholding his lips from the proffered wine—his hand from the tempting silver.

His companions, who had departed from honesty and simplicity, into that serpentine wisdom which uses its plausible pretences to lead others astray, advanced many specious arguments to persuade him to act as they did. Listening from time to time to their beguiling words, he was at length staggered; for he had not as yet learned, that man's only safety from sin depends on his turning away from the arguments, enticements and examples of unregenerate men, watching unto prayer, and seeking unto God for wisdom to know, and strength to execute His will. He saw that others were violating their oaths, regardless of their duty; and this strengthened the natural covetousness of his heart. Nothing that he heard or saw, had so great an influence on him, as the unfaithfulness of the members of the "Long Parliament," which was then sitting; and he had no hesitation in telling them afterwards, that it was through their evil example, he had been led to violate his trust.

He soon fell from his integrity, and again sought by unfair means to increase his wages. Yet the Lord, in love to his soul, followed him with reproofs and corrections; and in order to break his hard heart, judgment after judgment was administered to him. He continued, however, going on in the same course of iniquity, until through the inward rebukes of the Holy Spirit, he was filled with fear and terror. Being now devoid of comfort, he became very irritable. A small thing would ruffle his temper, and lead him to quarrel with his dearest friends. He who had been very loving and gentle towards his wife, was now so peevish, so fretful, and so froward, that he would often break out into fits of anger with her, even when she spoke mildly and pleasantly to him.

For a long time he felt the weight of condemnation upon him, and had many thoughts as to what he must do to find relief. Sometimes he thought of making restitution, confessing what he had done, and surrendering himself to the commissioners, to deal with him as they should think best. His heart, however, was not yet rightly subdued; and though for the last year he held the office he scrupulously refused to take more than his due, he still retained the gain of his former wickedness.

We have seen that Francis Howgill and Edward Burrough, in the year 1654, came from the north of England to London, preaching the gospel in the demonstration of the Spirit and of power, and that many being there gathered into communion with them, meetings were established in and about this great metropolis, that year and the next. One of these meetings Humphrey Bache attended; but what he then heard had very little effect upon him. Some time after, one of his acquaintance inquiring of him whether he had been to hear the Quakers, he replied, he had heard them once. "Yes," rejoined his friend, "but hear them five or six times, and then judge whether it be not truth that they declare." Humphrey accordingly attended two or three meetings more, still without appearing to receive any particular spiritual benefit. After a time, again feeling some inclination to try them, he went to the "Bull and Mouth" meeting, where were those three eminent ministers of the gospel of Christ, George Fox, Francis Howgill, and Edward Burrough. One of them, while speaking of the cross of Christ, which all true disciples must take up daily, said to this effect:—"The carnal mind is enmity against God. As any one comes to stand in the cross, which is the power of God, the enmity is broken down, and reconciliation is witnessed. The enmity is slain by the power of God—by that which crosseth the carnal mind—which is, the Light."

Under this testimony, the heart of Humphrey Bache was reached. The witness for God within him responded to the truth of what was uttered, and to its applicability to his own condition. He knew that "the Light which shineth in a dark place" had discovered his sin to him, and reproved him for that which his carnal mind urged him to do. He saw that as the cross was taken up, death must needs come on the carnal mind; sin must cease; and thus the partition wall between him and his God would be broken down.

Now, as the mysteries of the kingdom were opened before him, his inward eye was anointed to discover the mysteries of iniquity also. His heart was in measure turned to the Lord, and desires were raised in him for perfect redemption from sin. In order to witness this, he was led into inward waiting on the Lord, that he might receive the further manifestations of that divine Light, which he now knew had often convinced him of sin. He who had died to save him, now, by his Holy Spirit, instructed his soul, opening his inward condition, and showing him what yet stood between him and reconciliation with God.

The first thing which was then made manifest to him was his former unfaithfulness to his trust. In the remembrance thereof, trouble and anguish were again awakened within him, and he saw that he was not clear in the sight of immaculate Justice. He had given up his course of dishonesty; but he had not made restitution for that already committed. As he waited at "Wisdom's gate" for direction, it was made plain to his understanding that his covetousness—that which desired to retain the gain of iniquity—must be given up to die on the cross. He felt that all he had unjustly obtained, he must freely pay to the commissioners of excise, for the service of the commonwealth. This was a close trial to him, as it amounted to about one-half of all his outward substance. What added to the trial was, that he was now not easy to remain any longer in the excise, and had a wife and five children to provide for.

While he was in this tried condition of mind, George Fox was inwardly drawn to pay him a visit; and being partly informed by Humphrey of the struggles within him, he said to him, "He that confesseth, and forsaketh his sin, shall find mercy." Humphrey was made sensible that George's heart was raised up in prayer to the Lord on his behalf, and that the petition found acceptance. He has left the following record of what followed: "The Lord reached down His right arm of power, touched my heart with His grace, and made me willing to submit to His will, and give up the sum of money I had received unjustly. Waiting in the Light, this was made plain to me, to be near one hundred and fifty pounds. But it lay on my heart, to restore more, rather than less. So I was made free by the power of the Lord, and did give back at the excise office, London, one hundred and sixty pounds. Then I felt the truth of the words George Fox spake to me: 'He that confesseth, and forsaketh his sin, shall find mercy;'—for much ease, peace, and refreshment, I received into my soul."

He now resigned his station in the customs, and recommenced business at his original trade, at the sign of the Snail in Tower street.

A great care and dread came upon him, lest he should offend his Heavenly Father in word or deed. He now read some writings of the people called Quakers, and could unite with all he found. One of his acquaintance, who had frequented the meetings of this new Society, asked Humphrey what he thought of them; saying that for his part, he did believe that what they declared, would stand, when all else fell. Then specifying one of their more obvious characteristics, he further queried of Humphrey, whether he did not believe that "thee" and "thou" to one particular person, instead of the plural "you," was truth? Humphrey acknowledged that he did. Then he rejoined, "If thou dost not come into obedience to what thou art convinced is truth, thou must come under condemnation." This also Humphrey acknowledged was true; and continuing to follow, in obedience, the manifestations of the Light of Truth in his mind, he was brought to know it to be a "bridle to the tongue," and was strengthened to take up the cross in this respect, and soon afterwards in respect to the corrupt practice of putting off the hat in pretended honor of persons. This was the day of small things with him, which, as it was faithfully attended to, was to precede the days of greater experience in divine wisdom and usefulness; but without which, he would not have been led on, as he afterwards was, from one step of Christian progress to another, so as to know his feet at length established on "the Rock of Ages."

He was still at times under great temptations; yet as he abode in watchfulness towards the Light, he was preserved from falling. But at times forsaking that, and letting "the old man with his deeds which are corrupt" gain the ascendancy, he made work for bitter repentance. The swift witness for God then followed him with His judgments, until he was made to abhor himself in the dust, and unite with the Lord's Spirit in condemnation of that which had lifted itself up against the reign of Christ in his soul. He patiently bore these judgments, and after a time received power to stand, in the hour of temptation, against the fiery darts of the adversary. Then he saw, that several things in his business as a goldsmith, were not acceptable to his divine Master—that in providing rings and trinkets to sell to proud and vain people, he was not serving Christ, but the great enemy of all righteousness; and he was at length, by the power of the same Grace that discovered the practice of selling them to be evil, redeemed from that evil service.

Humphrey now joined himself in membership with the new society, and in 1656 a regular meeting was opened at his house, which continued to be held there for several years. He was a good example to his brethren, faithfully suffering several imprisonments for his Christian principles, and died soon after being released from prison, in 1662, from the effects of the hardships he had endured in his confinement for conscience' sake.

CHAPTER IX.

ACCOUNT OF JAMES PARNEL,—HE DIES IN PRISON,—GEORGE FOX IMPRISONED IN LAUNCESTON JAIL.

IN the forepart of the year 1656 died James Parnel, whose short history is of a very interesting character. He was born about the year 1638, at Retford in Nottinghamshire, and was educated in the schools of the neighborhood, and in the common way of worship which was then prevalent. This did not however change his heart, or bring him from the corrupt state in which mankind are by nature, into a state of grace; though he was often sensible of the secret reprovings of the Lord's Holy Spirit, in his solitary moments, and so clearly were life and death set before him at times, with a sense of the evil of his ways, that he would come to a resolution to forsake the sins for which he felt condemned; but this promise being made merely in the strength of his own will, it did not stand against temptation, and he made for himself fresh work for repentance. The judgments of the Almighty, nevertheless, followed him, and wrought true repentance in his soul; and as a brand he was plucked from the fire, to be made a vessel of honor in the Lord's house. When he was fifteen years of age, he was led to see the emptiness and idolatrous nature of the worship of the world; and George Fox being confined in Carlisle Dungeon, he came to visit him, and was effectually convinced of the truth, and submitted to the operation thereof in his heart. The Lord, more and more perfecting his divine work in an obedient heart, quickly made him a powerful minister of the word of life. In his eighteenth year he was moved of his divine Master to go to Cambridge, where he testified boldly against the corrupt practices of the magistrates and priests. For this he was shut up in prison, and after being there detained a considerable time, as his accusers could not substantiate any charge against him, he was violently thrust out of the town under the name of a rogue. He some time afterwards returned, and continued for about six months to preach the gospel in the neighborhood of that city; after which he passed into Essex, and was made an instrument to the conversion of many, and the great discomfiture of the priests. These, seeing that their craft was in imminent danger of being brought to naught, appointed a great meeting at Great Coggeshall in Essex, at which the people were "to fast and pray against the errors of the Quakers." James hearing of this, was pressed in spirit to attend the meeting, in order to defend the truth against the attacks of its adversaries. He stood still till the priest had finished his harangue, and then vindicated the cause of truth and his own right to speak there, in a masterly manner. They then bid him pull off his hat, and he declining to do so, told them that he would rather leave the house; which he did, followed by many people. But as he was passing along the road to a friend's house, he was arrested, and after a frivolous examination before four justices and six or seven priests, was committed to the common jail at Colchester. From this he was taken to the assizes at Chelmsford, being chained to five felons, and thus dragged eighteen miles through the country, having a man arrested for murder joined to him on the chain.

Being brought before the court, his hat was taken off his head, and thrown on the floor. The accusations against him were, that in a riotous manner he entered into the "parish church" at Great Coggeshall; that he there stood up and told the minister, he blasphemed, and spoke falsely, and that he used other reproachful words against him: he was also charged with being an idle disorderly person, who could not give a good account of his residence, or of his life and conversation, and with a contempt of the magistracy and ministry. He replied, that he by no means entered into the steeple-house in a riotous manner, but came thither quietly and alone; for that several boys wishing to go in after him, he bade them go in before, rather than occasion any disturbance by entering in a disorderly manner: that he there stood very orderly, and quietly listened to their revilings of himself and his friends, till their priest had finished and was leaving his seat. He denied not that he had told Priest Willis that he blasphemed by saying "the church in God" (an expression James had used in the meeting-house,) was nonsense; and he quoted 2d Thessal. i. 1, where the apostle addresses "the church of the Thessalonians, in God our Father and the Lord Jesus Christ." He asked them also to consider whether it was any more improper for a man to keep on his hat, than his shoe, or his glove, or whether this were not one of the vain customs of pharisaical men, who seek honor one of another, and not the honor which cometh from God only. With respect to the charge of being an idle disorderly person, he told them that his life and conversation might speak for itself, and challenged any to accuse him of disorder; adding that though he was not possessed of earthly property, yet he had a settlement in the Lord, where he had found a habitation, and was a laborer in the Gospel of God, in which none could tax him with idleness; and that it was indeed his great labor and diligence in laying open the delusions of deceivers and deceived men, that had raised up this persecution against him by those who loved to cherish those false prophets who would cry "peace, peace" when the word of the Lord would declare a "woe!" Thus boldly did this enlightened youth defend his cause. But the judge overawed the jury, and endeavored to make them find him guilty; and when the rest of the jury would have acquitted him, the judge and the clerk endeavored to draw forth expressions from their foreman, a notorious drunkard, not acquiesced in by his colleagues, to justify them in their determination, and finally sentenced him to pay a fine of about forty pounds, for contempt of the magistracy and ministry. This of course James could not pay consistently with his feelings of right, as he had committed no crime, and his payment of it would have sanctioned their unjust assumption. He was thereupon led back to his prison, which was an old ruinous castle, said to have been built in the times of the ancient Romans.

The jailer for a considerable time allowed no one to visit him, but such as came to abuse and beat him; and his wife not only sent her servant-man to beat him, but several times laid violent hands upon him herself, and swore that she would have his blood. She also set other prisoners to take away the victuals which his friends provided for him; and even denied him the comfort of a bed, which they wished to bring for his accommodation; so that he was compelled to lie on the cold stones; which, when the weather was damp, would run down with water. He was afterwards put into a place called "the hole in the wall," which appears to have been a vault, like a baker's oven, in the massive walls of that direful castle,* and was very high from the ground. There was a ladder placed under the mouth of this hole, by which he had to descend to obtain his food. But this ladder was too short by six feet, and he was under the necessity of raising himself into the hole from the top of the ladder, by catching hold of a rope. His friends wished to furnish him with a cord and basket, by which to draw up his victuals, but this the malice of his persecutors would not permit. By

---

* Thomas Scattergood visited this castle in 1796, saw the hole in which James was confined, and describes the walls as being about twelve feet thick.

continual subjection to the damp cold air of this dungeon, his limbs became benumbed; so that on one occasion, in climbing up with his victuals in one hand, and catching at the rope with the other from the top of the ladder, he missed his hold, and fell down upon the stones, and was so exceedingly wounded and bruised in his head and body, that he was taken up for dead. They then put him into a similar hole beneath the other, called "the oven," so small that some bakers' ovens are more capacious. Here, when the door was shut, there was no orifice for ventilation or light, and after he was a little recovered from his accident, they would not suffer him to take the air, even so much as by going to the door of the castle, though he was much exhausted by the close confinement. Some of his friends seeing the risk to which his life was exposed, offered to lie in prison for him if he could be permitted but for a short time to be nursed at one of their houses; but this also was refused by his enemies, who thirsted for his blood. And when, once that the door was left open, he ventured to breathe the air for a short time by walking in a narrow yard between two high walls, the jailer came in a great rage, locked up the hole where he usually lay, and shut him out in the yard all night, though it was in the coldest time of the winter. These continued severities at length completely undermined his constitution, and brought on a mortal sickness. As he felt death approaching, he said to those around him, "Here I die innocently:" a little afterwards, "Now I must go;" and turning to Thomas Shortland, he added, "This death I must die: Thomas, I have seen great things; do not hold me, but let me go." Then he said again, "Will you hold me?" meaning that he wished his friends freely to give him up, and not even to desire to retain him: to which one of them affectionately replied, "No, dear heart! we will not hold thee." He had often said, that one hour's sleep would cure him of all; and the last words he was heard to utter, were, "Now I go;" when he stretched himself out, and after sleeping about an hour, he breathed out his purified spirit to Him who had watched and inwardly supported him, during all his afflictions for His gospel's sake. He died in the nineteenth year of his age.

About this time, George Fox was taken up, with Edward Pyot, and imprisoned in Launceston jail, for many months. He had written, at Market-Jew, an address to the seven parishes at the Land's End in Cornwall, showing that Christ is indeed come to teach his people himself, and exhorting the people to take heed to the light of His Holy Spirit in their hearts, and prize the day of their visitation. One of these papers came into the hands of a servant of Major Ceely, a justice of the peace, who had George and his friends arrested, and carried by a party of horsemen with swords and pistols, to Redruth. His own account, somewhat condensed, of this remarkable transaction, will give a clear view of the bold and fearless character of this remarkable man, and of the nature of that persecuting spirit by which he was assailed.

At Redruth, he says, "several of the town's people gathered about us; and whilst I held the soldiers in discourse, Edward Pyot spoke to the people; afterwards Edward Pyot held the soldiers in discourse, whilst I spoke to the people; and in the mean time the other Friend got out and went to the steeple-house, to speak to the priest and people. The soldiers missing him were in a great rage, ready to kill us; but I declared the day of the Lord, and the word of eternal life to the people. In the afternoon, when we got to the town's end, I was moved of the Lord to go back, to speak to the old man of the house. The soldiers drew out their pistols, and swore I should not go back. I heeded them not; but rode back, and they rode after me. I cleared myself to the old man and the people, and then returned with them, and reproved them for being so rude. At night we were brought to Falmouth. There came into our inn the chief constable and many sober people, and a great deal of discourse we had with them concerning the things of God. Some of them were convinced, and stood faithful ever after.

"Next morning, Captain Keat brought a kinsman of his, a rude, wicked man, and put him into the room, himself standing without. This man walking huffing up and down, I bid him fear the Lord. Whereupon he ran upon me, struck me with both his hands, and clapping his leg behind me, would have thrown me down; but he could not, for I stood stiff and still, and let him strike. As I looked towards the door, I saw Captain Keat, and said, 'Keat, dost thou allow this?' He said, he did. 'Is this manly or civil,' said I, 'to have us under a guard, and put a man to abuse and beat us?' I desired one of our Friends to send for the constables, and then I told the captain he had broken his order; for we were to be 'safely conducted;' but he had brought a man to beat and abuse us; so I wished the *constable* to keep the warrant. Accordingly he did, and told the soldiers they might go their way, for he would take charge of the prisoners, and they should not have the warrant again. They walked up and down the house, pitifully blank and down.

"About the eleventh hour, upon the soldiers' entreaty, and promise to be more civil, the constable gave them the order again, and we went with them. We met Major General Desborough on the way; the captain of his troop, that rode before him, knew me, and said, 'Oh, Mr. Fox, what do you here?' I told him I was taken up as I was travelling. 'Then,' said he, 'I will speak to my lord, and he will set you at liberty.' So he rode up to the coach, and spoke to the major general. We also gave him an account how we were taken. He began to speak against the Light of Christ, for which I reproved him. Then he told the soldiers they might carry us to Launceston; for he could not stay to talk with us, lest his horses should take cold.

"So to Bodmin we were conveyed that night, and Captain Keat put me into a room, and went his way. When I was come in, there stood a man with a naked rapier (or sword) in his hand. I called for Captain Keat, and said, 'What now, Keat, what trick hast thou played now, to put me into a room where there is a man with his naked rapier? What is thy end in all this?' 'Oh,' said he, 'pray hold your tongue; for if you speak to this man, we cannot all rule him, he is so devilish.' 'Then,' said I, 'dost thou put me into a room where there is such a man with a naked rapier, that thou sayst, you cannot rule him? What an unworthy, base trick is this!' Thus his plot was discovered.

Next day we were brought to Launceston, where Captain Keat delivered us to the jailer. He required us to pay seven shillings a week for our horse meat, and seven shillings for our diet, a-piece. Then got up a great rage among the professors and priests; and they said, 'We shall see when the assize comes, whether they will dare to Thou and Thee the judge, and keep on their hats before him.' They expected we should be hanged at the assize. But all this was little to us; for we saw how God would stain the world's honor, and glory, and were commanded not to seek that honor, nor give it.

"It was nine weeks from the time of our commitment, to the assizes, to which abundance of people came, from far and near, to hear the trial of the Quakers. Captain Bradden's soldiers and the sheriff's men guarded us up to the court through the multitude of people that filled the streets. The doors and windows were filled with people looking out upon us. When we were brought into the court, we stood a while with our hats on, and all was quiet. And I was moved to say, 'Peace be amongst you!' Judge Glynne, Chief Justice of England, said to us, 'Why do you not put off your hats?' We said nothing. 'Put off your hats,' said the judge again. Still we said nothing. Then said the judge, 'The court commands you to put off your hats.' Then I said, 'When did ever any magistrate, king, or judge, from Moses to Daniel, command any to put off their hats when they came before them? And if the law of England doth command any such thing, show me that law.' Then the judge grew very angry, and said, 'I do not carry my law-books on my back.' 'But,' said I, 'tell me where it is printed in any statute book, that I may read it.' Then said the judge, 'Take him away—prevaricator! I'll *jerk* him!' So they took us away, and put us among the thieves. Presently after he calls to the jailer, 'Bring them up again.' 'Come,' said he, 'where had they hats from Moses to Daniel? Come, answer me; I have you fast now.' I replied, 'Thou mayst read in the third of Daniel, that the three children were cast into the fiery furnace by Nebuchadnezzar's command, with their coats, their hosen, and their hats on.' This plain instance stopped him: so that not having anything else to say to the point, he cried again, 'Take them away, jailer.' Accordingly we were thrust in among the thieves, where we were kept a great while; and they came into the jail to us, and violently took our books from us.

"In the afternoon, we were had up again into the court, and I seeing the jurymen and others swearing, it grieved my life, that such as professed Christianity, should so openly disobey the command of Christ and the apostle; and I was moved of the Lord to give forth to the jurors a paper against swearing, which I had about me. This paper passing among them, they presented it to the judge, who asked me, 'if that seditious paper was mine.' I told him, 'If they would read it up in open court, that I might hear it, if it was mine, I would own it.' He would have had me take it, and look upon it in my own hand: but I again desired that it might be read, that all might hear it, and judge whether there was any sedition in it. At last the clerk read it with an audible voice; and then I told them it was my paper: I would own it, and so might they too, except they would deny the Scripture. They let fall that subject, and the judge fell upon us about our hats again, bidding the jailer take them off; which he did, and gave them to us; and we put them on again, and asked the judge and justices, what we had lain in prison for these nine weeks, seeing they now objected nothing to us but about our hats: an honor which men seek one of another, but which God would lay in the dust; and we requested them to do us justice for our long imprisonment. But they brought in a strange indictment, which they had framed, full of lies, as, that we came 'by force and arms, and in a hostile manner, into the court!' I told them it was false: being taken up in our journey without cause by Major Ceely. Then Peter Ceely said, 'May it please you, my lord, this man (pointing to me,) went aside with me, and told me how serviceable I might be for his design; that he could raise forty thousand men at an hour's warning, and involve the nation in blood, and so bring in King Charles [who was then in exile]. I have a witness to swear it;' and called his witness. But I desired that my mittimus, in which my crime was signified, might be read in the face of the court. The judge said, it should not be read. I said, 'it ought to be, seeing it concerned my liberty and life.' The judge said again, 'it shall not be read.' But I said, 'it ought to be read; for if I have done anything worthy of death or of bonds, let all the country know it.' Then seeing they would not read it, I said to one of my fellow-prisoners, 'Thou hast a copy of it, read it up.' 'It shall not be read,' said the judge; 'jailer, take him away; I will see whether he or I shall be master.' So I was taken away, and a little while after called again. I still cried to have my mittimus read, which signified the cause of my commitment, and again spoke to my fellow-prisoner to read it.

He did read it, and the judge, justices, and whole court were silent; for the people were eager to hear it."

This paper was signed by Peter Ceely, justice of the peace, and charged G. Fox and his friends with acknowledging themselves to be Quakers, spreading abroad papers tending to disturbance of the peace, with travelling without any pass, or rendering any lawful reason, and with refusing to give sureties for their good behavior, or to take the oath of abjuration, &c.

"When it was read, I said to the judge and justices, 'You know that if I had put in sureties, I might have gone whither I pleased, and carried on the design (if I had one) which Major Ceely hath charged me with. And if I had spoken those words to him, judge ye whether bail could have been taken in that case.' Then turning to Ceely, I said, 'When or where did I take thee aside? Was not thy house full of rude people, and thou as rude as any of them? But if thou art my accuser, why sittest thou on the bench? This is not a place for thee to sit in, for accusers do not use to sit with the judge: thou oughtest to come down and stand by me, and look me in the face. Besides, I would ask whether or not Major Ceely is not guilty of this treason, which he charges against me, in concealing it so long? For he tells you here, that I went aside, and told him how serviceable he might be for my design—that I could raise 40,000 men, &c. He saith moreover, he would have aided me out of the country, but I would not go, and therefore he committed me. Now do you not see that Major Ceely is guilty of this plot and treason, and hath made himself a party to it, by desiring me to go out of the country, and not charging me with this pretended treason till now? But I deny and abhor his words, and am innocent of his devilish design. So the judge saw clearly that instead of ensnaring me he had ensnared himself.

"Major Ceely then got up again, and said, 'if it please

you my lord, this man struck me, and gave me such a blow as I never had in my life.' At this I said, 'Major Ceely, thou art a justice of the peace and a major of a troop of horse, and tellest the judge here, that I (a prisoner) struck thee. What, art thou not ashamed? Where did I strike thee? and who is thy witness?' He said, Captain Bradden was his witness. Then I said, 'Speak, Captain Bradden, didst thou see me give him such a blow?' But Captain Bradden made no answer; and the judge finding those snares would not hold, fined us twenty marks a-piece, for not taking off our hats, and to be kept in prison till we paid it.

"At night, Captain Bradden came to see us, and seven or eight justices with him, who were very civil, and told us they did believe neither the judge nor any in the court gave credit to those charges which Ceely had brought forward; and Bradden said, that Ceely had an intent to take my life, if he could have got another witness.

"Now we were kept in prison; and not being likely to be soon released, we broke off from giving the jailer seven shillings a-week a-piece for our horses, and the same for ourselves, and sent our horses into the country. On which he grew very wicked, and put us down into Doomsdale, a nasty, stinking place where they put murderers after they were condemned. The place was so noisome, that it was observed, few ever came out again in health. The filth collected had not been carried out (as we were told) for many years; so that it was all like mire, and in some places to the top of the shoes in water and filth; and he would not let us cleanse it, nor have beds or straw to lie on. At night, some friendly people of the town brought us a candle and a little straw, and we went to burn a little of our straw, to take away the stench. The thieves lay over our heads, and the head-jailer in a room by them, over our heads also. It seems the smoke went up into the room where the jailer lay; which put him in such a rage, that he took the most filthy matter he could collect in the thieves' room, and poured it through a hole upon our heads; whereby we were so bespattered, that we could not touch ourselves nor one another, and had like to have been smothered. We had the stench under our feet before, but now we had it on our heads and backs also; and he having quenched our straw with what he poured down, had made a great smother in the place. Moreover, he railed at us most hideously, calling us hatchet-faced dogs, and such strange names as we never heard of. In this manner we had to stand all night, for we could not sit down, the place was so full of filth. A great while he kept us after this manner, before he would let us cleanse it, or suffer us to have any victuals but what we had through the grate; and we had much ado to get water or victuals.

"This head-jailer, we were informed, had been a thief, and both he and the under-jailer had been burnt in the hand and shoulder, and their wives had also both been burnt in the hand.

"The quarter sessions drew nigh, and we drew up our suffering case, and sent it to the sessions; upon which the justices ordered, that Doomsdale door should be opened, and that we should have liberty to cleanse it, and to buy our meat in the town. We also sent up a copy to the Protector [Oliver Cromwell], whereupon he sent down an order to the governor of Pendennis Castle, to examine the matter about the soldiers abusing us, and striking me. One of the Protector's chaplains told him, they could not do George Fox a greater service for the spreading of his principles in Cornwall, than to imprison him there. And indeed my imprisonment was for the Lord's service in those parts. The Lord's light and truth broke forth, shined over all, and many were turned from darkness to light, and from Satan's power to God. A great convincement began in the country; for now we had liberty to walk in the Castle-green; and divers people came to us on First-days, to whom we declared the word of life."

These innocent sufferers were at length released from prison on the 13th of the Seventh month of this year, having been confined about six months, during which time their health appears to have been preserved in a wonderful manner.

CHAPTER X.

THE CONVINCEMENT, MINISTRY, AND FALL OF JAMES NAYLER—HIS REPENTANCE AND DEATH.

THE cruelties which Friends suffered about this time, for their faithful adherence to what was made known to them as their religious duty, were indeed excessive, and if mentioned in detail would fill many volumes.* They had also this year the additional affliction of a falling away from among their own ranks, of some, who, through unwatchfulness and spiritual pride, lost their way, and were taken in the snares of the enemy.

The occasion of this new trial to the church, was the excessive adulation paid by some to James Nayler, which, in an unguarded hour, got the better of his judgment, and carried him along with them to great and sorrowful extravagancies. He was born at Ardsley, in Yorkshire, about the year 1616, or '18, and during the civil wars served as quarter-master in the army of the Parliament under General Lambert. He was by profession an Independent, and was convinced of the truth of the principles of Friends by George Fox, near Wakefield, in the year 1651; and being a man of comprehensive intellect, though of limited education, he

---

* See Besse's "Sufferings of Friends."

brought into the service of the Society a great ability for being useful; especially as in the first period of his uniting with Friends, he exhibited an extraordinary gift of holy wisdom and humility. The year after his convincement, he believed himself bound in religious duty, to leave his habitation, and travel in the service of the ministry, in the northwestern parts of England. He suffered much personal abuse in Lancashire, in company with George Fox, and was imprisoned about twenty weeks at Appleby, for having said that Christ was in him, (in accordance with the apostle's doctrine: "know ye not that Jesus Christ is in you, except ye be reprobates." 2 Corinth. xiii. 5)—and that there is but one Word of God, even He that "was made flesh and dwelt among us." This, his enemies, the priests, construed into blasphemy, being afraid that if the sentiments promulgated by Friends, should be permitted to gain ground, "the craft by which they had their wealth would be set at naught."

After the termination of his imprisonment, James Nayler resumed his travels in the service of the ministry, and at length, in the year 1654, came to London. He declares that he entered that city with the greatest fear that had ever been his experience on entering any place; foreseeing in spirit that something would befall him in it, but not knowing what it was to be.

Edward Burrough and Francis Howgill, who had been fellow-prisoners of his at Appleby, had been the means, as before observed, of gathering a congregation of Friends in London; but Nayler now preaching there with eminent power, many of his admirers began to draw comparisons between him and his brethren in the ministry; and about the year 1656, some inconsiderate women thus undervaluing Burrough and Howgill, presumed to disturb them in their public ministry. Being reproved by the two ministers, they endeavored, though at first unsuccessfully, to enlist the feelings of James Nayler in their favor. But James, having too deep an understanding of the soundness of his brethren's judgment, was not forward to condemn them; whereupon one of these deluded persons, named Martha Simmons, fell into a kind of paroxysm, and exclaimed with a shrill, piercing voice, " I looked for judgment, but behold a cry!" — accompanying her words with such bitter lamentations, that poor James, too easily yielding to feelings of compassion, instead of rebuking her folly, became not only the dupe of her violent grief and of that of her associates, but was also further led aside by their flattery. From one step to another he at length arrived at such a height of spiritual pride, as to hear, even with a secret feeling of complacency, the wildest adulation of this woman, and of the other enthusiastic females who surrounded him. Among them was one Hannah Stranger, who, it is said, addressed to him several very wild and preposterous epistles; calling him "the everlasting Son of righteousness — the Prince of Peace — the fairest among ten thousand, &c.:" and she, together with some of the others, in their fanatical folly, would kneel before him and kiss his feet.

This was a time of great darkness, as James afterwards acknowledged. And "if the light that is in you be darkness, how great is that darkness!" It is remarkable that he declared it to have been his fear of opposing what might be right in his partisans, that prevented him from rebuking their extravagancies; and having lost the spirit of discernment, he was in a situation to accept almost any thing for the truth, more especially that which was gratifying to the natural feelings. He went to Bristol, accompanied by his frantic admirers, and after making a disturbance there, he was proceeding towards Launceston, in order to meet with George Fox (for what purpose it does not appear), when he was stopped by the way and imprisoned at Exeter. George Fox being released on the 13th of the Seventh month from Launceston jail, went to Exeter and warned James Nayler:

who, however, slighted his advice, though he testified affectionate feelings towards his friend. But the unflinching integrity of George Fox would not allow him to receive his proffered salute while mixed with so much wilful error; and he rejected it with the remark, that since James had turned against the power of God, he would not receive his show of kindness. "The Lord," says he, "moved me to slight him, and to set the power of God over him. I admonished him and his company; and when he was come to London, his resisting the power of God in me, and the truth that was declared to him by me, became one of his greatest burdens."

After his release from Exeter prison, James Nayler rode into Bristol, accompanied by his wild disciples; one of whom, named Thomas Woodcock, went bareheaded before him, whilst one of the women led his horse; Martha Simmons, Hannah Stranger, and others, spreading their scarfs and handkerchiefs before him, and the whole company shouting Hosanna! etc. in imitation of the manner of the entry of Christ into Jerusalem. It was to be expected that so extravagant an act should attract the notice of the police and magistrates. The procession had scarcely passed the suburbs, before they were all apprehended, and put in prison; and soon afterwards, James was taken to London, to be examined by the Parliament.

The fall of this eminent man was eagerly seized upon as a favorable opportunity for aiming a blow at the rising Society of Friends. Many of the members of Parliament were strict adherents to the settled forms of religion, but enemies to its true spirit; and could not tolerate the simplicity of the principles of Friends, because of the severe reproofs thereby administered to their own system of notions, and head-knowledge; and their animosity against the Society being afresh excited, they treated their victim with the greater severity, not caring to discern that his crime was a departure from the purity of his profession. The house took up the subject on the 30th of what was called November, 1656, and the report of the committee was received on the fifth of the following month. On the 16th, the business was brought before it for the *twelfth* time, after having been discussed, forenoon and afternoon in the interim, many members not approving the severity proposed to be used against him. A motion was made that the punishment should be death; but this was lost by a vote of eighty-two to ninety-six; and after a long debate, on the 17th they came to the following resolution, viz. "That James Nayler be set on the pillory, with his head in the pillory, in the palace-yard, Westminster, during the space of two hours, on Thursday next; and be whipped by the hangman through the streets, from Westminster to the Old Exchange, London; and there likewise be set on the pillory, with his head in the pillory, for the space of two hours, between the hours of eleven and one, on Saturday next; in each place wearing a paper containing a description of his crimes: that at the Old Exchange, *his tongue be bored through with a hot iron!* and that he be there also stigmatized on the forehead with the letter B; that he be afterwards sent to Bristol, and be conveyed into, and through the said city on horseback, with his face backward; and there also publicly whipped, the next market-day after he comes thither; that from thence, he be committed to prison, in Bridewell, London; be there restrained from the society of all people; and there to labor hard, till he shall be released by parliament; and during that time, be debarred the use of pen, ink, and paper, and have no relief but what he earns by his daily labors."

This sentence was considered by the public, to be too severe a judgment on a man whose sin seemed more the result of a clouded understanding, than of depraved intentions; and accordingly several persons of different persuasions in religion, offered petitions to the parliament on his behalf; which petitions it was resolved not to read, till the sentence was pronounced against him. James was denied the liberty of offering anything in arrest of judgment, and when he remarked, as the speaker was about to pronounce sentence, that "he did not know his offence," he was briefly answered, "that he should know his offence by his punishment." He received the sentence with great calmness, and was heard to say with a composed manner, "I pray God he may not lay it to your charge."

On the day appointed, he suffered the first part of his punishment. He remained two hours exposed in the pillory, and was then stripped, and being fastened to a cart, was dragged through the streets, receiving three hundred and ten strokes of the whip. The patience with which he sustained this severe treatment, astonished many, especially when they beheld the pitiable condition of his poor lacerated body, which was suffered to go two hours without the opportunity of being dressed, and on which, according to a certificate presented to parliament, "there was not the space of a man's nail free from stripes and blood, from his shoulders near to his waist!"

Two days after this, he was to have undergone the further punishment of being again put in the pillory, of being branded in the forehead, and having his tongue burnt through with a hot iron; but he was found to be so much exhausted by the severity of that cruel whipping, that several persons of note, not members of the Society of Friends, moved with commiseration of his pitiable condition, interceded with his judges, and obtained from parliament a respite of one week. In the mean time, another petition, numerously signed, was presented at the bar of the house, by about one hundred of the signers, in which they used the following expressions:

"Your moderation and clemency, in respiting the punishment of James Nayler, in consideration of his illness of body, hath refreshed the hearts of many thousands, altogether unconcerned in his practice:—wherefore we most humbly beg your pardon, that are constrained to appear before you in such a suit, (not daring to do otherwise,) that you would remit the remaining part of your sentence against the said James Nayler, leaving him to the Lord, and to such gospel remedies as He hath sanctified; and we are persuaded you will find such a course of love and forbearance more effectual to reclaim, and will leave a seal of your love and tenderness upon our spirits," &c.

This petition was followed by one addressed to Oliver Cromwell, the Protector; which occasioned him to send a message to the house for information respecting their proceedings on the subject; but the only result was empty discussion, the majority of the parliament appearing determined to make the most of this case, and some even disposed to carry their severity to the extent of taking the life of their victim. A delegation of five professed ministers of religion was sent to confer with him, who refused to allow any witness to be present at their interview. James, being alarmed at this, declined saying any thing to them, unless what was said should be written down, and a copy, signed by themselves, should be left either with him or with the keeper of the prison where he was confined. To this they agreed; but after considerable discourse, and James taxing them with seeking to ensnare him, they rose up in a fret, burned what had been written, and left him. It would seem by what James Nayler afterwards related of this interview, and his replies to them, that he, poor man, was still, in some degree, under the power of that delusion which had brought him into these sufferings; for he was not prepared to acknowledge that the extravagant behavior of his fanatical followers should have been reproved by him. He attempted to palliate their falling down before him, by the supposition that it was intended as an act of homage, not to him as a creature, but to the power of Christ which they believed to be manifest in him.

On the 27th of the month, he was conveyed from Newgate to the Old Exchange, where he was again exposed in the pillory, and suffered the boring of his tongue with a red-hot iron, (which was held for a short time in his tongue, that the bystanders might witness the fact,) and also the branding with a red-hot iron on the forehead, until smoke arose from the burning flesh! All this he bore with wonderful patience, and it would seem that compassion had been excited by his sufferings, in the public mind; for though many thousands were said to be assembled on the occasion, yet few were observed to revile him, or throw anything at him while in the pillory; and while he was undergoing the burning on the forehead, the people, as if with one simultaneous emotion, stood bareheaded.

After this, he was sent to Bristol, to undergo the remainder of his punishment; where he was whipped through the streets; and finally was returned to London, and kept in prison until the summer of 1658.

It may well be supposed that so great a fall in an esteemed member amongst Friends, would be cause of triumph to their numerous enemies. Such indeed was the case; and desiring to make what was bad still worse, the vilest calumnies were also set afloat against his moral character. From these, however, he was enabled fully to clear himself. His transgressions had their origin in spiritual pride, excited by the adulation of weak fanatics, and turned to the purpose of his destruction by the adversary of his soul, who goeth about as a roaring lion, seeking whom he may devour, and as an envious, cunning serpent, seeking whom he may betray. But though this wanderer from the flock had so grievously missed his way, and fallen among thieves, he was mercifully followed, by the reclaiming, redeeming power of Israel's

Shepherd. During the solitude afforded by his close confinement, his mind was more and more softened; and as the mists of error faded away under the reviving power of the Sun of Righteousness, he felt the healing virtue of his Saviour's wing, and was enabled to pour forth, in many touching effusions, the penitence of his soul.

On his liberation, which occurred very soon after the death of Oliver Cromwell, about the Seventh month, 1658, he went to Bristol, the chief scene of his offence; in which city, in a public meeting, he made a confession of his fault in so affecting a manner, as to draw tears from most of those who were present, and to occasion his reconciliation with many who had been estranged from him. The following expressions, forming part of a paper addressed by him to Friends, feelingly set forth his sincere repentance.

"Dear brethren," says he, "my heart is broken this day for the offence that I have occasioned to God's truth and people, and especially to you, who in dear love followed me, seeking me in faithfulness to God; which I rejected, being bound wherein I could not come forth, till God's hand brought me, to whose love I now confess. Unless the Lord himself keep you from me, I beseech you let nothing else hinder your coming to me, that I might have your help in the Lord. In the mercies of Christ Jesus, this I beg of you, as if it was your own case: let me not be forgotten by you. And I entreat you to speak to whoever I have most offended; and by the power of God, and in the Spirit of Christ Jesus, I am willing to confess the offence; that God's love may arise in all hearts as before, if it be his will, who only can remove what stands in the way; and nothing thereof do I intend to cover; God is witness."

And in another paper, after giving praise to the Lord Jesus Christ, his Saviour, and the rock of his salvation, who had lifted him out of the pit, delivered him from darkness, and given quietness and patience to his soul, he adds: "But condemned for ever be all those false worships, with which any have idolized my person in the night of my temptation, when the power of darkness was above. All their casting of their clothes in the way, their bowings and singings, and all the rest of those wild actions which did any ways tend to dishonor the Lord, or draw the minds of any from the measure of Christ Jesus in themselves, to look at flesh, or ascribe that to the visible, which belongs to Christ Jesus, all that I condemn. And all those ranting, wild spirits, which gathered about me in that time of darkness, and all their wild actions, and wicked words against the honor of God and his pure Spirit and people, I deny that bad spirit, the power and the works thereof. And as far as I gave advantage, through want of judgment, for that evil spirit in any to arise, I take shame to myself justly."

In another paper, relating how he was betrayed into this snare, he instructively attributes it in great measure to his "not minding to stand *single and low;*" and there can be no doubt that if he had kept humbly on the watch, with his eye single to the divine Light and Leader, he would have been preserved blameless by the same power that so livingly sent him forth at first to preach His gospel. But "there is joy in Heaven over one sinner that repenteth;" and there is joy also in the church over the healing virtue of that divine love in Christ Jesus, the holy unction of which is often effectual for the restoration of the diseased and crippled members to life, and health, and unity once more with the body. George Whitehead, who knew James Nayler well, testifies of his latter days, that "he was revived by the Lord's power, and in measure restored to his ancient testimony, and to bear the same publicly, as the Lord enabled him, both in ministry and writings; and he walked in much brotherly love and simplicity among us, until his end came."

He lived rather more than two years after his liberation

from prison, and spent his time in great self-denial and watchfulness. Departing from London, towards the latter part of the summer of 1660, for the purpose of visiting his family in Yorkshire, he was seen by a Friend at Hertford, sitting by the roadside, in a very solemn and retired frame of spirit. This Friend invited him to his house; but he expressed a wish to proceed. In passing on foot through Huntingdon, he was observed by another Friend to be in a particularly solid frame of mind, like one who felt himself to be a stranger in the earth, and seeking a better and an enduring inheritance. Soon after this, he was found towards evening by a countryman, very ill, on a field, near King's Rippon, having (as it was supposed) been robbed and personally abused. He was taken to a Friend's house, and attended by a physician, but gradually sunk away. He expressed his love for Friends, and to those around him he said, "You have refreshed my body—the Lord refresh your souls!" About two hours before his decease, he uttered, among others, the following heavenly expressions, evincing in a consolatory manner, his restoration to the divine favor: "There is a spirit which I feel, that delights to do no evil, nor to revenge any wrong; but delights to endure all things, in hope to enjoy its own in the end. Its hope is to outlive all wrath and contention, and to weary out all exaltation and cruelty, or whatever is of a nature contrary to itself. Its crown is meekness; its life is everlasting love unfeigned. It takes its kingdom with entreaty, and keeps it by lowliness of mind. In God alone it can rejoice. I have fellowship therein, with those who lived in dens and desolate places in the earth; who through death obtained this resurrection, and eternal holy life!" He quietly departed, about the 44th year of his age.

Such was the career of James Nayler, and such his peaceful close. Awfully instructive was his fall, as a warning to all to beware of that spirit which would lift us up above the pure teachings of the "still small voice" in the secret recesses of the heart. And sweetly edifying is it also to dwell on the depth and riches of that redeeming love which raised the poor soul from the horrible pit, and set his feet upon a rock, and put a new song into his mouth, even praises to his great and gracious Lord.

CHAPTER XI.

FIRST VISITS OF FRIENDS TO AMERICA—CRUEL PERSECUTIONS IN NEW ENGLAND, ETC.

THIS eventful year to the Society of Friends (1656) was also remarkable as being the era of the first arrival of any of the ministers of the Society on the continent of America.

Mary Fisher, a young woman of about thirty years of age, and Anne Austin, who had a husband and five children residing in London, were, in 1655, travelling together in the ministry of the Gospel in the island of Barbadoes; and in the spring of 1656, they sailed for Boston, under a concern of mind to spread the doctrines of the true spiritual religion among the high professing, but priest-ridden and intolerant inhabitants of Massachusetts Bay. Nearly twenty years before this, Rhode Island had been purchased from the Narragansett Indians for fifty fathoms of beads, and settled by a colony from Boston, who had left the latter town in disgust at the attempts made to introduce by force, a system of religious uniformity. Many of these original colonists of Rhode Island afterwards became Friends, and afforded a quiet resting-place for the poor persecuted members of the Society, when whipped or banished out of the adjoining patent.

Anne Austin and her companion arrived at Boston in the Fifth month, and their arrival was quickly announced to the deputy-governor; who in his zeal to prevent any inroads on the settled religious opinions of the colony, commanded that they should be closely confined on board the ship that brought them, and that their books should be burned by the common executioner, under the vague and false charge of heresy and blasphemy. The council also ordered that the women should be closely imprisoned, and that the captain of the ship should give security, on pain of imprisonment, to convey them back speedily to Barbadoes, at his own cost. So fearful were those bigoted people of the light of truth to discover their false opinions and evil deeds.

Being brought on shore, these harmless and innocent women were closely confined, and a penalty of five pounds threatened against any one who should even speak to them through the window of their prison. The window indeed was afterwards boarded up, and their pens, ink and paper were taken from them, to prevent any communication with the citizens. Their persecutors now raised the cry of witchcraft, doubtless with the hope of putting them to the same death as had already been meted out to two women a short time previous. Finding no overt act as evidence of this unfounded charge, they scrupled not to examine the persons of their prisoners, in a cruel and indecent manner, to see if there were no mark of witchcraft upon them, under the popular superstitious notion that some unusual sign was set upon the bodies of those who had thus sold themselves to satan. Their enemies now refused to supply them with food, or allow it to be brought to them by the citizens; but an aged inhabitant, touched with compassion for their sufferings, bribed the jailer to allow him privately to furnish them with provisions.

After an imprisonment of nearly five weeks, they were

shipped back to Barbadoes under strict guard. But scarcely had these two ministers of the Gospel sailed from the port, when a vessel arrived from London, bringing eight others, viz.; four men and four women. These also were immediately seized, carried before the court then sitting, and subjected to a long and frivolous examination. Their trunks on board the vessel were searched "for erroneous books and hellish pamphlets." During their examination they steadfastly maintained that the Scriptures were not the *main* or *only* guide of life, and that the "more sure word of prophecy," mentioned by Peter (2 Peter i. 19), was the eternal Word and sure guide to which we are to take heed. Sentence of banishment was pronounced upon them, and they were directed to be kept close prisoners, without paper or ink, and all communication forbidden with the citizens, until they could be returned by the same ship that brought them thither; the captain being also imprisoned for four days, to induce him to give bond to take them back at his own charge.

All that had hitherto been done against Friends, was without even the shadow of law; for they had been seized before setting their feet in the country, and thus prevented, even if so disposed, from violating any of the laws of the colony. But their persecutors now framed a law to sanction their past and future arbitrary proceedings, in which the "cursed sect of heretics, commonly called Quakers," were severely denounced, and all captains of vessels knowingly bringing any of them into the colony, were made liable to a fine of one hundred pounds, or to be thrown into prison till paid, and were to give security to carry them back to the place whence they should have come. It was further enacted, that any Quaker who should arrive should be forthwith committed to the house of correction, be severely whipped, and kept constantly at work, without being allowed to speak with any one during his or her imprisonment. The rest of the law was of the same spirit, providing for the punishment of any who should possess Friends' books, or advocate their principles. After it was passed, it was proclaimed through the streets by beat of drum. Nicholas Upshall, the aged inhabitant who had supplied Anne Austin and Mary Fisher with food, became much interested in Friends and in their principles; and when this law was proclaimed before his door, he publicly testified his disapprobation of it. For this offence he was cited before the court, where he spoke in much tenderness, but warned them to "take heed lest they should be found fighting against God." He was fined, imprisoned, and banished from Boston patent. This venerable man took refuge in Sandwich; but the governor of Plymouth patent forbade the inhabitants of Sandwich to offer him shelter, and directed him to be brought before him at Plymouth. These tyrannical proceedings, both at Boston and elsewhere, had the good effect of opening the eyes of some, to see the inconsistency of the rulers' conduct with the precepts of the Gospel, and tended to prepare the sincere-hearted among the people for sympathizing with the oppressed, and receiving with openness the doctrines of Friends, which, notwithstanding all these attempts to suppress them, were more or less spread abroad in the country. The eight Friends above mentioned were, on the passing of the new law, hurried on ship-board, to be conveyed away; and as all their bedding had been seized for the jailers' fees, some of the inhabitants of the neighborhood, affected at the idea of these innocent sufferers being obliged to take such a voyage without bedding to rest upon, subscribed a sum of money, and redeemed their goods for them out of the hands of the jailer. Such was the reception which Friends met with on first setting foot in New England, from a people who professed that for the sake of liberty of conscience, they had left their native land for a home in the wilderness of North

America. This, however, as will presently be seen, was but the beginning of a persecution, which did not stop until it had, on the gallows, taken the lives of several of these devoted people.

The next Friends who came to Boston were again two females; Anne Burden and Mary Dyer; who arrived early in the year 1657, without knowledge of the cruelties which had been already exercised, or of the law which had been passed to sanction still further inflictions. The former of these women came over to collect debts due to the estate of her deceased husband, with whom she had formerly resided in the neighborhood of Boston; and Mary Dyer was on her way to join her husband in Rhode Island. Both had probably become convinced of the principles of Friends in England. They were now seized by the authorities of Boston, and kept close prisoners, until Mary Dyer's husband came from Rhode Island, and became bound in a great penalty to take her away from the colony, without suffering any to speak with her; and Anne Burden, without being suffered to complete the business which had brought her over, and having received but six shillings of the debts due to her, was, after an imprisonment of three months, conveyed by the common hangman on board the vessel which had brought her from London.

Of the eight Friends above mentioned, who were sent away from Boston in 1656, six found it to be their religious duty the next year to return to America, and were joined by five others. They came over in a small vessel owned and commanded by Robert Fowler, making a company of twelve zealous advocates for the truth as it is in Jesus; and were remarkably guided and protected by their divine Master on the arduous voyage. As they came to land, which was on the same day on which Humphrey Norton, one of their company, had early in the voyage mentioned that he believed they should arrive, "the power of the

Lord," to use their own language, "fell upon them, and an invisible word came to them, that the seed of America should be as the sand of the sea." Several of them went ashore at New Amsterdam, (now New York,) and two of them, viz., Robert Fowler and Robert Hodgson, visited the governor, who received them civilly. Two others of their company, however, viz., Mary Weatherhead and Dorothy Waugh, for delivering Christian exhortations to the people, were committed to prison, and separately confined in wet and miry dungeons, for more than a week; when they were at length brought out by two negroes, their hands being tied behind them; and were thus led to the water-side, and placed on board a boat for Rhode Island. Robert Hodgson passed over into Long Island, and was made instrumental to the convincement of many. He was however arrested at Hempstead, and cruelly pinioned, tied behind a cart, and thus dragged nearly thirty miles in the night, over bad roads, and mostly through the woods to New Amsterdam, where he was thrown into a dungeon to await his sentence. This was of no light nature, he being denied a hearing in his own defence, and condemned, for preaching the Gospel freely and faithfully, to "work two years at a wheelbarrow, or pay, or cause to be paid, 600 guilders." The fine of course he could not pay, as he was innocent of any crime, and the paying of it would have been an acknowledgment of the authority of man to stop the progress of the gospel of Christ. The cruelties he underwent while thus in bondage, would have disgraced a heathen people. Twice he was so severely beaten by a negro, with a tarred rope more than an inch thick, that he fainted away. He was confined two nights and a day and a half without any food. Twice he was hung up by his hands, and weights were attached to his feet, and his back was then unmercifully beaten by a strong negro with rods. Being thus brought apparently very near the close of all mortal suffering, and desiring that some English people might be permitted to visit him and examine his body, a woman was admitted, who washed his stripes, and administered what she could to his necessities; but his strength was so reduced, his flesh so lacerated, and the dungeon so devoid of all comforts, that she told her husband she thought Robert could not live till the next day. A number of the inhabitants now offered to pay the fine for him; but Robert told them he was not easy to receive his freedom that way. He believed the Lord would heal him, and was free to labor, when restored to strength, for the sustenance he should need. In a few days he was favored to be sufficiently recruited to enable him to work, and was well contented with his mean fare of bread and water. At length the community at large became so dissatisfied with the cruelties and continued imprisonment to which he was subjected, that their entreaties prevailed on the governor to set him at liberty.

Christopher Holder and John Copeland, two of the fellow-passengers of Robert Hodgson, went over into the island called Martha's vineyard, where there was a mission established among the native Indians. But the priests of the mission would not suffer them to remain; and after a few days' hospitable entertainment by the poor Indians, they were by the governor's orders, taken from the island in a canoe, and landed on the coast near Barnstable. They were gladly received at Sandwich by some sincere seekers after truth, but being at length arrested and brought to Plymouth, and thence banished from the jurisdiction, they took refuge in Rhode Island.

Mary Clark was another of these fellow-passengers, who first proceeded to Rhode Island, and thence to Boston; regarding not what sufferings she might sustain, so that she might deliver the Lord's errand there, and "be discharged of that burden of the word which lay so sore upon her." Here she was arrested, barbarously beaten, receiving twenty stripes with a heavy three-corded whip on her naked back, and committed to prison for twelve weeks; during the latter part of which she suffered much from the cold. After her release, she labored in the gospel throughout New England, until the next summer, when, with Richard Dowdney and Mary Weatherhead, who also composed part of Robert Fowler's company, she suffered shipwreck, being suddenly called by her heavenly Master, from the scene of her sufferings in this world, to the eternal reward prepared for those who have come through much tribulation, and had their robes washed in the blood of the Lamb.

Christopher Holder and John Copeland were also called to suffer for their testimony to the truth. They proceeded from Rhode Island into Massachusetts, and freely preached the gospel; which found place among many, and took such root that all the endeavors of interested and bigoted men could not eradicate it. But going into the public worship house at Salem on a First-day, Christopher was moved to speak a few words after the usual service was over. On this he was furiously seized by the hair of his head, and a glove and handkerchief thrust into his mouth. The two Friends were violently carried away, and taken to Boston; where they received each thirty strokes of a three-corded and knotted whip, laid on with the executioner's utmost strength. Their bodies were thereby miserably torn and inflamed; yet they were allowed neither bed nor straw to lie on, and for three days the jailer furnished them neither food nor drink; the only sustenance they received, being a little water given them by one of the prisoners, who, for this act of charity, was fiercely threatened by the jailer. They were not however forsaken by their Divine Master, but sustained and preserved in this time of extremity, and enabled to rejoice in the sensible evidence of His approving presence. Richard Dowdney also, who had come through Long Island and Rhode Island to Boston, was imprisoned with them.

Humphrey Norton, before mentioned, remained some time in Rhode Island and Providence, and then went to visit the seed sown and springing up in Plymouth colony. He was not permitted long to minister among the new converts there, but was arrested by a warrant from the governor, as "an extravagant person," and detained long without an examination. At length he was brought before the court, where many of the magistrates appeared disposed to be moderate. But the governor was violent against him, and commenced an attack on the principles of Friends, denying that the Light which enlighteneth every one was sufficient to salvation. Humphrey, to manifest his blindness, showed him in express words of Scripture, that "the grace of God, *that bringeth salvation,* hath appeared unto all men;" and that Christ had said, "my grace is sufficient for thee." The governor then asked him, "whether the Scriptures were not *the rule* of life, and ground of faith?" Humphrey replied in the negative, and proved, from the Scriptures themselves, that they did not claim this character; informing them that it was "through faith in Christ Jesus," the great Author and finisher of our faith, and the true Rule and Guide of life, that the Scriptures were able to make wise unto salvation. The governor was unable to convict him of any breach of the laws, yet he banished him from the colony, and had him conveyed fifty miles on the way to Rhode Island. Some time after this, travelling near New Haven, he was arrested, confined a considerable time in prison, cruelly whipped and burnt in the hand, and banished the patent.

The rulers of Boston, finding that notwithstanding their persecuting law, the seeds of truth had taken root among many at Salem, and in other parts of the colony, and that the Quakers still continued to come in among them, drew the cords of persecution still tighter, and passed a law imposing a fine of one hundred pounds (or imprisonment till paid) on any one who should "bring or cause to be brought any Quakers or other blasphemous heretics into the jurisdiction;" and a penalty of forty shillings per hour upon any one who should entertain or conceal them in their houses; and enacting that every Quaker who should presume to enter the colony, after having once suffered what the former law inflicted, (if a man,) should, for the first offence, have one of his ears cut off, and be kept at work in the house of correction, till he can be sent away at his own charge; and for the second offence, shall have his other ear cut off, and be kept at work as before; or (if a woman) shall be severely whipped and kept at work; and that for the third offence, whether man or woman, their tongues should be bored through with a hot iron, and they should be kept at work. This law also included in its penalties, those who should join Friends among themselves; and as they had now a number of this devoted people in confinement, the jailer received orders that they should all be "severely whipped twice a week, beginning with fifteen lashes, and every time to exceed three!" The Plymouth colony also enacted severe laws against Friends; and the governor of New Amsterdam published a law, imposing a penalty of £50 sterling on any one who should receive a Quaker into his house, though but for a night; and enacting that any vessel bringing a Quaker into that jurisdiction should be forfeited, with all its goods. This law however produced great dissatisfaction among the more serious part of the community, particularly on Long Island; and indeed in this, as well as in the other colonies, the power and wrath of man were not able to stop the progress of the work to which the Lord had called his faithful servants. During the year 1657, meetings were established and regularly kept up, in private houses, in the neighborhood of Salem and of Sandwich; one was held at Providence, and another on Rhode Island. On Long Island there were many individuals convinced of our principles; and as far south as Maryland, there were found seals of the efficacy of the labors of these indefatigable and undaunted publishers of the glad tidings of the Gospel.

We have seen that some part of the West Indies had been visited by Friends in 1656. The hearts of many inhabitants of Barbadoes had been in measure opened to comprehend the spirituality of the Gospel, when John Bowran was drawn to visit them in the year 1657. This friend also, passing over to the South American continent, visited Surinam, and travelled along the coast of Guiana for several hundred miles, with an interpreter, preaching the word of the true God to the Indian natives.

Early in the year 1658, Sarah Gibbons and Dorothy Waugh left Rhode Island, "to visit the seed at Salem." It was a wilderness journey of more than sixty miles, and was performed on foot, and partly through a great storm of snow. Besides this, they were obliged to lodge without shelter in the woods. But the Lord their Master preserved them through all dangers; and after laboring in the gospel among their friends at Salem, they went bound in the Spirit to Boston. As might be expected, they were soon arrested, confined in prison about a week without food, and beaten with a three-corded whip, the knots of which cruelly tore their flesh. About the time that they were released, Horred Gardiner, of Newport, the mother of many children, believed it her duty to go to Weymouth, a town within the Boston patent, and there bear a testimony for the truth. Having a young infant, and travelling on foot, she took with her a girl named Mary Stanton, to assist her in carrying the child. She reached the place in safety, and her message found a witness to its truth in the hearts of the people; but some of the baser sort caused her to be arrested, and carried to Boston. Here she was abusively examined by Governor Endicot, and committed with her attendant to prison, where they each received a severe whipping from the three-corded and knotted whip. Her poor babe was at her breast during the execution, protected by the arms of a mother's love, and unconscious of the agony which that mother was enduring. When the infliction was over, she knelt down, and breathed forth a petition that her persecutors might be forgiven of her Father in Heaven, for they knew not what they did. Struck with the meek and forgiving spirit of the prisoner, a woman who stood by, was much moved, and gave "glory to the Lord," saying, "Surely, if she had not the Spirit of the Lord, she could not do this." They were detained after this, two weeks, in prison, during which time none of their friends were allowed to visit them.

The spirit of persecution during this year was very active, particularly in the Plymouth colony; and many instances were afforded of patient endurance of hard suffering, and of undaunted firmness in maintaining the cause of pure spiritual religion, which it is not necessary here to narrate. Yet we can scarcely pass away from the transactions of this year without briefly relating two other instances of wicked cruelty, which paved the way for the dreadful scene of the succeeding year, in which the blood of martyrs for the testimony of Jesus, was shed by the rulers of Boston.

In the fourth month of this year (old style), Thomas Harris, William Brend, and William Leddra, the first and last of whom had landed the previous year at Rhode Island from Barbadoes, passed towards Massachusetts. Thomas Harris entered Boston, and was soon committed to prison; where he was twice severely whipped, and was kept for five days without any nourishment, until food was secretly conveyed to him during the night, through the window of his prison. William Brend and William Leddra, passing on to Salem, were gladly received by Friends there; but afterwards were treacherously seized near Newburyport, and carried before the court then sitting at the former place.

Several other Friends were also arrested for having attended their meetings; and they were all committed on the second of Fifth month to Boston prison. William Brend and William Leddra were put into a room which had the window stopped, so as almost entirely to prevent the passage of air; none of their friends were allowed access to them, neither were they permitted to purchase food. The keeper sometimes brought a little pottage and a piece of bread; but as he would not take their money, and said they should not have the food without working for it, they were not free to touch it. They thus had no nourishment for several days. On the fifth of the month, the magistrates directed that two of the prisoners, Lawrence and Josiah Southwick, should be reserved to lose their ears, and that the rest should be whipped. In pursuance of this order they suffered; even Cassandra Southwick, Josiah's mother, receiving her portion of the cruel punishment. They were then detained for the fees, which they were not at liberty with a clear conscience to pay. The next day, the jailer put William Brend into irons for not working. He placed a fetter on each leg, and one round his neck, and drawing them with force together, left this aged man locked in this suffering position for sixteen hours. The next morning, on his again declining to work, the jailer took a piece of inch rope, and beat him with all his strength, till after striking about twenty times, the rope began to untwist. Dreadfully mangled, William was taken back to his close room; but the same day he was again brought down-stairs, and being commanded to labor, declined as before. The jailer now produced a much stronger rope, and continued to beat William therewith until he had given ninety-one blows, and his own strength was exhausted. The poor sufferer, beside that his back was beaten till it seemed almost like a jelly, had now been five days without food; and shortly after the keeper left him, he sunk down and seemed to be dying. The rulers became alarmed, for fear they should be charged with having murdered him, and endeavored by all means to revive him. The governor sent his physician to him, who reported that his recovery was not probable, as the flesh was in such a condition that it would decay from the bones. The populace became excited at the idea of murder perpetrated by a public functionary, and the whole town was in commotion.

Humphrey Norton and John Rouse came to Boston at this time from Rhode Island, in deep sympathy with their suffering brethren. They also were arrested, whipped, and shut up in prison. William Brend was favored to recover rapidly. But several of his companions were subjected to a new order of the magistrates; which was, that if they still refused to work, they should be regularly whipped twice a week, increasing three lashes each time, till they should submit. Having all of them been whipped but a short time before, the old wounds were still fresh, and opened and bled freely at the renewed application of the lash. The people of Boston became more and more excited, and in compassion for them, a sum of money was raised by subscription, wherewith the fines were paid, and all, except the five friends from Salem, were sent away from the colony. Two of the latter were soon afterwards released, but the remaining three were detained for twenty weeks.

Christopher Holder, John Rouse, and John Copeland, being again imprisoned at Boston in the ninth month, suffered the cruel punishment of having their right ears cut off by the hangman, and were afterwards again whipped.

CHAPTER XII.

MARTYRDOM OF WILLIAM ROBINSON, MARMADUKE STEVENSON, MARY DYER AND WILLIAM LEDDRA—GEORGE FOX IMPRISONED IN SCARBOROUGH CASTLE.

WE now approach the consummation of all these cruelties, which had often appeared to be the aim of the Boston rulers, even the taking away of the life of their innocent victims. In the Tenth month of this year, they enacted a law to banish all Quakers who should come among them, "on pain of death."

In the Ninth month of the next year, (1659,) William Robinson, Marmaduke Stevenson, Mary Dyer, and Nicholas Davis, who were prisoners for the cause of a good conscience in Boston jail, were by this law banished from the colony, with the provision, that their return would be the forfeiture of their lives. The two former left the town of Boston, but did not feel free (although at so great a peril) to leave the jurisdiction, until they should have a clear intimation from their Divine Master, that they were at liberty to depart. They therefore went to Salem and the neighborhood, endeavoring to build up their friends in the faith. It was not long, however, before they were arrested, again imprisoned, and chained by their legs. The next month, Mary Dyer returned also, and being recognized, was likewise taken into custody. On the twentieth, the three were brought before the Governor and court, and desired to listen to their sentence of death. William Robinson, who had prepared a paper, setting forth his reasons for not having departed from the jurisdiction, now asked liberty to read it. This was peremptorily refused. He then laid it on the table, containing among other things, a declaration "that he had not come thither in his own will, but in obedience to his Creator—that the Lord had commanded him to go to Boston, and there to lay down his life,—that he had felt an assurance that his soul was to enter eternal peace and rest—and that he durst not disobey, believing that it became him as a child, to show obedience to the Lord, without any unwillingness." The governor read the letter to himself, but would not suffer it to be read aloud in the court, and presently pronounced the sentence, "that William Robinson should be had back to the prison whence he came, and thence to the place of execution, to be hanged on the gallows till he should be dead." The same sentence was then pronounced against Marmaduke Stevenson and Mary Dyer; to which the latter replied, "The will of the Lord be done." The governor then said, "Take her away, marshal;" to which she returned, "Yea, joyfully I go." In going back to the prison, she uttered frequent praises to the Lord, being full of holy joy that she was counted worthy to suffer shame for His name, and told the marshal, he might let her alone, for she would go to the prison without him. To which he replied, "I believe you, Mrs. Dyer; but I must do what I am commanded." Marmaduke also gave forth a paper, after sentence was pronounced, in which he clearly stated his divine call into that colony, and that it was not in his own will, but in the will of God. And Mary Dyer, from her prison, addressed the court in writing, making a similar declaration, and solemnly warning them that if they put to death any of these, the Lord's servants, it would tend to their own destruction.

They remained a week in prison, and on the 27th of the Tenth month, were led to the gallows by the marshal, attended by a band of about two hundred armed men, besides many horsemen. The envious priest Wilson, also joined the company, who, when the court was deliberating how to deal with the Quakers, had said, "Hang them; or else"—(drawing his finger across his throat, as if he would have said,) "Dispatch them *this* way." As they proceeded to the place of execution, the drums were beaten, especially when any of them attempted to speak. Glorious signs of heavenly joy sat upon the countenances of these martyrs for the truth, who walked hand in hand, as if going to an everlasting feast. When they approached the gallows, the priest in a taunting way, said to W. Robinson, "Shall such jacks as you come in before authority with their hats on?" To which he replied, "Mind you, it is for not putting off the hat, we are put to death!" They now took leave of each other with tender embraces; and W. Robinson going cheerfully up the ladder, said to the people, many of whom were doubtless awfully impressed with the iniquitous proceeding, "This is the day of your visitation, wherein the Lord hath visited you: this is the day the Lord is risen in his mighty power, to be avenged on all his adversaries." He also declared that he suffered not as an evil-doer, and desired the spectators to mind the Light of Christ which was in them, of which he had testified, and was now going to seal his testimony with his blood. The rope being put around his neck, and his hands, legs and face being bound, and the executioner about to turn him off, he said, "I suffer for Christ, in whom I live, and for whom I die." He was then turned off; and Marmaduke stepping up the ladder, said, "Be it known unto all, this day, that we suffer not as evil-doers, but for conscience' sake." And adding, "This day shall we be at rest with the Lord;" he too was launched into the eternal world. Mary Dyer, seeing her companions hanging dead before her, also stepped up the ladder; but after her clothes were tied about her, the halter adjusted about her neck, and her face covered with a handkerchief, just as she was about to be turned off, a cry was heard, that she was reprieved. Her son, it seems, had interceded for her life, which was granted at the last minute.

She was roughly taken down from the ladder, and conveyed back to prison; and the magistrates perceiving that the people began to be much discontented at the violence of their proceedings, resolved to send her away. She was accordingly conveyed towards Rhode Island on horseback, guarded by four men, and thus returned home. She is said to have been a person possessed of some extraordinary mental qualities, of a comely and grave countenance, of a good family, and the mother of several children.

The bodies of the two Friends who suffered death, were barbarously thrown into a hole, without any covering; and when some of their friends would have laid them in coffins, this was denied them; as also was the privilege of fencing the place around, to prevent their being preyed upon by the wild beasts, which then abounded in this new country.

Mary Dyer, in the spring of the next year, (1660,) found herself constrained once more to return to Boston, notwithstanding the sufferings which she knew awaited her. She arrived there on the 21st of the Third month, and ten days afterwards was sent for before the governor and general court. Being questioned, she undauntedly acknowledged herself to be one of those in scorn called Quakers, and that she was the same person who had been there at the last session of the court. She was told that the sentence passed upon her before was now to be renewed, and that she must prepare herself to die the following morning. To which she replied, that she came in obedience to the will of God, to desire them to repeal their unrighteous laws. They would not hear her out, but cried, "away with her; away with her!" and sent her back to prison.

Next morning the marshal came, and called her hastily to come. And rudely entering the room where she was, she desired him to stay a little, and mildly added, that she should be ready presently. But he roughly replied that he could not wait upon her, but she should now wait upon him. Margaret Smith, her companion, being grieved at such unfeeling behavior, expressed her sense of the injustice of their proceedings; to which he threateningly said, "you shall have your share of the same." Mary was then led through the town with a band of soldiers, the drums being beaten before and behind her, to prevent her from being heard in speaking to the spectators. Being come to the gallows, and having ascended the ladder, she was told that if she would return home, she might yet save her life. To which she replied, "Nay, I cannot; for in obedience to the will of the Lord I came, and in His will I abide faithful to the death." The priest cried out to her to repent, and not to be so deluded. But she let him know that the work of repentance was not then to be entered upon by her. Several observations of a like nature were made to her, and in reply she spoke of the heavenly state of mind which had for some days been her portion, and of the eternal happiness into which she was now about to enter. She was then turned off, and finished her course, a martyr for the truth in Christ.

The next that suffered death was William Leddra. He had already been banished from Boston on pain of death; but was under such necessity of conscience, that he could not forbear returning. He was soon arrested, and being fastened to a log, was kept night and day locked in chains, in an open prison, during a very cold winter. Early in the spring of 1661, he was brought into the court, with his chains on, and the log at his heels: and asking the jailer when he would take off the irons from his legs, he unfeelingly replied, that it should be, when he was about to be hanged. Being brought to the bar, he was told that he was to die. He asked, what evil he had done. He was told that he had owned those Quakers who had been put to death, and had said that they were innocent; and besides, that he would not put off his hat in court, and that he said *thee* and *thou.* Then, said he, "You will put me to death for speaking English, and for not putting off my clothes!" To this Major-general Denison returned, "A man may speak treason in English." William Leddra inquired, "Is it then treason to say *thee* and *thou* to a single person?" No one answered; but a member of the court asked him, whether he would go for England? To which he replied that he had no business there. The member then, pointing to the gallows, said, "Then you shall go *that* way!" To which William returned, "What! will ye put me to death for breathing in the air of your jurisdiction? I appeal to the laws of England, and if by them I am guilty, I refuse not to die." Of this no notice was taken, but they endeavored to persuade him to conform to their wishes; to which with a grave magnanimity he answered, "What! to join with such murderers as you are? Then let every man that meets me, say, lo! this is the man that hath forsaken the God of his salvation." He was again assailed by the offer, that if he would promise to depart from the jurisdiction, and to come there no more, his life should be spared; but knowing that to purchase his natural life by making a promise, the fulfilment of which might forfeit his duty to his Lord and Master, would bring spiritual death to his soul, which was much more to be dreaded than the death of the body, he replied: "I stand not in my own will, but in the will of the Lord. If I may have my freedom [from Him], I shall go; but to make you a promise, I cannot." He was accordingly condemned to death, and was led back to his prison. The day before his execution, his mind was drawn out in an affectionate farewell address to his beloved friends. "The sweet influences of the morning star," says he, "like a flood distilling into my innocent habitation, have so filled me with the joy of the Lord in the beauty of holiness, that my spirit is as if it did not inhabit a tabernacle of clay, but is wholly swallowed up in the bosom of eternity, from whence it had its being." "Oh, my beloved," he afterwards adds, "I have waited as a dove at the windows of the ark,—and my heart did rejoice, that I might in the love and life of God, speak a few words to you, sealed with the spirit of promise, that the taste thereof might be a savor of life to your life, and a testimony in you of my innocent death." "Therefore, my dear friends, let the enjoyment of the life alone be your hope, your joy and consolation—let the man of God flee those things that would lead the mind out of the cross—stand in the watch *within*, in the fear of the Lord, which is the very entrance of wisdom—stand still, and cease from thy own working—confess Him before men, yea, before his greatest enemies—fear not what they can do unto you. Greater is He that is in you, than he that is in the world. He will clothe you with humility, and in the power of his meekness you shall reign over all the rage of your enemies, in the favor of God; wherein, as you stand in faith, ye are the salt of the earth; for many seeing your good works, may glorify God in the day of their visitation.

"Bring all things to the Light, that they may be proved, whether they be wrought in God. The love of the world, the lust of the flesh, and the lust of the eye, are without the light—therefore possess your vessels in all sanctification and honor, and *let your eye look at the mark.*"

Thus did he encourage them to faithfulness, and concluded by commending them to that grace which himself had experienced, and by which they also might attain to salvation. What must have been the emotions with which those words of exhortation were received, penned as they were on the eve of suffering martyrdom for that faith which he so earnestly pressed upon his friends.

The next day, being the 14th of the First month, (old style,) 1661, the awful sentence was executed. After the lecture, (solemn farce as it was!) Governor Endicot came with a guard of soldiers to the prison. William Leddra's irons by which he had been chained to a log, night and day, during a cold winter, were knocked off, and he was conducted to the gallows, where he was pinioned; and as he was about to ascend the ladder, he took leave of a friend who was then under sentence of banishment, saying, "all that will be Christ's disciples must take up the cross." On the ladder he said to the people, "For the testimony of Jesus, and for testifying against deceivers, and the deceived, I am brought here to suffer;" and continuing cheerful, as the hangman was putting the halter round his neck, he was heard to say, "I commit my righteous cause unto thee, O God!" And adding "Lord Jesus, receive my spirit," he was turned off, and finished his days on earth, to receive that "crown of life" which is given to those who are "faithful unto death."

The persecutors had also in confinement Wenlock Christison, on the same account, whom likewise after much dissension among themselves, the governor condemned to death. But from some cause which did not appear, he was with twenty-seven more of his friends, suddenly set at liberty. And now we may turn from these scenes of blood, from which the heart recoils, and see what was taking place in other parts of the Society.

In the year 1662, George Fox and Richard Hubberthorn addressed a letter to the king, setting forth the affecting facts, that during the protectorate of the two Cromwells, three thousand one hundred and seventy-three of their friends had been imprisoned for conscience' sake, and for bearing a testimony to the truth as it is in Jesus—that there still lay in prison seventy-three individuals, committed under the power of the Commonwealth—that thirty-two during the protectorate died in confinement, through cruel and hard imprisonments, upon nasty straw and in dungeons — and that during the two years since the king's restoration, three thousand and sixty-eight had been imprisoned on the like account; and their meetings were still broken up by violent men, and Friends were cruelly thrown into waters, or trodden down till the blood gushed from them — the number of which abuses, they said, could hardly be uttered. They therefore besought the king to consider their innocence, and put a stop to these grievous sufferings. But the next year, George himself was imprisoned at Lancaster; whence being removed in 1665 to Scarborough castle, he suffered much from exposure to cold and wet in a miserable room, open to the weather, and was not released until 1666, by appealing to the king, on the injustice of his case. The room in which he was first immured had no proper defence from the rain, nor exit for the smoke; and when George had spent a considerable sum of money in rendering it more comfortable, they speedily removed him into another room, overlooking the sea, and so open to the weather, that the wind drove the rain in forcibly, and the water came over his bed and ran about the room, to such a degree that he had to lade it up with a plate. There was in this room neither chimney nor fireplace. When his clothes were wet, he had no fire by which to dry them, and by this damp, and the cold weather, he became much diseased. They would frequently prevent his friends from bringing him food; so that he had to hire a soldier to bring him bread and water; a three-penny loaf of bread commonly served him three weeks, and sometimes longer; and his drink was mostly water, with wormwood bruised and steeped in it. One time when the weather was very sharp, and he had taken a great cold, he procured a little elecampane beer; but the soldiers contrived to have him sent for to the deputy-governor, and in his absence stole his beverage.

During the early part of this imprisonment, while in

Lancaster jail, he had a sense of the sufferings of his friends in New England, as above related, and likewise of the approach of that awful scourge, permitted by the Almighty to come upon a guilty people, in the memorable fire of London, by which a great part of that city was destroyed, commencing the next day after his release from Scarborough castle.

CHAPTER XIII.

THE CONVINCEMENT OF RICHARD DAVIES.

ABOUT the year 1657, Richard Davies, a Welchman, who had been educated in the Episcopal society, but had joined the Independents, became convinced of the truth of the principles held by the people called Quakers, and united himself in fellowship with them. As he was one of the first witnesses for these principles raised up in Wales, so he also became in after-time, one of the most valiant and useful instruments in the Lord's hand, in gathering and confirming that people in his own country, even through hot persecution. His simple narrative of his convincement, gives so clear a statement of the ground on which he embraced these principles, and of the gradual but steady development of Christian truth in his mind, through the successive manifestations of the Divine Light, inwardly received, cherished and obeyed, that we may do well to pursue it in some of his own words, as an example, out of many thousand similar instances, of the way and work of the Lord.

"About the year 1656," says he, "our ministers told us,

that there was a sort of people come up in the north, called Quakers, that were a people of strange posture and principles. They were represented to us to be such a dangerous sort of people, that we were afraid of any who had the name of Quakers, lest we should be deceived by them. Hitherto they had not been in these parts, neither did we know what were the principles held out by themselves; but only such as were reported to us, though falsely, by our preachers and others; which kept us in blindness, and from making further inquiry, from trying all things, and holding fast that which is good.

"About the year 1657,"—Richard Davies being then about twenty-two years of age,—he continues: "there came a poor man, in a mean habit, to my master's house, named Morgan Evan, of South Wales: he had met with the people called Quakers in his travels, and was convinced of the truth. This poor man discoursed with my master about the principles of truth, and I being in the shop about my calling, my mistress came to me, and said, 'Why do you not go out to help your master? for there is a Quaker at the door, that hath put him to silence.' I hearing this, made haste, and took my Bible under my arm, and put on what courage I could, to dispute with that poor man; but he proved too hard for us all. When I went to them, they were upon the words *thee* and *thou*. I very peremptorily asked him, what command he had to speak *thee* and *thou*. I acknowledged to him it was the language of God to Adam, and the language of Scripture; 'but,' said I, 'that is not enough for us now in this day; we must have a command for it.' To which he answered, 'Hold fast the form of sound words, which thou hast heard of me.' I told him, we heard the Quakers denied the Scripture, and would not read them. He said, there were many false reports of them. And truly, when he quoted the Scripture so readily, I concluded that what was reported of them was not true; and he saw that he had reached to the witness of God in me. Then he exhorted me to take heed to that light which shined in my heart, and showed my vain thoughts, and reproved me in secret for every idle word and action; saying, that was the true Light, which lighteth every man that cometh into the world; and in that light, I should see more light, and that would open the Scriptures to me, and I should receive a measure of the same spirit which gave them forth. And further, he told me, it was the more sure word of prophecy, unto which I did well to take heed, "as unto a light that shineth in a dark place until the day dawn and the day-star arise in the heart." And he spoke much of the inward work and operation of God's Holy Spirit on the soul; recommending me to the grace of God, that bringeth salvation, 'teaching us, that denying ungodliness and worldly lusts, we should live soberly, righteously, and godly in this present world.' And so he departed, and I set him along on his way.

"The consideration of his words took fast hold on me, that I could not go from under them; and the more I waited in that light to which he recommended me, the more my former peace, and that in which I formerly took comfort, was broken. Herein I came to see that our former building could not stand, for we built upon that which the apostle called 'wood, hay, and stubble.' Thus I came to a loss of all my former knowledge, and my former performances proved but a sandy foundation. Then I did, with much humility and poverty of spirit, beg of Almighty God, that I might build upon that Rock which the true church of Christ was built upon, that the gates of hell might not prevail against me.

"I was made willing to lay hold on the precious promises of Holy Scripture, *and waited for the fulfilling of them in myself*, and of that which Christ said to the Jews, 'It is written in the prophets, And they shall be all taught of God. Every man therefore that hath heard, and hath learned of the Father, cometh unto me.'

"When I came to know a little of the teachings of the Lord, I took my leave of all my former formal teachers, and many times went into the woods and other by-places, where none might see me, to wait upon the Lord; where I was much broken and tendered by the power of God. And though I began to see a little of myself, and something of the goodness of God, still I was afraid of being deceived; for I had read that 'Satan himself is transformed into an angel of light.' I desired of the Lord that I might see this poor man once again; for I knew not where to see the face of any called a Friend. And it pleased God that he came again that way. Then I queried of him their way of worship, and concerning those two great ordinances, so called, that we so much relied upon, namely, the bread and wine, and baptism; and respecting the Scriptures, to know what was their judgment of them;—to which he gave me some satisfaction. In the morning I parted with him, and to my knowledge I saw him no more for several years.

"In all this time I still kept my retirement in the woods, or some other private place; and there waiting, I desired of the Lord, that I might be farther satisfied by himself as to those things: first, Whether the Scriptures were the Word of God, as was said and preached unto us they were, and the way to life and salvation. Then the first chapter of John came under my serious consideration. ['In the beginning was the Word; and the Word was with God, and the Word was God,' &c.] I, with many more, was under that mistake the Jews were, who thought they might have eternal life in the Scriptures; whereas Christ saith, 'Search,' or, 'ye search the Scriptures; for in them ye think ye have eternal life: and they are they which testify of me. And ye *will not come unto* ME, that ye might have life.'—As He is the life, so he is the way to the Father: 'I am the way, the truth, and the life: no man cometh unto the Father but by me.' As for the Scriptures, I was a great lover and a great reader of them, and took great pleasure in searching them, thinking *that* would make me wise unto salvation. Paul said to Timothy, 'And that from a child thou hast known the Holy Scriptures, which are able to make thee wise unto salvation, *through faith* which is *in Christ Jesus.*'—This main thing was wanting in me, the true and saving faith, which 'is the gift of God.' 'For by grace ye are saved, through faith, and that not of yourselves: it is the gift of God.' So it is the *grace of God* that brings salvation, and not the bare historical knowledge of the Scriptures. Men may have a great literal knowledge of the Scriptures, and yet remain in error, because they know them not as they ought to do, nor the power that was in the holy men that gave them forth: as Christ said to the Jews, 'Ye do err, not knowing the Scriptures, nor the power of God.' That which gives the true knowledge of God, and a right understanding of the Scriptures, is therefore the power of God. 'For,' says the apostle, 'God, who commanded the light to shine out of darkness, hath shined in our hearts, to give the light of the *knowledge* of the glory of God, in the face of Jesus Christ.' And as men and women come to mind this light, that is, the Spirit of God, and to obey it, they shall come to the comfort of the Scriptures, of which the same apostle speaks: 'Whatsoever things were written aforetime were written for our learning; that we, through patience and comfort of the Scriptures, might have hope.'

"And being under a serious consideration of what I read in the sacred writings, I believed the Spirit of the Lord to be the interpreter thereof. Those great mysteries that were hid from ages and generations, and are hid now in this our age from many, are come to be revealed by the Spirit of God. And though formerly I read the Scriptures as too many do, without a true sense and due consideration, yet now, I can bless God for them, and have great comfort in the reading of them; they being no more as a sealed book to me, and many more, who wait for the assistance of God's Holy Spirit, in all their duties and performances · for without Him we know that we can do nothing that is pleasing unto him. Formerly we ran in our own time and wills to preach and pray, not having a due regard to the leading and moving of the Spirit of the Lord: but many times, when I arose from my knees in a formal way of prayer, the reproof was very near me, 'Who required this at thy hands? It is sparks of thy own kindling.' I was afraid that I should lie down in sorrow, as was said to some by the Lord. Isaiah i. 11.

"I had much reasoning in my mind concerning water baptism, and the bread and wine. And when I was satisfied as to those weighty concerns, I thought I might rest there, and keep my old customs, and fashions, and language. But that would not do; I had no peace therein. God showed me the vain customs of the nation, and that our language was not according to the language of God's people, recorded in the Scriptures of Truth. And withal I knew a little grammar, and how it was improper to say *vos* (*you*) to a single person, instead of *tu* (*thou*). I also believed that the Lord would return to his people 'a pure language,' as was promised in the days of old. Zeph. iii. 9. Thus I was conscientiously concerned to speak the 'pure language' of *thee* and *thou* to every one, without respect of persons; which was a great cross to me. Though it seems to some but as a weak and foolish thing, yet when the Lord lays the necessity of speaking the truth to all, in the language that God and all his servants used, it comes to be of greater weight than many light airy people think it is. This necessity being laid upon me, I spoke to my master in that dialect. He was not offended at it, because he was convinced of the truth of it, and that it ought to be spoken to every one. But when I gave it to my mistress, she took a stick, and gave me such a blow on my bare head, that made it swell and sore for a considerable time. She swore she would kill me, though she should be hanged for it; though before that time, she seldom, if ever, gave me an angry word. But I considered that, 'that which was born after the flesh persecuted him that was born after the Spirit.'

"The Almighty put it into my heart to consider the cost, and that through tribulation I was to enter into the kingdom of heaven; and I was faithful in this testimony that I had to bear. I was much encouraged to go on in that strait and narrow way, that God showed me I was to walk in; considering the saying: 'Whosoever doth not bear his cross, and come after me, cannot be my disciple.'—And my prayers unto Him were, that He would enable me to go through all things that He required of me.

"I was now first called a Quaker, because I said to a single person *thee* and *thou*, and kept on my hat, and did not go after the customs and fashions of the world, that other professors lived and walked in. Though some of these would complain of their own formalities, and were weary of the fashions of the world, yet they did not take up their cross and leave them. In thus doing I had great comfort from the Lord, and did receive from Him living satisfaction, and encouragement to go on in my way.—The Lord kept me, and his people, very meek and low in our minds, in a self-denying spirit. We waited for the living Word, that came with a living voice from Him that speaks from heaven to us by His Spirit; and the living voice is the voice of 'Christ in us, the hope of glory;' which voice we esteemed more than our necessary food. For obeying this voice, we came to be mocked and derided; and they spoke all manner of evil against us, and hated us for His name's sake.—These and the like afflictions I was to meet with, if I truly and faithfully followed the Lord Jesus Christ; therefore I labored to put on the whole armor of light, that I might be able to withstand the fiery darts of the wicked one.

"The rage of my mistress was not yet abated, though she

had nothing against me but my not conforming to the corrupt language and vain customs of the world; for I labored to keep a conscience void of offence both towards God and man. One time, when she thought it a fit opportunity to execute her cruelty, she fell into a great rage; and I was freely given up to die that hour by her; but the Lord was pleased to accept of my free-will offering. He appeared for my deliverance, and made her more moderate the rest of my servitude. And after I went away, the Lord visited her with a sharp fit of sickness; in which time she said that she thought she should not die till she had asked me forgiveness, desiring them to send for me, even if it were from London. And so they did. I could freely forgive her, for that I had done long since; and I prayed to my Heavenly Father that he might forgive her also. It pleased God to touch her with a sense of his love, and lengthen her days; she confessing often the wrong she had done to an honest careful young man, as she said I had been, who had minded her husband's inward and outward good, more than they themselves did.

"About this time (1657) it was the talk of the country, that I had become a Quaker. My parents were much concerned about me. I had not been yet with them, but waited for clearness in myself, and then I went to see them. It was a trouble to them to see that I did not, as formerly, go down upon my knees to ask their blessing, and bow to them, and take off my hat. My father soon turned his back upon me. I had heard of his displeasure, and of his having said he would leave me nothing—that they thought to have had comfort of me, but now expected none, but that I would go up and down the country, crying, Repent! Repent!—I remembered David's condition, when he said, 'Thou hast been my help; leave me not, neither forsake me, O God of my salvation. When my father and my mother forsake me, then the Lord will take me up. Teach me thy way, O Lord, and lead me in a plain path, because of mine enemies.'

"At length my mother came tenderly to me—and when I discoursed with her out of the Scriptures, her heart was much affected with the goodness of God towards me. She went for my father, and said to him, 'Be of good comfort; our son is not as was reported of him; we hope to have comfort of him yet.'

"A little after this, I came to hear that some of the people called Quakers were at Shrewsbury, distant from my abode about eighteen miles. I waited for an opportunity to go to see them, and the way of their worship, for as yet I had not seen any of them, but that one poor man before mentioned. I went first to the house of John Millington, where many Friends resorted, and they of the town came to see me in great love and tenderness, and much brokenness of heart was among us, though but few words. We waited to feel the Lord among us, in all our comings together. When the first day of the week came, we went to a meeting at William Pane's; and though it was silent as to words, yet the Word of the Lord was among us. It was as a hammer and a fire—it was sharper than any two-edged sword—it pierced through our inward parts—it melted and brought us into tears, that there was scarcely a dry eye among us. The Lord's blessed power overshadowed our meeting, and I could have said, *that God alone was Master of that assembly.* The next day, we heard that John ap John was to have a meeting there. I stayed to that meeting; where I heard, for the first time, one called a Quaker preach in a meeting. And when I heard him, I thought he spoke as one having authority, and not as the scribes, his words were so sound and piercing.

"I came home; where I was under many considerations, and especially that of Christ's words, 'Ye are the light of the world. Let your light so shine before men, that they may see your good works, and glorify your Father which is in heaven.' And afterwards the Lord required of me to go and give my testimony for Him, and to warn a company of people to think of their latter end, who were met to dance and to play, not far from my master's house. When I came within the room where they were dancing, the fiddler ceased playing, and they dancing; and I declared the word of the Lord among them. That which was chiefly before me was that of Job xxi. 11, 13. 'They send forth their little ones like a flock, and their children dance. They take the timbrel and harp, and rejoice at the sound of the organ. They spend their days in mirth, and in a moment go down to the grave.' When I had discharged myself of what lay upon me, I parted from them in love and peace. They thanked me for my good exhortation, and some of them came to set me home.

"After this, I still waited to know the will and counsel of God, and that he might direct me in my way, and order my steps in this my spiritual travel. For I had none to look unto but Him alone, who was all-sufficient to carry on the work which He had begun, though often by weak, poor, mean, and contemptible instruments in the eye of the world. Well might I say with the apostle, 'But God hath chosen the foolish things of the world to confound the wise; and God hath chosen the weak things of the world to confound the things which are mighty; and base things of the world, and things which are despised, hath God chosen, yea, and things which are not, to bring to naught things that are.'

"About this time I went to visit some young men, my former companions in profession of religion. Two of them were convinced, and received the Truth. When we were come to the number of four, it was with me, that we ought to meet together in the name of the Lord; for I remembered the promise of Christ, who said, 'Where two or three are gathered together in my name, there am I in the midst of them.' So we all agreed to meet together; but none of us had a house of his own to meet in. We determined therefore to meet on a hill in a common, as near as we could for the convenience of each other, we living some miles apart. There we met in silence, to the wonder of the country. When the rain and weather beat upon us on one side of the hill, we went to the other side. We were not free to go into any neighbors' enclosures, for they were so blind, dark, and ignorant, that they looked upon us as witches, and would go away from us, some crossing themselves with their hands about their foreheads and faces.

"Thus we continued for some time, till two of them left me [to live elsewhere]. The third was William Davies: and we met together for some time; but one time he stayed [away] longer than usual, and a dark spirit possessed him, so that the little time we were together was not comfortable to me; and when we had broken up the meeting, he asked me, 'How I did think we should stand, in the face of the whole country?' I answered him with great zeal, 'The serpent, the serpent, the same that beguiled the woman in Paradise, hath beguiled thee;—*thou* wilt not be able to stand.' And while we were yet discoursing, I saw my master coming; two women followed him, the one being his wife, my cruel mistress, the other his sister. They both had staves in their hands, and when they came to us, my mistress began beating William Davies. So his trial came very quickly, and he came no more to meet with me, nor any other Friends for many years. It so happened that I had not a blow among them.

"These young men going away thus, I was left alone again, but still I kept waiting upon the Lord, to know his will concerning me. And when the time of my apprenticeship was over, I found freedom to go to London; and finding many Friends there, I settled to my trade; and well satisfied I was that I could go to meetings and follow my business. When any thing would come into my mind of this my native country [Wales], barren and uninhabited with Friends and Truth, I endeavored to shut it out, and to keep where I was. But all my fair pretences and reasonings would not do. Disobedient to the Lord I was, and trouble and sorrow and judgment from the Lord came upon me, for not obeying his command, to go to my own country, and stand a witness for Him there. In this my disobedience I continued, till I lost His presence, and He smote me with trouble within, and pain in my bones, that I could not work. My pain of body and spirit increased, till at last I was forced to bow to the will of the Great God, who was too strong for me. And reasoning with Him one night upon the bed of my sorrows, he showed me clearly, that I was to go to my own country. And I was made willing to go, if He would be pleased to let me know his will and pleasure by this token, *that He would remove my pain.* I also reasoned with Him thus: that I was alone, like a pelican in the wilderness, or a sparrow on the house-top. The Lord still *commanded me to go*, showing that *He would provide a help-meet for me.* And when I had made a covenant with the Lord to go, *immediately my pain was removed*, and I had peace and quietness of mind. I arose next morning, and went to my work; and when those tender Friends that had a regard for me in my sickness, came to see me that morning, I was gone to work, to their admiration.

"The Lord, in a little time, provided a help-meet for me, for I prayed unto Him, that she might be of his own providing. We concluded to lay our proceedings before our elders, and especially George Fox—who desired the Lord to be with us. And when we saw our clearness in the Lord, we went to the meeting in Tower Street, London, in the morning, and in the afternoon to Southwark; and in that meeting, in the presence of God and that assembly, we took each other to be man and wife. God alone knew our innocency and integrity in coming together. It was not for gold, nor silver, nor any outward thing; but to be serviceable to Him in our age and generation, and to stand witnesses for Him and His blessed Truth, where he should send us. Soon after, in the Lord's time, we made what haste we could to come to the country where we believed the Lord would have us to be, and we said, 'O Lord, if thou wilt be with us in our way, and give us bread to eat and raiment to put on, then, O Lord, thou shalt be our God.' And the Lord was with us, and gave us His sweet and comfortable presence."

Richard Davies continued to reside in Wales for many years, and became an eminent instrument in the hands of his Divine Master, in gathering many from the barren mountains of an empty profession, to sit down in the silence of all flesh, and learn from the great Minister of ministers the manifestations of His holy will, and the mysteries of pure spiritual religion.

CHAPTER XIV.

GEORGE ROBINSON GOES TO JERUSALEM, AND MARY FISHER TO TURKEY.

ABOUT the year 1657, several of the ministers raised up to testify to the universal grace of God through Christ, as the free offer of salvation to all mankind, were called forth by their divine Master, to bear witness to his goodness, as with their lives in their hands, among the semi-barbarous inhabitants of the coasts of the Mediterranean sea.

George Robinson, of London, believed it required of him to travel in the service of the gospel to Jerusalem, and there bear his testimony to pure and spiritual religion. Embarking from Leghorn in Italy, he landed at the port of Ptolemais, now called Acre, in the Levant, and thence proceeded to Joppa, and Ramlah, or Arimathea. But the Romish priests at Jerusalem, hearing of him, and understanding that his object was to decry the superstition of pilgrimages, which was their chief means of support, procured his arrest and confinement. After a short imprisonment, an old Turkish inhabitant of the place took him to his house, and for several days entertained him with much hospitality. At length there came an Irish friar from the Popish priests and friars at Jerusalem, who began to question him, whether he would, on his arrival at that ancient city, visit the various holy places, as they were called, pay the usual sums of money, and wear the customary habit of the pilgrims? He was also enjoined not to speak anything about religion, or against the Turkish laws which were in force there. George, however, was not at liberty to submit to terms, which would have fettered the operations of the Holy Spirit through him as an instrument of the divine will; and steadfastly refusing to comply with their wishes, he was carried back by a guard of horse and foot soldiers to Joppa, and thence conveyed to Acre, where he had first landed. Here he was kindly entertained by an old French merchant, who was secretly drawn in sympathy towards him; and feeling still a necessity laid upon him to endeavor to prosecute his journey, this merchant assisted him to return to Joppa, whence he again reached Ramlah on foot. On the road he was attacked by three robbers, who plundered him, but afterwards, moved perhaps by his innocent behavior, or by the special interposition of Divine Providence, one of them returned what they had taken, and in a friendly manner conducted him on his journey. Arriving at Ramlah, he was again seized by the contrivance of the friars, and carried into one of the Mahometan mosques; where he was required, on pain of death, to profess the Mahometan religion, in compliance with the custom of the Turks, that whoever enters a mosque must embrace their religion or die. Some of their priests pressed him with much solicitation; but he persisting in his refusal, and in the true spirit of the martyrs declaring that he would rather die than violate his conscience by complying with their demand, they grew angry; and delivering him to the executioner, he was hurried away to the place of execution, to be burnt to death. Here he was made to sit down upon the ground, as a sheep among wolves; and as he sat, engaged in inward supplication, and resigned to the will of his divine Master, He whom he served was pleased to interpose for his deliverance; the Turks began to fall out among themselves; and a grave old man of note among them came up to him, and declared, that whether he would turn to their religion or not, he should not die. He was again interrogated, whether he would deny his Saviour; to which he firmly answered, No! The old man ordered his servants to conduct George to his house, where he treated him kindly for some days. But the friars still plotted against him, and hired a guard of horsemen to carry him to Gaza, before the Pacha, trusting that their insinuations had influenced this officer against him. But coming to Gaza, some of the Turks acquainted the Pacha with the malicious designs of the friars, and instead of complying with their wishes, he made them pay a considerable fine, and compelled them to convey George Robinson in safety to Jerusalem. Their own malice thus proving the means of his obtaining an official authority which they could not withstand, they now tried other arts on his arrival at their convent, to frustrate the object of his journey; and like sycophants, began to flatter him, telling him that his preservation through so many enemies was miraculous, pretending that they had been misinformed about him, and offering that if he would visit their pretended holy places, as other pilgrims, he should do it without cost, instead of having to pay them considerable fees. But George, faithful to his testimony against the superstitious veneration for those places, replied, "I shall not visit them in your manner; for in so doing I should sin against God." They told him that if he would conform, they would honor him as much as they had honored any Englishman that had ever visited them; but he told them he should not conform, and as for their honor, he mattered it not. They then became angry, and began to threaten to make him an example to all Englishmen who should come thither; but he said, I choose your dishonor rather than your honor; and told them, that they, under pretence of doing service to God, in visiting the places where the holy men dwelt, opposed and resisted that life which the holy men of God lived and walked in; adding that he would have them turn from those evil practices, else the wrath of the Almighty would be kindled against them. They did not like such discourse, and replied that whether he would go to see their places or not, the Turks must be paid, and insisted that if he would not visit them, he must pay twenty-five dollars, "for the Turks" as they pretended; though if he would visit their favorite relics, "they would pay the money for him." But, he told them that he would not comply with any such unreasonable demands.

They then brought him before one of the Turkish officers of the city, who, discoursing about the worship of the Christians, asked him the ground of his coming to Jerusalem. He answered, "that he came thither by the command of the Lord God of heaven and earth; and that the great and tender love of God was made manifest in visiting them; His compassionate mercies being such, that he would gather them in this the day of his gathering." Having now, as he believed, delivered the message with which he had been commissioned to these people, having practically testified against their bigotry, and cleared his conscience of their blood, he found great peace with the Lord, and returned home, magnifying His glorious name, who had preserved him through so many dangers, and provided a way for him in the midst of his enemies. It is remarkable, that the friars were compelled by the Turks to convey him back safely, and free of charge, to the port of his embarkation.

Mary Fisher, who had now returned from the scene of persecutions in New England, felt an extraordinary concern in her mind, to pay a visit to the Sultan of Turkey, Mahomet IV., then encamped with his army near Adrianople. She proceeded as far as Smyrna, where the English Consul stopped her, and sent her back to Venice. Still, however, endeavoring to obey her Maker rather than man, she prosecuted her journey by another route, and travelling overland she arrived safely at Adrianople, a journey of five or six hundred miles. There she requested some of the inhabitants to accompany her to the camp; but fearing the displeasure of the Sultan, they objected, and she was obliged to go alone. At the camp she sent a message to the Grand Vizier, that "there was an Englishwoman who had something to declare from the Great God to the Sultan;" who sent her word that the next morning he would procure her an opportunity of an interview. Accordingly returning to the city that night, she went back to the camp at the time appointed, and was brought before the Sultan and his great officers of state. He asked her whether it was true that she had a message to him from the Almighty, to which she answering that it was so, he bid her speak on. She stood silent a while, with her mind retired in inward waiting for the divine motion and power, to give weight and energy to what she had to deliver; when the Sultan, supposing she might be fearful of expressing herself before them all, asked her whether she wished any of the company to retire. She answered, no; and he then desired her to speak the word of the Lord to them, and not to fear, for they had good hearts, and would hear it; strictly charging her to deliver the whole message, neither more nor less, for they were willing to hear it, be it what it might. She then in a weighty frame relieved her mind of what lay upon it, to which the Turks listened with much seriousness and gravity; and when she had finished, the Sultan asking her if she had any more to say; she asked if he had understood what she had said? To which he replied, "Yes, every word;" adding that it was truth, and respectfully inviting her to remain in the country. When he found that she wished to go to Constantinople in order to return home, he offered her a guard, saying that it was unsafe for her to travel alone, and that he would not, for any consideration, have any injury occur to her in his dominions. This, however, she modestly declined, confiding in the protection of that Divine Arm which had brought her thither. Then some of them asked her, what she thought of their prophet Mahomet? To which she made a cautious reply, saying, "that she knew him not; but Christ she knew, who was the true prophet, the Son of God, the Light of the world, that enlighteneth every man that cometh into the world." After some more conversation, she took her leave, and departing for Constantinople without a guard, arrived there safely, without the least injury or insult, and thence returned to England; having experienced respectful kindness and attention from those called infidels, in remarkable contrast with the bigoted cruelty of men unworthily claiming the name of Christians, whom she had encountered in New England.

CHAPTER XV.

THE SUFFERINGS OF CATHARINE EVANS AND SARAH CHEE-
VERS IN THE INQUISITION AT MALTA—AND OF JOHN
PHILLY AND WILLIAM MOORE IN HUNGARY, ETC.

IN the year 1658, Catharine Evans and Sarah Cheevers, under a religious concern to propagate, in the dark lands of superstition and ignorance, the doctrine of the divine Light of Christ in the heart of man, took passage in a ship bound from London to Leghorn; where arriving safely, they stayed some time, discoursing on religion with the people who came to them, and distributing the books of Friends, explanatory of their principles. Hence they took passage in a Dutch ship bound to Alexandria; but the master put into Malta; and the women landing were met by the English Consul, gave him some books, and accepted an invitation to his residence. Curiosity now drew many of the inhabitants to visit them, whom they found it laid upon them to call to repentance, and several were seriously touched by their testimony. They went also to the nunnery, to see the governor's sister, where they conversed on religious subjects with the nuns, and distributed books. Here a priest found them, brought them into the chapel, and wanted them to bow before the high altar. But with abhorrence of such idolatry they firmly refused, and went back to their abode at the British Consulate. During three months of their stay there, they were several times called before the officers of the Inquisition, and examined about their religious principles; but through the wisdom with which they were furnished, they answered in such a manner as neither to give these men the advantage against them which they were seeking, nor to give away the cause of Truth by the least compliance with their superstitions. Indeed they often testified boldly against the bigotry so prevalent in that popish place. The Consul was at length bribed to violate the rights of hospitality and the duty of his official station; and treacherously withdrew his protection so far as to allow their being taken by the officers of the Inquisition. By the lord inquisitor they were required to change their religion; but steadfastly refusing, they were confined in a close, dark room, with only two little holes for light and air, and so extremely hot, that it seemed as if the intention was to stifle them to death.

They were brought under examination again and again, and continually beset with the impertinencies of monks and priests, to terrify or beguile them into conformity to their superstitions. But all their efforts were ineffectual; these innocent women being too well established in that pure religion whose efficacy they had experienced, to be perverted therefrom by flattery, or terrified by threats, though daily in danger of their lives, and under dismal apprehensions of being led to the stake. It seemed, however, as if the intention of their keepers was rather to put them out of the way quietly, than to execute them in a public manner. They were put into a room so exceedingly hot and suffocating, that it was thought they could not long survive. They were often compelled to rise from their bed, and lie down at the chink of the door, to draw a breath of air. Their skin became parched, their hair fell off, and they frequently fainted away. They now wrote a remonstrance to the inquisitor, pleading their innocence, and complaining of the hardships to which they were subjected; but he was so offended at it, that he ordered their ink-horns to be taken from them. He also gave orders for them to be separated, which added much to their grief, especially as Catharine's sickness increased greatly, so that she was broken out in sores from head to foot; and the doctor being sent for, declared that they must have air, or they would die. The inquisitor hereupon ordered the doors to be opened for six hours in the day. Ten weeks after this, they were separated, and told that they should never see each other more; the friars hoping that by attacking them separately, they might be more able to prevail upon them. But in this they were disappointed, the Lord himself being their companion, enduing them with strength to resist all the attempts of their enemies, and even enabling them to speak boldly at various times in His name, to those who came to see them. Some considerable repairs to the inquisition were going on, which occupied about a year and a half, and often drew to the place many workmen and some of the persons in authority in the island, to whom these women had opportunities of declaring the Truth as it is in Jesus. But the friars were indefatigable in their endeavors, both by persuasion and threats, to induce them to change their religion. Some of their language was exceedingly disgraceful to men professing religion, abounding as it did, in expressions bordering on blasphemy, and threats that these poor defenceless women should be covered over in a pile of chains, that they should be given to the devil, that they should never come out of the prison alive, that they should be burnt to death, or, that as Ananias and Sapphira were struck down dead by the word of the Lord through the apostles, so the friars would do to them. But their meek, yet firm reply was, that their persecutors might do what they would; they did not fear; that if they suffered, they were the Lord's, and trusted in Him; that they were settled and grounded in the Truth, and the more they persecuted them, the stronger they grew. Sometimes they spoke so effectually to those who came to them, that they could not contradict them, but were struck with conviction. And Catharine's prison being at one time so near the street that she could be heard by the passers-by, she frequently found it her duty to call them to repentance, and direct them to the Light of Christ, which would lead them from all sinful ways and worships, to serve and worship God in spirit and in truth. Some would stay to listen as long as they dared, for the people were narrowly watched. Others, however, were hardened in wickedness, and maliciously threw stones at her window, as they passed to their place of worship.

Several efforts were made by various persons to obtain their release. The treacherous consul, who had been miserable ever since their imprisonment, visited them, and made an ineffectual application to the inquisitor on their behalf, offering to return the money by which the friars had bribed him to allow of their arrest. But he died before any thing effectual was done towards their deliverance. Two Englishmen after this endeavored, but to no purpose, to accomplish the same object. One Francis Stuart also, a sea-captain, took great pains to obtain their liberty; but the inquisitor professed inability to grant it, without an order from the Pope. They were told that one impediment to their freedom was their having preached to the people while there: to which they replied, that they had testified to the truth, which they were willing to maintain with their blood. This Captain Stuart was, however, admitted to see them, and told them with tears what he had done on their behalf, but in vain. He declared that if they could be set free, he would gladly give them a passage, and provide for them in his ship; and he offered them money. This they declined, but made sincere acknowledgments for his great kindness, and prayed for his preservation unto everlasting life.

After Stuart was gone, they met with worse usage than before; the taking away of their lives was again conspired, and their doors were shut up for many weeks. But they were still kept in great resignation, not daring even to beseech the Almighty for their own deliverance, until it should be His will.

They had now been confined nearly three years. About the beginning of the year 1662, Daniel Baker, a friend, who had come from England to Leghorn with John Stubbs, and had thence travelled to Smyrna, preaching the gospel to Papists, Jews and Mahometans, came back by Malta, in sympathy with these afflicted women, and demanded their liberty of the inquisitor. His repeated solicitations, however, were ineffectual; but remaining nearly a month on the island, he frequently found means to visit the prisoners, at the hazard of his life; being narrowly watched, and daily threatened with the inquisition. He administered to them spiritual consolation, assuring them that the church of God owned their testimony for His cause, "and they were a sweet savor unto the Lord and His people." And though they could only commune with him through the iron gratings of their windows, yet even this imperfect intercourse with one of their own countrymen, and a brother in the same faith, was a source of great refreshment to them in their long and hard imprisonment.

They were still repeatedly plied with attempts by the friars to induce them to change their religion. Being promised a release if they would become "Catholics," they replied, "that they were already true Catholics"—the term properly signifying members of the universal church of Christ. They were told also, that if they would but kiss the cross, they should have their liberty: but conscious that this act, small in itself, would be sanctioning the idolatry and bigotry against which they had so long borne their testimony, they steadfastly refused to purchase their liberty or lives by such an act.

At length George Fox and Gilbert Latey found means to procure their liberation. They applied to Lord D'Aubigny, an English papist, for his friendly interposition by writing to the magistrates of Malta; and his mediation was so successful, that Catharine and Sarah were soon released, after an imprisonment of nearly four years. After eleven weeks spent again at the British consulate, waiting for a vessel, they embarked for Leghorn, and thence passed to Tangier, at that time besieged by the Moors; notwithstanding which they entered the town, and had many opportunities of exhorting the people to amendment of life. They also visited the governor, who courteously received them, took their admonition in good part, and would have given them money. The Portuguese and Irish papists here were ready to do them mischief; but the governor threatened any of the garrison who should abuse or insult them, with severe punishment. And such was the favorable opinion which their integrity procured for them, that when they took ship from Tangier for England, several embarked with them, in preference to going in another vessel, believing that on account of these pious women, they should have a safer passage. At length they arrived at home in safety, magnifying the divine mercy, manifested in their wonderful deliverance.

In the early part of this year, John Philly and William Moore, being in Germany with some other Friends, felt a concern to proceed into Hungary, and visit the Hortesche brethren, a kind of Baptists, who refused to swear or fight, and who lived by hundreds together in families, having community of goods. They accordingly proceeded to the nearest body of these people, residing near Cushart, about a day's journey from Presburg, and were hospitably entertained. Here they dispersed some religious books, and had favorable opportunities for gospel labor among them, endeavoring to promote their growth in pure Christianity. They were by these people informed of another of their communities, settled three hundred miles further, at Pattock, in Upper Hungary. They therefore continued their journey towards Comora, on an island in the Danube, having their religious books with them. Here they were seized by the

garrison, and carried before an inquisitor, who informed
William, that the bringing of their books into the country
was a capital crime, and would cost him his life; asking
them if they did not know that "Catholics" had laws to
burn and torment heretics, and any who carried such books.
For more than a week, they were beset with attempts to
induce them to profess the Popish religion, and threatened
with the rack: which threats at length were put in execution.
The inquisitor came to William, and told him that he was
to be subjected to the rack, and afterwards was to lose his
head. It seems that they professed to consider these Friends
as spies, in order to justify in some degree the cruelties they
designed to inflict upon them. It was in vain that William
pleaded his innocence; he was put to the rack, whereby his
thumbs were exceedingly pinched by iron screws, his arm
dislocated, and his back and many of his joints twisted and
bent by tight cords; his chin was drawn close to his breast,
and his mouth and throat so distorted, that he was almost
choked. Then John was brought, who not seeing his companion, supposed that he had been hung on a gallows which
was in the place: he also was put to the torture in the midst
of his protestations of innocence. They were now told, that
it would soon be determined by what mode they should lose
their lives. The inquisitor required William to put in
writing the principal tenets of his religion, and intercepted
a letter which they wrote to the governor remonstrating
against these cruelties. After about sixteen weeks' imprisonment, they were conveyed in chains to General Nadasti;
and passing under a sort of examination before him and
several other lords of that country, they were condemned to
be burned, if they did not submit to embrace the Popish
religion. Under this dismal sentence John Philly was
divinely supported, and encouraged his companion, in a full
persuasion that the power of the Almighty would still open
a way for the preservation of their lives, by dividing the

counsels of their persecutors; which proved to be the case. They were now sent to a place near Vienna, where they were searched by the priests, their books and papers taken away, and they were threatened with most cruel tortures. Manacles were locked on their wrists, so tight as to make them cry out with pain, and they were thrust into a narrow hole along with some Turkish prisoners, and not allowed straw, or scarcely room to lie down. William Moore became much discouraged at their disconsolate situation, being again threatened to be burned to death; and crying to the Almighty for help, he was encouraged, by means of a dream, to believe the Lord would provide for their safety. The very same day, a message came from a certain earl in authority there, expressing his displeasure at these rigorous proceedings of the priests.

It was now resolved by these men to separate the two Friends, and William was violently and clandestinely carried off in a sled over the snow, to a convent several miles distant in a wilderness, where he was laid in chains, and the next day blindfolded and put into a deep dungeon; a Jew there being threatened with death if he gave any intelligence of him. Here he was kept four days and nights, in severe frosty weather, with nothing to subsist upon but bread and water; and he was apprehensive that their intention was privately to murder him in this secret place.

After about twelve days' imprisonment, they renewed their attempts to convert him to the Romish religion; but he still remaining inflexibly firm to that faith, the divine efficacy of which he had experienced, they again had recourse to menaces, threatening at one time to cut out his tongue, and at another, to flay him alive, if he would not turn papist.

There was a man named Adam Bien, a barber to the above-mentioned earl, who at the place of their confinement, near Vienna, had found means sometimes to have access to them, and had been reached by their pious discourse, and in good degree convinced of the truth of their principles. This man commiserated much their suffering condition, and exerted himself indefatigably to obtain their release. By some means he found out the place of William's detention, notwithstanding the secrecy maintained by the priests, and supplied him with some refreshments. The earl being seized with sickness, from which his recovery was doubtful, Adam, who had influence with this nobleman, seized this opportunity of renewing his solicitations in their favor, and finally succeeded in obtaining an order for their release. They were then set at liberty, and though turned adrift without any money, which had all been taken away from them, and in a country infested with war, yet they were favored to arrive in safety among their friends.

CHAPTER XVI.

EDWARD BURROUGH AND RICHARD HUBBERTHORN, BEING VIOLENTLY SEIZED AT THE BULL-AND-MOUTH MEETING, DIE IN PRISON.

DURING the year 1662, died Edward Burrough, a witness unto death for the cause of a good conscience toward God. We have seen by what process of mental experience and refinement he was brought to a knowledge of the Truth as it is in Jesus, and how, about the eighteenth year of his age, his Divine Master saw fit to make use of him to sound the glad tidings of the Gospel to his fellow-men. His ministry was powerful and reaching, his doctrine sound, and his language eloquent; having learned in the best school, that of Christ himself, and been prepared for the ministry by the immediate teachings of the Spirit of Truth, gradually leading unto the living experience of holiness, and clothing him with ardent desires for the salvation of mankind.

His own example gave efficacy to his ministry. He lived as he advised others to live, in the fear of his Maker, and in a sense of His omnipresence. His natural disposition was bold and manly, tempered with innocence; his conversation affable and instructive, circumscribed by great watchfulness over himself. His Christian courage in the fulfilment of his duty was remarkable, an instance of which we may here mention.

On one of his frequent visits to London, he passed by a place, where a number of rude muscular men were exhibiting feats of wrestling, before a multitude of idle people, who stood gazing at them outside a ring. He saw how one strong and dexterous fellow had already thrown three others, and was waiting for a fourth champion, if any durst venture to enter the lists. At length, none being bold enough to try, Edward Burrough stepped within the ring; and looking upon the wrestler with a serious countenance, the man was not a little surprised, instead of an airy antagonist, to meet with a grave and awful young man. All stood amazed at the sight, wondering what would be the issue of this contest. But it was quite another fight that Edward aimed at. He began very seriously to speak to the by-standers, and that with such a heart-piercing power, that he was heard by this mixed and rude multitude with no less attention than admiration. His speech tended to turn them from darkness to light, and from the power of Satan unto God. To effect this, he labored with convincing power, showing how God had not left himself without a witness, but had graciously enlightened every man with the light of Christ. Thus zealously he preached; and though many might look on this as a novelty, yet it was of such effect, that some were convinced of the truth.

He travelled in many parts of England, Ireland, Scotland and Flanders, in the exercise of his ministerial gift, meeting with repeated sufferings and imprisonments. But his principal field of labor was London and its neighborhood, where his ministry was effectual to the conversion of many. His gospel solicitude for the inhabitants of that city was so warm, that when persecution grew hot, he said to his bosom friend, Francis Howgill: "I can freely go to that city, and lay down my life for a testimony to that truth, which I have declared through the Spirit and power of God." And being this year on a visit to Friends in Bristol, in taking leave of them, he said "he did not know that he should see their faces any more;" and therefore exhorted them to faithfulness; adding to some, "I am now going up to London again, to lay down my life for the Gospel, and suffer among Friends in that place."

About that time the rage of persecution was such, that it was estimated there were five hundred Friends in prison at one time in London alone; and the Friends who met for divine worship at the "Bull-and-Mouth" meeting, near the centre of the metropolis, were particularly exposed to the merciless violence of the magistrates and soldiery. The soldiers came several successive First-days, with muskets, lighted matches, pikes, and halberts, conducted by an officer, with a drawn sword in one hand, and a cane in the other. They usually entered with violent rushing and uproar, to terrify the assembly, commanding the people to be gone; and then shamefully attacked both men and women with canes and clubs, threatening to fire at them, and even striking them with swords, and the butt-ends of their muskets, in such a manner that some fainted away, and others survived their injuries but a short time.

On one occasion, when the meeting was near breaking up, Major-general Richard Brown entered the house with a party of men with drawn swords, in a manner rude and terrifying beyond expression; and ordering the doors to be made fast, they fell upon the innocent assembly, engaged in the most solemn act of worshipping their Maker; and without regard to age or sex, dealt such unmerciful and unmanly blows on men and women with their swords and cudgels, cutting, bruising, and levelling those before them, as bore an appearance of open hostility beyond what had ever been seen in a time of peace. Six or eight together being knocked down, were dragged out and laid in the gutters senseless, and apparently half dead, with the wounds and bruises they had received. Their blood flowed visibly in the street, so that the passers-by, struck with compassion for this unoffending people, cried, "Shame" upon the perpetrators, and for their compassionate expressions obtained also their share of similar abuse. Many of these Friends were so much injured, as to keep their beds for a considerable time, and one died of the wounds he there received. Thomas Ellwood was among those thus seized on one of these occasions, along with many more Friends; and the prisons in London were literally thronged with this people for several months.

Not long after Edward Burrough's arrival in London this year, he attended this meeting; and while he was preaching the gospel, he was violently pulled down by soldiers, and committed, with many others, to Newgate prison. Here, being thrust into crowded rooms, among the vilest felons, besides the great annoyance to which, from the filthy character of these criminals, and the dirty state of the prison, Friends were subjected, they were also witnesses of such vile and wicked conduct and conversation, as brought grief and sorrow on their souls. Having lain here some weeks, Edward was brought to trial at the Old Bailey, fined by the court twenty marks, without authority of any law, and condemned to lie in prison till he should pay the fine. As the deed for which he and his brethren were condemned, viz., meeting for the worship of God, was in their estimation no crime, but an act of indispensable duty to their Maker and Redeemer; and as a voluntary and active compliance with the penalty would have been a tacit confession of guilt, a giving away of the cause, and a balking of their testimony to the Truth; they durst not, for conscience' sake, pay the fine; so that this sentence amounted to perpetual imprisonment, unless released by the king.

Being thus immured in prison with six or seven score of his Friends, and so many crowded into one room as to make it even suffocating, many of them grew sick and died; of which number he was one. A special order from the king was sent to the sheriffs for his release and that of some others; but so implacable was the malice of some of the city magistrates, that they found means to evade the execution of this order. Edward being consequently still detained in prison, his disease gained upon him, and threatened approaching dissolution. But this holy man being raised above the fear of death, supported by the consolatory review of a life spent in the service of his Creator, and comforted by a consciousness of no wilful omission of duty, and an inward sense of freedom from the power and guilt of sin, through the effectual operation and atonement of Him who came to put an end to sin and take away its guilt, he made the following solemn and affecting appeal: "I have had the testimony of the Lord's love unto me from my youth; and my heart, O Lord, hath been given up to do thy will. I have preached the gospel freely in this city, and have often given up my life for the Gospel's sake. And now, O Lord, rip open my heart, and see if it be not right before thee!" Again he said: "There is no iniquity lies at my door; but the presence of the Lord is with me, and His life, I feel, justifies me." His friends about him he exhorted "to live in love and peace, and love one another:" and praying for his enemies and persecutors, he said, "Lord, forgive Richard Brown, if he may be forgiven"—who was the chief agent of the persecution. Being sensible that his dissolution drew near, he thus memorably expressed his faith: "Though this body of clay must turn to dust, yet I have a testimony that I have served God faithfully in my generation; and *that spirit that hath lived and acted and ruled in me, shall yet break forth in thousands.*" The morning before his departure, he said, "Now my soul and spirit is centred into its own being with God, and this form of person must return whence it was taken;" and shortly afterwards he expired, having been a zealous preacher of righteousness about ten years, though only in the twenty-eighth year of his age.

Richard Hubberthorn was another of those who, violently dragged away from the meeting at the "Bull-and-Mouth," finished their earthly course this year in prison, for the testimony of a pure conscience. He had been a soldier in the army of the commonwealth, but early joined George Fox in the better warfare against sin and spiritual darkness; and receiving ability to direct others in the sure way to the kingdom of Heaven, became one of the first and most eminent ministers of the society of Friends. But after many travels and deep sufferings for the cause of truth, being seized this year at the aforesaid meeting, he was carried before that implacable magistrate, Richard Brown; who giving vent to his passion as usual, pulled this inoffensive man down by the hat, with such fury that he brought his head almost to the ground, and then committed him to the noisome prison of Newgate.

His infirm constitution was so affected with the throng and vitiated air of this doleful place, that he presently grew sick, and after about two months imprisonment was taken away by death. His end exhibited the happy result of a life spent in righteousness and the pursuit of peace; being enabled in his last moments to look forward, in full assurance of faith, to the near approach of future happiness. To some of his friends he expressed, that "he knew the ground of his salvation, and was satisfied for ever of his peace with the Lord;" and at another time, he said: "That faith which hath wrought my salvation, I well know, and have grounded satisfaction in it." The greatest part of the time of his sickness he passed in inward retirement and meditation, in great resignation and stillness; and towards his close he requested his friends not to hold him, for the body was too strait for him, and he was to be lifted up on high, far above all mortal or corporeal restraints. And thus, in a frame of mind prepared for an entrance into the kingdom of glory, he finished his earthly course, and doubtless obtained that eternal reward laid up for those who are faithful unto death.

CHAPTER XVII.

THE SUFFERINGS OF ELIZABETH HOOTON AND OTHERS IN NEW ENGLAND.

BEFORE passing to other matters, we may revert for a short time to a continuance, this year and the next, of the dismal scenes of persecution, which still disgraced the profession of Christianity in New England.

Among the companions in prison of Wenlock Christison, before alluded to, were Elizabeth Hooton, the first female minister among Friends, and Joan Brocksup, each about sixty years of age; who on being released from captivity were driven into the wilderness, and left there exposed to the wild beasts of the forest, without provisions, to wander in great danger through places uninhabited and scarcely passable, until at length they came to Rhode Island. Thence they went to Barbadoes; and still feeling bound to testify in New England against the spirit of persecution prevalent there, they returned to that colony. On coming to Boston, however, they were presently apprehended, and sent away to Virginia, whence Elizabeth Hooton returned to England.

After remaining a short time in her native country, she found herself not yet clear, without making a third attempt to deliver the message of her Lord and Master. Accordingly, preparing for her departure, she made application to the King, and obtained from him a license to settle in any of the British colonies. She and her daughter set sail for Boston; and immediately on their arrival the magistrates would have fined the master of the vessel one hundred pounds for bringing her, but for the king's license which she carried with her. This instrument nevertheless did not prevent them from indulging their malicious dispositions against this devoted woman; for at Dover she was set in the stocks, and kept four days in prison in cold weather. At Cambridge she was imprisoned, two days and nights, in a close stinking dungeon, without anything to sit or lie down upon, and without so much as bread and water to sustain her. And when a friend in sympathy brought her a little milk, to prevent her from perishing under their hands, he was arbitrarily fined five pounds and sent to prison.

Elizabeth was then whipped through Cambridge, Watertown and Dedham, with a three-corded whip having three knots at the end; and in this mangled condition was carried on horseback many miles into the wilderness, in frosty weather, and there left at the hazard of her life, exposed to wild beasts, which at that time abounded in the forests. Her persecutors seem to have even expected that she would perish by this exposure, as they expressed their hopes that "they should never see her any more." But the Lord in mercy preserved his servant safe through the dismal forests and deep waters which she had to cross, to a place called Rehoboth, where she arrived the next day. Thence she made her way to Rhode Island, praising and magnifying the Most High, whose supporting hand had been mercifully displayed for her preservation.

But her sufferings had not yet satiated the malice of a persecuting magistracy, backed by the vindictive priests. As they had sent her away without her clothing, she returned, accompanied by her daughter, to a place near Cambridge, in order to obtain her property. But as they were coming back towards Rhode Island, they were apprehended, along with Sarah Coleman, an ancient woman who had fallen in company with them in the woods; and all three were taken back to Cambridge, abused by the scholars there, and then whipped and committed to the house of correction. No just cause was assigned for this cruel treatment of inoffensive women, who were going about their lawful occasions. They were sent out of the colony, being whipped in three towns on their way to Rhode Island. Elizabeth after this returning to Boston to preach repentance to the inhabitants, was again sent to the house of correction, whipped at the whipping-post, and afterwards at Roxbury and Dedham at a cart's tail, taken as before in a mangled condition into the wilderness, and left there in the cold weather, to make her way, twenty miles, back to Rhode Island. And soon after, returning to Boston once more, she was again imprisoned, whipped from the prison-door to the end of the town, and sent away with an order to whip her from town to town, and a threat that "if ever she came thither again, they would either put her to death or brand her on the shoulder." Thus was this devoted woman, who was of reputable character and substance, and perfectly peaceable and inoffensive, for her faithful endeavors to perform her gospel mission, cruelly persecuted with three imprisonments, nine severe whippings, and two perilous exposures in the wilderness to perish by wild beasts, or by cold and starvation. But though her afflictions thus abounded, yet her inward consolations did much more abundantly flow; under the precious enjoyment of which, she declared her willingness to endure much more, for the propagation of righteousness, and for her love for the souls of her fellow-creatures.

During this same year, three other women, Mary Tomkins, Alice Ambrose, and Anne Coleman, went into the neighborhood of Piscataqua River, to visit their friends in gospel love, and endeavor to confirm them in the truth. Soon after their arrival, one Rayner, a priest of Dover, exciting the magistrates to their usual persecuting measures, they were seized, condemned to be fastened to a cart's tail, and thus dragged through the country, and whipped in all the towns they passed through, until they should be out of the limits of that government. This order was cruelly executed at Dover, while the priest stood by and laughed at these innocent women's tortures. Being reproved for this cruel levity, by two by-standers, the magistrates caused them both to be placed in the stocks. The women were again whipped at Hampden and Salisbury; but afterwards a person to whom they were intrusted, commiserating their case, at his own risk set them at liberty, and thus saved them from the infliction of similar cruelty in several other townships through which they would have had to pass.

After a little time, not feeling released from their religious engagement, they returned to Dover; and being met together with other Friends on the First-day of the week, Alice Ambrose knelt in prayer to God. Whilst she was occupied in this most solemn engagement, two constables entered the meeting, and seizing her each by an arm, inhumanly forced her out of doors, and dragged her with her face downwards, over the snow, which was knee-deep, and over large stumps and logs, for nearly a mile. They then returned for Mary Tomkins, and treated her in the same barbarous manner. The next morning, which was excessively cold, they forced them into a canoe, together with their companion Anne Coleman, and carried them to the mouth of the harbor, threatening that they would now so dispose of them, that they would be troubled with them no more. And because these poor defenceless women were not willing to go, they forced them down a very steep place in the snow, dragging Mary Tomkins again over stumps of trees to the water side, whereby being much bruised, she fainted under their hands. Alice Ambrose they pulled into the water, and kept her swimming by the canoe, in great danger of drowning or of being frozen to death. It seems indeed as if their intent was nothing short of taking away the lives of their victims; in which however they were frustrated by a storm, which drove them back to the house where they had kept these poor women all the previous night. Here they detained them till near midnight, and then turned them out of doors in the frost and snow, although Alice's clothes were frozen as hard as boards. The barbarity exercised against these innocent women was such, that in all probability they must have perished, had not a merciful Providence interfered for their preservation.

The next year, Anne Coleman was again apprehended, and with several other Friends, cruelly whipped through Salem, Boston and Dedham; and the severity of the whipping was such—the thongs of the whip wrapping around her body and the knots tearing her breast—that it was thought her life must fall a sacrifice to the malice of her persecutors.

Edward Wharton, also, a respectable inhabitant of Salem, but who bore the hated name of a Quaker, was a particular mark for the malice of these unrelenting men. Not being able, after many cruel inflictions, to induce him to promise to come no more to the religious meetings of his Friends at Boston, he was, by order of Governor Endicot, led to the market place, bound to the wheels of a great gun, and barbarously whipped with thirty stripes to such a degree, that it was testified that peas might lie in the holes made in his flesh by the knots of the whip. His body was much swollen and black from his waist upwards. In this sad condition they led him about the country, as if to expose him to the people as a spectacle, and terrify them with the notion of their unlimited power.

The eyes of the people however began to be opened, to see the enormity of these rigorous measures exercised against an unoffending portion of their fellow-citizens; and Governor Endicot being taken away by death, and several of his coadjutors also removed, the magistrates became more cautious of provoking public sentiment by continued persecutions. Through all the severities which had been exercised, the Society of Friends had held on their way, trusting in the Lord their preserver, and had continued to spread over the colony, though trodden under foot of men.

CHAPTER XVIII.

THE EXTRAVAGANCIES OF JOHN PERROT.

THE Society of Friends was steadily pursuing its path, and increasing in numbers, notwithstanding the persecutions to which its members were everywhere subjected. But it was not to be expected that every individual who was found within its precincts should have been rightly prepared for the station which he might have assumed. It would have been indeed remarkable, if in the multitude of those who went forth in that day of zeal, in the service of the ministry, there had not been instances of men who had taken upon them (perhaps mistakenly) the office of a gospel minister, without waiting for the preparation and the call. And it would have been still more surprising if such forward spirits had proved firm in the day of outward trial, or of inward fascinations and snares of the enemy.

John Perrot was one who at this time caused great distress and trouble to the faithful members of the Society, from giving way to self-importance and extravagant notions. He had joined the Society early, and had probably too soon taken upon himself the ministerial office. He travelled considerably, and about the year 1660 conceived that he must go to Rome to convert the Pope. He obtained the company of John Love, and travelled as far as Leghorn; where they were both taken up and examined by the inquisition. But the answers they gave were so satisfactory that they were soon dismissed. Thence they proceeded to Venice, and afterwards to Rome, where they were soon again apprehended; John Love being put into the inquisition, and John Perrot being shut up in a madhouse. The former, who is supposed to have been a sincere man, died in prison, not without suspicion of being murdered there; for though the officers of the inquisition gave out that he had fasted to death, some nuns are said to have acknowledged that he was privately dispatched in the night, for testifying against their idolatry. It is clear that John Perrot was at this time exceedingly puffed up with spiritual pride; for he wrote, whilst in prison, some epistles to be printed in England, in so affected a style as bespoke him almost bewildered in his mind; signing only his first name, John, and otherwise making very extravagant assumptions, apparently in imitation of the manner of writing of the great apostle of Patmos.

At length, through the solicitation of Friends to some persons of influence there, he was released from confinement, and returned to England. And though he had come away without having accomplished the object of his mission, or so far as appears, having even seen the Pope, yet the exaggerated report of his sufferings abroad, and a great appearance of sanctity, gained him a sort of compassionate affection and esteem with weak minds; and his self-importance increased to such a degree, that he thought himself further enlightened than George Fox and the rest of his friends; and as an evidence of it, he maintained that the custom of putting off their hats in joining in public prayer, was only a piece of formality, and ought not to be practised. The next extravagance he adopted, was to let his beard grow, in which he was followed by several of his partisans. George Fox and the principal body of Friends, foreseeing the danger of the minds of the members being drawn off from attention to the necessary work of inward sanctification, into contention about outward observances of little or no importance, exerted their endeavors to prevent the spreading of the defection. This, however, went on for some years, till Perrot manifested more clearly, by the instability and enormity of his conduct, the error of his spirit and the depravity of his heart. He went to America, and was there led into fleshly liberties, fantastically putting on gaudy apparel, and wearing a sword; and under the pretence of being above forms, went so far at length as to reckon meeting for divine worship a form, and by his example and doctrine led many to forsake the assembling of themselves together. And after a time, having obtained some post under the government, he who had before professed that Christ had forbidden all swearing, is said to have rendered himself conspicuous, as a most rigid exactor of oaths.

Perrot's followers, as observed above, were not without

the faithful admonitions and warnings of their brethren. George Fox, ever alive to the welfare of the flock, felt it his duty to appoint a meeting in London with those who had been seduced into this separation, and also addressed them more than once by letter, endeavoring to restore them to a sound understanding, and to unity with the body; and through the divine blessing attending the labors of love extended by him and his friends, most of these people in England were at length recovered, acknowledged their error, and returned into the unity of the Society.

In America, the wild notions which Perrot had sown, continued in some places, for several years, to bear bitter fruit. John Burnyeat, in 1665, travelling in Virginia, found many who had been led astray into these fanciful notions. They had almost forsaken the practice of meeting for divine worship, scarcely assembling together once a year. Of course they lost ground in religion, which was manifested by a general backsliding. They had laid aside the plainness of their profession in dress and language, and were become loose and light in their conduct. The offence of the cross had ceased, and the power of godliness, as well as the form, was lost. So that John Burnyeat found it difficult to get a meeting with them. But he was not a man whose zeal was easily discouraged. When he saw their reluctance to grant him a public meeting, he did not leave them under their delusion, but sought private opportunities with them, to convince them of their mistakes, and to vindicate the principles and practice of the Society, in diligently meeting to wait together upon God, and endeavoring to walk before Him in all orderly conversation and sobriety, and to fulfil all their social and moral duties among mankind. By perseverance in repeated visits and conferences of this kind, he at length obtained a meeting with them; which being favored with the overshadowing of divine power, was very conducive to open the understandings of several to perceive their error, and to the revival of more regard to their religious duties. And by the continuance of his gospel labors, and the renewed convictions of the Spirit of Truth in their hearts, many came in time to see through the wiles of the enemy, and to be again serviceable in the Society. Some years afterwards, returning to Virginia, he found an open door for his labors, and was successful in promoting among them the establishment of meetings for discipline, for the further help of those who had not yet been entirely reclaimed.

After this, travelling in New England, at Salem he met with the devastating effects of the same spirit. But patiently laboring among them, several had their consciences so awakened, as to let them also see their mistake, condemn it, and return into unity with the body.

CHAPTER XIX.

RISE OF THE SOCIETY IN SCOTLAND.

HAVING traced the origin of the people called Quakers in England, and noticed the foothold which they had now obtained on the continent of America and some of the West India islands, we may next turn our attention to the progress of pure, evangelical truth in Scotland.

There were scattered in various parts of that country, about the middle of the seventeenth century, pious individuals, who, weary and heavy-laden under a sense of their own manifold shortcomings, believed there was to be known a more purely spiritual way of worship and of life and conduct, than that to which they, or any with whose profession they were acquainted, had attained. Being greatly burdened with the formality, superstition, and will-worship prevalent around them, under which the public preachers generally detained their hearers, these serious inquirers had separated from the several congregations of the people; and at length some of them began to meet together by themselves, waiting upon God in a holy silence and deep humility of soul, for ability to draw near to him in true spiritual worship. They were thus at times made sensible of the quickening virtue, power, and life of the Holy Spirit, enabling some of them to speak forth the praises of the Almighty, and from an inward experience of His goodness, to extend instrumentally a hand of help to others.

Such religious meetings appear to have been held at Drumbowy and Heads, in the south of Scotland, as early as the year 1653; and the first preachers thus raised up among them were William Osborne, a colonel in the army, Richard Rae, and Alexander Hamilton. These meetings had been established a full year, before any in actual connection with Friends found them out and visited them. The feet of several gospel messengers were, however, soon turned in this direction, as Christopher Fell, George Wilson, John Grave, George Atkinson, Sarah Cheevers, and Catharine Evans. In 1654, Myles Halhead, and James Lancaster, and in 1655, William Caton, and John Stubbs, travelled into Scotland; and George Fox was at Edinburgh in 1657. James Nayler is supposed to have preached in some parts of Scotland as early as 1651; but he does not appear to have fallen in with the above-mentioned little flock. John Burnyeat was led to travel as far north as Aberdeen, in 1658, and met with some meetings of Friends; and in 1659, Stephen Crisp, of Essex, who had then recently come forth in the ministry, found it laid upon him by his Divine Master, "to go and bear witness to His name in Scotland, that high professing nation." "Oh!" says he, "how I would have pleaded my own inability, the care of my family, my service in that particular meeting, and many more things; and all, that I might have been excused from this one thing. But after many reasonings, days and weeks by myself, I thought it best to speak of it to some of the faithful elders and ministers of the everlasting gospel, not knowing but they might discourage me; but they laid it upon me to be faithful. The winter drew nigh, and something [in my mind] would have deferred it till next summer; but the Lord showed me it was not to be *my time*, but *his time*. Then, I would have gone by sea; but the Lord withstood me, and showed me it must not be *my way*, but *his way;* and if I would be obedient, he would be with me and prosper my journey; otherwise his hand would strike me. So I gave up *all*, and with cheerfulness obeyed, went forth, and visited the churches of Christ. I quickly perceived that the Lord was with me;—my journey became joyful;—in every place, my testimony was owned, and divers were convinced of the everlasting Truth. I got into Scotland in the Ninth month, and travelled to and fro that winter, on foot, with cheerfulness—and in about five or six months time, was, by the good hand of God, brought home to my wife, and children, and relations; in all my journey having been sweetly accompanied with the presence of the Lord; and his power often filled my earthen vessel, and made my cup to overflow. Praises forever to his name! saith my soul."

The gospel messages of these and other zealous ministers, reached the consciences of many who heard them; yet with regard to Aberdeen and the district thereabouts, no open espousal of the principles of Friends took place, until William Dewsbury was drawn, towards the end of the year 1662, in love to these prepared and panting souls, to proclaim among them "the acceptable year of the Lord," even *deliverance* from the bondage of corruption, by the law of the spirit of life in Christ Jesus. Thus was the remarkable work of convincement — which had been secretly going on in some hearts for several years, through many deep conflicts of spirit, — helped forward to such a point, that they were made willing to take up the daily cross, though in various respects as bitter as death, and to follow the guidance of Christ by his Spirit within them, whithersoever he should be pleased to lead. Alexander Jaffray, formerly chief magistrate of the city of Aberdeen, and one of the foremost in this little but noble band, declared that when first he heard that God had raised up a people in England, directing all to His pure light, Spirit, and grace in their own hearts, as the most sure Teacher and Leader into all truth, religion, and worship, *his very heart did leap within him for joy.*

George Gray, a poor weaver, but a man of very good repute for sincerity and the correctness of his life, was another of the early instruments in gathering the church in the neighborhood of Aberdeen. He received from his Divine Master a gift in the ministry of the gospel; and though poor as to this world, and barely acquainted with the very rudiments of learning, the word of God's wisdom dwelt richly in him, and his understanding became much enlarged in heavenly experience. And being, through watchfulness, preserved and directed in the exercise of his ministerial gift, he was made instrumental to the edification and great refreshment of the Lord's heritage. Many indeed confessed their admiration at the excellent matter, utterance and connection observed in the preaching of one so devoid of human learning, and yet so thoroughly furnished, in all respects, unto his holy calling. Thus was clearly held up to view, what it is that constitutes the *best adorning* of gospel ministers, and what is the *only* right qualification for speaking "as the oracles of God."

Nancy Sim, who was also in low pecuniary circumstances,

readily opened her house, at a place called Ardiharrald, for religious meetings. But the people flocked to them so greatly, that her house would by no means contain them; and they were often obliged to meet in the open field. Thus did the word of the Lord prevail; and such as were made willing to yield to it, esteemed it more than their necessary food; so that they could unite with the prophet Jeremiah, in acknowledging: "Thy word was unto me the joy and rejoicing of my heart."

But the principal instrument in these parts, for the gathering of many from the barren mountains of an empty profession, to feed in the green pastures of life, under the leadings of the Shepherd of Israel, was Patrick Livingston. He was convinced about the year 1659, when about twenty-five years of age; and three years afterwards, coming northwards in the work of the ministry, from Montrose, his native place, he was the means of planting a flourishing meeting of Friends at Kinmuck, which afterwards grew to be the largest in the nation.

The public preachers of the established form of religion now took the alarm, and a series of persecutions soon commenced, with the intention of destroying this vigorous young plant which was growing up within their precincts. But the more they trampled it under their feet, the more did it spread its verdure abroad, to their discomfiture, and the opening of the eyes of many to see the emptiness of their pretensions as teachers of the people, and the inconsistency of their practice with the mild and lovely features of the Christian life.

In the year 1666, Colonel David Barclay, of Ury, and his son Robert, openly attached themselves to the Society, refusing the glory of this world, and the various opportunities within their grasp, of gratifying "the lust of the flesh, the lust of the eye, and the pride of life;" and accepting cheerfully "the reproach of Christ," *becoming fools for his sake*, that so they might be "to the praise of his glory."

David Barclay was born in 1610, at Kirktounhill, in Scotland, and received a liberal education. Growing up to man's estate, he travelled into Germany, and enlisted in the army of Gustavus Adolphus, king of Sweden; but after being engaged in many battles, he returned home on the breaking out of the civil wars in his native country. In 1646, having attained to the rank of Colonel in the Scottish forces, he was sent with an army to quell an insurrection of the Earl of Crawford, whom he entirely routed; and after being for several years successfully engaged in various military expeditions, was made governor of Strathboggie, then a place of much strength. He soon after married Catharine Gordon, grand-daughter of the Earl of Sutherland, and third cousin to King James I. of Great Britain. He continued to occupy a prominent station in the Scotch army for several years, until the success of the republican party placed them in temporary possession of the reins of government. He was soon afterwards elected member of Parliament, where he vigorously opposed the project for Oliver Cromwell's being made king. After this, he disentangled himself from public affairs, and retired into a life of privacy. His retirement from the world afforded an opportunity for becoming acquainted with himself, and with the uncertainty of all temporal things. He was now between fifty and sixty years of age; and thought it high time for him who had spent so many years in the service of the public, to bestow the remainder of his life wholly in that of his Creator. He betook himself to a close reading of the New Testament, and was brought clearly to see that the religion of Christ, "was righteousness, and peace, and joy in the Holy Ghost"—that it taught to be humble, patient, self-denying,—to endure and suffer all things,—and not to place our happiness or comfort on this world, or the things of it.

He now heard of a people, who, under great reproach for singularity and abstractedness from the world, bore, in much plainness and simplicity, a remarkable testimony both in their words and practice, against the follies and vanities of the world; and he considered, that if they were really such as even their enemies acknowledged, there must be somewhat extraordinary about them. Accordingly, with the greatest earnestness did he enter into an examination relative to *this way*, which was indeed "everywhere spoken against." And being in London, he conversed with several Friends, whereby his mind became convinced of the truth of their principles. Some months afterwards, being on a baseless political pretence connected with his former public career, imprisoned in Edinburgh Castle, along with the Laird of Swintoune, who had zealously embraced the views of Friends, he was still further confirmed in his belief of their accordance with primitive Christianity. His imprisonment took place soon after the decease of his wife, about the year 1663; and in 1666, he openly connected himself in membership with the Society of Friends; and eventually became eminent for his religious and exemplary life, as he had before been for military bravery. He had formerly been much unacquainted with the virtue of Christian meekness, and patient endurance of injuries: but now, when Friends were often mobbed by the very dregs of the community, it was remarkable that none bore these indignities with greater calmness than David Barclay. One of his relations lamenting that he should now be treated so differently from what he formerly had been; he answered, that he found more satisfaction in being thus insulted for his religious principles, than when, some years before, it was usual for the magistrates, as he passed the city of Aberdeen, to meet him several miles, and conduct him to a public entertainment in their town-house, and then convey him so far out again, in order to gain his favor. His humility and sincerity as to religion was most remarkable in his whole conduct; and his deportment is said to have been particularly awful and striking, when engaged in public prayer.

His son Robert was born in 1648, and having from a child the appearance of a promising genius, was sent by his father to finish his education, at the Scotch college at Paris, of which his uncle was rector. Here he became so great a favorite, and made such proficiency, that his uncle desired to adopt him, and offered to make him heir to his large estate, if he would consent to remain. His father, however, in his seventeenth year, fearing, and not without reason, lest he might become tainted with the superstitions of Popery, went to Paris to bring him home. His uncle still endeavored to prevent his return, and offered to present to him immediately, an estate greater than his paternal one. But mindful of his filial duty, Robert replied, "he is my father, and must be obeyed;" and the uncle, disappointed, left his property to the college, and to other religious institutions in France.

It was in 1664, that he returned to Scotland; and having strictly examined into the principles of Friends, he soon found himself constrained, upon the same ground of real conviction as his father had been, to embrace their doctrine and life. One of his intimate friends has testified that this change was not consummated through the means of outward instruments; but that in one of their meetings, he was effectually "*reached* in the time of silence," and made to bow before the Truth. He himself declares, that he "came to receive and bear witness to the Truth," "not by strength of argument, or by a particular disquisition of each doctrine, and convincement of the understanding thereby; *but by being secretly reached by this life.* For, when I came into the silent assemblies of God's people, I felt a secret power amongst them which touched my heart; and as I gave way unto it, I found the evil weakening in me, and the good raised up; and so I became thus knit and united unto them, hungering more and more after the increase of this power and life, whereby I might find myself perfectly redeemed."

Thus did he travail in spirit for his soul's delivery out of the power and bondage of corruption, "into the glorious liberty of the children of God;" and through great love, watchfulness, and fidelity to the inward appearance of Jesus Christ by his light and Spirit, he early came forth a zealous and able witness thereof; taking up his cross to the glory and friendship of this world, and "esteeming the reproach of Christ greater riches than the treasures of Egypt." Thus he rapidly advanced to such a growth in grace and saving knowledge, as has been the admiration of many; and it was not long, before he was called to the public ministry of the Gospel.

About the year 1670, he married Christian Molleson, a young woman who had, through much suffering and hardship, publicly embraced the principles of Friends, in her sixteenth year. But though he was now favored with the greatest of all temporal blessings, a pious and devoted partner, yet he did not consider himself at liberty to surrender up the ripening powers of manhood to selfish ease or supineness. Indeed, he seemed to receive the gifts of a gracious Providence, as fresh signals for grateful and vigorous engagement in the warfare of the Christian life. He was not only diligent in laboring in the ministry which he had received, but also remarkably drawn forth to advocate, by a divinely guided pen, the simple principles of the pure religion which he professed. His works, which were all published within nine years after his marriage, and when he was between the ages of twenty-two and thirty-one years, formed, when collected, a folio volume of nine hundred pages. His "Catechism and Confession of Faith" appeared in 1673; about a year afterwards, he wrote a Treatise on Christian Discipline, entitled "The Anarchy of the Ranters," &c.; and in the twenty-eighth year of his age, he published (first in Latin) his celebrated "Apology for the True Christian Divinity, as held by the people called Quakers;" a work surpassed by no modern disquisitions of religious doctrine; a work which has never been refuted; and an argumentative declaration of pure Christian principles, which can scarcely fail to bring conviction to the candid mind, seriously seeking the truth.

In common with many of his fellow-laborers in the glorious cause of spirituality and real holiness, Robert Barclay came under that humbling description of exercise and service, which often engaged them to testify, in various ways, against the unsound, mixed, and even corrupt profession of religion, so much prevailing in the world; and he gave up to obey the call to some hard and weighty requisitions of this kind; sometimes visiting the congregations of such people, with a word of warning or of rebuke. On one occasion in particular, in the year 1672, he was constrained, under a strong sense of duty, to pass through three of the principal streets of Aberdeen, *clothed in sackcloth*, and exhorting the people to repentance. After he had thus submitted to become "a spectacle to men," he wrote an address to the inhabitants, declaring the still extended love of God to be waiting for their souls, and desiring to lead them by His Light and Spirit revealed in their hearts, "out of all unrighteousness and filthiness of flesh and spirit, unto all righteousness, truth, holiness, peace, and joy in the Holy Ghost." He reminded them that many among them had despised the meek and lowly appearance of God's witness in their hearts: "Therefore," says he, "was I commanded of the Lord God, to pass through your streets covered with sackcloth and ashes, calling you to repentance." . . . . "And some whom I called, to declare unto them this thing, can bear witness, how great was the agony of my spirit,—how I besought the Lord with tears, that this cup might pass away from me!—yea, how the pillars of my tabernacle were shaken, and how exceedingly my bones trembled, until I freely gave up unto the Lord's will. And this was the end and tendency of my testimony, *to call you to repentance* by this signal and singular step; which I, as to my own will and inclination, was as unwilling to be found in, as the worst and most wicked of you can be averse from receiving or laying it to heart." And after an earnest and affectionate expostulation, he thus concludes: "I have peace with my God in what I have done, and am satisfied that his requirings I have answered in this thing. I have not sought *yours*, but *you;* nor entertain evil towards any; but continue in pure and unfeigned love towards all; being ready to 'bless those that curse;' to 'do good to those that despitefully use' me; and to be spent in the will of the Lord *for your sakes*, that your souls may be saved, and God over all may be glorified! for which I travail and cry before the throne of Grace, as becometh a servant of the Lord Jesus Christ."

It is remarkable that most of the persecutions of the early Friends were instigated by the jealousy of the professed teachers of religion; who were keen-sighted enough to perceive, that the success of the principles of the new Society would give a mortal blow to the hireling system, by which they lived upon the credulity and money of the people. Robert Barclay's marriage was one of the circumstances which greatly raised their anger. In this important undertaking, he could not swerve from his principles, and by submitting to the common mode of accomplishing his marriage, sanction the unholy trade in religious things. In accordance therefore with the practice of the Society, his marriage was solemnly accomplished in an assembly of his Friends and others, and in the presence of the Most High. The public preachers were so much exasperated at this neglect of their authority, that they procured letters to summon him before the Privy Council, for an unlawful marriage; though they never had power to put their threats in execution against him.

Another matter which much provoked the priests, and nearly allied to the above, was the practice of Friends in burying their dead, to abstain from all the customary performances of ministers appointed by man, and acting under the promptings of man's will and judgment. This also struck at the emoluments of the *clergy*, as they arrogantly named themselves, and afresh excited their jealousy and rage. By their influence with the magistrates, in 1672, they procured the destruction of the walls of Friends' burial-ground at Aberdeen, in which a child of one of the members had been, a few days before, interred. The body was taken up, the coffin shamefully broken open, and carried for re-interment to a neighboring village. They continued to remove every corpse that was interred in that ground, until by means of a representation made to the King's Council, they were checked in this uncommon inhumanity. They found, however, other means to persecute this innocent people, often casting them into prison for their faithful attendance of their religious meetings, and fining them for non-payment of the hire of the priests. But through all, Friends in Scotland continued to increase, and a considerable number of meetings were soon established in various parts of the country.

CHAPTER XX.

ACCOUNT OF THOMAS LURTING AND THE ALGERINE PIRATES.

THE Christian behavior of Thomas Lurting under very trying and dangerous circumstances, in the year 1663, was of too remarkable a character to be passed over in silence, illustrating as the narrative does, the contrast between that spirit which seeks the destruction of our fellow-creatures, and that which breathes "peace on earth and good will to men."

Thomas Lurting, in early life, occupied the station of boatswain's mate in a man-of-war under Admiral Blake; in which occupation he eminently displayed those qualities which are by men of this world called bravery and courage; and being accordingly put into the post of danger, he met with many remarkable preservations of his life in times of close engagement in battle.

About the year 1654, several of the ship's company were favored with a divine visitation to their minds, under which some of them became convinced in degree of the principles of Friends, and began to decline hearing the hired services of the chaplain of the vessel, and to meet in silence among themselves. Thomas was informed of this by the priest, and his passions being excited by this man's false representations of them, he fell to beating and cruelly abusing his shipmates, when he found them thus religiously met together to wait on the Most High. This conduct however was far from producing ease of mind. The judgments of the Lord soon overtook him, and he became exceedingly distressed with what he had done; and dwelling under the condemnation, he became more and more enlightened, to perceive his own state of alienation from God; his heart became tendered and broken; and he sought for retirement, that he might freely pour out the burden of his contrited soul to the Lord. This change was observed by the ship's crew, so that at length it came to his share to be mocked and ridiculed.

Being alone one evening waiting on the Lord, and earnestly seeking to know his duty, it was clearly shown him that he must join himself to that little band whom he had so often abused. Remembering his aversion to them, and his contempt of their apparently foolish way of religion, he felt as if he would rather give up his natural life than comply in so repulsive a matter. But the Lord reminded him of his many wonderful preservations; which mollified his heart, and being still followed by inward reproofs and judgments, he came at length, after much struggling, to the conclusion, that " whether Quaker or no Quaker, he was for peace with God." After a while, he opened some of his feelings to one of them, named Roger Dennis, and when First-day came, he resolved to go to the little meeting on board, which was now of six in number. It soon got wind among the sailors, that Thomas was among the Quakers; and many of the ship's company leaving their own worship to look at him, greatly disturbed the quiet of their little gathering. He was summoned after this, before the captain and priest, but their arguments only tended to confirm him in the rectitude of his present position; and continuing to meet with his friends, some others also joined them, so that in less than six months, their number was doubled.

Hitherto Thomas and his friends had not perceived the inconsistency of war with true religion. Their minds however were undergoing the process of preparation for seeing more clearly the peaceable nature of the Messiah's kingdom in the heart, and they declined partaking of any of the booty seized in skirmishes with the enemy. They were caressed by many on board, as brave and useful men; and indeed they displayed such alacrity and boldness in fulfilling the requisitions of their officers, that the captain said he cared not if all his men were Quakers, for they were the hardiest men in his ship. But it was not long before their duty was clearly manifested to them in this particular, and then came a time of close trial.

This occurred while they were bombarding a castle at or near the town of Barcelona. Thomas and his friends were fighting with as much earnestness as any, and the vessel being annoyed by the shots fired from one corner of the castle, he proposed to beat down that part of it; and went into the forecastle, stripped to the waist, to level the ship's guns towards that spot. This being done, he was coming out of the forecastle to see where the shot would fall, when suddenly the query ran through his mind, "What if now thou killest a man?" This struck him instantly with strong emotions; and He who alone can turn the hearts of men, so suddenly and completely changed his views, that he immediately felt that he must not proceed in the destruction of his fellow-creatures, even if it were to gain the whole world. Putting on his clothes, he walked the deck, as if he had not seen a gun fired; and being under great mental exercise, some asked him if he were hurt. He replied, "No; but under some scruple of conscience on the account of fighting." Though he knew not at that time that this was one of the doctrines held by Friends, yet he clearly saw that they who had been so active in fighting must now bear their testimony against it, and abide the consequences. Soon afterwards, one of his friends also informed the captain that he could no longer continue to fight. The latter threatened to run his sword into any one who refused to fight in time of engagement, and severely beat the friend with his fist and cane, for attempting to reason with him upon it.

Some time after this, while cruising in the Mediterranean, a ship was discovered bearing down upon them, supposed to be a Spanish man-of-war. Orders were of course given, to prepare the ship for an engagement; and Thomas, who saw that a time of trial was approaching for himself and friends, called them together, and encouraged them to faithfulness to their convictions; and at the same time exhorted them not to deceive the captain, who placed confidence in them, but publicly to show him, in good time before the engagement, what their intentions were. His friends agreeing with him, collected round the capstan, and one of them informed the lieutenant that he could no longer fight. This was immediately reported to the captain, who came furiously down upon him, flung his hat overboard, and taking him by the collar, beat him with a great cane, and dragged him to his quarters. He then retired to the half-deck, called for his sword, and drew it with great passion. Thomas now fe... constrained to go to him, and under great exercise of mind turned round to his friend Roger Dennis, and said, "I must go to the captain:" to which Roger returned, "Be well satisfied in what thou doest." Thomas replied, that there was a necessity laid upon him; and then seeing the captain coming forward with his drawn sword, he stepped towards him, keeping his eye fixed upon him in much seriousness, and his mind intent upon the secret pointings of the Divine finger. The captain saw him; was struck with the authority in which he came; his countenance turned pale; and turning away, he gave his sword to an attendant, and went off. The ship which they had taken for an enemy, soon proved to belong to a friendly nation, and the captain, ashamed of his conduct, sent the priest before night to apologize to Thomas for his passionate behavior. Thus was the latter preserved through outward dangers and inward trials of faith, until at length he got safe home.

Now leaving ships of war, his subsequent voyages were in merchant-vessels; but from these he was several times pressed into the king's service; and being carried on board the men-of-war, he suffered greatly for not feeling himself at liberty to do any work on board such vessels. On one occasion, the captain of the ship on board of which he was carried, was very violent, threatening either to hang him or take him before the Duke of York, for not being willing to do any work on board; but the next night being exceedingly troubled in mind on his prisoner's account, he sent for "the Quaker" in haste, and put him ashore, in order to be able to rest peaceably in his bed.

In the year 1663, Thomas Lurting being mate of a vessel commanded by a Friend, they were chased in the Mediterranean by an Algerine pirate; which coming up with them, compelled the captain and several of the men to come on board their vessel, leaving only Thomas with three men and a boy behind. The Algerines then put about fourteen of their own men aboard the English ship. While they were coming in the boat, Thomas was under great exercise of mind, not knowing what the event might be; but retiring mentally to the Lord his ever gracious Preserver, he felt an inward assurance that he should not be carried to Algiers, as many were, and sold into slavery. His confidence in divine protection was renewed, and meeting the Algerines at the ship's side, he received them in a friendly manner, and showed them the vessel and cargo. The pirates also behaved towards him personally with civility. Thomas afterwards endeavored to cheer the men of the ship, by telling them of his assurance that they should not go to Algiers; and exhorted them now to be willing to obey the Turks, as the people of Algiers were called by the English. This they promised to do; and he soon perceived that they gained the favor and confidence of these barbarous people, who gradually grew careless and easy, and several of them returned to their own ship with some small matter of plunder. Soon afterwards the captain and men were returned on board from the other vessel, which relieved Thomas's great anxiety for their safety. He still assured the seamen of his belief that they should not go to Algiers, and told them that if they would be ruled by his directions, he would act for their delivery as well as his own; though he saw at present no way to effect it. The vessel having been commanded by a Friend, though the sailors were not of that persuasion, had of course no arms on board, except what were in possession of the pirates, who were well armed. Thomas said to the seamen, "What if we should overcome the Turks, and go to Majorca?" at which the men rejoiced, and began to boast of their intentions of killing their captors; but this being very far from the mate's intentions, he was much grieved, and plainly told them that he intended not to hurt any, and if he knew that any of them would touch a Turk for that purpose, he would tell the Turks himself; adding, "but if ye will be ruled, I will act for you; if not, I will be still." To this the men agreed; and he strictly charged them to do all that the pirates should tell them, with the utmost diligence, so as to gain still more their confidence. Divulging his plans to the captain, the latter agreed to let him do what he would, provided no blood should be spilt; which Thomas of course engaged, as he said he would rather go to Algiers, than to kill one of the Turks.

The weather now becoming stormy, they lost the company of the Algerine vessel, which was favorable to the mate's wishes; and the pirates had by this time grown extremely easy and careless, from the good behavior of the sailors. The second night after the vessels parted company, the leader of the pirates and one of his company having gone to sleep in the cabin with the captain, Thomas persuaded another of them to lie in his own cabin, and about an hour afterwards, another in another cabin; and as it rained very hard, he at length persuaded them all to lie down and sleep. When they were all fast asleep, he came to them, and fairly got possession of their arms; and going to the sailors, he said to them, "Now we have the Turks at our command, no man shall hurt them—but as they are under deck, we will keep them so, and go for Majorca." And having ordered some to keep the doors, and not to let more than one out at a time, he steered for that island; and having a brisk gale, when morning came they were in sight of it. The Turks finding this, were struck with consternation, and began to beg that they might not be sold; which the mate assured them they should not; and when they came towards the shore, they concealed the pirates in the ship, to prevent the Spaniards from discovering that any were on board. But by the treachery of an Englishman, to whom they confidentially divulged what they had done, the Spaniards got wind of it, and would have seized these men to sell them for slaves; and they had much difficulty, with the assistance of the pirates themselves, in getting clear of the island, so as to enable them to save their prisoners from such a fate. They at length got safely out to sea, thus placing themselves again in great danger, in order to save those men from their enemies.

Several times these ungrateful people attempted to rise against them, notwithstanding they were treated with great kindness; but the Christian intrepidity and prudence of the mate, kept them from their purpose. On one occasion, when the ten pirates were for some purpose all on deck, and none of the English there but the captain, the mate, and the man at the helm, they began to behave in such a way as to awaken Thomas's suspicions of intended mischief; whereupon, stamping with his foot on the deck, he brought up the men from below; who began to look about for something wherewith they might fall on the Turks. He bade them however not to hurt them; but hearing some of the pirates threatening the captain, he stepped up to their leader, and laying hold of him, told him to go below; which he did very quietly, and the rest followed him. Two days after this, they came off the coast of Barbary, about fifty miles from Algiers, and began to consider the best means of putting the pirates ashore, with safety to themselves. Thomas, who trusted in the Lord's preserving power, undertook this hazardous business; and taking with him two men and a boy, he put these ten Turks into the boat, all loose and unbound, in order that, if necessary, they might be able to swim ashore. In order to provide against a sudden rising, whereby they might get possession of the boat, he made them sit in each other's laps, the leader being the lowest at the stern of the boat, and he himself sitting with a boat-hook in his hand on the bow. Thus the boat stood for the shore; but as they came near it, the sailors becoming afraid, suddenly cried out that there were Turks in the bushes on the shore; and the pirates perceiving their fright, took advantage of it, and all rose up in the boat. But the mate in this emergency preserved his presence of mind, and with the boat-hook in his hand he struck the leader a smart blow, and bid him sit down; which he did instantly, and the rest followed his example. After the boat was come so near the shore that they could easily make to land, he bid the pirates jump out; which they did; and giving them some provisions, and afterwards putting the boat closer in, he sent them off, and got safe back to the ship. The Algerines, getting up to the top of the hill, waved their caps at the English, and so took their leave. Thomas Lurting had the satisfaction of reflecting that he had followed the injunction of his Divine Master, even to love our enemies, and do good to them that hate us; and having by his prudence, under the guidance of heavenly wisdom, thus saved the ship and his companions, he was favored to return to England with a prosperous wind. On his arrival in the river Thames, this extraordinary transaction having become known in London, the king, with the Duke of York, and several other nobles, came in the royal barge, to have the narrative from Thomas's own mouth; though it appears that the monarch did not duly appreciate the principles under which he had acted.

About this time there were a number of Friends held in captivity at Algiers; who by faithfully serving those who claimed them as slaves, gained the esteem of the inhabitants, and were suffered to go at large in the town, without being chained as others were. These met together for religious worship, and one of them received a gift in the ministry, for the edification of his Friends. Some other English slaves also frequented the meeting, and came to be united with them; and the name of Quaker came to be known in Algiers, as that of a people that might be trusted beyond all others.

CHAPTER XXI.

DEATH OF SAMUEL FISHER—ACCOUNT OF HIS CONVINCE-MENT, ETC.

AMONG the great numbers of the people called Quakers who laid down their lives in prison during the year 1665, was Samuel Fisher. He was a man of good abilities, and had received a liberal education, having, when a young man, been sent to one of the universities to complete his studies. Being a youth of circumspect and pious conversation, his mind was burdened with many practices which he found prevalent at the university. But at the conclusion of his studies there, he was ordained a priest, and became first a chaplain to a person in authority, and afterwards was presented to the living of Lidd, in Kent, with a stipend of about two hundred pounds a year.

Before he became acquainted with Friends, being conscientiously engaged in seeking after truth, he discovered that infant baptism was a mere human institution, and that to preach for hire was contrary to the command of Christ: "Freely ye have received—freely give." And being requested by a person of his acquaintance, to converse with a young man who had been in some degree convinced of the principles of Friends, but as yet had no acquaintance with any of that people; in his endeavors to remove this young man's scruples in respect to some of their religious performances, he was himself convinced of the impropriety of the common practice of giving out psalms for a mixed congregation to sing, whose minds must be in very different stages of religious attainment, and consequently unfit in many instances to take the words of the holy psalmist as expressive of their own condition. At length his continuing to preach for hire, contrary to his convictions, became a burden too heavy for him to bear; and he voluntarily resigned his pastoral charge, and trusted to the protection of Divine Providence, in an endeavor by honest industry to provide a subsistence for himself and his family. He rented a farm, and commenced the business of a grazier; by which he was favored to procure a comfortable competency, with the consolation of the testimony of an approving conscience.

Having discovered a great mixture of human tradition and invention retained from the papal system, among the Episcopalians, he withdrew from their communion, and joining the Baptists, became for a time a favorite teacher among them. But his mind was still seeking the further discoveries of the Divine will; and about the year 1655, it pleased the Father of mercies to open his understanding to behold more "wondrous things out of his law." William Caton and John Stubbs, two eminent ministers among Friends, came to Lidd; and Samuel Fisher, remembering the apostolic exhortation, "Be not forgetful to entertain strangers," received them into his house. John Stubbs going to the meeting of the Baptists where Samuel officiated, and obtaining an opportunity to preach the gospel, delivered the sound principles of Christian truth with such clearness and authority, that Samuel was deeply affected. And observing that the life and conversation of these gospel messengers were consonant to the testimony they held forth, he was so much impressed, that giving up all his dependence on his own wisdom and learning, he soon became thoroughly convinced, and openly professed the religion of this persecuted people.

Whilst Samuel Fisher's mind was undergoing this change, Hammond, his colleague in office, took upon him to utter in a sermon many bitter invectives against the Quakers. On which, Samuel, incited by a more Christian temper, and a dispassionate regard for truth, thought that his duty to his misinformed flock required him to bear his testimony against the calumnies of his colleague. "Dear brother," said he, with the moderation and charity of a Christian, "you are very dear and near to me, but the truth is dearer and nearer: it is the everlasting truth and gospel which they hold forth." "Our brother Fisher is also bewitched," retorted Hammond, in a very different spirit. But Samuel's faith was not of that cast to return reviling for reviling; and having sincerely borne his testimony, he then left it, and followed his own convictions to his great peace. Soon after joining the Society of Friends, he received a gift in the ministry, and travelled much both in England and other countries. In Flanders, he faithfully testified against the idolatry of the papists: and afterwards, in company with John Stubbs, crossed the Alps on foot, and travelled through Italy to Rome; where they bore a faithful testimony to the simplicity of true religion, and exposed the superstitions of that seat of bigotry and pomp. They also distributed some books among the ecclesiastics of that city, and having finished their service, passed away without molestation.

But though Samuel escaped persecution among the

Romanists, he met with his full share of it from the protestants of his native country; and spent the greatest part of the last four years of his life in prison. In 1662, in company with William Ames and some other Friends, he was violently seized by a party of soldiers, with no warrant but their drawn swords; and after six weeks' confinement was committed to Newgate, for refusal to take an oath, and without any form of trial. Here he continued about twelve months, and in a short time after his release, was again taken, and committed to the White-lion prison in Southwark. This was his last imprisonment, and only ceased with his life. He remained nearly two years in confinement, until in 1665, the plague broke out in London, and soon raged to such a degree that seven thousand persons died of it in that city in one week. Of course it reached the filthy and crowded prisons, where many Friends were at that time confined; and in Newgate prison alone, no less than fifty-two of that people laid down their lives, twenty-two of whom were under sentence of transportation.

Whether this was the disease by which Samuel Fisher was called to his everlasting home, we are not informed; but he finished his course in prison in perfect peace.

CHAPTER XXII.

THE SUFFERINGS OF RICHARD SELLER, FOR HIS TESTIMONY AGAINST WAR, ON BOARD THE FLAG-SHIP "ROYAL PRINCE."*

WE have seen how Thomas Lurting was preserved through sufferings, a faithful witness of the peaceable nature of the Redeemer's kingdom, and finally overcame the malice of his enemies. We now have to narrate the simple story of another soldier of the Lamb's army, who knowing that the weapons of the Christian's warfare are not carnal but spiritual, endured uncommon cruelties, and refused to save his life, by uniting in the destruction of his fellow-men.

Richard Seller was a fisherman of Kilnsea, on the coast of Yorkshire, who had been convinced of the truth of the principles of the Society of Friends. During the war between the English and Dutch about the year 1665, he was pressed at Scarborough into the king's service, and forcibly conveyed on board the flag-ship "Royal Prince," commanded by Admiral Sir Edward Spragg, and having on board nearly one thousand men. Being commanded to go to work at the capstan, he declined, and told them that not being free to do the king's work, he would not live at his charge for victuals. Upon this the boatswain's mate beat him severely; and he was ordered on the quarter-deck; where the captain asking him the reason of his refusing to fight, or partake of the ship's provisions, he replied that he was afraid of offending God, and durst not fight with carnal

---

* See Besse's "Collection of the Sufferings of the Quakers," vol. ii. p. 112.

weapons; whereupon the captain also fell upon him with his cane, knocking him down three or four times on the deck, and beating him very severely as long as he had strength to do it. One Thomas Horner coming up, who had had some acquaintance with Richard, entreated the captain "to be merciful, for he knew him to be an honest and good man;" but the captain in his fury exclaimed, "he is a Quaker,—I will beat his brains out!" and falling upon him again, beat him until he became exhausted, and then called another person to help him. After this they tied two ropes to his wrists, and reefing the ropes through two blocks in the mizzen-shrouds, hoisted him up aloft, and fastened the ropes, so that he hung there by his wrists for some time, a butt for the vulgar jests of this wicked crew. Then they let fly the ropes, and he fell upon the deck. The captain called to the boatswain's mate, to "take the Quakerly dog away, and put him to the capstan, and *make* him work, and beat him, and spare him not." This man performed his officer's command thoroughly, beating Richard unmercifully, tying his hands to the capstan, and making the men thus haul him round with them by main force. But the fastenings of his hands coming loose by some means which no one could explain, the conscience of this guilty man appears to have been aroused; he thought it was done by an invisible hand; and his mind was so strongly affected by the circumstance, that he "promised before God and man, that he would never beat or cause to be beaten, either Quaker or any other man that refused for conscience sake to act for the king; and if he should, he wished he might lose his right hand."

This man's turn came now to suffer. He was called up before the admiral, for refusing any longer to beat Richard Seller: and being desired to answer for himself, he said, "I have beaten him very sore; and I seized his arms to the capstan's bars, and forced them to heave him about, and beat him,—and in three or four times of the capstan's going about, the seizings were loosed, and he came and sat down by me. Then I called the men from the capstan and had them sworn, whether they had loosed him or not; but they all denied that they either loosed him or knew by what means he was loosed; neither could the seizings ever be found. Therefore I did and do believe that it was an invisible power that set him at liberty, and I did promise before God and the company, that I would never beat a Quaker again, nor any man else for conscience sake." At this the admiral told him, he must lose his cane (the insignia of his office); which he willingly yielded. He added, that "he must also lose his place;" which also he was willing to do. He then told him "he must lose his right hand;" when he held it out, and said, "take it from me if you please." So they took his cane from him, and displaced him, but did not fulfil the other barbarous threat.

Richard was given in charge by the admiral to seven men, who were commanded to beat him wherever they met with him, for seven days and nights, and to make him work; the first of which they did till they were weary, and desired to be excused. Another man then undertook it, and beat him occasionally for a day and a night; when he also desired to be excused. The admiral having him stripped, and examining his body, could find no bruises; at which he grew angry with the men for not beating him enough; but Captain Fowler replied to him, "I have beaten him myself as much as would have killed an ox." The jester, (a silly man often in those days retained about the persons of the nobility to make merriment by his fooleries,) who had instigated them to the hoisting punishment, said "he had him hung a great while by the arms up aloft in the shrouds;" and the men declared, "they also had beaten him very sore, but they might as well have beaten the mainmast." The admiral, however, was inexorable; Richard was laid in irons, and the ship's company by proclamation prohibited on pain of similar punishment, from providing him with food. So he lay in irons day and night for nearly two weeks, and would probably have famished, but that two Friends of Bridlington had, early after his seizure, sent him a supply of provisions. As it was, he grew very ill with a fever. After some days, the remainder of his food being taken away, the carpenter's mate secretly provided him with some refreshment, telling him that he had of his own, independent of the ship's provisions, and that before he came on board he was strictly charged by his wife and mother, "that if any Quaker came on board, he should be kind to them;" he added that he had also lately received a letter from them, wherein they repeated their charge, "to remember his promise, and be kind to Quakers, if any were on board." This man, however, was soon sent away from the vessel on some occasion, and Richard remained without sustenance for three days and nights.

After suffering in this way for a considerable time, the admiral called a council of war, composed of the officers of that and other ships, to decide on the final punishment to which Richard Seller should be condemned. Being so lame with the irons that he could not stand, he was set on a bulkhead to hear his sentence. The judge or president, who was governor of Dover Castle, was a papist; and when they were much divided in sentiment, to what death to subject their prisoner, this man proposed that he "should be put into a barrel or cask driven full of nails with their points inwards, and so rolled to death." But the council of war thinking this too horrible a punishment, agreed that he should be hung. The poor innocent prisoner meanwhile was lifting up his heart to the God of his life; who left him not in his extremity, but raised his mind above all earthly things, endued him with sudden strength, and enabled him to declare to the assembly, that "the hearts of kings themselves were in the hand of the Lord, and so were theirs and his; that he valued not what they could do to this his body, for

he was at peace with God and with all mankind, even with
them, his adversaries; that he could never die in a better
condition, for the Lord had satisfied him that his sins were
forgiven, and he was glad in His mercy that He had made
him willing to suffer for His name's sake—that he was
heartily glad and did really rejoice with a seal to the same
in his heart." His accusers and judges could not bear this,
and most of them slunk away. A man came and laid his
hand on Richard's shoulder, saying, "where are all thy
accusers?" And looking round he found them gone. The
admiral, however, being still there, he showed him his terrible sores, produced by the irons on his limbs; and an old
soldier coming up, put off his cap, and kneeling down on his
bared knees before the commander, with the obsequious
etiquette of the navy, begged his pardon three times, and
having got liberty to speak, thus addressed him: "Noble
Sir Edward, you know that I have served his majesty under
you many years, both in this nation and other nations by
sea, and you were always a merciful man: therefore I do
entreat you in all kindness, to be merciful to this poor man,
who is condemned to die to-morrow, and only for denying
your order, for fear of offending God, and for conscience
sake; and we have but one man on board, out of nine hundred and fifty, which doth refuse for conscience-sake; and
shall we take his life away? Nay, God forbid. For he
hath already declared, that if we take his life, there shall a
judgment appear on some on board within eight and forty
hours; and to me it hath appeared; therefore I am forced to
come upon quarter-deck before you, and my spirit is one with
his. And therefore I desire you in all kindness, when you
take his life, to give me the liberty to go off; for I shall
not be willing to serve his majesty any longer on board ship.
So I do entreat you once more, to be merciful to this poor
man."

The chief gunner also, who had been formerly a captain,

came in the same humble manner, and begged for Richard's life. The admiral however persisted, and desired him to go down, and spend the day in taking leave of his acquaintances on board. That night, one of the men kindly offered him the use of his hammock, and he obtained the luxury which had long been denied him, whilst he lay continually in irons, of a good night's rest. About eight o'clock the next morning, the captains of the other ships, who had joined in the council of war, having come on board, and a rope being fastened on the mizzen-yardarm, with a boy ready to turn him off, Richard was brought out to be executed. And coming to the spot, the commander asked the council, how their judgment stood? And most of them consenting, he turned to the prisoner, and desired him freely to speak, if he had any thing to say before his execution. He replied, that he had little at present to say. Then came a man who bid him go forward to be hung; and he stepping on the gunnel to go towards the rope, the commander bid him stop there, if he had any thing to say. At this juncture, when perhaps the hearts of some were softening, at the fate which seemed impending over this innocent sufferer, the person who had acted as judge on the trial incautiously showed his popish bigotry by the remark, "Sir Edward is a merciful man, that puts that *heretic* to no worse death than hanging." The word *heretic* struck the ear of the admiral, who professed himself a protestant; and scorning to be made a tool to execute the vengeance of a papist, he turned quickly about, and asked him what he said. "I say," replied he, "that you are a merciful man, that puts him to no worse death than hanging." "But," said the commander, "what is that other word that thou saidst?—that heretic—I say, he is more a Christian than thyself; for I do believe thou wouldst hang me, if it were in thy power." And turning to his prisoner, he said, "Come down again; I will not hurt a hair of thy head, for I cannot make one hair grow." He immediately caused it to be proclaimed three times over, that if any credible man on board would give evidence that Richard had done any thing deserving of death, he should have it; but no one appearing, he proclaimed, "that the Quaker was as free a man as any on board." So the men, who filled the shrouds, tops, and decks, heaved up their hats, and loudly cried, "God bless Sir Edward, he is a merciful man." And thus did the Almighty Care-taker of his lowly dependent children, defeat the evil intentions of those who sought the life of this faithful sufferer for the cause of a pure conscience, and for his testimony to the peaceful nature of true Christianity. Great was the peace with which his soul was filled on this memorable day. Much kindness was shown to him by all on board; but he declared that "the great kindness of the Lord exceeded all."

Being thus preserved from death, he was soon after made instrumental to the saving of the ship, and the lives of many on board. It appears that he was visited by a remarkable dream or vision, in which it was shown him that the vessel would be engaged with the Dutch on a certain sand-bank, and in imminent danger of running aground, and so becoming a prey to the enemy. And though it was death by the rules of the navy, for any one to say any thing calculated to discourage the crew in time of battle, yet he was not easy without mentioning the circumstance to one or two of the officers; and when afterwards they were engaged in battle, he from the shrouds pointed out to the pilot the very sandbank, which had been marvellously manifested to him several days before, when he and the rest were entirely unacquainted with such a shoal. The vessel was immediately put about, in spite of the commander's orders to the contrary, who knew nothing of the danger; and they were thus suddenly rescued from running aground, through the instrumentality of this despised and abused man. During the engagement, he was employed in attending to the poor wounded and dying men; and again saved the ship from danger, by pointing out a fire-ship rapidly approaching them through the smoke, filled with combustibles, in order to set them on fire by the collision which would soon have taken place.

About a week after this, they were again engaged with the Dutch, and Richard was as before employed in carrying down and attending to the wounded men. This day they lost about two hundred of their ship's company. In describing this day's work, he says, "The lieutenant meeting me, asked me if I had received any wound? I told him, none. He asked, 'How I came to be so bloody?' Then I told him, 'It was with carrying down wounded men.' So he took me in his arms, and kissed me; and this was the same lieutenant that persecuted me so with irons at the first."

Soon after this, the vessel arriving near Chatham, the admiral came up to Richard, and laying his hand on his head, said, "Thou hast done well, and very well too," and gave him liberty to go ashore. Richard requested from him a certificate, to show that he had not run away. The admiral, knowing he was a fisherman, and likely, from his occupation, to be exposed again to be pressed on board some ship of war, said, "thou shalt have one to keep thee clear at home, and also in thy fishing;" and having it made out, he signed it, and gave it to Richard, wishing him well, and desiring to hear from him if he got well home. His pay was offered him; but he refused it, and told them that he had money of his own, which he hoped would serve him till he reached his home.

Such is the remarkable narrative of the sufferings of this faithful man, who, rather than violate his conscience by being instrumental to destroy other men's lives, endured with patience many sore trials, "loving not his life unto the death;" but was freely resigned to martyrdom for his testimony against war, and was preserved from it at the last extremity, by a memorable interposition of Him who can change the hearts and purposes of men at his will. And thus was he enabled to triumph over the malice of his enemies, who conscious at length of his innocence and virtue, became his friends and favorers.

CHAPTER XXIII.

WILLIAM PENN'S EARLY LIFE AND CONVINCEMENT.

ABOUT the year 1666, the Society was joined by one whose talents, education, and rank in life opened to him the fairest prospects of promotion to the favor of courts, and the various gratifications which this world has to bestow; but who, preferring a life of self-denial and suffering, with and for the people of God and the cause of eternal Truth, forsook the pleasures of Egypt at an early age, and entering heartily into the ranks of the Lord's army, became eminently serviceable in advancing the cause of true Christianity, both in the old world and in the new.

William Penn was born in London, in the year 1644. His father, Admiral Sir William Penn, was a man of good estate and reputation, and distinguished himself in some of the highest stations of the British navy. He was knighted by King Charles the Second; and became a peculiar favorite with the Duke of York, afterwards James the Second. William received a liberal education, and made so early improvements in learning, that about his fifteenth year he was entered as a student in the university of Oxford. He soon however began to display an ardent desire after pure and spiritual religion. He had been much impressed on one occasion, by the ministry of a member of the Society of Friends, named Thomas Loe; and yielding to the feelings which were secretly implanted in his mind, he, with certain other students of the university, withdrew from the national ceremonious way of worship, and held private meetings for devotional purposes, preaching and praying among themselves. He was now sixteen years of age; and this practice giving great offence to the heads of the college, he was fined for non-conformity; and still persevering in what he believed to be more consonant with the gospel, than the practices of the established form of religion, he was expelled the college, and returned home in 1661.

His father, who had fondly hoped for great worldly preferment for his son, was much disappointed in finding the change which had taken place in his views. For feeling a secret sympathy spring up in his heart for sober and religious people, William took great delight in their company, to the neglect of those associations and occupations which would have promoted his entrance into a courtly life. His father endeavored to persuade him to conform to his wishes, though at the risk of wounding his conscience; but finding that neither his entreaties nor blows were sufficient to induce his son to obey him, rather than his Maker, in a fit of anger he turned him out of doors.

Relenting however in some measure from his severity, the next year he sent him to France, in company with some persons of quality who were making a tour on the continent, hoping by this means to wean him from the serious thoughtfulness and strictness of life to which he was so strongly inclined. This snare was wellnigh succeeding; for being thrown for a year or more among the fashionable and dissipated circles of the continent of Europe, his mind became diverted from the concerns of his soul's salvation, and he came back, to his father's great gratification, an accomplished man of the world. But He who watched over him for good, suffered him not to remain long in this state of ease. He was mercifully made sensible that the pleasures of the world, and the maxims dictated by its spirit, were at enmity with God, and incompatible with an earnest seeking after that crown immortal, which was renewedly presented to his view as the only object worthy of his supreme desires. He was thus brought into great conflict of spirit; for his natural inclination, his lively and active disposition, his acquired accomplishments, the respect of his friends and acquaintance, and above all, the favor of a fondly attached parent, combined strongly to entice his youthful mind to embrace the glory and pleasures of this world, then courting his acceptance. The earnest supplication of his soul was put up to the Lord for preservation; and He was pleased to grant him such a portion of His holy power and Spirit, as enabled him in time to overcome all opposition, and with holy resolution to follow Christ, whatsoever reproaches or persecutions might attend him.

In the year 1666, and the twenty-second of his age, his father sent him to Ireland, to manage a considerable estate there; and being at Cork, and hearing that Thomas Loe, whom he had heard preach several years before at Oxford, was expected at a meeting in that city, he went to hear him. Thomas began his declaration with these words: "There is a faith that overcomes the world, and there is a faith that is overcome of the world:" and enlarging upon it with much clearness and energy, his living and powerful testimony made such impression upon William's spirit, that under the baptizing power thereof, he was effectually convinced that this was the people to whom he must attach himself; and he constantly afterwards attended the meetings of Friends, and was united in close fellowship with them.

The next year he was called to testify, by patient suffering, his faithfulness to the principles he had espoused; for being again at a meeting in Cork, he was apprehended, and with eighteen others, carried before the mayor, and committed to prison. The Earl of Orrery, however, Lord President of the province of Munster, with whom he was well acquainted, on William's laying his case before him by letter, and pleading for liberty of conscience as a just right, ordered his discharge.

And now came on another distressing conflict between his father and himself. The former, by a letter from a nobleman of his acquaintance in Ireland, was informed of his son's attachment to this despised people, and promptly sending for him home, once more earnestly endeavored to dissuade him from a course, which seemed to him to shut up from his son all avenues to the promotion which he desired for him. William deeply felt the affliction of being obliged by his regard for his own eternal welfare, to refrain from complying with these entreaties of an affectionate though mistaken parent; and in agony of spirit, when his father threatened to disinherit him for his non-compliance, he lifted up his heart to God, for strength to support him in that hour of trial. When his father, finding him firmly fixed against a general acquiescence in the customary compliments, seemed inclined to bear with him at length in other respects, provided he would agree to take off his hat in the presence of the king, the duke of York, and himself, William, desiring, if he possibly could with a clear conscience, to comply with his father's wishes, requested time to consider of it, and promised to retire to his chamber until he should be prepared to return him an answer. Accordingly he withdrew; and humbling himself before God, with fasting and supplication, to know His heavenly will, he became so strengthened in his resolution, that returning to his father, he signified that he could not disobey his heavenly Parent by the desired compliance. On this, his father, utterly disappointed, and convinced that all his endeavors to shake his son's constancy were in vain, and accustomed to the implicit obedience of the British navy, could no longer endure him in his sight, but again turned him out of doors. This was indeed a severe affliction to one of William's ardent and affectionate disposition; but supported by an inward sense of rectitude, he endured the cross with Christian patience and magnanimity.

His father, after a time, became willing for him to return home once more, though he did not publicly appear to countenance him.

About the year 1668, being the twenty-fourth of his age, he first came forth in the ministry of the Gospel, rightly called to and qualified for that office; being sent of God to teach what himself had learned of Him; commissioned from on high to preach to others that holy self-denial himself had practised; and exemplifying in his own course the following beautiful description given by himself of the ministry of the early Friends.

"As God," says he, "had delivered their souls from the wearisome burdens of sin and vanity, and enriched their poverty of spirit, and satisfied their hunger and thirst after eternal righteousness, and filled them with the good things of His own house, and made them stewards of his manifold gifts; so they went forth to all quarters of these nations, to declare to the inhabitants thereof what God had done for them; what they had found, and where and how they had found it, viz.: the way to peace with God; inviting them to come, see, and taste for themselves, the truth of what they declared."

"But these experimental preachers of glad tidings of God's truth and kingdom, could not run when they list, or pray or preach when they pleased; but as Christ their Redeemer prepared and moved them by his own blessed Spirit;

for which they waited in their services and meetings, and spoke as that gave them utterance; which was as those having authority, and not like the dreaming, dry, and formal Pharisees."

"And truly they waxed strong and bold through faithfulness; and by the power and Spirit of the Lord Jesus became very fruitful; thousands, in a short time, being turned to the truth in the inward parts through their testimony in ministry and suffering; many meetings were settled, and daily there were added such as should be saved. For they were diligent to plant and to water, and the Lord blessed their labors with an exceeding great increase, notwithstanding all the opposition made to their blessed progress, by false rumors, calumnies and bitter persecutions."

"It may be said of this abused and despised people, they went forth weeping and sowed in tears, bearing testimony to the precious Seed, the Seed of the kingdom, which stands not in words, (the finest, the highest that man's wit can use,) but in power — the power of Christ Jesus — who empowered them, as their work witnesseth, by the many that were turned through their ministry from darkness to the light, and out of the broad into the narrow way of life and peace, bringing people to a weighty, serious and godlike conversation."

"They were changed men themselves, before they went about to change others. Their hearts were rent, as well as their garments; and they knew the power and work of God upon them. This was seen by the great alteration it made, and their stricter course of life, and more godly conversation that immediately followed it. They went not forth, or preached in their own time or will, but in the will of God; and spoke not their own studied matter, but as they were moved by His Spirit, with which they were well acquainted in their own conversion; which cannot be expressed to carnal men, so as to give them any intelligible account;

for to such it is, as Christ said, like the blowing of the wind, which no man knows, whence it cometh, or whither it goeth. Yet this proof and seal went along with their ministry, that many were turned from their lifeless professions, and the evil of their ways, to an inward and experimental knowledge of God, and a holy life, as thousands can witness. And as they freely received what they had to say, from the Lord, so they freely administered it to others.

"The bent and stress of their ministry was conversion to God, regeneration, and holiness.—They directed people to a principle in themselves, though not of themselves, by which all that they asserted might be known to them, through experience, to be true; which is a high and distinguishing mark of the truth of their ministry, both that they knew what they said, and were not afraid of coming to the test. For as they were bold from certainty, so they required conformity upon no human authority, but upon conviction of this principle, which, they asserted, was in them that they preached unto; and unto that they directed them, that they might prove the reality of those things which they had affirmed of it, as to its manifestation and work in man. This is more than the many ministers in the world pretended to. They declare of religion, say many things true, in words, of God, Christ, and the Spirit; of holiness, and heaven; that all men should repent and amend their lives, or they will go to hell, &c. But which of them all pretend to speak of their own knowledge and experience; or ever directed to a divine principle or agent, placed of God in man, to help him; and how to know it, and wait to feel its power to work that good and acceptable will of God in them? Some of them indeed have spoken of the Spirit, and the operations of it to sanctification, and performance of worship to God; but where and how to find it, and wait in it to perform our duty to God, was yet as a mystery to be declared by this further degree of reformation. So that this people did not only in words, more than equally press repentance, conversion and holiness, but did it knowingly and experimentally; and directed those to whom they preached, to a sufficient principle; and told them where it was, and by what tokens they might know it, and which way they might experience the power and efficacy of it to their souls' happiness. Which is more than theory and speculation, upon which most other ministers depend: for here is certainty; a bottom upon which man may boldly appear before God in the great day of account."

In this spirit did William Penn go forth in the work of the ministry, and many were the sufferings and trials to which he was subjected, for his devotion to the cause which he had so heartily espoused. Some of the remarkable transactions of this enlightened man we shall have to review as we pass along.

CHAPTER XXIV.

REMARKABLE CONVERSION OF A WOMAN IMPRISONED FOR MURDER. — DEATH OF FRANCIS HOWGILL IN PRISON.

A REMARKABLE circumstance occurred during the imprisonment of William Bennit for conscience sake, in Bury jail, in the year 1668.

One day, he seriously accosted a certain young woman, who was a criminal, asking her, whether during the course of her life she had not many times transgressed against her conscience? and whether thereupon she had not often felt some secret checks and inward reproofs, and been troubled in her mind on account of the evil committed? This he did in such a convincing way, that she not only assented to what he laid before her; but, her heart being reached by his discourse, she came clearly to see, that if she had not been so stubborn and disobedient to these inward reproofs, she would not have come into this miserable condition. For man not desiring the knowledge of God's ways, and departing from Him, is left helpless, and cannot keep himself from evil, even though it be such as he would formerly have abhorred in the highest degree.

William thus opening matters to her, by his wholesome admonitions so wrought upon her mind, that she who never had conversed with the Quakers, and was altogether ignorant of their doctrine, now came to apprehend that it was "the grace of God which bringeth salvation," which she had so often withstood; and to perceive that this grace had not yet quite forsaken her, but was now making her sensible of the greatness of her transgression. This consideration weighed so powerfully with her, that from a most grievous sinner, she became a true penitent, and with hearty sorrow she cried to the Lord, that it might please Him not to hide his countenance. Continuing in this state of humiliation and sincere repentance, and persevering in watching unto prayer for the pardon of her sins, she was at length favored with a sure hope of forgiveness, through the precious blood of the "Immaculate Lamb," who came into the world to save sinners, and call them to repentance, and who died also for the sins of the world.

Of this change, graciously wrought in her by the Spirit of Christ revealed in her heart, she gave clear evidence, at her trial before Judge Hale; who, having heard how penitent she was, wished much to save her from the capital punishment due by the law to her offence, and accordingly had procured the insertion in the indictment, of the words "wilfully and designedly," hoping that thence she might find occasion to deny the charge, and so to quash the indictment. But she, being as usual asked whether "Guilty or Not Guilty?" readily answered, "Guilty." This astonished the judge, who told her that she seemed not duly to consider what she said; since it could not well be believed, that such a one as she, who, it might be, had inconsiderately handled her child in a rough manner, should have wilfully and designedly killed it. Here the judge was opening as it were a back door for her to avoid the penalty of death. But now, the fear of God had obtained so much room in her heart, that no tampering would do—no fig-leaves could be made use of for a cover—she knew that this would have been adding sin to sin, and covering herself with a covering but not of God's Spirit. She therefore plainly acknowledged to the court, that she had indeed committed this wicked act intentionally; adding, that "having sinned thus grievously, and being now affected with true repentance, she could by no means excuse herself, but was willing to undergo the punishment the law required. She could not therefore but acknowledge herself guilty, since otherwise how could she expect forgiveness from the Lord?"

This undisguised and free confession, spoken with a serious countenance and demeanor, so affected Judge Hale, that with tears trickling down his face, he sorrowfully said, "Woman, such a case as this I never met with before. Perhaps you, who are but young, and speak so piously, as being struck to the heart with repentance, might yet do much good in the world. But now you force me, that *ex officio* I must pronounce sentence of death against you, since you will admit of no excuse." Standing to what she had said, the judge then pronounced the sentence of death.

When afterwards she came to the place of execution, she made a pathetic speech to the people, exhorting the spectators, especially those who were young, to have the fear of God before their eyes, to give heed to His secret reproofs for evil, and so not to grieve and resist the good Spirit of the Lord: she not having timely attended to this, had run on in evil, and thus proceeding from one wickedness to another, had brought herself to this dismal exit. But since she firmly trusted in God's infinite mercy, nay surely believed that her sins, though of a bloody dye, were washed off by the pure blood of Christ, her Redeemer, she could contentedly depart this life. Thus she preached at the gallows, a doctrine very consonant with the views of the people called Quakers, and gave heart-melting proofs that her immortal soul was to enter into paradise, as well as in ancient days that of the thief on the cross.

This year, died Francis Howgill, a prisoner for the cause of Truth, in Appleby jail. He had been imprisoned in the year 1663, and the next year sentenced under premunire, to be confined during his life, and his property confiscated to the king; without any other crime being found against him, than that he could not transgress the command of his Divine Master, to "swear not at all," nor bind himself by any agreement to forsake the assembling together with his Friends for the worship of Almighty God, in spirit and in truth. "Hard sentence," he remarked to the court, "for obeying the command of Christ: but I am content and in perfect peace with the Lord; and the Lord forgive you all—it is for Christ's sake I suffer, and not for evil doing." Being by this sentence "put out of the king's protection," he was remanded to the prison where he first suffered for his righteous testimony, and remained there until released by death, towards the end of the year 1668, after an illness of nine days.

During his long imprisonment in this filthy jail, he evinced the peaceful condition of his soul, by great patience and resignation to all his sufferings; and his outward losses were abundantly compensated by that inward consolation which the Lord alone can bestow. As he approached the close of life, having passed the time of his sojourning here in fear, he met his change with great serenity, and felt the sting of death to be taken away. He said he was content and ready to die — praised the Almighty for the many sweet enjoyments and refreshing seasons, wherewith he had been favored, while lying on that prison-bed, — and freely forgave all who had had a hand in his restraint. To his wife and others, two days before his death, he gave a message of his dear love to his friends, adding, "As for me, I am well, and content to die — I am not afraid at all of death." And the mayor of Appleby visiting him, and some persons present, praying that God might speak peace to his soul, he answered emphatically, "He hath done it."

A few hours before he departed, some friends from a distance came to visit him in his prison. He inquired after their welfare, and prayed fervently, "that the Lord by his mighty power might preserve them out of all such things as would spot and defile." His voice soon afterwards failed through weakness; but recovering, he said, "I have sought the way of the Lord from a child, and lived innocently among men; and if any inquire concerning my latter end, let them know, that I die in the faith which I have lived in and suffered for." After this, he uttered a few words in prayer, and so finished his earthly course in perfect peace, in the fiftieth year of his age. Conspicuous for his virtues, and the innocence and integrity of his life, the malicious efforts of his enemies were unable to sully his reputation; he was generally respected and esteemed by those who knew him, even though not of his religious persuasion; his sufferings were commiserated, and the unmerited cruelty of his persecutors justly condemned.

CHAPTER XXV.

MEETINGS FOR DISCIPLINE INSTITUTED IN THE SOCIETY.—
GEORGE FOX GOES TO AMERICA—AND RETURNING, IS
IMPRISONED AT WORCESTER.

IT was about this time that the Society of Friends assumed the form of a more regularly organized body, under the advice of George Fox and those deeply experienced men and women who felt and labored with him, by the institution of meetings held periodically, for the good ordering of the affairs of the church. It will therefore be appropriate in this part of our history, to consider briefly the steps by which this important and highly useful feature was gradually introduced.

Many of the early members of the Society were poor as to this world's goods, though rich in faith; and the constant persecutions to which for many years they were subjected, reduced many of them to great destitution. But brotherly kindness abounded. Those who possessed pecuniary means remembered to do good and to communicate; they dared not esteem all that they possessed as exclusively their own; but felt bound to use it freely, in relieving with a noble liberality the necessities of their suffering brethren, remembering that they were all members of one body, "striving *together* for the faith of the gospel," and when one member suffered, all the members must suffer with it. This feeling being general, and the necessities of families deprived of their means of subsistence by the imprisonment of one or both of the heads being often pressing, the propriety of meeting together occasionally, to consider the circumstances of such, became apparent; and hence the first meetings for the affairs of the church had their origin. In the accomplishment of their marriages also, they could not conscientiously follow the practice, either of those on the one hand, who, forgetting the religious nature of the compact, and considering it as a merely civil act, were accustomed to accomplish it before a magistrate; or on the other, of those who called in the assistance of a hireling ministry, and thus sanctioned an interference with the prerogative of the Lord alone to join persons in that solemn covenant. They were thus led to the performance of their marriages among themselves: and remembering the apostolic advice, that "all things be done decently and in order," they were especially careful in this solemn undertaking, that no cause of offence should be given, either by any appearance of secrecy in the manner of accomplishing it, or by joining persons already entangled in other engagements, or so nearly related as to render such connection improper. In connection also with this subject, was the due recording of births and deaths, taken care of by these early meetings for business.

Strict integrity and uprightness was one of the first fruits of that spirit by which our early Friends were led to forsake the ways of a corrupt world. They considered the prevailing standard much below the morality required by the Gospel; and regulating their conduct towards their fellow-man by the rule laid down by our blessed Saviour, "Whatsoever ye would that men should do unto you, do ye even so to them;" their truthfulness and honesty drew upon them the observation of their neighbors. George Fox was anxious that all should walk consistently with the high character the Society had obtained, and not be induced to extend their business improperly, or promote their worldly advantage by unfair means. Several of his early epistles recommended well-concerned Friends to watch over their brethren in love; and many of his fellow-laborers earnestly endeavored to promote that Christian moderation which avoids rather than seeks riches, as well as the exercise of caution in contracting, and promptness in paying debts.

The care also of granting certificates to those who travelled in the work of the ministry, testifying the unity of their Friends at home with their so doing; and for those who removed to settle within other monthly meetings; the religious education of the youth, which was a subject very near the heart of George Fox, as vitally affecting the progressive welfare of the Society; the purchase and care of burial-grounds, where the deceased members might be interred, free from the officious interference of the priests, and away from the crowd of costly and pompous monuments, which they considered inconsistent with the profession of a Christian, and designed to gratify the pride of survivors;—these were among the subjects which early engaged the attention of those gatherings of the church, which George Fox had seen it right to recommend to his Friends to establish, for the regulation of their common affairs. And last, though not least in importance, the preservation of the conduct of the members clear from inconsistencies and stains, and breaches of those testimonies which they were as a body holding forth before the world, rendered the necessity obvious, as the Society rapidly increased in numbers, that some mode of church government should be instituted, by which the conduct of the members might be inspected and restrained. George Fox considered the church as a harmonious and compact body, made up of living members, having gifts differing according to the measure of grace received, yet all dependent one on another, and each, even the weakest and lowest, having his proper place and service: and as the very design of religious society is the preservation, comfort, and edification of the members, and all have a common interest herein, so he considered every faithful member religiously bound to contribute, according to his capacity, toward this attainment. Our Lord himself laid down a rule for the observance of his church, in the treatment of those who should commit offences. "If thy brother shall trespass against thee, go and tell him his fault between thee and him alone. If he shall hear thee, thou hast gained thy brother. But if he will not hear thee, then take with thee one or two more; that in the mouth of two or three witnesses, every word may be established. And if he shall neglect to hear them, tell it to the church; but if he neglect to hear the church, let him be unto thee as an heathen man and a publican." And the apostle Paul, in writing to the Galatians, thus exhorts them: "Brethren, if a man be overtaken in a fault, ye who are spiritual, restore such an one in the spirit of meekness; considering thyself, lest thou also be tempted." These injunctions were the fundamental principles of the discipline established by the Society of Friends, simple, beautiful, and when fully carried out in practice, often efficient, under the influence of the Holy Spirit, in reclaiming the wanderer from the fold.

The first General Meeting of the Society was perhaps that held at Balby, in Yorkshire, in 1656, which issued certain wholesome advices. Quarterly Meetings were soon afterwards established, which appear to have exercised much the same functions as our Monthly Meetings now have. In the year 1668, the Monthly Meetings were generally settled through England. The same year there was a General Meeting held in London, from which an epistle was issued to the Society; and in 1672, another General Meeting of ministers, held also in London, at which it was agreed that a representative General Meeting should be annually held in London, "for the better ordering, managing, and regulating of the public affairs of Friends." The Representative Yearly Meeting, however, which met in the succeeding year, concluded to leave the management of these affairs, and the general care of the church, for the present, in the hands of the annual General Meeting of Ministers; and it was not till the year 1678, that they were again convened at the suggestion of the latter meeting. Monthly Meetings in some parts of America, were established about the year 1669; and a Yearly Meeting was held in Rhode Island, for the Society in New England, in 1671, if not a year or two previously. Other Yearly Meetings were subsequently established in the North American colonies, as the increase of the Society rendered it necessary.

The Society has now for many years been thus organized. The members residing at convenient distances from each other, whether composing one particular meeting for worship, or more than one, united to form a "Monthly Meeting," for the transaction of the affairs of the church, composed of one or more subordinate or "Preparative" meetings, in which some portions of the business were prepared for the action of the former body. Several of these monthly meetings united, formed a "Quarterly" meeting, to which representatives were sent from each of the constituent monthly meetings; and again the quarterly meetings situated in a particular country or state, or in contiguous states, formed a "Yearly" meeting. These yearly meetings were the highest assemblies known to the Society, and only amenable to the judgment of Truth in the body at large, as a part of the great brotherhood of the church.

Besides the above, there are Monthly or Preparative, Quarterly and Yearly Meetings of the Ministers and Elders, in connection with the respective meetings for discipline. These "select meetings" are designed to be composed of such ministers as, having given proof of a divine gift for the ministry, have been officially recognized in that capacity by their Friends, and of elders appointed to watch over the ministry particularly, and generally over the flock. Besides the elders, there are overseers appointed in each Monthly Meeting, to take a more special charge of the conduct of the members, and to see that all walk orderly, according to their Christian profession.

It early appeared to the clear and comprehensive mind of George Fox, that advantage would arise to the body, from the concerns of the female members being attended to by their own sex: and accordingly, women's meetings for discipline were recommended by him to be held in the same manner as those for the men, to whom they might be helpmeets, in the restoration of offenders, in the care of their own poor, and in other affairs of the church, as they are outwardly in civil and temporal things. They were instituted soon after those for the men, and served to complete that system of order and government, in which a field was opened for the exercise of the various gifts by which the church, the body of Christ, is edified.

A new field of operation now opened before the expansive mind of that remarkable man, who was so eminent an instrument in the good work which we have just contemplated.

George Fox's wife had lain for several years in prison, under a sentence of premunire; but was finally released in 1671; and shortly afterwards, George finding it laid upon him to visit the churches beyond the Atlantic, took leave of her and his numerous other friends in England, and sailed in company with several Friends for Barbadoes. Two remarkable interpositions of the protecting care of Divine Providence attended him during this voyage. The ship was chased by a Sallee * man-of-war, when about three weeks at sea, and seemed to have no way of escape from her. She gained rapidly upon them, though they altered their course with the hope of eluding her pursuit. At night the captain and others came into George Fox's cabin, asking him "what

---

* Sallee, or Salé, a town on the coast of Morocco, about halfway between Cape Blanco and Tangier. noted for the boldness of its pirates, but now much in ruins.

they must do?" He told them, "he was no mariner." They said, "there were but two ways of escape—either to outrun the enemy, or to tack about." George replied, that "they might be sure the enemy would tack about too; and as for outrunning him, it was to no purpose to talk of that, for they saw he sailed faster than they did." They asked him again, in consternation and perplexity, "what they should do? for," they added, "if the mariners had taken Paul's counsel, they had not come to the damage they did." George answered them, that "it was a trial of faith, and therefore the Lord was to be waited on for counsel;" and retiring, himself, in spirit unto the Almighty, the Lord showed him "that His divine life and power was placed between them and the ship that pursued them." He told this to the captain, desiring that all the lights, except the one used to steer by, should be put out, and that all should remain very quiet. About eleven o'clock at night, the man on watch called out that the enemy was just upon them; which alarmed some of the passengers. George looking out of the port-hole of his cabin, by the light of the moon, which had not quite set, saw them very near the vessel; and was getting up to go on deck; but remembering the Lord's word, which had been whispered into his mental ear, "that His life and power was placed between them," he quietly lay down again, and awaited the result in faith. In a little time, the moon went down, a fresh breeze arose, the Lord hid them from the enemy, and they sailed briskly on, and saw them no more. The next day, being the First-day of the week, Friends had a public meeting for worship on board, in which the Divine presence was eminently felt: and George Fox exhorted the ship's company "to mind the mercies of the Lord, who had delivered them; for they might all have been by that time in the hands of the Turks, had not the Lord's hand saved them." It afterwards appeared, by the testimony of a merchant who arrived in Barbadoes from the port to which this piratical vessel belonged, that its captain had been struck with the remarkable deliverance of their ship out of his hands, when he thought himself sure of the prize, and acknowledged his belief that "there was a spirit in her which he could not take."

Soon after George Fox's arrival in Barbadoes, he was informed of the death of a young man who had imbibed an implacable enmity against him, and meditated his destruction. This young man, a person of some worldly account, but a common swearer and very bad man, when in London some time before, had addressed the daughter of a Friend in order to marriage, having an eye to her property. George being one of her guardians, had plainly told him that "he should betray the trust reposed in him, if he should consent that he, who was out of the fear of God, should marry her; and that he would not do it." The young man returned to Barbadoes greatly incensed, and afterwards, hearing that George was likely soon to arrive in the island, he swore desperately, and threatened that "if he could possibly procure it, he would have him burned to death when he came there." Repeating this threat to a Friend, who was expostulating with him, the latter warned him: "Do not march on too furiously, lest thou come too soon to thy journey's end." About ten days after this, he was struck with a violent burning fever, of which he died, and was carried to the grave three days before George arrived in the island.

The constitution of this indefatigable laborer in the Lord's vineyard had been much shattered by the severe sufferings he had undergone for many years in the service of truth; so that the voyage greatly affected him, and he was, for many weeks after his arrival, laid up with severe illness. But being favored at length with a recovery, he was diligent in strengthening the Society in that distant part, and building them up in comely gospel order. Here also, in conjunction with some other Friends, he drew up an address to the governor and council of Barbadoes, setting forth, in the name of the Society, their true Christian belief in the divinity and atonement of our Lord and Saviour Jesus Christ, and in the divine inspiration of the Holy Scriptures; and vindicating Friends from the malicious charge, which some had brought against them, of teaching the negroes to rebel, because they felt it to be their Christian duty to treat them kindly, to give them instruction, and to hold meetings with them for divine worship and religious edification.

Having remained in Barbadoes about three months, George Fox, William Edmundson, Elizabeth Hooton, and some other Friends, departed to Jamaica, where they travelled up and down the island, and had much service. Many were convinced of the truth of their principles, and they met with no opposition. Here Elizabeth Hooton, who had received a gift in the ministry as early as 1650, and was consequently the first female minister raised up among Friends, peacefully laid down the body, and departed to her heavenly rest.

George Fox, William Edmundson, and Robert Widders, having spent about seven weeks in Jamaica, embarked for Maryland. They had a very tempestuous voyage, and ran short of provisions; but through the goodness of the Lord, in whose protecting care they trusted, they were favored to arrive safely. A vessel which sailed in company with them, the captain of which had offered to convey the Friends to Maryland, but demanded an exorbitant price for their passage, fell among the Spaniards; by whom she was taken and plundered, and the master and mate were made prisoners.

Near the place where they landed, they held several meetings with Friends, and with the native Indians of the country; and then George Fox and his companions travelled through the woods to Newcastle on the Delaware, crossed that river in canoes, with great risk to their lives, and dived into the forests of what is now called New Jersey; but which was then inhabited only by Indians. They had a wilderness journey, sometimes lying at nights in the woods by a fire, and at other times in the Indians' wigwams. They hastened to be at the half-yearly meeting of Friends at Oyster Bay, on Long Island; where they labored successfully for the establishment of wholesome discipline in the church, to the exposing and confounding of some ranting spirits, who had "run out from truth into prejudice, contention, and opposition to the order of Truth, and to Friends therein." These, George Fox says, "had been very troublesome to Friends — but I would not suffer the service of our men's and women's meetings to be interrupted and hindered by their cavils." A subsequent meeting was appointed for a conference with these opposers, at which, he adds, "the glorious truth of God was exalted and set over all, and they were all brought down and bowed under; which was of great service to truth, and satisfaction and comfort to Friends; Glory to the Lord forever."

Thence they proceeded by sea to Rhode Island; and attended the Yearly Meeting for New England; in which also George Fox was much concerned for the establishment of meetings for discipline, "that all might be kept clean," and "to take care of the poor, and other affairs of the church; and to see, that all who profess truth, walk according to the glorious gospel of God." He was very gladly received by the people generally in Rhode Island and the parts adjacent; but finding they began to talk of hiring him to be their minister, not understanding the principles of Friends, he told some, that " it was time for him to be gone; for if their eye was so much to him, or any of his companions, they would not come to their own Teacher," even Christ Jesus, the Minister of ministers. He accordingly departed to Shelter Island, had some good meetings there with the white inhabitants and with the native Indians; then returned to Long Island; and afterwards crossed to New Jersey again. They rode thirty miles through the woods and over very bad bogs, the descent into one of which was so steep, that they had to slide down with their horses, and then let them lie to take breath, before they could proceed. Among Friends in New Jersey, who, it seems, were principally about Shrewsbury, he was again instrumental in promoting the establishment of men's and women's meetings for the discipline of the church, "to see that all who profess the holy truth, live in the pure religion, and walk as becometh the gospel."

While they were at Shrewsbury, an accident occurred, which was near proving fatal to one of their company. John Jay, a Friend of Barbadoes, who had accompanied them from Rhode Island, and was escorting them through the woods to Maryland, was thrown from a horse, and supposed to have "broken his neck." He was taken up as dead, and laid upon a log. George Fox got to him as soon as he could, and feeling him, concluded he was really dead: but as he stood by him, pitying him and his family, he found his neck was so limber, that his head would turn any way. Whereupon, he took the Friend's head in both his hands, and setting his knees against the log, he raised the head with all his might, and restored it to its place. The dislocation of the neck being thus reduced, he soon began to breathe; and other measures being taken for his restoration, he quickly recovered, so as to be able to resume his journey with them the next day.

They now had a long and dreary wilderness journey again to encounter, across New Jersey and down towards the Delaware Bay. Philadelphia was not in existence, and they met with few except Indians, had many rivers to cross, were often very wet with exposure to storms, and had to lie generally in the woods at night. This autumn and much of the ensuing winter, they spent in travelling through

Maryland, Virginia, and some parts of Carolina; and towards the spring of 1673, "having," as Geo. Fox expresses it, "alarmed people of all sorts where they came, and proclaimed the day of God's salvation amongst them, they found their spirits began to be clear of those parts of the world, and to draw towards Old England again." Accordingly, after attending the general meeting of Friends for Maryland, which "was a wonderful, glorious meeting, and the mighty presence of the Lord was seen and felt over all," George and his companions took leave of their Friends in great tenderness, and sailed for England; where, after a prosperous voyage, they were favored to arrive in safety, on the 28th of the Fourth month, 1673.

This indefatigable servant of Christ had not been long returned to his native land, before he was called to suffer a long and hard imprisonment, for preaching at a religious meeting in Worcestershire. He was sentenced under premunire to imprisonment for life. Interest was made by some to the king to get him released; but he knowing his innocence, would not accept of a pardon, which was the only way in which the king could release him. As the acceptance of this would have implied a confession of guilt, George Fox declared that he would rather have lain in prison all his days, than come out in any way dishonorable to the truth; and therefore, knowing that his imprisonment was not only unjust but illegal also, he chose to have the validity of his indictment tried before Judge Hale; who released him by proclamation, after having been a prisoner nearly fourteen months. He was thus fairly set at liberty without any pardon, or coming under any engagement or obligation to compromise his principles.

CHAPTER XXVI.

THE TRIAL OF WILLIAM PENN AND WILLIAM MEAD AT THE OLD BAILEY — DESTRUCTION OF FRIENDS' MEETING-HOUSES.

AN Act of Parliament, called the Conventicle Act, was passed in the year 1670, the intent of which was to suppress all meetings for divine worship except those of the established form of religion, particularly those of the Presbyterians, who were obnoxious to the court; though its force fell principally upon Friends, who stood most exposed to its action, from their well-known practice of standing firmly for their principles, and not flinching from suffering for the cause of their Divine Master.

The zeal of the magistrates of London in carrying into effect this oppressive law, and the noble intrepidity of William Penn in defence of his inalienable rights, brought about this year one of the most memorable judicial trials in English history; which did more to promote clear views of the liberty of conscience, and to establish the great privilege of trial by jury on its just foundation, than perhaps was ever effected by the personal exertions of any other man. Its importance will warrant our pursuing it in some of its details.

Friends being forcibly kept out of their meeting-houses in Gracechurch street, found themselves constrained to meet as near the premises as practicable; and accordingly held their meeting in the open street, as a public testimony of their allegiance to the God of the spirits of all flesh. William Penn was one of the number thus assembled, and addressing the people in the love and authority of the Gospel, he and William Mead were apprehended and committed to Newgate prison; and at the next sessions at the Old Bailey were indicted for "being present at, and preaching to, an unlawful, seditious, and riotous assembly."

The indictment set forth, that William Penn and William Mead, with other persons to the number of three hundred, on the 15th of August, with force and arms tumultuously assembled, and that William Penn, by agreement between him and William Mead, had preached there in the public street, whereby was caused a great concourse of people, to the great disturbance of the peace, and terror of the king's subjects. To this indictment they both pleaded "not guilty;" after which they were detained in court five hours, waiting for the trial of some felons, and then returned to Newgate prison. Two days after, they were brought up again; when the court more openly manifested a preconcerted design to treat them with the utmost severity, and take every unfair advantage against them; although they had before promised William Penn on his urgent remonstrance, that no advantage should be taken of them, but that they should have liberty to be heard in their own defence. On this occasion, coming into court, the officers had taken off the hats of the prisoners; but the mayor sharply reproved their officiousness, as it did not suit his present intentions, and ordered their hats to be replaced; and when they thus appeared in the court covered, they were fined for it forty marks apiece, the injustice of which was particularly evident in William Mead's case, inasmuch as he had not even been spoken to by the court on the subject. The jury were desired to take notice of this arbitrary act: after which three witnesses deposed that they saw William Penn speaking to the people assembled in great numbers in the street; but they could not hear what he said. William Penn, to this, after requesting silence in the court, addressed them thus: "We confess ourselves to be so far from declining to vindicate the assembling of ourselves, to preach, pray, or worship the eternal, holy, just God, that we declare to all the world, that we do believe it to be our indispensable duty to meet incessantly upon so good an account; nor shall all the powers upon earth be able to divert us from reverencing and adoring our God, who made us." One of the sheriffs told him he was not there for worshipping God, but for breaking the law; though they had made the act of worshipping according to conscience, a breach of the law. William Penn denied having broken any law, or of being guilty of the indictment, and demanded to be informed by what law he was prosecuted, that the jury might understand on what ground they were asked to give a verdict. The recorder answered, "upon the common law;" to which William Penn desired that the law might be produced; which was declined; and he still persisting in demanding it, as otherwise it would be impossible for the jury to determine their verdict clearly, the recorder suffered his passion to carry him beyond the bounds of decency, and freely lavished on William Penn, the epithets of a "saucy, impertinent, troublesome, and pestilent fellow,"—and told him it was not for the honor of the court to allow him to go on. William Penn remarked, "I have asked but one question, and you have not answered me; though the rights and privileges of every Englishman be concerned in it." The recorder replied, "If I should suffer you to ask questions till to-morrow morning, you would be never the wiser;" to which William Penn promptly rejoined, "That is according as the answers are." The recorder said: "Sir, we must not stand to hear you talk all night." William Penn then observed: "I design no affront to the court; but to be heard in my just plea; and I must plainly tell you, that if you will deny me the '*oyer*' [hearing] of that law which you suggest I have broken, you do at once deny me an acknowledged right, and evidence to the whole world your resolution to sacrifice the privileges of Englishmen to your sinister and arbitrary designs." And going on in earnest expostulation with the court on the arbitrary nature of their proceedings, and showing how the dearest social rights of man, guaranteed to Englishmen by their ancient fundamental laws, were thus invaded, he was rudely ordered to "be silent, there!" and sent into the bail-dock. William Mead followed his companion in pleading for their privilege to be informed of the law under which they were indicted, and told the jury he stood there to answer an indictment which was full of lies and falsehoods, for therein he was accused of meeting with force and arms, unlawfully and tumultuously; and boldly claiming his rights as an Englishman, he was told by the Lord Mayor that he deserved to have his tongue cut out, and he was also taken aside into the bail-dock.

The recorder then proceeded to charge the jury, urging them, at their peril, to attend to the evidence that had been produced against the prisoners. But William Penn, who from a distance heard what was going on in the court, raised himself up by the rails of the bail-dock, and with a loud voice thus remonstrated against this unjust proceeding: "I appeal to the jury, who are my judges, and this great assembly, whether the proceedings of the court are not most arbitrary, and void of all law, in offering to give the jury their charge in the absence of the prisoners. I say, it is directly opposite to, and destructive of the undoubted right of every English prisoner;" referring to Coke on *Magna Charta*. He added that the jury could not legally leave the court before he had been fully heard, and that he had at least ten or twelve material points to offer, in order to invalidate the indictment. But the recorder cried out, "Pull that fellow down — pull him down! Take them away into the hole;" and they were accordingly thrust into a noisome hole, and detained there, while the jury went up to agree on their verdict.

After staying about an hour and a half, eight of them came down agreed; but four being dissatisfied, remained above. The bench was highly provoked that these jurymen should obstruct their designs; and using many threats against them, very unbecoming the seat of justice, sent them back to consider their verdict. After some time, returning to the court, they rendered a verdict against William Penn, of "guilty of speaking in Grace-church street," and declared William Mead "not guilty." This the court refused to accept, and insidiously endeavored to extort expressions from some of the jurymen, to procure a verdict more to their purpose; as "that William Penn was speaking to an unlawful assembly:" but several of them firmly refused to admit any alteration in the verdict to which they had agreed. The court thereupon repeated their abusive language towards them, and sent them away again to bring in a verdict more to their mind. On their return, they produced a verdict in writing, to the same effect as before, signed by the whole jury; at which the Lord Mayor and recorder fell into a great rage, and the latter swore that they would have a verdict, or the jury should starve for it; telling them they should be locked up, without meat, drink, fire, or tobacco.

This drew the following remonstrance from William Penn: "My jury, who are my judges, ought not to be thus menaced. Their verdict should be free, and not compelled. The bench ought to wait upon them, but not forestall them. I do desire that justice may be done me, and that the arbitrary resolves of the bench may not be made the measure of my jury's verdict."

"Stop that prating fellow's mouth," cried the recorder, "or put him out of the court." And the lord mayor telling the jury "that William Penn had gathered a company of tumultuous people," William Penn replied, "It is a mistake; we did not make the tumult, but they that interrupted us; the jury cannot be so ignorant as to think we met with a design to disturb the civil peace. We were with force of arms kept out of our lawful house, and met as near it in the street as the soldiers would give us leave. It is no new thing, nor with the circumstances expressed in the indictment; but what was usual with us. It is very well known that we are a peaceable people, and cannot offer violence to any man." He then insisted that the agreement of twelve men is a verdict; requiring the clerk to record it; and addressing himself to the jury, said, "You are Englishmen — mind your privileges — give not away your right." To which some of them replied, "Nor will we ever do it."

The prisoners were now remanded to prison, and the jury shut up all night in their room without fire, food, or any accommodations.

The next morning, which was the First-day of the week, the court resumed its sitting, and the jury being called, declared they could give no other verdict than that which they had already agreed on; which answer occasioned the magistrates again to burst forth with rage and disappointment, and endeavors to browbeat and intimidate them into a compliance with their wishes. William Penn inquired whether the jury's finding William Mead "not guilty" was not a verdict? But the recorder would not admit it.

Again were the jury remanded to their room, and again they returned with the same verdict as before; on which the lord mayor, transported with anger, and referring to one of the jurors whom the recorder had singled out as the most obnoxious, exclaimed, "Have you no more wit, than to be led by such a pitiful fellow? I will cut his nose!" And William Penn protesting against his jury being thus illegally threatened, the recorder said to the mayor, "My lord, you must take a course with that same fellow;" at which the lord mayor cried out, "Stop his mouth! Jailer, bring fetters, and stake him to the ground."—"Do your pleasure," calmly observed William Penn; "I matter not your fetters."

The jury, after considerable discussion, were once more shut up for the night; and the next morning being called upon for their verdict, unanimously brought both the prisoners in "*not guilty,*" to the disappointment and chagrin of the bench, but to the great satisfaction of the large assembly of the people who had witnessed these arbitrary proceedings. The recorder immediately fined each of the jurors forty marks, with imprisonment till paid, for venturing to bring in a verdict so contrary to the views of the court; and maliciously detained the prisoners for the fine, for coming into the court at first with their hats on, though he was reminded that the great charter of English liberties declared that "no free man should be amerced but by the oath of good and lawful men of the vicinage;" whereas they had not had even the form of an examination on this matter. The jury remained some time in prison, and were at length released by a lucid decision of Judge Vaughan, having by writ of *habeas corpus* procured the hearing of their case in the court of Common Pleas. And thus ended this famous trial, which, from the firm stand taken by the prisoners and the jury, and two full statements of it appearing soon after in print, aroused the attention of the people of England to the arbitrary and oppressive proceedings of the courts, by which the benefits of the trial by jury were sought to be invaded, and the most flagrant violations of justice were practised with impunity.

William Penn's father, who had become reconciled to his son's change, now feeling himself drawing near to the close of life, was very desirous of the company of his son in his last hours; and contrary to William's express desire, sent to the prison, and paid the fine for which he was detained. He lived only eleven days after the termination of the trial; and before his close, addressed his son in the following memorable language.

"Son William, if you and your friends keep to your plain way of preaching, and keep to your plain way of living, you will make an end of the priests, to the end of the world. Let nothing in the world tempt you to wrong your conscience; I charge you, do nothing against your conscience; so you will keep peace at home, which will be a feast to you in the day of trouble;" — a remarkable testimony from one who had formerly stoutly opposed the very course, which he now, at the verge of the grave, so solemnly recommended.

The violence of those who were bent on exterminating the Society of Friends showed itself this year, among many other shameful acts, in the destruction of two meeting-houses of that people in the suburbs of London. And what made the deed still more to be regretted, was that it was sanctioned by the king and privy-council.

The meeting-house at Horslydown in Southwark was first attacked. A party of soldiers had twice broken in upon the peaceful assembly, met there to wait upon their Maker; and having forced those present out of the house, had endeavored to disperse them by riding among them, and had wounded several. But on the 20th of the month called August, a party of soldiers with carpenters and others, came and pulled the house down, carried away the benches, windows, and boards, and sold them. The next day being First-day, the Friends came as usual to meeting, but had to meet on the rubbish of their demolished house. The soldiers denied them even this privilege, and dragged them into the street; and the captain ordering his men to knock their brains out, they pulled and dragged them from the place, and lodged them in prison without warrant from any civil magistrate. For nearly three months, did the soldiers continue to persecute the Friends who attended this meeting; beating men and women in an outrageous manner with their muskets and pikes, and endeavoring by provoking their horses, to ride furiously over them. Friends keeping faithfully to their meeting, exasperated them still more. One of them provided himself with a shovel, and threw the dirt from the gutters shamefully over men and women promiscuously. After him advanced both horse and foot soldiers in a furious onset, dealing about their blows, and knocking down all before them without regard to sex or age, to the shedding of the blood of many. On various occasions, twenty, thirty, and fifty individuals were sorely wounded at one time. But at length the civil authorities were aroused to the enormity of these flagrant breaches of the peace, and put a tardy stop to them.

The proceedings at Ratcliff meeting-house were of a similar character, though not attended with so much personal outrage. A few days after the destruction of the Horslydown meeting-house, the lieutenant of the Tower came with a party of soldiers, and caused the building to be demolished. Twelve cart-loads of doors, windows, and floors, with other materials, were carried away; and some of the materials were sold on the spot for money and strong drink. Friends here also continued to meet on the ruins of their meeting-house, or as near thereto as the constables and other officers present would permit; but many of them were seized, fined, and committed to prison.

CHAPTER XXVII.

THE SEPARATION OF WILKINSON AND STORY; AND THE HERESY OF JEFFERY BULLOCK.

THE Spirit of Truth by which our Friends professed to be guided, was abundantly able to preserve the sincere and obedient and persevering followers thereof from all the wiles of the enemy. But when any slackened in watchfulness, and gave no longer unremitting heed to its monitions, it was no marvel that they were suffered to become entangled in the mazes of error. They had practically abandoned the ground of their profession, though they might still pertinaciously adhere to it in words; and having therefore only themselves to blame for the bitter fruits of their unfaithfulness, the integrity of the principles remained unshaken, and the Society pursued the even tenor of its way.

About the year 1675, a spirit of dissatisfaction crept into the minds of some members in the north of England; who giving themselves up to a headstrong spirit of party, opposed the wholesome discipline which had been established by the body, and particularly the institution of women's meetings. John Wilkinson and John Story were at the head of this disaffected party, and by plausible insinuations engaged in their favor a considerable number of persons of weak minds and strong wills, who from one cause or another had imbibed disgust and unsettlement. They inveighed severely against George Fox, who had been a prominent instrument in establishing the discipline, and they endeavored to introduce the fallacious doctrine, that inasmuch as the Divine Spirit was given to every man to guide him aright, any attempt by rules and laws to introduce order into the Society, was a departure from that principle, and an imposition on their gospel liberty. Wilkinson and Story had been in the station of ministers: but beginning to thirst after pre-eminence, and to look for greater deference from their fellow-members than the most sensible of their brethren thought it right to pay them, they became restive under the admonitions and warnings which these believed themselves called upon to extend, in gospel solicitude for their welfare, and for the integrity of the church.

The Quarterly Meeting of Westmoreland, to which they belonged, observing with pain the dangerous tendency of their proceedings, used Christian efforts to reclaim them, but without success; and in order to prevent, if possible, an open breach, concluded to refer the case to the judgment of impartial and disinterested Friends of the neighboring counties. Accordingly six of the most judicious and eminent Friends of Cumberland, and several from Yorkshire, went over to a meeting appointed by Westmoreland Quarterly Meeting, on purpose to hear and determine the matter of difference. But the disaffected persons refused to give their attendance. The committee being desirous, if possible, to give them a fair and full hearing, appointed another day, and themselves personally waited on the heads of the secession, to request their attendance. But their message and advice were treated with slight and contempt; and seeing that these men were not by any means to be induced to a reconciliation, they drew up a testimony against them, and left it with Friends of the Quarterly Meeting of Westmoreland.

Still another attempt was made the next year, to reclaim and recover those who had thus gone out of the way. A meeting was appointed at Drawell, near Sedburgh, on the borders of Yorkshire and Westmoreland, at which they were again offered a fair opportunity of being heard upon the subjects of their discontent. On this occasion, they condescended to attend, and were fully heard by the Friends formerly appointed, and by many other aged and experienced Friends from other parts, who spent four days in the investigation. But as it plainly appeared that the defection proceeded from a spirit of contention and opposition to all regularity and good order in the church, they were affectionately entreated to return to the unity of the body. Obstinately persisting, however, in their opposition, they were testified against by this meeting also; and soon afterwards detached themselves entirely from the Society, and set up a separate meeting.

John Story travelled over the country, endeavoring to propagate the dissent in various parts of the nation, and gained some adherents in the western counties, particularly at Bristol.

This defection drew forth from William Penn a small treatise on Church Discipline, designed to inform the judgments of the discontented; and Robert Barclay also came forth with his well known work entitled "The Anarchy of the Ranters," &c., in which, with his usual clearness and strength of reasoning, he vindicated the discipline established among Friends, against those who accused them of confusion and disorder on the one hand, or of tyranny and imposition on the other. These books elicited contentious replies from William Rogers, one of the prominent seceders; which, however, being more remarkable for passionate intemperance of language than soundness of reasoning, and abounding in personal invectives against many of the most eminent members of the Society, particularly George Fox, soon ran their ephemeral course and sunk into oblivion.

William Rogers becoming puffed up by the applause of his party, went to London at the time of the Yearly Meeting, and challenged Friends to an open dispute. He was met accordingly, and was so completely foiled in all his sophistry, and his errors and petulancy were so fully exposed, that framing a frivolous excuse, he left the meeting, and departed abruptly from the city, refusing a second opportunity for further discussion.

Thomas Ellwood and George Whitehead were also engaged in this controversy, both replying to William Rogers's books, and defending the principles and practices of the Society. The compact by which these separatists were bound together, was found too slight to maintain their union, and was soon dissolved. The more sincere among them coming in time to perceive the groundless nature of their separation, were united once more to the body, and the rest fell to pieces and dwindled away; leaving only, as their memorial, a solemn warning on the page of history, of the unsubstantial nature of all attempts, made in the spirit of party and of self-aggrandizement, to divide and scatter the church of Christ.

About the same time that this defection of Wilkinson and Story broke out in the north of England, a spirit of unsoundness showed itself in the east; which, though confined in its sorrowful effects to one individual, became important as a matter of history, inasmuch as it once more drew forth the testimony of the faithful members of the body, to their belief in the divinity and atonement of the Lord Jesus Christ, as a fundamental and integral part of the doctrines of the Society of Friends. A certain Jeffery Bullock, of Sudbury, elated by a fond conceit of his own attainments, and mistaking the vagaries of a deluded imagination for the pure influences of the Spirit of Christ, adopted and promulgated the false and anti-christian notion, that the gift of divine grace in the soul superseded the necessity, and cancelled the benefits, of the coming and sufferings in the flesh, of our blessed Lord and Saviour, Jesus Christ.

Being rebuked for this and other errors, he assumed an

air of great importance, and inveighed with much acrimony against the faithful elders, whose concern it was to administer counsel and reproof, in order to reclaim him from the gross delusions into which his self-confidence had betrayed him; and he denounced the good order and government of the church, as tyranny, oppression, and usurpation of power; declaring that every one should be left to the guidance of the Spirit in himself, with no control of outward rules. Becoming, notwithstanding the brotherly admonitions of his friends, still more refractory and overbearing, and going on to propagate his unsound opinions, he was, about the year 1675, disowned by Friends, who issued several clear and cogent testimonies against his anti-christian errors.

Irritated by this disownment, he made use of the press, and published a book against the Society, upbraiding its members with much bitterness. Giles Barnardiston and Isaac Penington stepped forward in defence of the truth, replying to his charges and false assertions; vindicating the faith of the Society in our Lord Jesus Christ, as the Son of God, and the only Justifier and Saviour of the repenting sinner; and showing that as those are to be blamed who despise the doctrine of the Light within, relying on the death and sufferings of Christ, without coming to an experience of his cleansing and sanctifying operations in the soul, so those, on the other hand, who, pretending to exalt this Light, despised the loving-kindness of the Lord in sending his Son Jesus Christ into the world, to lay down his precious life a sacrifice for the sins of man, cannot be owned as maintaining sound doctrine; for that such as speak and act under the promptings of that divine Light, can never disregard or deny the efficacy of what the Son of God did and suffered in the prepared body.

This unhappy man was afterwards mercifully enabled to see the delusion into which he had fallen: and in 1686, he gave forth a paper of condemnation, not only of his gross doctrinal errors, but of his supercilious and injurious treatment of Friends, and animadversions against the wholesome order and government of the Society.

CHAPTER XXVIII.

WILLIAM PENN'S TRAVELS IN HOLLAND AND GERMANY.

IN the year 1677, William Penn found it laid upon him to visit Holland and Germany, in the service of the Gospel. He had been before on the continent, about 1671; but no account of that journey is now to be found.

Sailing from Harwich on the 26th of the Fifth month, in company with George Fox, Robert Barclay, George Keith, and several other Friends, he landed on the 28th at the Briel in Holland, and soon proceeded to Rotterdam, where many Friends of that city immediately came to see them. They held two meetings there, and visited Friends in their families, and William Penn then proceeded with George Fox to Leyden, Haarlem and Amsterdam; at which place was then held the first general meeting of Friends for Holland, embracing also those in the Palatinate, Hamburg, Lubeck, Frederickstadt, &c. This meeting agreed upon several salutary minutes, to be sent forth among the members for their edification, and for the better conducting of the affairs of the church, which document may be considered as in some degree embodying their code of discipline. The first item ran thus:

"Be it known to all men, that the power of God, the Gospel, is the authority of all our men's and women's meetings; and every heir of that power is an heir of that authority, and so becometh a living member of right, of either of those meetings, and of the heavenly fellowship and order in which they stand: which is not of man, nor by man."

The practice to be observed in laboring with offenders for their restoration is thus described:

"Though the doctrine of Christ Jesus requireth his people to admonish a brother or sister twice, before they tell the church; yet that limiteth none, so as they shall use no longer forbearance, before they tell the church;—and it is desired of all, that before they publicly complain, they wait in the power of God, to feel if there is no more required of them to their brother or sister." "And further, when the church is told, and the party admonished by the church again and again, and he or she remain still insensible and unreconciled; let not final judgment go forth against him or her, till every one of the meeting hath cleared his or her conscience, that if any thing be upon any, further to visit such a transgressor, they may clear themselves, if possibly the party may be reached and saved. And after all are clear of the blood of such an one, let the judgment of Friends in the power of God go forth against him or her, as moved for the Lord's honor and glory sake: that no reproach may come or rest upon God's holy name, truth, and people."

Amongst other things which then engaged their attention, was the subject of marriage; which they declare, "as the universal and unanimous sense of Friends," to be "the work of the Lord only, and not of priest or magistrate; for it is God's ordinance and not man's."

They also directed that committees of Friends should be appointed to judge of such writings as were designed to be published, and that "no book may be published but in the unity."

William Penn bears testimony that at this meeting "the

sound of the everlasting gospel went forth, and the Lord's fear, and life, and power was over all."

Here William Penn addressed a letter to the king of Poland, in the name and on behalf of his fellow-believers of Dantzick, who had for some time been great sufferers for conscience' sake, some banished from their homes, and others closely imprisoned, for meeting together for the worship of their Divine Master. This cogent appeal, however, did not prevail to stop the persecution; which continued for some years, so that those poor people were subjected to much cruelty, being confined in the house of correction, chained together by their hands, fed only with bread and water, and forced to lie upon straw through the severe winter.

Hence William Penn, Benjamin Furly, George Keith and Robert Barclay, went to Osnaburg, and then to Herwerden, to visit the Princess Elizabeth Palatine of the Rhine, granddaughter of King James I., and sister of the famous Prince Rupert. She and the Countess De Hornes, who lived with her, had for some time been acquainted with Robert Barclay and other Friends, and were seeking after best things, and lovers of those who separate themselves from the world for righteousness' sake. This Princess came measurably to appreciate the truth of the principles held by Friends, and not only maintained an affectionate correspondence for several years with Robert Barclay and William Penn, but made her house an asylum and a meeting-place for Friends on various occasions. These were now very cordially received, and held several meetings in her house, one of which, at the suggestion of the Countess De Hornes, was with the domestics of the establishment, to the great satisfaction of the princess: another was a public meeting for the family and the towns-people, "which began," says William Penn, "with a weighty exercise and travail in prayer, that the Lord would glorify his own name that day. And by his own power he made way to their consciences, and sounded his awakening trumpet in their ears, that they might know that He was God, and that there is none like unto Him. Oh! the day of the Lord livingly dawned upon us, and the searching life of Jesus was in the midst of us. The Word, that never faileth them that wait for it, and abide in it, opened the way and unsealed the book of life: yea the quickening power and life of Jesus wrought and reached to them; and virtue from him in whom dwelleth the Godhead bodily, went forth, and blessedly distilled upon us his heavenly life." "As soon as the meeting was done," he adds, "the princess came to me, and took me by the hand, to speak to me of the sense she had of that power and presence of God, which was amongst us; but was stopped—and turning herself to the window, she broke forth in an extraordinary [emotion,] crying out, 'I cannot speak to you—my heart is full,'—clapping her hands upon her breast."

In taking a solemn leave of these interesting persons, the Friends recommended to them a "holy silence from all will-worship, and the workings, strivings, and images of their own mind and spirit; that Jesus might be felt by them in their hearts, and his holy teachings witnessed and followed in the way of his blessed cross, which would crucify them unto the world, and the world unto them; that their faith, hope, and joy might stand in Christ in them, the heavenly Prophet, Shepherd, and Bishop."

Leaving Herwerden, they passed through Paderborn, Cassel and Frankfort; except Robert Barclay, who prepared to return to Amsterdam. Soon after they arrived at Krisheim, where they found a meeting of tender and faithful people; and notwithstanding Friends there were desired by the chief officer of the place, through fear of the leading Calvinists, not to suffer any preaching amongst them, yet they had a comfortable meeting. At Manheim, William Penn addressed a letter to the Prince Elector Palatine of

Heidelberg, encouraging him in the Christian virtue of charity towards those who conscientiously dissented from the established form of religion: they then went by the Rhine to Worms, and thence on foot to Krisheim again, where they had a good meeting, and the Lord's power was sweetly felt by many. This meeting had been chiefly gathered by William Ames and George Rofe, about twenty years previously.

Passing through Mentz and Cologne, and not being permitted to enter the town of Mulheim, they came to the walls of Duysburg, at night; but the gates being shut, and no houses outside the walls, they lay down together in a field until near the dawn of day, soon after which, the gates being opened, they entered the city. Here William Penn wrote a letter to the Countess of Falkenstein and Bruck, of whom he had some knowledge as a person of much religious feeling, who saw the vanity of this world, and in some degree the emptiness of its religions; but whom they had not been able to visit, being rudely turned away by her father, with a guard of soldiers. He encouraged her closely to attend to the divine Visitor in the soul, which had shown her the fading nature of all earthly glory, and the joys of the world to come, and had wrought in her heart the change which she had witnessed from the spirit of the world. And he recommended her to stay herself upon Christ Jesus, the everlasting Rock, and feel him a fountain in her soul— whom God had given for the life of the world. He wrote also at the same time to her father, the Graef or Earl of Bruck and Falkenstein, exhorting him to repentance, and remonstrating with him on his illiberality and unchristian behavior, in turning out of his dominions at sunset, innocent strangers of good character in their own country, and thus subjecting them to exposure in the fields at night, in an unknown country, merely for being what the world called Quakers, and not giving him the usual empty compliment of putting off the hat.

They were met, the same day, after a meeting with some serious people, by a messenger from the countess, telling them of her grief at the behavior of her father, and advising them not to expose themselves on her account, to such difficulties; for her father set his dogs at some who came in the love of God to visit her, and at others his soldiers, to beat them; adding, however, that even this ought not to hinder them from doing good. After some serious discourse with the tender young man, her messenger, it being now afternoon, and they having neither eaten nor drank anything since the morning of the previous day, and having lain out in the field all night, they retired for some refreshment, and afterwards left the city, being compelled to walk eight miles to a town called Holten, where they lodged.

Proceeding through Wesel to Cleve, they paid a visit to a certain noblewoman of religious disposition. They told her, their message was to those of that city who had any hunger or thirst after the true and living knowledge of God. She told them there were some who searched after God; but she feared that the name of *Quaker* would make them shy; for they were called Quakers themselves, by people of the same profession, merely for being more serious and retired in their conversation. They replied, that it was an honor to the name, that all sobriety throughout Germany was called by it; and that this ought to make the way easier for those who were Quakers indeed — to all such, God had committed to him and his friends the word of life to preach, and such they sought out wherever the Lord brought them. This person, as well as an attorney whom she sent for to meet them, was reached by their testimony to pure spiritual religion, and they both confessed to the truth of what was said. "A blessed sweet time we had," says William Penn; "for the power and presence of the Lord, our staff and strength, plenteously appeared amongst us."

Soon after this, at Utrecht, William Penn parted from

his companions, and went to Amsterdam, where he received a letter from the Princess Elizabeth, who longed for greater experience of the baptism of fire and of the Holy Ghost, and for power to bear the cross of Christ.

From Amsterdam he joined George Fox at Harlingen, where was held at that time the first Monthly Meeting of Friends for Friesland, Groningen, and Embden, and a public meeting also for the inhabitants generally. There was a Presbyterian minister present, who sat with much attention and sobriety, but who, having to preach that evening, went away, while George Fox was speaking. However, he speedily returned and sat at the door till George Fox concluded; when he stood up, and putting off his hat, with his face towards heaven, and in a solemn manner, exclaimed, "The Almighty, the All-wise, the Omnipotent great God, and his Son Jesus Christ, who is blessed forever and ever, confirm His word that hath been spoken this day;" and apologizing for having to leave the meeting, withdrew. Just as the meeting ended, he came again, and said in the hearing of some Friends, that he had made his sermon much shorter than common, that he might enjoy the rest of the meeting. From this place William Penn wrote a letter of religious counsel to Joanna Eleonora Malane, a noble young woman of Frankfort, who had been sweetly visited by the ministry of life, through himself and his companions. He soon afterwards paid an interesting visit to Anna Maria Schurmans, a noted religious woman among the followers of John De Labadie, who seeking a more spiritual fellowship and society, had separated themselves from the common Calvinistic churches, and were a serious, plain people, having approximated towards Friends as to silence in meetings, women's speaking, preaching by the Spirit, and plainness of garb and furniture. This woman, with some others of the same persuasion, resided in the family of the Somerdykes, daughters of a nobleman of the

Hague. They gave William Penn a serious account of the work of the Almighty among them; having evidently tasted of the heavenly gift, but appearing to place too great reliance on their beloved John De Labadie. William Penn then addressed them in an earnest appeal, opening the true nature of religious experience, and exhorting them, that since God had given them a divine sense of himself, their eye should be to him, and not to man; that they might come more into true silence, and a growth into that heavenly sense — that the work of the true ministry was not to keep the attention of the people to the preacher, but to turn them to God, the new covenant teacher, and to Christ, the great gospel minister — and closely recommending to them not to be of those who begin in the Spirit, and end in the flesh; but to wait in the light and the spirit of judgment that had visited them, that all might be wrought out that was not born of God, and they might become a holy priesthood, offering up a living sacrifice with God's heavenly fire.

Leaving this little company, with much exhortation to "know no man after the flesh," but to have their fellowship in Christ, he went to Lippenhausen and Groningen, at both which places were meetings of Friends: and thence to Embden, where Friends had suffered most grievous persecutions for some years. Here he found it laid upon him to visit the president of the council, at whose instigation these persecutions had taken place, who received him respectfully, and gave some expectation that the visit would not prove in vain.

After this, at Bremen, he went to see two ministers under some suffering for their zeal against formality in the reformed churches; and though one, through fear, reluctantly declined the visit, he had with the other a satisfactory open interview of about three hours; testifying "that the day was come, and coming, in which the Lord would gather out of all sects that stand in the oldness of the letter, into His own holy Spirit, life, and power; and that in this, the unity of faith and bond of peace should stand."

He and Jacob Claus, his companion, visited some other serious individuals, and had in their inn, frequent opportunity to declare the way of Truth; and leaving books among the people, they took their leave of them, and went again to Herwerden. Here they had much satisfaction in the company of those pious women, the Princess Elizabeth and Countess De Hornes, and held several meetings in the house, which appear to have been remarkable opportunities of divine overshadowing, to the tendering of the hearts of those assembled. Having at length taken an affectionate and solemn leave of this family, they travelled by wagon to Wesel, about two hundred miles, riding three nights and days without rest; and arriving at Amsterdam, they had on the tenth of Eighth month, a "blessed public meeting, never to be forgotten." In this city they had a dispute with Galenus Abrahams, the great father of the Socinian Menists in those parts, who came accompanied by several of his congregation, and some of their preachers, and affirmed in opposition to Friends, that there was no Christian church ministry, or apostolical commission now in the world. But the Lord assisted them with His wisdom and strength, to confound his attempts.

From Amsterdam they went to Delft and Rotterdam, where they had a large and favored meeting among Friends and others; thence to the Hague and Leyden, and on the 21st embarked at Briel for Harwich, on their return to England.

CHAPTER XXIX.

ACCOUNT OF ISAAC PENINGTON.

IN the year 1679 died Isaac Penington, a man remarkable for his sweet Christian spirit, and extraordinarily clear views of the mysteries of godliness, and the true character of pure and undefiled religion. He was born about the year 1617, and was the eldest son of Alderman Penington, who was twice elected lord mayor of London, a noted member of the Long Parliament, and nominated, though he never acted, as one of the judges for the trial of King Charles the First. Isaac's education was suited to his quality and expectations in life, having all the advantages which the schools and universities, and the conversation of some of the most considerable men of the age, could afford. His natural abilities enabled him to avail himself of these advantages, being possessed of a quick apprehension, an acute mind, sound judgment, and good general understanding. His disposition was remarkably mild and affable, free from pride and affectation; his common conversation cheerful but guarded, equally divested of moroseness and levity. Tempering easy affability with serious gravity, he was pleasing in the manner, and instructive in the matter of his discourse.

His father's station in public employments, and his rank in life, opened for him a fair prospect of worldly greatness, if his views had been turned that way; but actuated by higher and nobler considerations, he was induced to relinquish the short-lived glories of this world, as unworthy to engage the principal attention of man born for immortality; and with Moses he "chose rather to suffer affliction with the people of God, than to enjoy the pleasures of sin for a season."

"Very early," says his intimate friend, William Penn, who married his step-daughter Gulielma Maria Springett, "very early did the Lord visit him with a more than ordinary manifestation of his love; and it had that good effect upon him, that it kept him both from the evils and vain worships of the world; and he became the wonder of his kindred and familiars, for his awful life and serious and frequent retirements, declining all company that might interrupt his meditations." He was frequent in reading the Holy Scriptures, and faithful in practising what was thereby manifested to his understanding, though in this he met with much reproach and opposition. But in reading the lives of holy men of God, recorded in the Scriptures, he perceived in himself and in the generality of professing Christians, a great falling short of the power, experience, and spiritual attainments, which the Scriptures testified to have been acquired in former times. So that the religion of that age, though very high in profession, appeared to him for the most part but a talk, in comparison with what was enjoyed, possessed, and lived in by the primitive believers.

Under this view, he was led to separate himself from the public worship he had usually frequented, and to join a select society of pious persons similarly dissatisfied with the prevailing empty professions. Amongst these he found a good degree of sincerity, and Divine help was often near them. But still there was wanting a greater degree of inward watchfulness, and retirement to the gift of Christ in the heart; and they fell into a mistake, and lost ground. For whilst they should have pressed forward into the spirit and power of godliness, they ran too much outward into the letter and form; in consequence whereof they became darkened in their minds, and confusion and scattering overtook them.

Isaac being now left alone, connected with no visible society, and in a state of darkness and uncertainty, fell under great trouble of mind for a long season, secretly mourning and praying to the Lord, night and day. At length he met with some of the writings of the people called Quakers; but he cast a slight eye over them and threw them aside with disdain, as falling very short of that wisdom with which he supposed the living faith which he was seeking would be attended. Some time afterwards, he had opportunities of conversing with some of them; and although (to use his own expressions) they reached the life of God in him, and that life answered to their discourse, and engaged his affectionate regard towards them, yet he seemed to himself to have such an advantage over them in the power of reasoning, and superiority of understanding, that he viewed them rather in a contemptuous light, as a poor, weak and despicable people, who had some smatterings of truth in them, and some honest desires towards God, but who were very far from the full understanding of His way and will.

One of these opportunities was at Reading in 1656, where Alexander Parker met with him. Alexander thus mentions the interview: "Though at that time he had not the outward garb and appearance of a Quaker, yet did mine eye behold an inward beauty and hidden virtue of life in him; and my soul in the love of truth, did cleave unto him, and I could have embraced him in the sense thereof; but in those early days we were cautious, and laid hands on no man suddenly." He did not hastily join Friends; but for some time reasoned about things, without being able to arrive at a clear view of the Divine will, because he sought it not yet in that low and humble state, wherein the still small voice was to be discerned from the insinuations of the adversary of truth.

But in the year 1658, being invited to a meeting of Friends at John Crook's in Bedfordshire, he went with a fixed disposition and desire to receive nothing as truth, which was not of God, nor withstand anything that was. George Fox was at that meeting; who spoke so clearly to Isaac's state, and expounded the mystery of iniquity, and the gospel of peace and salvation, with such energy, that he gained his full assent to the truth; and from that time forward, Isaac heartily joined in society with this people; though for a season he endured great spiritual conflict, as well as much opposition and reproach from his father and other relations, and from the people and powers of the world.

Being well prepared by the religious exercises through which he had passed, previous to his convincement, as well as after, he soon became an eminently serviceable member of the Society of Friends. His piety was manifested in his humble and reverent adoration of the Most High, and circumspect conversation as in His divine presence. His benevolence and Christian charity was displayed in the diligence with which he visited and administered to the afflicted in body or mind; and his hospitality, in opening his heart and house for the reception of the messengers of peace, and for the religious meetings of his friends. He was a man of quick apprehension, and when any spark arose from the coals of God's altar, it soon kindled in him a flame of holy zeal for God and his truth. Through his ministry many were converted to the truth he had received, and many more confirmed in it; his preaching being with divine authority, in the demonstration of the Spirit and of power. In all his declarations, and writings too, which were numerous and highly edifying to the spiritual traveller, he ever pointed to *the life*—the living efficacy—of religion; and pressed all to mind the *power* of godliness, and not to settle or content themselves in the letter or form. Indeed this was the very bent of his mind; and the strong cries of his soul to the Lord were, that all might partake of this living efficacy, even the life of Jesus, of which he, through the death of the cross, had been made a partaker; in which life re lived unto God, and was a striking pattern of humility, walking in uprightness and innocence before the Lord. He was weaned from the world, and redeemed from the earth; his mind being exercised in things of a higher nature, drinking daily of the water that Christ gives; which was in him "a well of water, springing up unto eternal life."

His conduct and conversation were a seal to his ministry, exhibiting the fruits of the Holy Spirit, and affording an excellent example of piety and virtue in every relation of life. He was a most affectionate husband, a careful and tender father, a mild and gentle master, a sincere and faithful friend; compassionate and liberal to the poor, affable and kind to all with whom he conversed, ready to do good to all men, and careful to injure none.

Having embraced the truth from a firm persuasion of its inestimable value, he patiently and meekly submitted to the sufferings which were, in that day, the lot of most of those who faithfully stood for the cause. His first imprisonment was in Aylesbury jail, in 1661 and 1662, being taken from a meeting in his own house, and confined seventeen weeks, in winter, in a cold and very incommodious room without any chimney. From this severe treatment he contracted so violent a disease, that for several weeks afterwards he was not able to turn in his bed.

His second imprisonment was likewise for meeting with his friends for divine worship, and was in the same jail, and for nearly the same space of time. His third also was in the same place, on the following occasion; which affords an instance of the arbitrary temper, and illegal assumption of power, of many of the magistrates of that period. A Friend of Amersham having died, several Friends and others of the neighborhood assembled as usual to attend the funeral. It happened that one Ambrose Bennett, a justice of the peace, accidentally riding through the town, heard of this funeral. He alighted, and stayed at an inn until the company came by, carrying the corpse to the grave in a solemn manner, becoming the occasion; upon which he rushed out, attended by some constables and rude people, and with his drawn sword struck one of the foremost bearers of the coffin, and commanded them to set it down. But they, knowing that he had no legal authority for so arbitrary a proceeding, as they were not engaged in any unlawful act, were not forward to comply with his order; whereupon this justice of the *peace* violently pushed the coffin off their shoulders into the street, and there left it to the rudeness of all passengers until evening; when it was forcibly taken away from the widow, and buried. The funeral company, on the coffin being thrown down, were seized or dispersed by his order, and ten of them, among whom was Isaac Penington, were committed to Aylesbury jail. Here they were detained until the assizes, when they were again committed for one month, on the act of banishment.

Isaac had scarcely enjoyed his liberty again more than a month, when he was once more taken out of his own house, in a manner still more arbitrary than before, by military force. A rude soldier, without any other warrant than his weapon, took him before one of the deputy lieutenants of the county; who sent him with a guard of soldiers to Aylesbury jail, with a very unusual kind of mittimus, importing that the jailer should receive and keep him in safe custody, *during the pleasure of the Earl of Bridgewater!* This earl had causelessly imbibed a particular antipathy to this inoffensive man, to that degree, that although the plague was then raging, and had reached that town, and the jail was supposed to be infected, he could not be prevailed upon, by the intercession of a person of considerable rank and authority in the county, to permit Isaac to remove to another house in the town, until the jail should be free from infection. After a time, one of the prisoners dying in the jail, of that disease, the jailer's wife, in her husband's absence, gave him liberty to remove into another house: and at length, by the interposition of the Earl of Ancram, after suffering a causeless imprisonment of three quarters of a year, he was discharged. But before the end of a month, another party of soldiers, under the same authority as before, came to his house at night, seized him in his bed, and carried him to the same jail again; where, without any cause, or being charged with any offence, he was imprisoned in rooms so damp and unhealthy that he was thrown into a disease in which he lay for several months, and his life was greatly endangered. During his long confinement, he was never called for at the sessions, but by some illegal means was returned on the calendar to remain in prison. At length in 1668, procuring a removal by writ of *habeas corpus* to the court of King's Bench, when he appeared there, no cause of imprisonment appearing, the court released him, with plain indications of surprise, that a man should be so long kept in prison for nothing.

Last of all, he was imprisoned in 1670 at Reading; whither he had gone in the exercise of Christian charity and fraternal sympathy, to visit his friends in prison there. This was, in the eyes of that rigid and implacable magistrate, Sir William Armourer, sufficient cause for his arrest, and he was committed to the same prison with his friends whom he came to visit. Here he continued a prisoner, a year and three quarters, being condemned under a sentence of premunire, until at length he was released by the king's letters-patent, in 1672.

A fellow-prisoner gives the following testimony of his deportment under these repeated tribulations. "I have had knowledge of him near twenty years, especially in suffering; for it pleased the Lord so to order it, that our lot fell together in prison several times, and I may say, it was well it was so; for, being made willing by the power of God, to suffer with great patience, cheerfulness, contentedness, and true nobility of spirit, he was a good example to me and others. I do not remember that I ever saw him cast down, or dejected in his spirit, in the time of his close confinement, nor speak hardly of those that persecuted him. Indeed I may say, in the prison he was a help to the weak, being made instrumental in the hand of the Lord to that end. Oh, the remembrance of the glory that did often overshadow us in the place of confinement; so that indeed, the prison was made by the Lord unto us as a pleasant palace." Many of his excellent letters were written during his incarcerations.

Being thus, by divine assistance, preserved through all his trials, steadfast in the faith, he was well prepared for death. In the year 1679, being at Goodnestone Court in Kent, a farm belonging to his wife, (who was the widow of Sir William Springett,) he was there taken ill of a painful disorder. The anguish of his body, however, gave no shock to the inward peace with which he was favored. He died, as he had lived, in the faith that overcomes the world, leaving to posterity, by his life, and by his excellent writings, an animating example of that Christian purity and wisdom, which can only be attained by unremitting watchfulness, and attention to the inspeaking, quick, and powerful Word of divine Grace.

23

CHAPTER XXX.

PENNSYLVANIA GRANTED TO WILLIAM PENN — PERSECUTION AT BRISTOL.

WE have seen by the occurrences narrated to have taken place in the colonies of New England, that notwithstanding the plea of liberty of conscience with which those colonies set out, they furnished a very imperfect kind of refuge to our Friends from the persecutions rife in the old world. But the time now approached, when their Divine Master saw fit to grant to his servants an asylum on the Western Continent under circumstances which assured to them, at least for many years, the peaceable enjoyment of their religious rights.

William Penn had for some years been interested in promoting the colonization of West Jersey as a trustee of the estate of Edward Byllinge. His attention had thus been attracted at times across the great ocean, and probably a remembrance occasionally renewed of the prospect which he seems to have had at an early period of his life, of usefulness in the Western World. And now having long witnessed the sufferings to which his friends were subjected for their faithful adherence to their religious convictions, he became desirous of obtaining a grant of a tract of country in the wilderness of America, where he might furnish them a retreat from the malice of their enemies, and found a government based on the principles of Christianity. Accordingly, in 1680, he applied to King Charles II. for a grant of territory, and power to found a colony. After considerable deliberation the request was acceded to, and a charter granted on the fourth of the month called March,

1681, by which William Penn was constituted Proprietor and Governor of the new colony, named by the king, Pennsylvania.

By this charter William Penn became possessed of very considerable political power, and, as far as the royal grant was competent to give him possession, of an extensive country, nearly covered with woods, and chiefly occupied by wandering tribes of Indians. These, he was well aware, were the real owners of the soil, and he early determined not to overlook their rights, or follow the example of those who had preceded him in other colonies, of robbing and oppressing this poor defenceless people.

Soon after obtaining the charter, he commenced preparations for settling the province: he published such an account of the country as could then be obtained, with a copy of the charter, and a statement of the terms on which the lands would be sold; and a large number of purchasers coming forward, he drew up, and presented to them certain conditions, which may be considered as the first step to a constitution of government. This document contained twenty-four articles, which were consented to and subscribed by the first settlers; the first article being on a matter which was very near to his feelings, and expressed as follows:

"In reverence to God, the Father of light and spirits, the author, as well as object, of all divine knowledge, faith, and worship, I do, for me and mine, declare and establish, for the first fundamental of the government of this country, that every person that doth or shall reside therein, shall have and enjoy the free profession of his or her faith, and exercise of worship towards God, in such way and manner as every such person shall in conscience believe is most acceptable to God: and so long as every such person useth not this Christian liberty to licentiousness, or the destruction of others; that is to say, to speak loosely and profanely or contemptuously of God, Christ, the Holy Scriptures, or religion, or commit any moral evil or injury against others in their conversation; he or she shall be protected in the enjoyment of the aforesaid Christian liberty by the civil magistrate."

He wrote also on the eighteenth of the Eighth month, 1681, a kind letter to the Indian inhabitants of the country, recognizing the same Lord over all, for the red as for the white man, to whom we must all give account; mentioning the royal grant of a tract of country to himself, but desiring to enjoy it with their love and consent; and informing them that he should shortly appear among them personally, but in the mean time had sent commissioners to treat with them about the land, and a firm league of peace.

These commissioners were enjoined, in negotiating with the natives for the sale of their lands, to treat them with all possible justice, candor, and humanity.

Having at length completed the arrangements for his departure, he wrote a beautiful and touching letter to his wife and children, exhorting them by the most tender entreaties of a father's love, to a godly life, and a cultivation of the true graces and virtues of the genuine Christian; and going on board the ship "Welcome" in the Sixth month, 1682, he addressed on the 30th, from the Downs, an affectionate farewell epistle to his Friends in England.

He had about one hundred fellow-passengers, chiefly of his own Society, but the small-pox breaking out among them, carried off nearly one-third of the number. In this trying situation, he administered to the sick all the comfort and assistance in his power, not seeking his own ease when his exertions could be of any use to his fellow-creatures. After a voyage of six weeks, they came in sight of the American shores, and sailing up the Delaware Bay and river, received the hearty congratulations of the inhabitants, and landed at Newcastle on the 24th of the Eighth month. Here he took possession of his territory, having obtained from the Duke of York, before his departure, the three lower counties on the Delaware Bay to annex to his province; and soon afterwards proceeded to Chester, then called Uplands, and convened an assembly there, consisting of an equal number of freemen from Pennsylvania and from these lower counties. This assembly, though only three days in session, passed several important laws, the first of which was to insure liberty of conscience to every one who should "confess one Almighty God to be the Creator, Upholder, and Ruler of the world, and profess himself obliged in conscience to live peaceably and justly under the civil government. By these laws, the officers of the government were required to be such as professed faith in Jesus Christ. Scandalous vices of every description were prohibited, and provision was made for training children to business, to prevent pauperism. Some new views were introduced into the penal system, prisons being considered as places of reformation, and not merely of vindictive punishment.

In a letter written from this place soon afterwards, he declared himself "much satisfied with his place and portion, yet busy enough, having much to do to please all;" and comparing his allotment with what he had elsewhere witnessed, he exclaimed, "Oh, how sweet is the quiet of these parts, freed from the anxious and troublesome solicitations, heresies, and perplexities of woful Europe."— "Blessed be God—my soul fervently breathes, that in His heavenly guiding wisdom we may be kept: that we may serve him in our day, and lay down our heads in peace."

It was not long before he redeemed his promise to the Indians, of coming among them in person; for in the autumn of this year, he held his celebrated treaty with these people at Shackamaxon, about two miles north of the original site of the city of Philadelphia, and since included within its limits. It is much to be regretted that the records of this treaty have been lost, and nothing remains respecting it but tradition, and the deep and indelible impression which it made in the heart of the red man. This impression was one of lasting gratitude for the justice and kindness with which they had been treated by William Penn, and of unwavering confidence to this day in the sincerity and friendship of his brethren in religious fellowship. The immediate object of the treaty was probably the formation of a league of perpetual friendship and mutual confidence; the purchase of land having been previously effected by William Penn's commissioners, as far as was necessary for the early requirements of the colony. A celebrated writer has designated this treaty as the only one between the Indians and Christians which had not been ratified by an oath, and the only one that was never infringed. It was, too, a commencement of that system of peaceful and Christian practice, by which, during a series of several years, whilst the colony of Pennsylvania was under the control of Friends, was fully exemplified that great and important truth, that war is not an unavoidable part of the intercourse of nations, but that by a firm adherence to the dictates of Christian principle, the occasions which call it forth may be entirely avoided. This was a grand experiment, and its success was to the honor of that great Name, under whose promptings it was conceived, and who having vouchsafed to his servants a clear sense of His will, granted them strength also in the time of need, to carry out his blessed designs.

Before this year was concluded, William Penn proceeded to lay out the plan for his intended metropolis, in a very favorable situation, then called by the Indians Coaquannock; and displayed the prominent social feeling of his mind, in naming it the city of Brotherly Love. There were on William Penn's arrival, about four thousand inhabitants in the province, chiefly Dutch and Swedes; and in little more than a year after the arrangements were made for the settlement of the province, more than two thousand emigrants arrived, a large portion of them being members of the Society of Friends. These scattering along the Delaware, according as their choice or convenience led them, the country was soon peopled, though thinly, from Chester to the Falls at Trenton. Before William Penn's arrival, a meeting of Friends had been held at Shackamaxon, and in 1682, a meeting was held in a frame house erected for the purpose, within the present limits of Philadelphia. A brick meeting-house, near the centre of the plot of the intended city, was built two years afterwards. The house on the bank of the river in Front street, called the Bank meeting-house, was erected in 1683; and the great meeting-house on High street, in 1695. These are all that were erected in the city during William Penn's lifetime. A meeting of Friends was held at Upland, now Chester, several years before the arrival of William Penn, and at that place, a meeting of record, probably the first in the province, was held as early as 1681. A meeting was also settled at Darby in 1682, and in the course of this year, great numbers of emigrants arrived from England, Ireland, Wales, Germany, and Holland. The Welsh settled on both sides of the Schuylkill river; and among the German emigrants were a number of Friends from Krisheim in the Palatinate, among whom William Penn had travelled in the service of the gospel in 1677, and who formed the flourishing settlement of Germantown.

During the year 1683, the legislature held a session in Philadelphia, the members being chosen as representatives by the freemen of the province. Considerable progress was made in the erection of the new city, so that by the end of the year, one hundred houses had arisen from the former forest; the land in the vicinity was in places cleared and brought into cultivation; and the grains of Europe were beginning to flourish in the soil of Pennsylvania.

After about two years' residence in the country, having settled the colony in a thriving and prosperous condition, and addressed a tender and affectionate epistolary exhortation to the members of his own Society in his province, William Penn thought it best to return to England, and arrived there on the 12th of Sixth month, 1684.

In the year 1682, a dismal scene of persecution had been opened in the city of Bristol, in England. The meetings of Friends were grievously disturbed, their houses broken into, and almost all manner of violence and abuse committed, chiefly at the instigation of a cruel sheriff. It is true, the meetings of other Protestant dissenters were then also disturbed; but it seems *they* did not so much persist in their religious testimony, and were accordingly not by any means so obnoxious to that insolent outrage, to which this people, from their constancy and non-resistance, were liable. The vilest characters were permitted and encouraged to commit every kind of "excess of riot," without regard to sex, age, or condition. Nay, even ancient men and women were hurried to prison with force and blows, and the little children beaten on the head till they became giddy, and then taken to Bridewell, and terrified by the prospect of whipping, unless they would promise to go no more to their meetings.

But the malice and threats that were used, even to this youthful class of sufferers, did not succeed in subduing their constancy; though scarce a stone was left unturned, in their attempts to afflict Friends, and deter them from assembling to worship their Maker. These disturbances continued till nearly all the men were taken to prison.

Even there, however, their persecutions did not cease, but were greatly increased by privations and ill treatment. They were so closely thronged, that there was barely room for them to rest themselves at night on the floors; and in other respects also their health and lives were so far endangered, that four physicians of Bristol thought fit to give forth a certificate to that effect.

After this, the religious meetings of Friends continuing to be kept up chiefly by women, they also were seized, till at length few or none but children, that remained with the domestics in the houses of their parents, were left free. It is, however, very remarkable, that these pious children, mostly under the age of sixteen, now performed what their parents by being imprisoned, were prevented from doing. They met for the purpose of Divine worship, and continued faithful without fainting, through all the insults of a wicked rabble, from whom they suffered exceedingly. Nineteen of them were carried to the House of Correction, and kept some time there, though from their tender age they were not within the reach of the law. When threatened with whipping if they returned to their meeting, so great was their zeal, that, despising all reproach and insolence, they remained steadfast to their duty. This persecution lasted till the next year, as it did with unrelenting cruelty in many other parts of England; so that more than seven hundred Friends were confined in jails throughout the kingdom during the year 1683.

Some of the prisoners would have willingly worked in prison, to earn something for their sustenance; but the jailer, who was one of the chief instruments of the cruelties exercised upon them, would not permit it. One venerable man near ninety years of age, was kept three nights without a bed, though others offered to pay for accommodations for him, if the jailer would allow it. Other prisoners fell sick of the "spotted fever," and some of them died.

Yet all this did not soften this hard-hearted man. At length, however, a heavy stroke fell upon him. He was taken ill, and was seized with terrible anguish of mind, and in his distress he desired some of those called Quakers to pray for him, and to forgive him for what he had done. They freely answered that they forgave him; but advised him to ask forgiveness of God. His anguish increased; and when the physicians ordered him to be bled, he said, "No physic would benefit him; his distemper was another thing; that no man could do him good — his day being over — and there was no hope of mercy for him from God!" Friends told him, they desired, if it was the will of God, he might find a "place of repentance." But whatever was advanced, encouraging him yet to try to obtain peace and mercy, he would repeat, that his day was over, and that he had no faith to believe. He remained about a month in this lamentable condition, and died without any visible signs of forgiveness; but the judgment thereof must be left to God, the "Judge of quick and dead."

CHAPTER XXXI.

THE DEATHS OF DAVID AND ROBERT BARCLAY, AND GEORGE FOX.

AMONG those champions of the truth whom we have seen to have fearlessly withstood the persecuting spirit of intolerance in Scotland, was David Barclay. The latter part of his days he passed chiefly at his estate of Ury, enjoying the tranquillity of a country life, after many years of hardship and trial, and favored with that inestimable treasure, "the peace of God, which passeth all understanding." About the 76th year of his age, he was attacked by a fever, which in about two weeks, removed him to an "inheritance incorruptible, that fadeth not away." During his sickness, though under much bodily suffering, he was preserved in a quiet, contented mind, freely resigned to the will of God; and several times testified in a lively manner, to the truth of the principles and practices into which he had been led, and to the love of God shed abroad in his heart by the Holy Ghost. On one occasion, being in much pain, he thought he was dying; but expressed his confidence, that he should go to the Lord, and be gathered to many of his brethren, who had gone before him, and to his dear son David, an amiable, exemplary youth, and acceptable minister among Friends, who had died at sea on his voyage to America, about a year before.

On the 11th of Eighth month, about two or three o'clock in the morning, he grew weaker; and his son Robert approaching him, expressed his desire, that He who had loved him might be near him to the end. He answered, "The Lord *is* nigh;" repeating—"You are my witnesses in the presence of God, that the Lord is nigh." A little after, in reference to the convincement of the truth which he and his family had experienced, he exclaimed,—" The perfect discovery of the 'Day-spring from on high!'— how great a blessing it hath been to me and to my family!" Being asked to have something to refresh him, he laid his hand on his breast, saying, "he had *that inwardly* which refreshed him;" and after a little time, added several times, "The Truth is over all."

After kissing his grandchildren, and desiring the divine blessing upon them, he spoke in a serious weighty manner to the father and sisters of his son Robert's wife; and perceiving one of them who was not a Friend, weeping much, he desired that she might come to the Truth, and bade her not to weep for him, but for herself. The medical attendant coming near, he took him by the hand, saying, "Thou wilt bear me witness, that in all this exercise, I have not been curious to tamper nor to pamper the flesh." He answered, "Sir, I can bear witness, that you have always minded the better and more substantial part; and rejoice to see the blessed end the Lord is bringing you to." David enjoined him to "bear a faithful and true witness;"—"yet," added he, emphatically, "it is *the life of righteousness*—it is the life of righteousness, that we bear testimony to, and not to an empty profession." Then he said several times, "Come, Lord Jesus, come, come!" And again, "My hope is in the Lord." He sent by his son, Robert, a message to the carpenter: "See thou charge him to make no manner of superfluity upon my coffin."

Several Friends from Aberdeen coming to see him, and one of them, his faithful fellow-laborer, Patrick Livingstone, having supplicated and praised the Father of all mercies, David held up his hands, and said, "Amen, amen, forever!" And afterwards, when they stood looking at him, he said, "How precious is *the love of God* among his children, and *their* love one to another. Thereby shall all men know that ye are Christ's disciples, if you love one another.—My love is with you—I leave it among you." About eight at night, several Friends standing around the bed, he, perceiving some of them weep, said, "Dear Friends! all mind the *inward man*—heed not the *outward:*—there is One that doth regard—the Lord of hosts is his name!" After he heard the clock strike three, in the morning, he said, "Now the time comes." And a little afterwards he was heard to say, "Praises, praises, praises to the Lord!—Let now thy servant depart in peace.—Unto thy hands, O Father! I commit my soul, spirit, and body.—Thy will, O Lord! be done in earth, as it is in heaven!" These sentences he spoke by short intervals; and at a little after five in the morning, his spirit passed away, in remarkable sweetness and quietness.

The loss sustained by Friends in Scotland, in the removal of this pious man, was soon followed by one felt through the Society at large, in the death of that eminent Christian advocate, his son, Robert Barclay. This greatly gifted man spent the last two years of his life in much retirement. In the year 1690, however, he accompanied James Dickenson, of Cumberland, in a religious visit to some parts of the north of Scotland: and returning to Ury, from a meeting at Aberdeen, he was immediately seized with a violent fever; and in about eight or nine days, it pleased the Lord to take him out of this world, to a kingdom of eternal glory. James Dickenson was with him during his illness, which was a solemn season; and while he sat by him, the Lord's power and presence bowed their hearts together, and Robert Barclay was sweetly melted in a sense of God's love. Though much oppressed by the disorder, an entirely resigned, peaceful, and Christian frame of mind shone through all. With tears, he expressed the love he bore towards "all faithful brethren in England, who kept their integrity to the Truth," and added, "Remember my love to Friends in Cumberland, and at Swarthmore, to dear George, [meaning George Fox,] and to all the faithful everywhere;" concluding with these comfortable expressions:—"God is good still: and though I am under a great weight of sickness and weakness as to my body, yet *my peace flows*. And this I know, that whatever exercises may be permitted to come upon me, they shall tend to God's glory and my salvation; and in that I rest." He died on the third of the Eighth month, 1690, in the 42d year of his age.

Robert Barclay was distinguished by strong mental powers, particularly by great penetration, and a sound and accurate judgment. His talents were much improved by a regular and classical education; but it does not appear that his superior attainments produced that elation of mind, which is too often their attendant. He was meek, humble, and ready to allow to others the merits they possessed. His passions were under the most excellent government. Two of his intimate friends have declared, that they never knew him to be angry. He had the happiness of early perceiving the infinite superiority of religion, to every other attainment; and Divine Grace enabled him to dedicate his life, and all that he possessed, to promote the cause of piety and virtue. For the welfare of his friends he was sincerely and warmly concerned; and he travelled and wrote much, as well as suffered cheerfully, in support of that Society and those principles to which he had conscientiously attached himself. This was not a blind and bigoted attachment: his zeal was tempered with charity; and he loved and respected goodness, wherever he found it. His uncorrupted integrity and liberality of sentiment, his great abilities, and the suavity of his disposition, gave him much interest with persons of rank and influence; and he employed it in a manner that marked the benevolence of his heart. He loved peace, and was often instrumental in producing reconciliation between contending parties. In the support and pursuit of what he believed to be right, he possessed great firmness of mind; and this firm and resolute spirit in the prosecution of duty, was united with great sympathy and compassion towards persons in affliction and distress. They were consoled by his tenderness, assisted by his advice, and as occasion required, were relieved by his bounty. His spiritual discernment and religious experience, directed by that Divine influence which he valued above all things, eminently qualified him to instruct the ignorant, to reprove the irreligious, to strengthen the feeble-minded, and to animate the advanced Christian to still greater degrees of virtue and holiness.

In private life, he was equally amiable. His conversation was cheerful, guarded, and instructive. He was a dutiful son, an affectionate and faithful husband, a tender and careful father, a kind and considerate master. Though the period of his life was short, he had, by the aid of Divine Grace, most wisely and happily improved it; and he lived long enough to manifest, in an eminent degree, the temper and conduct of a Christian, and the virtues and qualifications of a true minister of the Gospel. Of his deep and excellent writings we have already spoken.

Scarcely had the Society recovered from the shock occasioned by the early removal of this upright pillar from the church, when it was called upon to surrender into the abodes of everlasting peace, that eminent servant of Christ who had been, more than any other man, instrumental in gathering it from the "lo! heres," and "lo! theres," of the barren mountains of empty, though plausible profession, into the green pastures and fruitful fields of substance and of life.

The latter part of the life of George Fox was chiefly passed in or near London. His bodily health had for some years been declining, in consequence of his many and grievous imprisonments and other sufferings and exercises of body and mind, his long travels for the promotion of the cause of truth, and his incessant labors in defence of the Gospel, against the clamor and opposition of apostate brethren, and the unfounded imputations of open enemies to the Truth as it is in Jesus.

His solicitude, however, to promote the welfare of the Society, remained undiminished. He wrote many epistles to his Friends, some of sympathy and consolation, to encourage and strengthen them in their deep sufferings; others of counsel, exhortation, and reproof, "stirring up the pure mind by way of remembrance," and laboring to build them up in the most holy faith. On the 10th day of the Eleventh month, 1690, he wrote an epistle to Friends in Ireland, full of consolation to them under the sufferings which then lay heavy upon them; and the next day being First-day, went to the meeting at Grace-church street, London: where the Lord enabled him to preach the truth fully and effectually, opening many deep and weighty things with great power and clearness. After which, having prayed, and the meeting being ended, he went to a Friend's house near the meeting-house; and some Friends accompanying him, he told them, "he thought he felt the cold strike to his heart, as he came out of the meeting;" but added, "I am glad I was here; now I am clear, *I am fully clear.*" When those Friends had withdrawn, he reclined on a bed, complaining still of cold. And his strength sensibly declining, he soon took to his bed entirely; where he lay in much contentment and peace, and very sensible to the last. And as, in the whole course of his life, his spirit, in the universal love of God, had bent its main energies to the promotion of righteousness and piety in the earth; so now, when the outward man was wasting away, his mind seemed absorbed in desires for the spreading of the cause of Truth. He sent for some Friends, and expressed to them his dying wishes for the wide dissemination of the writings of Friends in the world at large. To some who came to visit him, he said, "All is well; the Seed of God reigns over all, and over death itself. And though I am weak in body, yet the power of God is over all, and the Seed reigns over all disorderly spirits." Thus lying in a heavenly frame of mind, his spirit wholly exercised towards the Most High, he gradually grew weaker, until on the Third-day of the week, the 13th of Eleventh month, 1690, between the hours of nine and ten in the evening, he sweetly fell asleep in the Lord, whose blessed truth he had livingly and powerfully preached in the meeting but two days before. He died in the 67th year of his age.

This extraordinary man, as Thomas Ellwood testifies, "was valiant for the truth, bold in asserting it, patient in suffering for it, unwearied in laboring in it, steady in his testimony to it, immovable as a rock. Deep he was in divine knowledge, clear in opening heavenly mysteries, plain and powerful in preaching, fervent in prayer. He was richly endowed with heavenly wisdom, quick in discerning, sound in judgment, able and ready in giving, and discreet in keeping, counsel; a lover of righteousness, an encourager of virtue, justice, temperance, meekness, purity, chastity, modesty, humility, charity, and self-denial in all, both by word and example. Graceful he was in countenance, manly in personage, grave in gesture, courteous in conversation, weighty in communication, instructive in discourse, free from affectation in speech or carriage. A severe reprover of hard and obstinate sinners; a mild and gentle admonisher of such as were tender, and sensible of their failings. Not apt to resent personal wrongs; easy to forgive injuries; but zealously earnest where the honor of God, the prosperity of truth, and the peace of the church, were concerned. Very tender, compassionate, and pitiful he was to all that were under any sort of affliction; full of brotherly love, full of fatherly care; for indeed the care of the churches of Christ was daily upon him, the prosperity and peace whereof he studiously sought."

His character has been thus beautifully portrayed also by his intimate friend William Penn.

"He was a man that God endued with a clear and wonderful depth; a discerner of others' spirits, and very much a master of his own. And though that side of his understanding which lay next to the world, and especially the expression of it, might sound uncouth and unfashionable to nice ears, his matter was nevertheless very profound — and as abruptly and brokenly as sometimes his sentences would seem to fall from him, about divine things, it is well known they were often as texts to many fairer declarations. And indeed, it showed beyond all contradiction that God sent him, in that no art or parts had any share in the matter or manner of his ministry; and that so many great, excellent, and necessary truths, as he came forth to preach to mankind, had therefore nothing of man's wit or wisdom to recommend them. So that as to man he was an original, being no man's copy. And his ministry and writings show that they are from one that was not taught of man, nor had learned what he said by study. Nor were they notional or speculative, but sensible and practical truths, tending to conversion and regeneration, and the setting up of the kingdom of God in the hearts of men.

"In his ministry, he much labored to open truth to the people's understandings, and to bottom them on Christ Jesus, the Light of the world; that by bringing them to something that was from God in themselves, they might the better know and judge of Him and themselves. He had an extraordinary gift in opening the Scriptures. He would go to the marrow of things, and show the mind, harmony, and fulfilling of them with much plainness, and to great comfort and edification. The mystery of the first and second Adam, of the fall and restoration, of the law and gospel, of shadows and substance, of the servant's and son's state, and the fulfilling of the Scriptures in Christ, and by Christ the true Light, in all that are his, through the obedience of faith, were much of the substance and drift of his testimonies. In all which he was witnessed to be of God; being sensibly felt to speak that which he had received of Christ, and was his own experience, in that which never errs nor fails. But above all, he excelled in prayer. The inwardness and weight of his spirit, the reverence and solemnity of his address and behavior, and the fewness and fulness of his words, have often struck even strangers with admiration, as they used to reach others with consolation. The most awful, living, reverent frame I ever felt or beheld, I must say, was his in prayer. And truly it was a testimony that he knew and lived nearer to the Lord than other men; for they that know Him most, will see most reason to approach him with reverence and fear.

"He was of an innocent life, no busybody, nor self-seeker, neither touchy nor critical. What fell from him was very inoffensive, if not very edifying. So meek, contented, modest, easy, steady, tender, it was a pleasure to be in his company. He exercised no authority but over evil, and that everywhere, and in all; but with love, compassion, and long-suffering. A most merciful man, as ready to forgive, as unapt to take or give offence. Thousands can truly say he was of an excellent spirit and savor among them; and because thereof, the most excellent spirits loved him with an unfeigned and unfading love.

"He was an incessant laborer: for in his younger time, he labored much in the word and doctrine and discipline, in England, Scotland, and Ireland; — and towards the conclusion of his travelling services, he visited the churches of Christ in America, in the United Provinces, and in Germany, to the convincement and consolation of many. And besides his labor in the ministry, he wrote much — but the care he took of the affairs of the church in general, was very great. He was often where the records of the business of the church are kept, and where the letters from the many meetings of God's people over all the world used to come. Which letters he had read to him, and communicated them to the meeting weekly held for such services. And he would be sure to stir them up to answer them, especially in suffering cases; showing great sympathy and compassion upon all such occasions, carefully looking into the respective cases, and endeavoring speedy relief.

So that the churches or any of the suffering members thereof, were sure not to be forgotten or delayed in their desires, if he were there.

"As he was unwearied, so he was undaunted in his services for God and his people. He was no more to be moved to fear than to wrath. His behavior at Derby, Litchfield, Appleby, before Oliver Cromwell, at Launceston, Scarborough, &c., did abundantly evidence it.

"But as in the primitive times, some rose up against the blessed apostles of our Lord Jesus Christ, even from among those that they had turned to the hope of the gospel — so this man of God had his share of suffering from some that were convinced by him, who, through prejudice or mistake, ran against him, as one that sought dominion over conscience, because he pressed a ready and zealous compliance with such good and wholesome things as tended to an orderly conversation about the affairs of the church, and in their walking before men. That which contributed much to this ill work, was in some, a grudging of this meek man the love and esteem he had and deserved in the hearts of the people; and weakness in others, that were taken with their groundless suggestions of imposition and blind obedience. In all these occasions, though there was no person the discontented struck so sharply at, as this good man, he bore all their weakness and prejudice, and returned not reflection for reflection; but forgave them their weak and bitter speeches, praying for them, that they might have a sense of their hurt, and see the subtilty of the enemy to rend and divide, and return into their first love that thought no ill.

"And truly, I thought God had visibly clothed him with a divine preference and authority; and indeed his very presence expressed a religious majesty; yet he never abused it, but held his place in the church of God with great meekness, and a most engaging humility and moderation.

For upon all occasions, like his blessed Master, he was a servant to all; holding and exercising his eldership in the invisible power that had gathered them, with reverence to the Head and care over the body; and was received only in that spirit and power of Christ, as the first and chief elder in this age: who, as he was therefore worthy of double honor, so for the same reason it was given by the faithful of this day, because his authority was inward and not outward, and that he got it and kept it by the love of God, and power of an endless life. I write my knowledge, and not report, and my witness is true; having been with him for weeks and months together on divers occasions, and those of the nearest and most exercising nature; and that by night and by day, by sea and by land; in this and in foreign countries; and I can say, I never saw him out of his place, or not a match for every service or occasion. For in all things he acquitted himself like a man, yea, a strong man, a new and heavenly-minded man, a divine and a naturalist, and all of God Almighty's making. I have been surprised at his questions and answers in natural things: that whilst he was ignorant of useless and sophistical science, he had in him the grounds of useful and commendable knowledge, and cherished it everywhere: civil beyond all forms of breeding, in his behavior; very temperate, eating little, and sleeping less, though a bulky person.

"Thus he lived and sojourned among us. And as he lived, so he died; feeling the same eternal power that had raised and preserved him, in his last moments. So full of assurance was he, that he triumphed over death; and so even in his spirit to the last, as if death were hardly worth notice, or a mention. He had the comfort of a short illness, and the blessing of a clear sense to the last: and we may truly say, with a man of God of old, that being dead, he yet speaketh; and though now absent in body, he is present in spirit: neither time nor place being able to interrupt the communion of saints, or dissolve the fellowship of the spirits of the just."

CHAPTER XXXII.

THE PERSECUTION OF FRIENDS DURING THE CIVIL WARS IN IRELAND, IN THE REIGN OF JAMES II.

IN the year 1685, that faithful apostle of Ireland, William Edmundson, had seen with the eye of faith that a time of great exercise and trials to Friends was approaching, when the carcasses of men would even be spread as dung upon the earth. And being under a weighty sense of the need there was for a fleeing unto "the Strong Hold" for safety and preservation, he faithfully and plainly warned Friends and others in many public meetings, and often advised them to lessen their concerns in the world, so as to be ready to receive the Lord in his judgments which were at hand. These troubles came in a few short years thickly upon that distressed island, in all the horrors of civil war.

The Earl of Tyrconnel, then lord deputy of Ireland, disarmed most of the English, and armed the native Irish, who were chiefly Papists; so that the Protestants were struck with fear, and many left their habitations and property, and fled for England; while others took refuge in garrisons from the violence which threatened the whole country. Friends, of course, felt restrained from thus trusting to the arm of flesh, and remained at their homes. An open war soon broke out, and abundance of the Irish who were not of the army, but went in bands, called **Raparees**, plundered and spoiled many of the English inhabitants and Protestants, who had remained in their dwellings. Many of the army also, being countenanced by some of their officers, became very abusive and violent.

A party of Sir Maurice Eustace's troop coming into the neighborhood of Mount Melick, went to William Edmundson's house, and seizing him by the hair of his head, dragged him about the yard among their horses' feet, without any further provocation than the fact of his not being a Papist. Some of them with clubs, and others with pistols, swore they would kill him; which being heard by his wife, she came out to them in great alarm, and desired them to take all their property and save the life of her husband.

They then left William and turned after his wife, swearing and calling bad names; shot several times at his mastiff dog which was kept chained, and then rode off like madmen, abusing and beating all the English they met with, and almost killing some. The poor Protestants became much alarmed, and many began to hide themselves in the woods and bogs, apprehending a general massacre.

At the earnest request of some of the principal inhabitants of the town, William Edmundson, with two others, proceeded at the risk of his life, to Dublin, to lay before the men in power a statement of the outrages which had been committed against the inhabitants. Through the friendship of Lord Chief Justice Nugent, he was admitted into the presence of Tyrconnel, but was only permitted to speak of his own wrongs; they would not listen to anything else; and it plainly appeared that their object was to frighten all the Protestants out of the country, and take possession of their property and of all power in the island. He afterwards went to several of the officers of the army, expostulating with them on the violence of the troopers; and was so indefatigable in his representations, that Tyrconnel was compelled by the attention publicly excited to the matter, reluctantly to give them a hearing; and on examination, the parties concerned being fully identified, were disarmed and sent to jail.

Soon after his return home, these troopers had leave from the jailer and sheriff to come to Mount Melick; and one of them went to William's house, to solicit his forgiveness, saying they would make what satisfaction he pleased. Accordingly going to the town, he expressed to the soldiers his forgiveness, and a hope that what had occurred would be a warning to them for the future, desiring them to make satisfaction to others whom they had similarly abused. They begged him to write to Lord Nugent, requesting their pardon, which he did, succeeded in his solicitation, and gained their gratitude in place of hatred.

This year the trouble daily increased; most of the leading men among the Protestants were gone, and those who stayed were afraid of appealing to the government for the preservation of the country. Anarchy and destruction stalked abroad, and seemed to threaten the total ruin of the sober inhabitants; in a sense of which William Edmundson, who was well known to several of the chief men of the nation, again felt himself religiously called upon to use his influence with the rulers in behalf of the suffering Protestants, and in particular for those of his own Society. He was often accordingly in Dublin, pleading for the oppressed, and using what interest he had among them for the public good. The Irish army being now about to proceed against the Protestants in arms in the north of Ireland, he with some other Friends in that city earnestly solicited the principal officers to spare the members of the Society of Friends, and treat them kindly, as they had not taken up arms; which they promised to do, and afterwards fulfilled their engagement.

The next year (1689) these calamities still increased. The Raparees on one hand, plundered and spoiled many of the English; and on the other hand, the army marching and quartering took what they pleased from the inhabitants, and compelled the families where they came to set before them whatever they had, and wait upon them as servants; so that many seemed likely to be deprived of sustenance for themselves and families. King James coming into Ireland, William Edmundson several times went to see him, and laid before him the calamities to which the Protestants were subjected. The king heard him attentively, but had it not in his power at that time to restrain the disorders. Wickedness was let loose through the country; and violence and cruelty had so much prevailed that most of William's Protestant neighbors had been forced from their homes. Several families took refuge in this Friend's house, until every room was full. Most of the cattle also that were left to them they brought to his land, thinking themselves and their property safer there than elsewhere; and his house being thus crowded with refugees, their situation brought great concern upon him, as they were in continual danger of losing not only their property, but also their lives, at the hands of exasperated bands of ruffians and bigots.

At the battle of the Boyne, the Irish army being beaten, many of them fled in the direction of Mount Melick, plundering wherever they came. They plundered William Edmundson's house several times over; and so violent were they, that the family were compelled to go out of the way. William's wife, preferring to venture her own life to save that of her husband, desired him to secrete himself, lest he should be killed; but he could not do it, trusting in the Lord's protecting arm; whose secret hand restrained these murderers, and preserved the lives of his confiding servants. All his horses were taken away, and whatever else they could find that suited their rapacious wills.

The next year (1690), notwithstanding a proclamation

from King William, (who had supplanted James II.,) that such of the Irish as would remain quietly at home should not be molested, the same disorders continued. The Protestants who remained in the neighborhood of William Edmundson's residence, fled into the parish worship-house at Rossenallis for safety; but after a while the British army gaining the ascendancy, a party of three hundred Protestant soldiers came and drove away about five hundred head of cattle and horses, taking also many prisoners. William Edmundson hearing that one of the prisoners was about to be hung, on empty suspicion of his being a Raparee, he took horse and rode swiftly after the soldiers, to endeavor to prevail on them to relinquish their purpose. After riding four miles, followed by many of his Irish neighbors in expectation of getting their cattle and people released, he came up with the soldiers; and the two captains perceiving who it was, made a halt and met him. He reasoned with them, and reminded them of the king's proclamation, and at length persuaded them to promise a release, if the soldiers could be prevailed on. He then rode with the captains to the head of the party; but they were very angry, and seemed ready to kill the Irish who followed for their cattle. Whereupon he quitted his horse, and ventured with his life in his hand among the rude soldiers, to save these poor people, and at length, with much ado, and the captain's assistance, he prevailed with them to release the greatest part of the booty. He then remounted his horse, and sought out the man whom they had stripped for hanging. Having found him, he threw him his riding-coat to wrap around his almost naked body, and then hunting out the person who had possession of his clothing, he reasoned with the men and officers on the unmanly action of stripping a man thus, telling them he had been a soldier himself, and would have scorned so base an act. By much persuasion he at length prevailed, so that the soldier had to put off the man's clothes and restore them to him; and this poor man and some others of the prisoners were released, with all their cattle.

On several occasions, when the English soldiers took away the cattle of the Irish, William Edmundson persuaded them to restore them, or bought them off for a small sum of his own money, to give them back to the owners; and he let them pasture their horses on his own land, to save them from the plunderers.

Towards the latter part of this year, the English army having gone into winter-quarters, the Irish were more at liberty, and the Raparees increased. They burned many excellent houses, and some towns, and killed several of the Protestants; but through the wonderful mercies of God, Friends were enabled to hold their meetings regularly, though many times in danger of their lives in travelling to and from them. Not more than four Friends were known to have lost their lives by violence during all this widespread calamity.

In the Ninth month (old style) William Edmundson attended as usual the Half-year's National Meeting at Dublin, where a spirit of thankful rejoicing prevailed among Friends, in having been preserved through so many dangers to meet each other once more. During the meeting, tidings were brought to William Edmundson, that the Raparees had taken about twenty of his cows, but that none of his family were hurt. When the service of that meeting was over, he returned home, and found his wife and family well; but spoil and cruelty increased, and imminent dangers seemed to hover over them. Yet he dared not to remove, considering that his example was much looked at, and that his removal would discourage not only Friends, but the English neighbors around, who thought they were safer for his remaining in his place. And he also believed that one hair of his head should not fall without God's providence.

On the 23d of the month, he went to Colonel Biarly, then governor of Mount Melick, and told him of the danger to which they were exposed, expecting every night to have his house burnt down; but this man took little notice of it; and that same night, while William and his family were asleep, some hundreds of Raparees beset his house, firing several shots in at the windows. The noise was heard at Mount Melick, two miles distant, and several went to the governor to request a party of men to render him succor; yet he not only refused to grant it, but when a certain lieutenant voluntarily offered to relieve him or lose his own life, he even threatened to hang any man that would leave the garrison. So the Raparees set fire to his house, William Edmundson remaining in it until much of it was destroyed. When the fire would not permit them to stay longer, he made conditions with these lawless people, and opening the doors, went out. But they soon broke their engagements, though bound by many oaths, and took what plunder they could get from the fire, which however had destroyed the greatest part. One mare was burnt to death in the stable, and two more were rescued from the flames, exceedingly scorched. All his cattle they took as booty, leaving not a single one. They took away his wife's upper garment, and so left her; but William and his two sons they took prisoners, bare-legged and bare-headed, and not much better than naked. One of them lent him however, at his request, an old blanket of his own, to wrap about him, the weather being cold; and that night they dragged him and his sons through rough places, bushes, mire, and water to the knees, whereby their bare feet and legs were sorely hurt and bruised with the bushes, gravel, and stones. The next morning they took them into the woods, and holding a consultation over them, concluded to shoot William, and to hang his two sons. He expostulated with them on the injustice of their conduct, appealing to **many** that knew him and his family, challenging them all to prove that either he or his sons had wronged any of their country-people in the smallest matter during all these troubles, and on the contrary reminding them that he had done what he could to protect them, sometimes with the hazard of his life, among the English soldiers. Several of them acknowledging that they knew he was an honest man, he told them that if he died they were his witnesses that he was innocent, and God would avenge his blood. They proceeded, nevertheless, in their murderous preparations, blindfolding his sons to hang them; and having prepared two fire-locks to shoot William, they came to blindfold him also. But he calmly told them they need not do that, for he could look them in the face, and was not afraid to die.

At this juncture there came up one Lieutenant Richard Dunn, whose father William Edmundson had got released, together with his cattle, from the English soldiers, and whose brother was the man whom William had so remarkably saved from death and got released when he was stripped to be hanged. This Lieutenant Dunn, expecting to obtain preferment, determined to carry the prisoners to Athlone, which was twenty miles distant; and so the Almighty defeated their intention of taking the lives of these innocent men. Dunn taking possession of them, kept them three nights at a cabin on the way, cold and without food, so that even their persecutors wondered how they endured it. William told them, that they had taken or destroyed his provisions, and the Lord had fitted him for the privation by taking away his appetite.

As they went through Raghan, there came out of a cabin an ancient Irishman, who looked on William with a sorrowful countenance. William asked him if he could give him a piece of bread, knowing his sons were very hungry. The man replied that he would give him some bread, if he had to buy it with gold, for he did not believe William was

one that was accustomed to beg his bread. So he went into
the cabin, and brought a piece of extremely coarse bread,
expressing regret that he had nothing else to offer him; on
which William, telling him that it was very acceptable,
gave it to his sons. That night they got straw to lodge on,
and consequently rested well; and the next day they came
to Athlone. On their entrance into the main street of the
town, they were saluted by a mob, encouraged by the high
sheriff of the county, with the epithets of traitors, rebels,
&c.; and scarcely escaped injury. They were taken to the
main guard, and afterwards to the castle, before the governor and chief officers. William Edmundson coming in,
wrapped in the old blanket, the governor asked him where
he lived, and what was his name; to which replying that
he was old William Edmundson, the governor stood up,
and with tears in his eyes said he was sorry to see him
in that condition, for he knew him well, having been sometimes at his house; and the lieutenant who brought them
there accusing them of things which he could not prove,
the governor placed William and his fellow-prisoners in
charge of another officer, and sent them some refreshment.
But having nothing to lie upon but the bare floor, without
even straw to cover it with, and the weather being very
severe, and they very destitute of clothing, William would
probably have fallen a sacrifice to the hardships he endured, but for the succor providentially afforded by that
Divine Hand who never yet forgot the wrestling seed of
Jacob in their time of need.

A Friend named John Clibborn, residing about six
miles from the town, who had himself been so sorely plundered that he had but little clothing left, hearing of William's confinement, was moved to visit him. When he saw
this venerable man in that distressed condition, he wrung
his hands with sympathetic emotion, crying out that they
had taken prisoner as honest a man as trod on the earth.

The next day he brought them some food; but still they could get no straw to lie upon; and William was much spent, and so grieved with the profanity of this wicked crew, that he desired rather to die quietly in a dungeon, than to continue among them. John Clibborn wrote to the governor to desire that he would either bring William to a fair trial, or suffer him to be removed into the dungeon. The governor, however, still expressed his sorrow, that so honest a man as he believed him to be, should be so oppressed; but he dared not release him, for there were many eyes over him, and yet he could not find in his heart to commit him to the dungeon. But John Clibborn persevering in his efforts for the relief of his friend, offered to be answerable by all that he possessed, for William's appearance, if he might be allowed to take him with him to his house; to which at length the governor assenting, the prisoners gladly changed their quarters for the house of their friend.

In the beginning of the Twelfth, or as it was then called the Tenth month, William Edmundson's wife ventured to the ruins of their late abode, with a number of horses, and some English neighbors, in order to bring off a stock of hides and leather from the tan-yard, which had escaped destruction when the house was burnt. Whilst they were loading the leather, they were attacked by a party of Raparees, who carried off the property and compelled them to run for their lives. But William's wife being ancient, and not able to escape, they overtook her, and stripping her entirely of clothing, left her in that cold time of the year under the necessity of going two miles naked; from which exposure she was taken ill, and never recovering her health, died in a few months afterwards. These Raparees threatened to burn the town of Mount Melick, but the next day they were attacked by the English soldiers, their two leaders were killed, and their wicked project was frustrated.

During William Edmundson's stay at John Clibborn's, many of the Irish came daily to get what they could; and a Colonel Bourk also came with about three hundred men, to intercept the English. This man showed kindness to William, and soon going to Athlone, procured his discharge from the governor. But there were still those abroad who had evil designs against this upright man, and who scrupled not the most wicked means to put them in execution. Soon after his return to Mount Melick, he narrowly escaped an ambush, laid for the purpose of taking his life. Eight or nine Raparees secreted themselves about the road from that place to Rossenallis, near which place were the ruins of his former habitation, and procured some to endeavor to persuade him to go to Rossenallis, under various pretexts. He was however restrained by an unseen hand, from yielding to their importunities; and the next morning, three other persons passing by the place of ambush, were shot at, one of them being killed on the spot, and the others dragged into the woods and barbarously murdered. Thus the Lord preserved his servant out of the hands of cruel and bloodthirsty men. The Irish Papists, that night, generally joined the Raparees; as indeed it would appear that from the first they had been the instigators of the insurrection. The English troops however began now gradually to suppress them, and the roads became safer for travellers. William Edmundson went into the north with some other Friends, on a religious visit to their fellow-members in that section; and during his journey, he observed where the hostile armies had been engaged in the work of mutual destruction, that many bones appeared on the ground, and tufts of rank grass had grown from the carcasses of men, as if it had been from heaps of manure; so that he was led to remind Friends of what he had some years before publicly and prophetically declared, "that the Lord would spread the carcasses of men as dung upon the face of the earth;" which was now literally fulfilled.

The above-mentioned John Clibborn was one who, though at one time strongly prejudiced against the Society of Friends, had joined this despised people, from a settled conviction of duty, and became a serviceable member thereof. He was born in the county of Durham, England, in 1623, and when about twenty-six years of age, went into Ireland as a soldier in the army of Oliver Cromwell. Here he married, and settled at Moate-a-Grenoge. The people called Quakers established a meeting on part of his property. He was much displeased at this; and looking on them, in the pride and ignorance of his heart, with aversion and contempt, he determined to burn down their meeting-house, and thus to clear them from his premises. Accordingly, he provided himself with fire, and went thither at a time when he supposed there would be no one in the meeting-house: but to his surprise, he found the Friends assembled in solemn worship, and one of them, named Thomas Loe, was preaching. Being suddenly impressed with new and strange emotions, he put away the fire, went in, sat down behind the door, and was sensibly touched by the solemn covering over the assembly, and the power which accompanied the words spoken. On his return home, his wife asking him if he had burned the Quakers' meeting-house, he told her, "No;" and even proposed her accompanying him thither the next First-day. They both accordingly went, and Thomas Loe again preached. John Clibborn, and his wife, both received the truth of his doctrine into their hearts, and eventually became members of that Society which had been the object of such displeasure and dislike. This was about the year 1658. John, some time afterwards, attended a General Meeting in the above-mentioned meeting-house, and perceiving it inconveniently crowded, promised Friends that they should have a larger house the next time; and accordingly built a meeting-house at his own expense, which, with a burial-place adjoining, he bequeathed to Friends forever.

John Clibborn's situation in the time of the civil wars was peculiarly perilous; being, as we have seen, only a few miles from Athlone, where the Irish army had established one of their principal garrisons, whence they issued in parties to distress and plunder the country. John and his friends continued at great hazard, to keep up the religious meetings at his house; and here he remained for some time, affording succor and hospitable assistance to many in distress, and endued with the patience and courage of the Christian. But at length his own day of suffering arrived. His house was beset in the night by a party of violent men, who dragged him by the hair of his head from that home which had so often afforded an asylum to the distressed, but which was now devoted to plunder and the flames. His life was attempted three times, by those bloodthirsty men, who at length, desperate in their wickedness, laid his head on a block, and raising the hatchet, prepared to strike the fatal blow. He requested a little time. His request was granted. The pious man kneeled down, and in the words of the martyr Stephen, prayed that this sin might not be laid to their charge. With the prospect of a better world before him, he prayed not for his own life. Just then another party arrived, and inquiring, "Who have you got there?" were answered, "Clibborn."—"Clibborn!" re-echoed they, "a hair of his head shall not be touched!" He was then set at liberty, and having been stripped almost naked, he wrapped a blanket about him, and presenting himself before the commanding officer at Athlone, informed him of the treatment he had met with. The officer desired John to point out the men who had committed this outrage, "and they should be hanged before his hall-door." But this the benevolent sufferer refused to do; declaring that, owing them no ill-will, he desired not to do them the smallest injury; and that all he wanted was, that his neighbors and himself might be allowed to live unmolested.

Many other instances of unprovoked and patient suffering occurred during this calamitous period; but those which we have detailed, may be sufficient to show the fidelity with which Friends adhered to their principles, and the divine protection which rewarded their faithfulness.

CHAPTER XXXIII.

ACCOUNT OF THOMAS STORY'S CONVINCEMENT

IN the year 1691, Thomas Story, a native of Cumberland, joined the Society of Friends, from immediate conviction of the truth of their principles, and not from the outward ministry of any instruments. He had had the advantage of a liberal education, as his father had designed him for the practice of the law. Having an early inclination to solitude and religious thoughtfulness, he delighted in reading the Holy Scriptures, and spent many hours in their perusal. He was, however, in accordance with the usual routine of a genteel education in that day, set to learn fencing and music; by which he found his mind drawn away from serious considerations, and habits and associations contracted, which were unfavorable to religion.

He was next placed with a counsellor in the country, to commence his studies of law, preparatory to entering one of the inns of court; and being situated in a sober and religious family, of the most moderate sort of Presbyterians, he had again the advantage of solitude, and little exposure to company; so that he recovered in some degree his former seriousness. And though he indulged himself at times in some youthful airs, yet through divine grace he was preserved from gross evils, and his agreeable manners gained him respect with all the family.

He had been educated among the Episcopalians; but his mind being intent on investigating truth, he was enabled to perceive that some of their practices were relics of superstition, and in no way conducive to the advancement of pure religion. For when the family moved from the country into Carlisle, and he had frequent opportunity of attending the public worship, especially in the cathedral, the congregation turning their faces towards the east at the repetition of the apostles' creed, and at the mention of the word Jesus bowing and kneeling toward the altar-table, surmounted as it was with the letters I.H.S.* painted on the wall; these forms gave him uneasiness, as they appeared to him to be relics of Popery; and although he continued to go thither for a while, yet he could not comply with several of the ceremonies in use. Afterwards, being invited to the *christening* (as it was called) of a relation's child, his mind was renewedly offended at the ceremony of baptizing the infant with water, as he apprehended that we have neither precept nor example in Scripture for that practice, and saw the impropriety of placing any reliance thereon, as producing regeneration.

Being attentive to the reproofs of instruction felt in the secret of his soul, he experienced them to be a law condemning those thoughts, expressions, passions, and affections, which belong to the first nature, and are rooted in the carnal mind. The spiritual warfare was begun, which was to bring into captivity every thought to the obedience of Christ; and in which the spirit of judgment and of burning was to pass upon the lust of the flesh, the lust of the eye, and the pride of life. The elegant airs of a well-

---

* The initials of the words, "*Jesus Hominum Salvator*," Jesus, the Saviour of Men.

bred youth, his strength, activity, and comeliness of person; his mental endowments, and competent acquisition of literary knowledge; and even the glory, preferments, and friendships of the world, which were beginning to fawn upon him, were all to be given up, and thrown as it were," to the moles and to the bats," that the Lord alone might be exalted in his renewed and quickened soul. And as he followed on to know the Lord, he was favored from time to time with deeper and clearer manifestations of the purity of true religion. To his spiritual eye it was discovered, that the Son of God was not yet effectually revealed in him, nor "the old man" sufficiently crucified and slain by the power of the cross. This sense increased his inward inquiry after essential truth, and his attention to the monitor in his own breast for instruction; as he did not know of any in all the world to teach him, or that the Lord had any people then on earth, owned by His presence with them, as his flock and family.

After a season of deep humiliation, being strengthened to resign himself to the divine will, the Sun of righteousness arose in his soul with healing and restoring virtue; whereby the carnal mind, with all that belonged to it, self-love, pride, evil thoughts and desires, with the whole corruption of the first nature, were wounded and slain; and his mind became like that of a little child, serene and free from anxiety. A great alteration was perceived in him; but the cause was unknown to his friends. He put off his usual airs, his jovial conduct and address; laid aside his sword, which at that time it was the fashion to wear; burnt his musical instruments; and divesting himself of the superfluous part of his apparel, confined himself to what was decent, plain, and useful. He declined the public worship, though not with any design to join any other society; for he knew not but that these inward manifestations were peculiar to himself, and was not acquainted with any people with whom he could unite. At one time indeed, beginning to fear lest it might be his own fault, that he did not enjoy the Lord's presence among the people with whom he had been accustomed to worship, he determined once more to make the trial; and accordingly he went to one of the Episcopal meeting-houses in Carlisle, and endeavored to retire mentally, and feel after the divine presence. But he found himself so enveloped in darkness and distress, that it was only from regard to decency, that he could prevail with himself to remain till the worship was ended. He returned to his chamber in trouble, and went no more among them. Although, however, he now declined all merely outward worship, determining to follow the Lord whithersoever He might see good to lead him; yet he found his mind clothed with universal charity and benevolence to all mankind.

Continuing to seek after God in silence and solitude, he advanced in religious experience, and his peace and consolation increased. At a certain time, to his surprise, the people called Quakers were suddenly brought before his mind during his solitary meditations, in so impressive a manner, as to induce a secret inclination to inquire after them, their principles, and their manner of worship.

In the Fifth month of this year, 1691, an opportunity presented. Meeting with a member of this Society, he perceived, on inquiry, no material difference between their sentiments and his own; and being invited by the Friend to accompany him the next day to their meeting at Broughton, he willingly complied. The meeting was fully gathered when they arrived; and he sat down among the crowd of people, in inward retirement. Though one of their ministers began to speak, yet his attention was particularly turned to what passed in his own mind, desiring to understand whether the Most High owned them with his presence in their religious assemblies; and he soon received a convincing evidence of what he desired to know. For not long after he sat down among them, the same divine power with which he had of late been favored in his private meditations, overshadowed his mind with abundant consolation. And as he had been distressed with the prevailing formality of religious professors, who generally contented themselves in that kind of religion which was merely the effect of education or tradition; he now perceived on the other hand, and was convinced beyond a doubt, that the divine presence and holy influence of Truth attended the greater part of that meeting, and that under the shadow of the wing of divine power and love they sat with great delight. He was thus enabled to rejoice with them, in the view of reformation so far advanced in the earth: though not long before this, he had thought there was scarcely any true and living faith, or knowledge of God in the world.

From this time he continued to attend their meetings; and becoming more intimately acquainted with them, he felt the bonds of near unity with them strengthened, and was not ashamed openly to acknowledge himself a member of this despised Society, on the following occasion.

At the time of the assizes at Carlisle, an acquaintance applied to him, in regard to a suit he had to come on the next day, involving the greater part of his property; and Thomas being the only witness for the deeds of conveyance, whom he could at present procure, he desired him not to fail giving his attendance at the court early the next morning. Thomas, in answer to this request, said to the man, for whom he had a friendly regard, and saw that his case was a hard one: "I am concerned it should fall out so; but I will appear, if it please God, and testify what I know in the matter, and do what I can for you in that way; but I cannot swear." At this answer, the man, in a passion. replied with an oath: "What! you are not a

Quaker, sure?" As Thomas had hitherto neither received from others, nor assumed for himself this appellation, nor indeed as yet had seen whether he had so much unity with all their tenets as to justify him in adopting the name, he continued silent for a while, and attentive to the Spirit of Truth in his own mind, till clear in his understanding what reply to make; and then he said, "I must confess the truth—I am a Quaker."

This plain confession increased his own peace, but his acquaintance's perplexity and vexation, whose case appeared to himself thereby rendered desperate; so that in the height of his anger, he threatened to have Thomas fined and proceeded against with the utmost rigor, exclaiming, "What! must I lose my estate for your groundless notions and whims?" Thomas was not free from anxiety in consequence of this threat, under the prospect of probable fine and imprisonment; but after some time of silent meditation, he felt strength to resign himself to the divine disposal, and therein found his anxiety vanish, and his mind centre in serenity. The next morning, as he was going to the court-house to give his testimony, his acquaintance met him with a cheerful countenance, and in a very different disposition from the night before, and informed him that his adversary had yielded the cause, and they were agreed, to his satisfaction.

He continued diligently to attend the meetings of this people; where, in silent worship, his heart was frequently tendered and broken, and at times, likewise, under a powerful living ministry. Some years after he had joined Friends, he himself received a gift in the ministry; and he devoted much of the remainder of his life to travelling in the service of the gospel, on both sides of the Atlantic. Few of his contemporaries were more diligent, or more esteemed for their gospel labors; and the meetings which he visited were frequently attended by a numerous concourse of people of other professions.

He gave up his profession as an attorney, perceiving that the practice of the law, and being continually mixed up in the frequent suits and contests of worldly men, would disturb the peace and serenity of his mind, expose him to many temptations, and probably be the means of preventing his advancement in religious experience, and present an obstruction to the fulfilling of his religious duties.

CHAPTER XXXIV.

THE LABORS OF JOSEPH PIKE AND OTHERS IN IRELAND, FOR A REFORMATION FROM THE SPIRIT AND HABITS OF THE WORLD.

THE well known testimony of the Society of Friends to Christian simplicity, arose not from any desire for singularity or distinction from the rest of mankind; but was the necessary result of a clear view of the self-denial and redemption from the fashions and customs of a vain world, required of the followers of Christ. The most serious religious people, in the sixteenth and seventeenth centuries, had from conscientious motives discarded the frivolous ornaments of attire which were very generally indulged in, and had adopted a plain, simple and useful style of dress. From among these, the Society of Friends in the beginning was chiefly gathered; and for a considerable time, it would appear that they were not greatly distinguished from them by their apparel. But their principles restrained them from following the changeable fashions of the world; and as others varied from time to time, their own continued adherence to the simple mode of dress into which they had been led, produced, in process of time, a marked distinction between Friends and the rest of the community. Thus this Christian testimony arose into a more prominent point of view than, from the above circumstances, it had held when the members were recently gathered; though George Fox had at an early date declared against indulging in gay attire, and encouraged his friends to faithfulness in this respect.

This testimony to Christian simplicity was not confined to personal attire alone, but extended to the furniture of houses, and the general life and conversation; and for many years after the rise of the Society, a remarkable consistency of conduct was apparent among the members generally. Isaac Penington once challenged the production of a single instance among Friends, of one who was taken captive by the spirit of the world, and thereby led under the power of covetousness. But alas! this beautiful example of a whole society of people bearing with one accord in their bodies the marks of the dying of the Lord Jesus, of a crucifixion to the world and a deaf ear to its false allurements, gradually became clouded over. Temporal prosperity was the portion of many Friends, whose children, growing up in ease and affluence, began to despise the cross which their parents had faithfully borne. Little by little, things crept in among families, which the pure word of truth could not sanction; there was an eager pursuit of business, bringing great encumbrance upon the minds of some who might otherwise have been eminently serviceable in the church; and a luxurious tasty spirit got afloat, which craved to have household furniture, and even personal clothing, more delicate and showy than what pure Christian simplicity would have led into. Some faithful men and women in various places saw the inroads which the enemy was thus silently making in a camp, which had nobly withstood all the powers of persecution, and had held up, through evil report, a banner for the truth of God.

In Ireland particularly about the year 1692 was a standard raised against these inroads, and some advances were made towards a reformation. That eminent instrument for the gathering and preservation of the Society in this island, William Edmundson, with Joseph Pike and Samuel Randall, felt deeply concerned for the revival of ancient simplicity, and began to arouse their brethren to the necessity of a united effort for this very desirable object. They had, however, great difficulties to encounter. Many had gone out into extravagant furniture and apparel, to gratify the natural mind in things which the Divine Spirit in the beginning had led Friends to put away. Some from wearing dresses of plain colors, had got lighter ones; and others seeing these, had themselves gone a degree further, adding a small or a larger figure; until at length such vain fashionable colors and patterns were indulged in, and so excessively fine and superfluous furniture, that many could scarcely be recognized as belonging to the Society.

At length the attention of the Half-yearly Meeting in Dublin was called to the subject; and under a pressure of spirit it issued advice to the members, counselling them against these hurtful things, and exhorting to a faithful uniting together for solemn waiting in spirit on the Lord; to the right education of the children in godliness, industry, humility, and self-denial; and to a solid grave deportment, on all occasions, becoming the Christian. It was also recommended, that every Quarterly Meeting appoint *clean-handed and faithful Friends*, who had a true concern for a reformation, to inspect and visit every particular meeting, family, and person; and to advise, exhort, and admonish Friends to a compliance with the advices, as they found occasion.

Joseph Pike had returned to Cork from England, under a strong apprehension of duty to join hand and heart in the work of reformation. Being a young man, he had felt much diffidence of his own fitness for undertaking such a work; it was very trying to him to have to appear as one of the foremost; and he often said in his heart, "Oh, that I could shelter myself under some worthy elders! then would I heartily assist them in spirit, and, as under their wing, do what little I could." But being appointed by his meeting with other Friends, to this weighty and arduous work, he heartily joined his brethren in first searching their own houses, and clearing themselves from marks of superfluity or luxury; so that they might with clean hands go to exhort their fellow-members to greater simplicity, and accordance with their holy profession. In doing this, they had to part with many things which the world esteemed lawful, but which they believed were standing in the way of entire conformity to the will of Him, who seeketh a people crucified to the spirit of the world and the gratifications of the carnal mind. Not that they placed religion barely in outward conformity and plainness. Far otherwise—they were well aware that though we may outwardly conform in everything to which the Holy Scriptures direct us, or that may have been practised or advised by the worthy men who were instrumental in raising up this people in the beginning; yet if our hearts are not right in the sight of God; and we do not witness a grafting into the true Vine, and a growth in the holy Truth, all the external conformity and plainness in the world, though good in itself, will avail us nothing as to divine acceptance, but be as sounding brass and a tinkling cymbal. Yet they were equally convinced that true religion leads into a deep searching of heart and of the secret springs of action, and allows not of the fostering of those natural propensities which have a life in show and parade, in delicacy and superfluity; but leads us to deny ourselves, and by a holy and circumspect walking, to redeem the time, and to testify our heartfelt conviction, that "we have here no continuing city," no permanent abiding-place, but that "we seek one to come," as the chief and all-absorbing good. And though some might frivolously argue, "Where is the *standard* of plainness and simplicity; and what is the *exact rule* by which we are to square ourselves; or who are the proper judges of what is our duty in these respects, but ourselves?" these would nevertheless find, if they were really willing to obey, without reserve, the inspeaking Word in the deep recesses of the heart, that the Spirit of Truth is sufficient to guide in these as in all other things, and that it will so guide those who sincerely desire to be made conformable to Christ's death, into a holy consistency, and a certain degree of uniformity, by which they shall be known to be one another's brethren in that which changeth not; and will produce a tenderness and caution to be preserved from even edging or tending towards the side of a luxurious world, in copying after its vain and foolish fashions. They would see also that the church has authority, under its blessed Head, to claim the consistent walking of all its professed members, with their high and holy calling.

The committee thus appointed, after first searching their own houses, and clearing their hearts to each other in great freedom, proceeded in the work with a deep concern for the prosperity of truth, and the welfare of the members. They visited every family of Friends, and those who attended the meetings of Friends in the city of Cork, sitting down in quietness together with them; and as they found a concern to come upon their minds, giving them advice and counsel suitable to their respective states; particularly exhorting them to keep close to the witness for God, the gift and measure of His Holy Spirit in their souls, whereby they might come to experience a growth in His holy truth; and the inside being thus made clean, the outside would be clean also. The Lord owned them in their service, breaking in upon the spirits of those visited as well as the visitors, by his living and powerful presence, to the bowing of many hearts into tenderness; so that some would acknowledge their deficiencies, and in brokenness of heart desire to be found more faithful. No opposition appeared in any of the families visited, but a general condescension to put away superfluities; so that in a short time there was a pretty thorough reformation in that city, as to things that were contrary to truth and the rules of the Society.

After this, Joseph Pike and other Friends visited the province of Munster generally, more than once, and found a general disposition to accede to the concern and counsel of the committee. And similar visits were performed by committees in the other provinces, with the same blessed result.

CHAPTER XXXV.

THE APOSTASY OF GEORGE KEITH.

THE unsound and dangerous notion, that a man once under the powerful influence of the Grace of God cannot fall therefrom, received a signal contradiction in the melancholy instance of George Keith; whose history is an instructive warning to those who may have tasted largely "of the good word of life, and the powers of the world to come;" lest wandering from the place of watchfulness, and giving way to a spirit of self-exaltation, they become vainly puffed up by their supposed attainments, and fall into the snares ever laid for the feet of the unwary.

George Keith had been an eminent instrument in the

gathering of the people called Quakers from the barren mountains of empty profession, to the green pastures and still waters of pure and life-giving Christianity. He was a native of Scotland, and had received a liberal education in the university of Aberdeen; and having joined the Society of Friends, was called into the ministry, and suffered imprisonment for his testimony to the truth, so early as 1664. The next year, believing it required of him to enter the steeple-house at Aberdeen with a gospel message, he was there violently assaulted and beaten to the ground by the bell-ringer. Shortly after this, the bell-ringer going up the steeple to toll the bell, fell through a hole above four stories high, and was instantly killed by the fall, upon the very same spot of pavement where he had beaten down George Keith.

George was afterwards, for several years, involved with numbers of his Friends in confiscations and long imprisonments for the cause of a pure conscience; and also exerted himself, both in verbal disputations and on many occasions in print, in defence of the principles he had embraced. Indeed for nearly thirty years he fully participated in the concerns and sufferings of the Society, and was in unity with its most esteemed members. But alas! in a time of unwatchfulness, the enemy found an entrance into his heart; he became wavering in mind and impatient under sufferings; and was shaken from his steadfastness in the faith. That inward turning of the soul constantly towards the Lord with humble breathings for preservation, in which alone is true safety, gave way to self-sufficiency and empty speculations; and he began to indulge himself in curious, uncertain, and unprofitable questions, the fanciful notions of one Van Helmont, concerning the transmigration of souls, the resurrection, and other matters calculated to subvert the mind, and carry it away from the right object of its meditation and its love. But finding no room amongst his Friends for the propagation of these airy notions, he let in secret jealousy and contempt, which afterwards broke out in open opposition and contention; first with individuals, and then with the body at large.

Becoming meanwhile more and more impatient under the sufferings to which Friends were then subjected, he declared that as nothing but persecution was to be met with in England, he would seek an asylum in a land of liberty; and accordingly sailed for America. He had not yet placed himself in an attitude of open opposition to Friends, and still retained a place in their esteem; and on his arrival in Philadelphia he was chosen by Friends to superintend a school there, with a comfortable remuneration. But his restless spirit was not satisfied. He aimed at having pre-eminence in the church; and George Fox having died in the year 1690, symptoms began to appear in George Keith's conduct, which led to a conjecture that he was aiming to succeed that eminent servant of the Lord, at least in America, in that esteem and influence which he had so rightly and disinterestedly held in the minds of his Friends. He even came forward in several instances to vindicate with his pen before the world, the principles of the Society, particularly against Cotton Mather, and the New England Presbyterians. But many of his friends became increasingly uneasy with his restless aspiring spirit, and some were concerned in brotherly love and solicitude to communicate to him their apprehensions; and he, finding that he could not obtain that pre-eminence which he coveted, nor carry things in all cases as he pleased in .the church, at length allowed his secret disgust and disappointment to break out into open dissension. He began with objecting to the discipline which the Society in America had established; from this he went to captious remarks and bitter sarcasms on the general conduct of Friends, their manner of preaching, &c., and soon raised a contest with two of his fellow-members. He also undertook to deny the doctrine which he had before faithfully defended, that the universal love and grace of God in Christ Jesus is sufficient, if abode in, to procure salvation, without the outward knowledge of Christ's death and resurrection.

Friends in England were made acquainted with the discord which he was thus sowing in America; whereupon George Whitehead, Patrick Livingston and some others wrote an affectionate epistle to their brethren in Pennsylvania, earnestly pressing them to "keep the unity of the Spirit in the bond of peace," and warning them against disputations on subjects not tending to edification. But this was not sufficient to stop the efforts which George was making to obtain a party in his favor. Being baffled in his principal aim, of taking the lead in the Society, he let loose his malicious disposition without bounds, and vented his passionate resentment in illiberal reproaches, in violation even of decency and common sense. He railed against Thomas Lloyd, the deputy governor, from whom he had received many favors, calling him "an impudent man and pitiful governor," tauntingly asking him why he did not send him to jail, and otherwise endeavoring to draw him and other magistrates into some measure which he might represent as persecution for religion. But the men he had to deal with were of a different cast, being restrained by their religious principles from returning railing for railing; they bore his reproaches with patience, and exerted their endeavors in the spirit of meekness to recover and pacify him, and prevent an open breach; but without success. At length, after quarrelling with various individuals, and applying opprobrious epithets freely, as his passion dictated, he went a step further, and brought a reproachful charge against a reputable part of the body at large, accusing a meeting of ministers with coming together "to cloak heresies and deceit;" and declaring that there were more heresies and erroneous doctrines among the Quakers than among any profession of Protestants; in direct contradiction to what he had himself advanced, when opposing Cotton Mather, within a year from that time.

Hitherto Friends had treated with him in a private way in much meekness and patience; but it was now thought that this public reproach demanded public reparation; which George contemptuously refusing to make, the Monthly Meeting of Philadelphia proceeded to disown him. This they did by a testimony addressed to the several Monthly and Quarterly Meetings, containing a plain narration of his offensive conduct, and of the reasons of their procedure.

George having succeeded in drawing around him a number of discontented spirits like himself, now set up a separate meeting, which assumed the title of "Christian Quakers and Friends," and made nearly its whole business, the vilifying of those among whom they had formerly walked in harmony and fellowship. George had gained over to his party one William Bradford, the only printer at that time in Philadelphia, and by his means readily published his malicious invectives.

His old friends at Aberdeen were much distressed at hearing of his defection; and wrote to him and his wife a tender, expostulatory letter, beseeching them to return into the unity of the body. It was addressed to "our ancient Friends George and Elizabeth Keith;" whom they tenderly reminded how useful they (particularly George) had been in building up the Lord's church and people in Scotland; and after reminding George of his former labor in demonstrating the free unmerited love of God to all mankind, and referring him to two of his own treatises, they added, "How glad should our hearts have been to have found thee, George, going on, as moved thereunto, to improve thy talents, which the Lord hath liberally given thee, for further spreading the beauty, fame, excellency, and loveliness of this precious inward plant of renown; and so edifying, comforting, and strengthening the flock of Christ, as in pastures of love, that the beauty of the love of brethren in unity might flow as sweet ointment, to make the lamp of truth shine with lustre throughout the world,— as in due time we believe it shall."—"O George! bear with us in love, for we can say it is in tender breakings of heart we utter it, and in tender breathings for thee, that if that sweet, healing, meek, self-denying spirit of lowly Jesus had been kept and abode in, your breaches thereaway would have been handled after another manner; and such a sad occasion to amuse the world, sadden the hearts of God's children, and rejoice the enemies of Zion's peace and prosperity, had never been told in Gath, nor published in Askelon." Here they appeared to allude to some of his publications pretending to set forth his grievances, which it is probable he had sent to Aberdeen; and with other affectionate judicious counsel, they thus concluded: "So, our dear and ancient Friends, we earnestly desire you to receive in a right mind our innocent freedom and love: and in the cool of the day, go forth again with your brethren into the ancient green pastures of love, and to the healing springs of life; giving up to fire and sword that which is for it; so the *first* and the *last* works shall be precious together; then 'righteousness and peace shall kiss each other.' And we can say, appealing to the Lord our God, the searcher of hearts, our joy shall be great, to hear that the sweet, healing and uniting life hath or shall make up all those breaches in Israel's camp, by all of us submitting to it, and the true judgment thereof in His church. And in this sweet, ancient spring of our Father's love, wherein we have often been sweetly refreshed together, many years ago, shall we truly rejoice to hear from you, and also to see **your faces**, who remain your friends and well-wishers."

But neither did the tender entreaties of these his early fellow-laborers avail to stop his angry career. In the spring of 1694, he returned to England, in hopes apparently of gaining upon the good will of Friends there. But after a patient investigation of his case, which occupied nearly ten days, the Yearly Meeting of London came to the conclusion that the fault lay at George Keith's door; and charged him to retract his accusations, call in those malicious books of his by which the Society had been traduced, and sincerely use his best endeavors to terminate the separation. He rejected, however, this advice of the Yearly Meeting, and endeavored to rend the Society in England; but his rude and intemperate conduct frustrated his intentions, and he gained but few adherents. The next Yearly Meeting, seeing that he went on still in his disorderly course, confirmed the judgment of Friends of Philadelphia, by issuing themselves a testimony against him.

He was now totally separated from the Society, and set up in London a separate meeting at Turner's Hall, continuing to write against Friends; who, however, found an able advocate in Thomas Ellwood. George having for some time endeavored to court the favor of the Episcopal clergy, and raised their hopes of his bringing over to their communion, many of his late fellow-members, was after a time ordained a priest by the bishop of London, and received employment as a curate. His party in America dwindled away; and when, in 1701, he was sent over thither as a missionary, he met with little success, and was looked on with disdain. Returning in about a year to England, he received the benefice of Edberton in Sussex. But his restless spirit involved him in contention with his parishioners about the tithes: for displaying an unusually extortionate disposition, and extending his claim to the very utmost, even to the tenth of the eggs of a single fowl, and of the garden roots of the poorest inhabitant, he lost the affections of his hearers, who were quite disgusted with his meanness and avarice. He fell into general disrepute, and many of his neighbors were accustomed to say, they should be glad if the Quakers would take him back again, so that they might be rid of so turbulent a spirit.

There is ground to hope, that near his latter end, he had some hours of serious reflection, wherein he was sensible of the peaceful state he had once enjoyed in fellowship with Friends, and felt remorse for its loss; for, paying a visit to Hurst-pierpoint, and a conversation arising concerning the Quakers, he owned before several persons, "that since he had left them, he had lost one qualification they had amongst them, that in their religious meetings they could stop all thoughts which hindered their devotions, which he very much admired he could never attain to since." And near the close of his life, a Friend paid him a visit; which he appeared to receive kindly, amongst other remarks expressing himself to this effect: "I wish I had died when I was a Quaker, for then I am sure it would have been well with my soul." His decease is supposed to have occurred about the year 1714.

This case of George Keith is one of deep instruction. A neglect of inward watchfulness and daily self-denial had left his mind exposed to the darkening cloud of speculative error; and the pride of a deceived heart prevented his accepting in meekness the labors of love extended for his recovery. "Let him that thinketh he standeth, take heed lest he fall." But the downfall of individuals is not the downfall of the church. This is founded on a rock, and the Lord can still "send the rod of his strength out of Zion, and rule in the midst of his enemies." Let therefore, the humble, careful traveller be encouraged to look to the great Head of the church, and endeavor to stand faitnful to His cause, watching over his own heart, lest at any time the cares of this world, and the deceitfulness of riches, and the lusts of other things, entering in, choke the word, and it become unfruitful;"—"looking diligently, lest any man fail of the grace of God; lest any root of bitterness springing up, trouble" the church, "and thereby many be defiled."

CHAPTER XXXVI.

PETER GARDINER'S JOURNEY TO SCOTLAND, AND DEATH.

IN the year 1694, Peter Gardiner, a Friend who lived in Essex, England, had a religious concern to visit Scotland; but being low in circumstances, and having a wife and several children, was under discouragement about it. The Lord in mercy condescended to remove his doubts, by letting him know He would be with him; and though he had no horse to ride, and was but a weakly man, yet that He would give him strength to perform the journey, and sustain him so that he should not want for what was sufficient. Having faith in the Divine promise, he laid his concern before the Monthly Meeting to which he belonged, with innocent weight; and Friends concurring with him therein, he took his journey along the east side of the nation, through Norfolk, Lincolnshire, and Yorkshire; and coming to a meeting in Bridlington, where John Richardson then resided, he lodged at his house. In the evening, the doors being shut, Peter asked him "if any Friend lived that way," pointing with his finger. John told him he pointed towards the sea, which was not far distant. Peter said he believed he must go and see somebody that way in the morning. John asking him if he should go with him, he replied that he believed it would not be best, and so went to bed.

In the morning, when John's wife had prepared breakfast, their guest not appearing, he thought he would go to his chamber and see if the Friend were well; but to his surprise, he found that he was gone. Soon afterwards Peter came in; to whom John said, "Thou hast taken a morning walk; come to breakfast." Before they had done eating, a Friend from the harbor, which lay in the direction to which Peter Gardiner had pointed overnight, came in, and said, "I wonder at thee, John, to send this man with such a message to my house;" and related as follows, viz.: "That he came to him as he was standing at the fish-market-place, looking on the sea to observe the wind, and he asked him if he would walk into his house? To which Peter answered, that he came for that purpose. This was in the twilight of the morning. When he went into the house, Peter inquired whether his wife were well; to which the man answered, that she was sick in bed, and invited him to go in and see her. He said, he came so to do. Being conducted into the chamber, he sat down by the sick woman; and after a short time told her, that the resignation of her mind was accepted instead of the deed, and that she was excused from the journey which had been before her mind, and should die in peace with God and man. Then turning to her husband, he said, 'Thy wife had a concern to visit the churches beyond the sea; but thou would'st not give her leave; so she shall be taken from thee;' adding, 'Thy wife will be happy; but behold, the Lord's hand is against thee, and thou shalt be blasted in whatsoever thou doest, and reduced to want thy bread.'" The man seemed angry with John Richardson, who said to him, "Be still, and weigh the matter; for I knew not of the Friend's going to thy house, but thought he was in bed; and did not inform him about thee nor thy wife;" at which he went away.

Peter pursued his journey towards Scotland, John Richardson and another Friend going with him to Scarborough, on horseback, for he would not let them go on foot with him. He kept before them as fast as they chose to ride; and when they had gone about halfway, he gained on them, and John was filled with admiration, for he seemed to go with more lightness and ease than ever he had seen any man before. Riding fast to overtake him, he remarked, "thou dost travel very fast;" to which Peter replied, "My Master told me, before I left home, that He would give me hind's feet, and he hath performed his promise to me."

When they came in sight of Scarborough, Peter said, "Do take me to some Friend's house — *a Friend's indeed* — for I am greatly distressed." John replied, "I will take thee to the place where I lodge, and if thou art not easy there, I will go until we find a place, if it may be." And just as they entered the door, they heard some one go up stairs; and the woman of the house coming down, invited them to be seated. In a little while, Peter appeared very uneasy, and said to John, "I cannot stay in this house: here is light and darkness — good and bad." After the woman had got them some refreshment, she came and asked John, "Who hast thou brought here?"—"A man of God," he replied; whereupon they went away. Peter had a meeting at Scarborough the next day, and had good service. He also went to several Friends' houses, and frequently spoke his sense of the state of the families; but as they were about entering one house, he stopped and said to John, "My Master is not there — I will not go in;" so they turned away. When John was about leaving him to return home, Peter asked him "if the small-pox was in any town on his way?" John replied, "Why? Peter, what hast thou to do with that?" To which he answered, "I am satisfied I shall die of that distemper; and my Master told me to make speed in this visit, for I had but a short time to do it in." John Richardson was much affected; and wishing to facilitate Peter's journey, who, he saw, bore the appearance of a poor man, asked him how he was prepared in money; telling him it was expensive travelling in Scotland, Friends were thinly scattered, and the journey was long. Peter answered, "I have enough: my Master told me I should not want; and now a bit of bread or some water from a brook, refreshes me as much as a set meal at a table." John, however, insisting to see how much money he had, found it was but two half-crowns; and feeling an immediate impulse to tender him some money, he took from his pocket a number of small pieces. Peter modestly refused them, saying he doubted not his Master's provision; but John forced him to take it, telling him the Lord had put it into his heart; and so they parted.

In about two weeks afterwards, the man's wife at the sea-shore, before mentioned, died, as Peter had foretold. At that time, this man had three ships at sea; his oldest son was master of one, his second son was on board another; and in their voyages they were all wrecked or foundered, their cargoes chiefly lost, and his two sons and several of the hands were drowned. So that, from considerable affluence, he was soon after reduced so low as to be maintained by Friends. The woman at whose house Peter was so uneasy at Scarborough, had put her husband to bed in a state of intoxication; which John Richardson had not before known him to be guilty of.

Peter proceeded into Scotland, and paid a very acceptable visit among Friends of that nation. In the Eleventh month, he was at Aberdeen, Ury, Montrose, &c., where a remarkable out-pouring of the gift of the gospel ministry attended his labors. Robert Barclay, Jun'r, David, Christian, and Catharine Barclay, Robert Gerard, and Margaret Jaffray, among the young, and John Forbes and Jane Molleson, among the older members, had their mouths opened to declare of the Lord's goodness, and invite others to partake of it.

His visit to the neighborhood of Ury was remarkable. Robert Barclay, the Apologist, as we have seen, was deceased, but his widow still resided there, with her seven children. On the death of her eminently gifted husband, George Fox had addressed to his bereaved widow, an epistle of affectionate sympathy; in which, after setting forth the consolations which flow from a union and communion with the Lord, the Husband and Father of His people, he endeavored to encourage her to do her day's work, to put on strength in the divine name, and to hope for a blessing on her faithful discharge of duty, as a spiritual nursing-mother over her household. And further, he subjoined his fervent prayer, that her children might be established upon the Rock, Christ Jesus, and thus be favored of the Most High, through the fervent exercise of their surviving parent. She was indeed a faithful mother, and lived to see some of the blessed fruit of her religious care. John Grattan, who passed several days under her roof about this time, relates that, "when her children were up in the morning, she sat down with them before breakfast, and in a religious manner waited upon the Lord — which pious care doubtless had its desired effect upon them; for as they grew in years, they also grew in the knowledge of the blessed Truth; and since that time," he adds, "some of them are become public preachers thereof." Thus cherished and watered, did Peter Gardiner find this group of young "olive plants," when he entered their abode. His visit is thus described by some who were present.

"When he came to Ury, he had a meeting there on

Fourth-day. From thence he went to Stonehaven on Fifth-day, being accompanied by most of them of Ury; and there he and Andrew Jaffray [who had accompanied him from Aberdeen] had a good opportunity among the people. Thence, we came that night to Springhall; [a house on the estate of Ury;] and had there a good meeting, only he said, he felt *the life stopped* in some there, who would not give up to the Lord's requirings. The same night, after supper, he had a blessed opportunity with Robert, David, and Patience Barclay, John Gellie, David Wallace, and Robert Gerard;—and Robert Barclay [aged 22 years] was opened in a few living words of exhortation to the young people then present, which reached and melted our hearts in a wonderful manner. He said, it was himself, who had occasioned the life to be stopped in the foregoing meeting, by not giving up to the Lord's requirings; and he concluded in a few living words of prayer.—Next day, we had a blessed meeting among the children; where Christian Barclay, the younger [aged 14 years], had her mouth opened in prayer, to the refreshment of us all. That same day, we had a more general meeting at Ury;—and on Seventh-day, we had another blessed meeting among the children; and the First-day of the week following, we had a good meeting, where there were more people than usual; and Robert Barclay bore a living testimony among them. Life so went along with him in it, that it reached the hearts of many of them, and astonished others. In that meeting was also his aunt Jane Molleson's mouth opened in a few words of testimony. That same night, we had a blessed meeting at Springhall; where David, [aged 12 years,] Catharine, [aged 16 years,] and Christian Barclay, Jun'r, bore, each of them, a testimony to the Truth. Yet, notwithstanding all this, our Friend Peter Gardiner could not obtain ease, but felt *the Life stopped* in one there, and at last named the person, and desired him *to clear himself*.

And so, John Chalmers, their teacher, [aged about 19 years, afterwards an acceptable minister in Dublin,] stood up, and said a few words by way of testimony. Then Peter ended the meeting in prayer, and came away easy. — Next morning, he had his farewell meeting at Ury: and so he, together with Robert and David Barclay, took his journey. But as we were parting at the end of the garden, Robert Barclay had some living words to those who accompanied us there.

"We came to Montrose that night, where, after we had rested a while, we had a little meeting. Next morning we had a meeting among ourselves. About the middle of the day, we had a meeting of all the Friends of the town; and some other people came in: both Peter and Robert Barclay preached on that occasion. We had also another meeting that night, where Peter fully relieved his mind. Robert and David Barclay both declared the Truth among them, also John Gellie had some words of prayer. The substance of the testimonies borne in the meeting, was much to this purpose:—That none should sit down in Zion at their ease, but that they should travail for the prosperity of the Truth *in themselves and others;* that none should love the world or the things of it too much, nor be covered with any other covering but the Spirit of Truth; and that a profession of the Truth would not do, *till persons came to the life, and possession of it.* Next morning, we had a blessed farewell meeting; and so parted from each other in much tenderness of heart. Peter Gardiner, David Wallace, and their companion went towards Edinburgh.

"After they were gone, Robert and David Barclay, John Gellie, and Robert Gerard, returned to Ury that night; and next day, we all had a blessed meeting among the children. The day following, we had a glorious meeting, where Patience Barclay, [aged 19 years,] was opened both in testimony and in prayer, to the refreshing of all our hearts.

"And so, the Lord God, as he hath begun a good work, will carry it on, *if we be but faithful to him*, over all that the enemy or his instruments can do to hinder it."

Peter Gardiner having proceeded on his journey through the other meetings of Friends in Scotland, arrived at Carlisle on his way homeward: whence, as it is supposed, he wrote an epistle to Friends of Aberdeen, in which he spoke of the success which had attended his labors also in the west of Scotland—where the Lord was pouring out of his Spirit in a glorious manner—and besought them "in the eternal love of God," not to "despise the day of small things, *in themselves or others.*"

Having faithfully accomplished his extraordinary mission, it now pleased his Divine Master to take him to his everlasting reward. In accordance with what he had expressed to John Richardson in the early part of his journey, he here fell sick of the small-pox, and "made a very sweet and heavenly end." John Bowstead, a Friend of Carlisle, coming into the room where he lay sick, asked him how it was with him; to which he replied, "Ah, John! I am sick in body, but the Lord reigns gloriously in Zion." He expressed a sense he had of an awful day to come upon the nation of Scotland: and after a time of silence, John Bowstead being moved to prayer, Peter after him prayed very powerfully,—"That the Lord would preserve his people together in unity, and would spare and overshadow them with the wing of His power, until the storm be passed over." And the power of the Almighty being felt over all, they that were in the room were melted and broken into tenderness; and some who had fallen from the Truth being present, were also tendered, and made to confess that the Lord was with him. As he lay quietly for a little time, there came into the room one that was not a Friend, but under convictions in his heart. Peter was so full of the small-pox that he could not see; but asked who that was, who came into the room. Being told by some one in mistake, that it was a Friend; "Ah!" said he, "it is no Friend; is it not *such a one?*" (which it was;) and called him near. He then spoke to the young man, saying, "Thou hast no peace in thy lying down, nor in thy uprising; therefore, I charge and warn thee in the name of the Lord my God, that thou speedily return, and draw near unto the Lord, whilst thou hast a day afforded thee; for now is the day of thy visitation. — I tell thee, thou wouldst be heir of *two kingdoms*, but wilt never obtain them *both*." He uttered many other weighty expressions to particular individuals; and dictating a last message to Friends of his own country and elsewhere, he declared, "I have sweet peace with Him, that is the Redeemer of Israel, and am now waiting for my Pilot to conduct me to my long home."

This Heavenly Pilot at length arrived, and his spirit was conducted to the haven of eternal rest and peace.

CHAPTER XXXVII.

SAMUEL BOWNAS COMES FORTH IN THE MINISTRY — ACCOUNT OF HIS EARLY LIFE. — FRIENDS' PEACEABLE TESTIMONY MAINTAINED DURING THE INDIAN WARS IN NEW ENGLAND.

ABOUT the year 1696, Samuel Bownas came forth as a minister of the gospel; who was afterwards an eminently serviceable instrument in confirming the churches, both in England and America. He was born in Westmoreland, about the year 1676, and received a religious education, his parents being upright and zealous Friends, who suffered much for their faithfulness to their Maker.

When a child, his mother often took opportunities of admonishing him to a holy life, and to the fear of God, as the only way of obtaining His favor and blessing: and occasionally she would relate to him some circumstances of his father's sufferings in times of persecution, who had been removed by death before his son Samuel was a month old. And when she took him to meetings, where she frequently had a testimony to bear in public to the Lord's power and goodness, he would particularly notice, even when very young, the tenderness and brokenheartedness that prevailed over those present, and would inquire of her, why they wept so much, and why she wept.

But when placed out as an apprentice, though with an honest sincere-hearted Friend, he grew up with very little consideration about religion, or any taste for it, addicting himself to the pleasures of the times. And when at meeting, for want of a proper engagement of mind, he often shamefully spent those precious opportunities of religious improvement in sleep; for preaching, of which there was much, he took slight account of. Thus passed two or three years of his apprenticeship, with very little inward sense of God or religion. He was indeed considered a witty and sensible young man; (for he took much liberty in conversation;) but often on his bed he ruminated on his way of life with sorrowful reflection, and yet he fell into the same course again and again. No one could charge him with any gross vice; but what he gave way to most, was jesting and foolish talking, and turns of wit to promote mirth, which the apostle tells us are not convenient; (Ephes. v. 4;) and Samuel often found it so after it was over, and that the end of that mirth was heaviness of heart. However, the Lord, who is plenteous in mercy, even to the rebellious, gave him a remarkable visitation, which doubtless he remembered with gratitude through life, as it appears to have been the means of awakening him to a sense of his condition, and impressing him with a deep conviction of the necessity of a change of heart and life. Being one First-day at meeting, Anne Wilson, a young woman, was present and preached. She was very zealous, and Samuel looking upon her, she with great energy pointed her finger at him, uttering these words with much power: "A *traditional* Quaker, thou comest to meeting as thou wentest from it, and thou goest from it as thou camest to it, but art no better for thy coming;—what wilt thou do in the end?" This language came so home to his state at that time, that like Saul it might be said he was smitten as it were to the ground, being pricked to the very heart; and turning his mind inward, he cried in secret, "Lord, what shall I do to help it?" A voice spoke within him, "Look unto me, and I will help thee." Then he found such comfort to flow through him as made him shed tears abundantly. From that day he experienced the Scriptural assertion to be true, that *what is to be known of God* and true religion, *is manifested within:* for upon this eventful circumstance his conduct and even his countenance became much altered, his soul being bowed down under heavy exercise; so that he could for a time neither eat nor sleep as he used to do. Yet his work never succeeded better in his hands than it did at that time, nor was his mind ever less in it. He longed for the next meeting-day; and when the hour of meeting came, his mind was soon fixed and stayed upon the One great object of worship and dependence, and he felt therein an uncommon enjoyment and satisfaction.

Relying on the Lord for strength and salvation, who had begun thus wonderfully to reveal His power in him, his understanding became opened, and all his faculties so sensible, that he appeared to himself another man; a divine and spiritual sweetness abiding with him night and day for some time. The Scriptures also became wonderfully clear and plain to his view, and the truths of the Gospel, there spoken of, he readily understood and embraced. He came clearly to see wherein he had before failed of the grace of God, in relying on a mere education in the way of truth, and outward conformity therewith, being thus a mere "traditional Quaker," instead of coming, as he now did, into an earnest travail of soul that he might be made acquainted for himself with the way to true peace, through Christ revealed in his heart, and operating there as the sanctifier and enlightener, and the only way to the Father. And as he gave up his heart to the cleansing and purifying baptisms of the Holy Ghost, and abode in deep humility and watchfulness unto prayer, he became gradually prepared for service in the Lord's church, and in a short time received a gift in the ministry of the Gospel. Going one day to meeting as usual, he had not sat long therein before his spirit was impressed with a very solemn weight, and a few words were presented to his mind, accompanied with a sense of duty to give them utterance. But giving way to his own reasoning powers, which suggested to him that it was too early for him to undertake so awful a service, being but an infant in religion, he was not faithful to the divine call, and the burden of the word was taken from him. Now came a feeling of condemnation. He was made deeply sensible of his unfaithfulness, and of the loss he had sustained, and was much cast down in fear of being entirely given up of his Lord and Master. But mercy and forgiveness were still with Him, that He might be feared and obeyed. When the next meeting-day came, Samuel went in great weakness and fear, and sitting therein with his mind deeply exercised towards the Lord, after a time he felt the same concern as before. He sat under this feeling until the meeting was almost over, and then giving up to the renewed call, he rose upon his feet, and delivered the message wherewith he felt himself intrusted. The joy and sweetness with which he was now rewarded were inexpressible; and the next time that he was in like manner required to stand as a spectacle to the world, it was not quite so difficult for him to give up to the heavenly vision. For about three years however he did not speak frequently, nor much at a time; but after that his gift was enlarged; and through obedience he became an able minister of Christ, to the edification and comfort of the church and the convincement of many seeking minds.

The motives inducing him to undertake the office of a preacher of the Gospel, it will be well to remember, as they appear to have been perfectly consonant with the precepts and practice of Christ and his apostles: viz., 1st a clear, cogent, and convincing evidence of a Divine call, and heavenly impulse thereto—2d an indispensable sense of his duty necessarily obliging him to yield obedience to that call—and 3d the sweet returns of inward peace and divine consolation accompanying his obedience therein; which greatly conduced to his confirmation and perseverance in the way cast up for him.

To the performance of this he found himself measurably prepared and qualified; for his own experience of the love of God, and of the operations of His Holy Spirit, in gradually purging out the corruptions of his own heart, had excited in him a Christian love to his fellow-creatures, attended with an ardent zeal and desire for their conversion. His preaching was attended with divine authority and innocence, which commanded the attention of the hearers; and his voice being clear, strong, and distinct, was capable of conveying his exhortations, replete as they were with sound judgment and doctrine, to the ears and understandings of a very numerous auditory. He stood much upon his guard, as his gift enlarged, lest through self-love and conceit, he should depart from that humility, which is the ornament of every gospel minister.

The importance of a faithful adherence to the peaceable principles of true Christianity even in times of great apparent danger, was well exemplified by some circumstances which occurred about the year 1704 to Friends in New England. The Indian natives of the country, exasperated by repeated wrongs inflicted on them by the white settlers, had become very barbarous in the destruction of the English inhabitants, scalping many, and knocking out the brains of some; by which the country was kept in continual alarm. But, as Thomas Chalkley says, the great Lord of all was pleased wonderfully to preserve our Friends, especially those who kept faithful to their peaceable principles. But because Friends could not join with their neighbors in fighting, some of them were subjected to imprisonment; many people railing and speaking very bitterly against them, and wishing the Quakers might be cut off. Among, however, the many hundreds that were slain, the same Friend, who was then travelling in New England in the service of the gospel, remarks that he heard but of three Friends being killed, and that their destruction was very remarkable. One of these was a woman, and the other two were men. The men had been accustomed to go to their labor without any weapons, trusting to the protection of the Most High in a faithful maintenance of their testimony. But a spirit of distrust taking place in their minds, they took weapons of war to defend themselves; and the Indians who had often seen them without any, and had let them alone, saying that they were peaceable men, and would hurt nobody, and therefore they would not hurt them, now on the contrary seeing them have guns, and supposing their design was to kill the Indians, shot the men dead.

The woman had remained in her habitation when many were fleeing to fortified places. Neither could she, her son, nor her daughter, be easy to seek their preservation and that of their little ones by such means. But after some time, the poor woman in a time of unwatchfulness lost her trust in the Lord's all-powerful arm, and letting in a slavish fear, advised her children to go with her to a fort not far from their dwelling. Her daughter Mary Doe, was one who had confidence in that "Strong Tower to which the righteous flee and find safety," even the name of the Lord Jehovah; and her account of this sorrowful circumstance is very instructive.

"When," she says, "the cruel Indians were suffered to kill and destroy, it was showed me that I must stand in a testimony for Truth, and trust in the name of the Lord. I often desired my mother and husband to sit down, and wait upon the Lord, and He would show us what to do. But I could not prevail with him: he would say, it was too late now, and was in great haste to be gone. But I could not go with him, because I was afraid of offending the Lord. He would say, I was deluded by the devil; so that my mother would often say, 'A house divided could not stand;' and she could not tell what to do; for although she had most peace in staying, yet she had thoughts of moving, and said to me, 'Child, canst thou certainly say it is revealed to thee we should stay? If it be, I would willingly stay, if I was sure it was the mind of God.' But I being young, and afraid to speak of it so high, said, 'Mother, I can say, that when I think of staying, and trusting in the name of the Lord, I find great peace and comfort—more than I can utter—with a belief we shall be preserved; but when I think of going, oh, the trouble and heaviness I feel, with a fear some of us should fall by them!' My dear mother sighed, and said she could not tell what to do. But I said to them, 'if they would go, I should be willing to stay alone: if they found freedom, I was very willing; for I was afraid of offending the Lord.'

"But still my poor husband would say, 'I took a wrong

spirit for the right.—How should I know?—if I was right, I should be willing to condescend to him?' Then I said, 'in condescension to him I would move; but I hoped the Lord would not lay it to my charge; for, was it not to condescend to him, I would not move for the world.' After I had given away my strength, in a little time there came men from the garrison with their guns, saying, they came for us, and thought the Indians might be near. And then away we went; and my mother went in with my brother-in-law, although I persuaded her not to do it. But oh, the fear and trouble that I felt! and I told my husband, it seemed as if we were going into the mouth of the Indians.

"The next day was the First-day of the week: and our friend Lydia Norton, coming with my dear mother, in her testimony said, there was there that was very near to her life, that was very near death. Oh, then I was ready to think it would be I, because I believed we had done amiss in moving; and great trouble was I in, and told Lydia thereof. But she comforted me as much as she could, saying, she did not think it would be myself. My mother went again to the garrison; where she found herself not easy; but, as she often said, she felt herself in a beclouded condition, and more shut from divine counsel than she had ever been since she knew the Truth. And being uneasy, she went to move to a Friend's house in the neighborhood: and as she was moving, the bloody cruel Indians lay by the way, and killed her. Oh then, how did I lament moving! and promised, if the Lord would be pleased to spare my life, and husband and children, and carry us home again, I would never do so more. But oh, the fear, trouble, and darkness that fell upon me and many more at that time! Three or four of us kept our meeting, yet we sat under a poor beclouded condition till we returned home again; then did the Lord please to lift up the light of His love upon our poor souls Then I told my husband, although he had built a little house by the garrison, I could not move again. So he was willing to stay the winter; but told me he could not stay when summer came, for then the Indians would be about; and that if I could not go to the garrison, I might go to a Friend's house near it. I was willing to please him, if the Lord was willing; and then applied my heart to know the mind of Truth; but it was showed me, that if I moved again, I should lose the sense of Truth, and should never hold up my head again. Still he would say, it was a notion; till our dear friend Thomas Story came, and told him he did not see that I could have a greater revelation than I had; and satisfied my husband so well, that he never more asked me to go, but was well contented to stay all the wars. Then things were made more easy; and we saw abundance of the wonderful works and mighty power of the Lord, in preserving us, when the Indians were at our doors and windows, and at other times—and how my dear children stayed at home alone, when we went to meetings, the Lord putting courage into them, and preserving them, so that no hurt came upon them. If I had not feared the Lord, and felt the comforts of His Holy Spirit, I never could have stood so great a trial, when so many judged I was deluded; but the Lord was near, and gave me strength, courage, and faith to trust in Him; for I knew his name to be a *strong tower*, yea stronger than any in the world; for I have often fled there for safety. Oh blessing, and honor, and everlasting high praise be given to the Lord and to His dear Son, our Saviour and Mediator Christ Jesus; Amen!"

Though the Indians were at this time frequently shooting people as they rode along the highways, knocking them on the head in their beds, and barbarously murdering many; yet Friends travelled in the country in safety, and had large meetings, and the good presence of God was abundantly with them. The people generally rode armed to their places of worship; but Friends went to their meetings without either sword or gun, having their trust and confidence in God.

CHAPTER XXXVIII.

SHIPWRECK AND REMARKABLE PRESERVATION OF SUSANNA MORRIS. — EXAMPLES OF ZEAL AND SIMPLICITY IN IRELAND.

SUSANNA MORRIS, a minister of North America, about the year 1731, felt constrained in gospel love to pay a religious visit to Friends of Great Britain and Ireland. Having the unity of her friends, she embarked in a vessel in which Joseph Taylor, from Raby, in England, was returning home from a similar engagement in America. The occurrences which befell them on this voyage were memorable, tending to strengthen her faith in the superintending care of Him who had sent her forth in His name, and are thus mentioned by herself.

"Soon after I got out to sea, I dreamed that our ship would be lost, and there remained on my mind a solid weight, for fear it should be so. But at times, I thought it had been as some other dreams; and yet I thought it safe to dwell humble and low before the Lord. I again dreamed the same; and was weak as to being fixed in a belief of the truth of it, until the Lord was pleased to favor me with his goodness, and in one of our meetings to make it known to me, that we should surely suffer shipwreck. And then, for a season, I was in trouble; but oh! blessed forever be the name of our God; for I had soon a good answer returned into my bosom, of our preservation, and that if we would be faithful, we should have our lives for a prey. I hinted something of my mind to the captain, who seemed somewhat startled; and lest he should be too much discouraged, I had it given me to tell him, that I should see him safe on shore.

It was some time before it came to pass; and when I hinted a little of what was made known to me, to Joseph Taylor, I found that it seemed like idle tales to him. So I forbore to go further in the relation of it to him; yet I was preserved so as not to stagger in my mind, or disregard the manifestations made known to me, from Him that is true. And as I endeavored to dwell near Him who is faithful and true, my habitation was pleasant, until the sudden outcry was proclaimed, and nothing appeared but the destruction of our lives." The ship had struck upon a rock off the coast of Ireland, near Dungannon. "Then, for a time, my outward tabernacle greatly shook and trembled. But, blessed be the great Lord of all our mercies, the time of trembling was soon over, and what had been made known to me was renewed, that the all-wise God would command the proud waves, that they should not come at his servants to hurt them; as it was said, 'Touch not mine anointed, and do my prophets no harm.' And so it was, the Great God did preserve us, I believe, for his own name's sake. It was the time called Christmas-eve, and very cold; and we had for two days, little sustenance for our bodies; and many times our heads were under the great waves, which rolled over us after she sunk, by reason of the strokes she got on the dreadful rocks. Afterwards she drove, until she settled on a sand bank. In that distress I had no help of man, or counsellor but the Lord alone; and thought it best for me to get to the upper side of the vessel, and fix my seat by the shrouds, where I was favored so that I kept my hold, when the waves rolled over us: and we remained in that wet condition about nine hours, in a cold time of frost and snow, before any of us got relief. And yet I was not hurt—the Lord is pleased to favor his heritage—though many of the ship's company lost their lives, some perishing with the cold, and others being drowned."

John Griffith, who speaks of Susanna Morris as "a truly

evangelical minister of Jesus Christ," mentions the following additional particulars of this event, narrated to him by Joseph Taylor. "The ship was driven on her broadside, yet did not soon break; but the sea, running high, broke over her, and several of the crew were washed overboard, and drowned. The captain, Susanna Morris, Joseph Taylor, and perhaps one more, scrambled up to the upper side of the ship, and held fast to the shrouds, the sea frequently breaking over them. Susanna never discovered the least impatience, in word or countenance, all the time; but Joseph Taylor confessed that he once, in a flutter or impatience, did say to this effect, 'We might as well have gone at first, for we *shall* be drowned.' She looked upon him and said nothing; but her looks were a sufficient rebuke for his impatience and distrust. After they had held a considerable time by the shrouds, this extraordinary woman had a sense given her, that they would not be safe on that side of the vessel much longer; and although it seemed very hazardous to move and fasten to the lower side of the ship, she urged them all to attempt it, believing it would be the means of their preservation. She at length prevailed, and they moved, in the best manner they could, to the lower side of the ship; and soon after they had fixed themselves, there came a great swell of the sea, and threw the vessel flat on the other side; so that if they had not moved, they would all have been drowned. A priest on shore being informed there were some alive on board in great distress, came down to the beach and charged his people not to hurt them, but use all means to save their lives; which if they refused to comply with, they should never have their sins forgiven. And through the assistance of a merciful Providence, they brought them safe to land, and treated them with great hospitality." "And now," says S. Morris, in concluding her account of this wonderful preservation, "I write not this relation because

I would have any one think the better of me; no, that is not what I aim at; but that the poor in spirit, or weak in their own eyes, (if willing to serve the Lord,) may take a little courage, to trust in the Lord, and be truly willing to serve him in all that He may require of them."

Great was the zeal and exemplary the simplicity of many members of the Society of Friends in Ireland in the early part of the eighteenth century. James Gough, a minister who went thither about the year 1737, has testified to their holy and circumspect walking, in terms so animating that we shall do well to ponder the example thus beautifully set before us.

"'God hath said, I will dwell in them, and walk in them; and I will be their God, and they shall be my people. *Wherefore come out from among them, and be ye separate, saith the Lord*, and touch not the unclean thing; and I will receive you, and will be a father unto you, and ye shall be my sons and daughters, saith the Lord Almighty.' 2 Cor. vi. 16, &c. By this call were our honorable predecessors in the beginning *separated* from the spirit and ways of the world, and incited to refuse touching the unclean thing, or whatever sprang from an unclean source, what persecution soever that refusal might cost them; knowing that He whom they obeyed and in whom they trusted, would carry them through all opposition. This they experienced, to their unspeakable joy, to be fulfilled, and testified to the world, many of them, both living and dying. In those days the meetings of Friends were more eminently favored with divine power, as they lived more devoted to Christ, and consequently more abounding with His love flowing in their hearts.

"I remember when a child,[*] some whose very countenances seemed to command awe, and impress observers with

[*] James Gough was born in the year 1712.

serious consideration; *as the salt of the earth*, seasoning those amongst whom they walked, with a sense of the Truth which lived and predominated in them. Those happy men and women left the Lord's vineyard (through their faithful labors with the Divine blessing upon them) well fenced and clean, (having gathered out the stones thereof,) and abounding with the excellent fruits of the Holy Spirit of Christ.

"At my first going [to Ireland] there were yet living in most parts of the nation, where meetings were settled, some of the good old stock, both ministers and elders, who loved God and mankind, and were esteemed and beloved, being kind and open-hearted, as well as faithful and circumspect in all branches of our Christian testimony, closely united in tender love one with another in supporting and keeping things in good order in the church. Their pious care herein was like a fence about the flock, which kept them together in nearer unity and greater safety, so that the young people in most parts were generally trained up in innocence of manners, and in plainness of habit and speech."

In another place, he relates of a friend of Kilconimore, named John Ashton, that "he with his wife, when at liberty [from imprisonment for conscience' sake] constantly attended the meeting at Birr twice a week, generally walking on foot thither, being about seven English miles and a very bad road, wading through a river both going and returning. In winter they sometimes had the ice to break in crossing this river; and John had wept to see the blood on his wife's legs in coming through it. In those days truth was precious to its professors, who also possessed it; and no difficulties or dangers could prevent them from getting to their religious meetings, to enjoy the renewings of divine love and life with their brethren."

The same writer, as a lively illustration of that great truth, that "a man's life consisteth not in the abundance of the things which he possesseth," records the following simple but instructive instance of the mode of living, devotedness, and hospitality of some of the early Friends; showing that a man may live on little of this world's goods, if his mind be kept in humility, and his appetites subjected to the cross of Christ. "John Goodwin, of Escargogh in Monmouthshire, lived and maintained his family on a farm of four pounds a year; but at length had purchased and improved it, so that he reckoned it worth six pounds a year. The first journey he travelled in the ministry, which was to visit Friends through Wales, he had then got of clear money about forty shillings in all; and he was free to spend it, if there were occasion, in the Lord's service, knowing that He could give him, or enable him to get more. The first time he began to entertain travelling Friends, (most of that meeting being gone to Pennsylvania,) he had but one bed, which he left to them, he and his wife taking up their lodging in the stable."

CHAPTER XXXIX.

THE TRIALS TO WHICH FRIENDS WERE SUBJECTED DURING THE AMERICAN REVOLUTIONARY WAR.

THE breaking out of hostilities between the British American colonies and the mother country, about the year 1775, which resulted in the acknowledged independence of the United States of America, was a signal to the Society of Friends, to flee to the strong-hold of faith for safety during the storm. Many experienced brethren foresaw that in this time of contention, those who stood firm to their peaceable principles, and imitated the example of the ancient Christians in resolutely refusing to unite in war, would be subjected to great trials: and they earnestly endeavored to strengthen and confirm their fellow-members in bearing a noble and unflinching testimony to the peaceful nature of Christianity, even when property, liberty, and life itself were at stake. Some superficial individuals, nevertheless, in various places, were caught by the prevailing martial spirit, or induced by fear to relinquish their faith, and to trust in the arm of flesh; but generally the Society stood firm through all that was permitted to assail it. Many of its members were exceedingly persecuted by one party or the other; but it may be truly said that the Lord of hosts encamped round about his poor afflicted people in their time of deep distress; and even during the greatest commotion, a remnant felt the sweetness of His love, and the calming influence of that voice which said to the waves formerly, "Peace! be still!"

Even the outward circumstances of many who stood faithful appeared to be eminently preserved from serious harm; whilst a different result attended some who lost their confidence in the God of Truth. One instance in New York was remarkable. A family descended from the worthy Isaac Penington resided in the city of New York; and while many of their fellow-members and neighbors were thinking of removing to Long Island and other places around, the female head of this family could feel no peace in contemplating such a step. Accordingly they with some others remained in the city when the British troops took possession of it; and while those who had retired found themselves more perplexed than before by the scouting parties of the troops, which lay all around the neighborhoods to which they had retreated, these families who remained, were preserved from injury. A great part of the city was on one occasion consumed by fire, which surrounded the dwelling of the family above mentioned; yet their house was preserved unhurt by the flames.

The next year, as the conflict became more close and doubtful, the enmity increased against Friends, who could not conscientiously take up arms in any cause; and many of whom felt restrained from using the paper money put in circulation in order to carry on the war. Heavy penalties were ordered for refusing this money. On the first night of the year 1777, Thomas Watson, of Buckingham, Pennsylvania, was taken from his home and family by a number of armed men, who conveyed him to Newtown, and detained him forty-eight hours in heavy irons, and three nights without a bed to rest upon. Mark Miller and Thomas Redman, of New Jersey, were imprisoned soon afterwards for reading in their respective meetings an epistle issued by the Meeting for Sufferings of Philadelphia, in which the members of the Society were exhorted to stand fast to their ancient faith, and not to let the fear of suffering prevail with them to unite in any warlike operations. These Friends were confined eight weeks in Gloucester jail; and several others were imprisoned the same year on a similar account.

On the second day of the Ninth month, John Pemberton, a minister among Friends, and clerk of the Meeting for Sufferings, which had, as above mentioned, thought it their duty to exhort their fellow-members to faithfulness to their principles, was arrested in his house by three officers with a guard of ten men, his desk broken open and rifled of the papers of the Meeting for Sufferings, and other documents, and himself dragged through the streets to the Masons' Lodge. His brothers, Israel and James Pemberton, John Hunt, also a minister, Henry Drinker, Samuel Pleasants, Edward Penington, and sixteen other Friends, were also arrested, and confined without any examination, notwithstanding their demand of a hearing from the Council and Congress, under whose authority their liberty was taken from them. A few days after their arrest, an order of Council appeared, for the banishment of these Friends into Virginia, and they were desired to prepare for their removal. On the ninth of the month they were conveyed from the city in wagons towards Reading; and although they had obtained writs of *habeas corpus* from the chief justice, the assembly overruled them, and these innocent men were conveyed over the Susquehanna, and through Maryland to Winchester in Virginia, where they arrived in about three weeks. Here they were often treated with great harshness, and at times were much cast down; but possessing their souls in patience, and relying on the help and preservation of their Divine Master, they frequently had to acknowledge the comforting virtue of His presence whose favor is better than life, were made sensible that "the power of the Highest is able to stay the wrath of man, and preserve his dependent people," and were at times enabled to bless and praise his holy name. They held their meetings for divine worship regularly in their prison, which was a private house, guarded by soldiery; and were often refreshed in sympathy with each other. For a time they were allowed to ride or walk to a short distance from their place of confinement; though afterwards this was rescinded, and they were kept closely confined, sometimes with guards stationed at the front and back doors of their quarters. During the time of comparative liberty, John Pemberton attended the neighboring Monthly Meeting of Hopewell, where a deep concern had been felt on account of the manner in which the lands in that part had come into possession of the white inhabitants, and a fear that the Indian natives who formerly owned them had not been fully remunerated for giving them up. A committee had been appointed on this important subject, which now proposed the raising of a fund to be applied for the benefit of the descendants of the natives formerly resident there, or any others where it might be truly useful. The meeting approved of the measure, thus affording a striking contrast with the unprincipled conduct which was prevalent in the community at large. Two months after this, he again attended Hopewell Monthly Meeting, in company with his fellow-sufferer, John Hunt, who had to speak of the judgments of the Lord upon the country, mentioning that he had heard, with his inward ear, a voice proclaiming mourning, lamentation, and woe, unless the people repented and sought the Lord; and contrasting the balls, revelling, and dancing, now prevalent among the people, with that humiliation of heart which ought to be experienced. He mentioned also an apprehension that he should not have the like opportunity again among Friends there, though he wished to leave the event to Divine Providence. A short time after this, John Hunt was taken very ill. In one of the solemn interviews which John Pemberton had with him during his sickness, his spirit was much contrited and broken into tenderness, and he expressed a thankful sense of the continued regard of the Most High: but added that he "had a prospect that an exceedingly trying time would attend Friends as a people, more deeply exercising than they had ever experienced; and that our deepest sufferings would be from some of the same family; that many would make submission to this and the other: but that the poor and some weak ones would be established;" and he desired it might be noticed. He intimated that having in this time of great exercise made a narrow search, and desired the Lord to manifest if in any particular he had done wrong, he could not find anything laid to his charge; but felt sensible "there was need of becoming still more pure and holy, and inwardly refined throughout." Some days after this he seemed better; and expressed to Israel and John Pemberton, that he had thought much of some expressions of John Woolman's, in a time of great affliction, respecting true prayer: that it was deep, and the place thereof was a precious habitation; that it was not to be truly come at in the commotions of the mind, but in pure stillness; adding that he thought he could at times say, "Not my will, O Lord, but thine be done." About a month subsequently, after passing through much bodily suffering, and submitting to the amputation of his leg, he quietly departed this life, after a banishment of about six months from his house and near friends, being the second of the prisoners who had died during their captivity.

At length, on the 18th of Fourth month, 1778, an order came from Congress for their restoration to the Pennsylvania authorities; and returning from Virginia, they were at Pottsgrove discharged from custody, and reached their homes in safety. The arbitrary nature of this transaction will be at once perceived from the fact that these innocent men were subjected to a banishment and imprisonment of nearly eight months, without ever being permitted even the form of a trial, or being able to discover who were their accusers, or of what crime they were supposed to be guilty.

Many were the instances of hardship and oppression exercised against Friends during the whole time of the war. A Friend in Virginia suffered greatly for his testimony. Being drafted to stand guard over part of the army of General Burgoyne, prisoners in Virginia, he declined having anything to do with military proceedings. He was accordingly tried by a court-martial, and sentenced to be flogged with thirty-nine lashes. Forty stripes, however, were heavily laid on him in the presence of several hundred spectators, with a nine-corded whip; but the Friend, though much lacerated, was supported in faithfulness; and both threats and persuasions were afterwards tried in vain, to move him from his constancy. His faithfulness, under this severe suffering, was thought to have been instrumental in spreading the testimony of truth; the procedure gave great disgust; and one officer laid down his commission, declaring that if innocent, conscientious men were thus treated, he would serve in the army no longer.

In Carolina, about ten Friends were dragged along by soldiers when about to engage in battle, in order to force them to fight; and when the two hostile armies approached near each other, with their guns presented, ready for firing, these Friends still refusing to bear arms, were placed in front in order to receive the discharge. But Divine Providence preserved them in this extreme peril; for falling down flat upon their faces at the moment the firing commenced, the discharge passed over them; and though many were slain close by them, and the party who had brought them thither were entirely routed, yet they escaped unhurt.

About this time Moses Roberts and John Hughes were on the same account cruelly detained in confinement at Lancaster, Pennsylvania, more than eleven months, without form of trial.

The case of an officer of the American army is worthy of commemoration. A part of the forces lay near the Gunpowder Falls meeting-house; but Friends were not thereby deterred from holding their usual meetings for worship. Among these troops was a colonel of dragoons, whose resentment against Friends was raised to such a pitch of malice, that one day, when traversing the country, he came to the most extraordinary and cruel resolution, of putting to the sword the Friends who were then collected at their place of worship; considering them as no better than a company of traitors, merely because they steadfastly refused to take any part in war. Drawing up his men accordingly, near to the spot, he ordered them to halt, in order to make arrangements for the execution of his dreadful purpose. But at this moment, an awful silent pause took place, in which he felt his mind so powerfully smitten with conviction, that he not only drew off his men, but conceived very favorable sentiments of the Society; and continuing to yield to the convictions which were from time to time impressed on his mind, he after a while actually joined in communion with Friends, and continued faithful to the principles of Truth professed by them.

A remarkable incident occurred to David Sands, an esteemed minister among Friends, furnishing incontestable evidence of divine communication to the mind of this servant of Christ. A detachment of the American army, comprising about five hundred men, was stationed near his dwelling a few miles above the city of New York. A secret uneasiness pressed upon David's mind, and his wife felt a presentiment that some trial was approaching them. One night, after they had retired to bed, she was alarmed by a noise about the house, which her husband thought might be the rustling of the wind among the neighboring trees. In a few minutes, however, they heard some one near their room say, "Some of the family are awake — we will shoot them!" Their sleeping-room being on the first floor, David and his wife easily escaped by the window; but in passing through it they were discovered, and a pistol was discharged at them, the ball of which grazed David's forehead. Having on but a scanty supply of clothing, and the night being cold, they suffered severely before morning. After the day dawned, they returned to their dwelling, which they found plundered of all the cash, about fifty pounds, most of their bedding, and even some of the furniture. A domestic and two children, who were sleeping in a different part of the house, were not disturbed.

David soon felt that it would be right for him to go to the encampment. On his arrival, he found several officers conversing together, who thus accosted him: "Mr. Sands, we have heard of the depredation committed at your house, and desire to know what you think can be done, to discover the offenders." David, after a time of solid consideration, informed them that he believed, if the men were drawn up in rank and file of fifty in a company, he should be able, by following divine direction, to detect those concerned in the robbery. The officers wondered at this, thinking it impossible that with no outward knowledge of their persons, he should be able to point them out. Nevertheless, they ordered out the troops, and David commenced his review. As he passed down the first rank, he made a short pause near the bottom, and then went on to the next company. Here he soon paused before one of the men, and looking him in the face, said, "Where wast thou last night?" He replied, "Keeping guard, sir; and a very cold night it was." "Didst thou find it so when at my house?" asked David. At this, the man trembled so much, and discovered such evident marks of guilt, that he was immediately ordered out of the ranks, and placed under arrest. In like manner four others of the men were discovered. David then went to a young officer, and asked him how he came to aid and accompany his men to pillage his house? He denied the charge. David placed his hand on the officer's breast, saying, "Let me feel thy heart, and see if that do not accuse thee;" and finding the heart throbbing so that it could be felt even up to the neck, he called the other officers to draw near, and see for themselves how his own heart had become his accuser.

There had been eight concerned in the robbery, two of whom belonged to the company near the foot of which David first stopped, and should have been at that very spot; but they had deserted before the search commenced. The greater part of his furniture, and about one-half of the money, was returned; the rest was reported as lost. The offenders were brought to trial before a civil tribunal, where David not appearing against them, they were discharged; but the officers informed him that by martial law they had forfeited their lives. They were brought bound to his house, and he was told that he should determine their sentence. Upon this he administered suitable advice to them, forgave them the injury they had done to him, and perceiving them to be weary, ordered suitable refreshment. Whilst thus returning good for evil, David's wife said to one of the men, "Thou art he that shot at us." Her husband added, "he has been told of that before." The staff officers seemed to think that the young officer at least must suffer death, because he should have been an example to the men; but on David's earnest entreaty, they suffered him to desert. The men received some corporal punishment, to deter others from similar practices, and were then restored to the ranks.

Several years after this occurrence, David Sands being from home on a religious visit, a man came up to him, begging his pardon, and would have gone down on his knees if he had not been prevented. He confessed himself to have been one of the two above alluded to, who had deserted, to avoid detection. He declared he had never been easy in his mind since, and expressed a hope that David would forgive him. David Sands replied, that it was out of his power to forgive sins, but he hoped the Almighty would forgive him, as he himself had long since forgiven all those concerned in the robbery. The other individual of the two then came up. He also acknowledged that he had not had true peace since he committed the crime. He appeared to be a reformed character, had comfortably married, and had applied to be received as a member of the Society of Friends. He desired that David, in token of forgiveness, would go with him, and partake of the hospitalities of his house; which he did, and doubtless had much more satisfaction than if, pursuing him at law, he had avenged the injury received by prosecuting the offender.

CHAPTER XL.

RISE AND PROGRESS OF THE SOCIETY'S TESTIMONY AGAINST SLAVERY.

AT the time when the Society of Friends arose, great numbers of slaves were held in bondage in various parts of the world, particularly in the West Indies, Virginia, and the Carolinas. Some of their owners were among the early converts to our Society in those lands, and Friends who emigrated thither from England, inadvertently fell also into the custom, and purchased slaves.

But there were not wanting, even at that time, faithful men among them, whose souls yearned for the greater prevalence of the spirit of the gospel, in the intercourse between man and his fellow-man, and who, though their attention had not been drawn to this subject so closely as it has been in the present age, yet felt that the immutable principles of justice and equity were for the whole race of mankind, and that the divine injunction of the Saviour of men, "whatsoever ye would that men should do to you, do ye even so to them," was not limited by any varieties in the form of features or the color of the skin.

George Fox earnestly exhorted Friends that had slaves, to treat them with Christian care and humanity, and to prepare them for freedom. In addressing Friends in Barbadoes in 1671, he desired them "to endeavor to train them up in the fear of God, that all might come to the knowledge of the Lord; that so with Joshua, every master of a family might say, 'as for me and my house, we will serve the Lord.'" He desired also, "that they would cause their overseers to deal mildly and gently with their negroes, and not use cruelty towards them, as the manner of some hath been and is; and that after certain years of servitude they should make them free." And in a public discourse spoken to the people of that island, he used this remarkable language: "Let me tell you, it will doubtless be very acceptable to the Lord, if masters of families here would deal so with their servants, the negroes and blacks, as to let them go free after they have served faithfully a considerable term of years, be it thirty years, more or less; and when they go and are made free, let them not go away empty-handed."

William Edmundson, who visited Barbadoes in company with George Fox, united with him in his labors on behalf of the slaves. He also addressed an Epistle to Friends of Maryland, Virginia, and other parts of America, in which he reminded them that God made all men of one mould, and that our blessed Saviour shed his blood for all without distinction — that God is no respecter of persons, and Christ hath taken away the partition-wall of enmity between one people and another; and reviving the command of Christ, to do unto others as we would have them do unto us, he asks, "which of you all would have the blacks or others to make you their slaves, without hope of liberty? Would not this be an aggravation upon your minds, that would out-balance all other comforts? So make their conditions your own; for a good conscience void of offence, is of more worth than all the world, and Truth must regulate all wrongs."

From this time forward, many bore a faithful testimony against the sin of slaveholding. The attention of the Yearly Meeting of Pennsylvania and New Jersey, was, by a cogent appeal from Friends of Germantown, near Philadelphia, drawn to the subject in 1688; but this assembly at that time felt diffident of coming to a positive judgment in a matter which concerned the whole body of

Friends. The first official step of the Society on the subject appears to have been taken by that Yearly Meeting in 1696, when in its collective capacity it sent down advice to its members, "that Friends be careful not to encourage the bringing in of any more negroes; and that such as have negroes, be careful of them, bring them to meetings, and restrain them from loose and lewd living, as much as in them lies, and from rambling abroad on First-days or other times."

William Penn felt and mourned over the state of the slaves; but his attempts to improve their condition by legal enactments were defeated in the House of Assembly of Pennsylvania. In the year 1700, he laid before the Monthly Meeting of Philadelphia the deep concern of his mind, respecting these poor people and the Indian natives, desiring that Friends should carefully discharge a good conscience towards them in all things for their good; whereupon that meeting concluded to appoint a meeting for worship to be held monthly for the negroes, and advised their masters to endeavor to be present with them.

The advice of the Yearly Meeting of 1696 was repeated in 1711, at the instigation of Chester Quarterly Meeting, which then comprised the whole southern branch of the Yearly Meeting, as far as Hopewell, in Virginia; and the following year, the Yearly Meeting still feeling the subject to be of general interest to Friends in various parts, drew to it the attention of their brethren in England, requesting them, as they corresponded with the other Yearly Meetings, where the slaves were more numerous than in Pennsylvania, to express to them their sense and judgment on this important subject.

About the year 1717, the Yearly Meeting of Rhode Island had the subject brought before it by some Friends, who had felt much concern on account of the importation and keeping of slaves; but no decisive minute was then made.

In 1729, the faithful Friends of Chester queried of the Yearly Meeting of Pennsylvania, whether, as the members were restricted by former advices from *importing* slaves, it were not equally reasonable that they should be prohibited from *purchasing* them when imported; and the Yearly Meeting, uniting in this view, issued advice accordingly. This advice was repeated in 1735, and annually renewed afterwards, with one exception, till 1743; and frequent labor was from this time forward extended by the Monthly Meetings, to induce those members who were in the way of buying or selling slaves, to cease from the unchristian practice. In this year, a query as to the clearness of Friends from importing or buying negroes, was added to those heretofore annually answered by the Monthly Meetings.

The Yearly Meeting of London, in its printed epistle of 1758, "fervently warned all in profession with us, carefully to avoid being in any way concerned in reaping the unrighteous profits of that iniquitous practice of dealing in slaves, whereby one man selleth another as he does the beast that perisheth, without any better pretension to a property in him than that of superior force." This advice was adopted by the Rhode Island Yearly Meeting as a part of their discipline; and a query was also adopted the same year, whether Friends were clear of importing or buying slaves, and whether, when possessed of any by inheritance or otherwise, they used them well, and endeavored to train them up in the principles of religion.

While the Society as a body was thus clearing itself of importing, buying, or selling slaves, the concern was spreading among the members on account of slavery itself; and Friends in various parts felt more and more deeply its utter repugnance to the spirit of the gospel. Among the foremost of these were John Woolman and Anthony Benezet; the former of whom, in 1754, published his "Considerations on the Keeping of Negroes," which was widely and usefully circulated among Friends. And in the same year, the Yearly Meeting of Pennsylvania issued an excellent epistle on the subject, the substance of which was sent up from Philadelphia Monthly Meeting, and is believed to have been from the pen of Anthony Benezet. In this epistle, Friends are earnestly reasoned with, and entreated "in gospel love, seriously to weigh the cause of detaining them in bondage;" and in 1758, the Yearly Meeting again earnestly pressed upon Friends who had any slaves, "to set them at liberty, making a Christian provision for them, according to their ages, &c.;" and appointed a committee, consisting of John Woolman and others, to visit all such Friends as held slaves, and endeavor to persuade them to set them free. Slaveholders were now also declared incapable of being employed in the service of the Society.

For several years the subordinate meetings were exhorted to labor in Christian love and meekness with those who still continued this practice; and from 1767, regular statements of this labor, and of the success which attended it, were forwarded to the Yearly Meeting. It does not appear that many were disowned for purchasing or selling slaves. The earnestness of the labor, coupled with forbearance, had the happier effect of inducing the greater number to abstain from doing either; and by the year 1774, this Yearly Meeting may be said to have cleared its members from dealing in slaves. A further step was taken this year, by the Yearly Meeting, directing that the cases of such as still persisted, notwithstanding the labor of their Friends, to retain their fellow-men in bondage, should be brought up the next year for further consideration and adjudication by the body. The practice of hiring slaves, on wages to be paid to their masters, was also declared against, as promoting the unrighteous system.

The Yearly Meeting of 1776 repeated the injunctions of

former years, to earnest and continued labor with the offenders on this subject; and declared its sense that those who could not be induced to desist from the practice of holding slaves should, after such patient, persevering, and ineffectual labor, be testified against as no longer members of the Society. The subordinate meetings, on receipt of the minute, appointed committees to carry out the views of the Yearly Meeting; but through the divine blessing which had rested on the endeavors of Friends, the principal portion of the labor had been already accomplished, and the greater part of the slaves held by the members of this Yearly Meeting had been set free. It does not appear that many were disowned on this account; and it is believed that by the year 1782, the Yearly Meeting had cleared its hands entirely of this unrighteous practice.

The Yearly Meeting of Rhode Island, in 1769, appointed a large committee to visit such Friends as were concerned in keeping slaves, and endeavor to dissuade them from the practice; and the next year, enjoined that all should be set at liberty that were of age, capacity, and ability suitable for freedom, and the rest should be well treated, educated, and encouraged in a religious and virtuous life. And in 1773, they further declared, "that Truth not only requires the young of capacity and ability, but likewise the aged and impotent, and all in a state of infancy and non-age among Friends, to be set free from a state of slavery, that we do no more claim property in the human race, as we do in the brutes that perish." Four years after this noble testimony, a committee was appointed to aid the meetings in laboring with individuals for effecting the discharge of all who were held in bondage; which reported the next year, that most of the slaves were manumitted in their presence, and encouragement was given to hope that the rest would all be set at liberty.

In 1782, this Yearly Meeting recorded, doubtless with a

feeling of thankfulness to the Author of all good: "We know not but all the members of this meeting are clear of that iniquitous practice of holding or dealing with mankind as slaves."

The Yearly Meeting of New York, previous to 1759, had manifested its disapprobation of the slave-trade; and in 1767 the question was sent up for its judgment from Purchase Quarterly Meeting, whether the holding of our fellow-men in slavery were any more consistent with the Christian spirit, than the buying or selling of them. But it does not appear what notice was taken of this question. Four years after this, however, a communication from Philadelphia Yearly Meeting on the subject of keeping slaves was read, and copies sent to the Quarterly Meetings; and a committee was appointed "to visit them that have slaves, and see if there can a freedom be obtained for them that are suitable for it; and such as are not set free, suitably instructed and provided for." And in 1777, after laboring for several years with those who adhered to the practice, the Yearly Meeting directed that such as persisted in refusing to comply with the advice of their Friends, should be testified against. The answers to the queries from this time, state the care exercised by meetings in these respects, and few slaves appear now to have been left among Friends. A solitary one was reported in 1784 and 1785; and in 1787 it was recorded that no Friends of that Yearly Meeting were concerned in negroes, as slaves.

The first step taken in this concern by the Yearly Meeting of Virginia, was the adoption of a query, in 1757, designed to forbid the traffic in slaves, and to enjoin the religious care of those already in possession of their members. But their minds, like those of their brethren in other parts, were gradually enlightened to a full view of the inconsistency of slavery itself with the benign precepts of the gospel. The subject at various times engaged the attention of the body, until in 1773, the Yearly Meeting earnestly recommended all their members who had slaves to give them their liberty when of mature age, declaring that they believed "the time is come when every member of our religious Society who continues to support or countenance this crying evil, either by continuing their fellow-creatures in bondage, or hiring such who may be kept in that state, should be admonished and advised to discontinue such practices." The members were also tenderly reminded that a proper sense of their religious duty to these poor people would lead them "to advise and assist them on all occasions, particularly in promoting their instruction in the principles of the Christian religion, and the pious education of their children; also to advise them in their worldly concerns, as occasions offer,"—"it being the solid sense of this meeting, that we of the present generation are under strong obligations to express our love and concern for the offspring of those people, who, by their labors, have greatly contributed towards the cultivation of these colonies, under the afflictive disadvantage of enduring a hard bondage; and many amongst us are enjoying the benefit of their toil."

A deep concern prevailed in the Yearly Meetings of 1782 and 1783 on this subject; and in 1784, as some individuals still declined to comply with the advice of their Friends, the Monthly Meetings were directed to extend such further care and labor, as they apprehended would be useful; and where these endeavors proved ineffectual, were authorized to disown the offenders. Three years after this, as it appeared that some still continued unfaithful, the Monthly Meetings were again exhorted to enforce the discipline; and thus, by patient and continued exertion they cleared their hands of this stain on any Christian community.

We have thus seen the calm, cautious, and Christian-like manner in which this great subject was approached by the Society, and the success which crowned their persevering efforts to free every slave within their borders. But they did not stop here. As the Society dwelt under the religious exercise which had been brought over it by the participation of its members in this grievous sin, a concern spread for making reparation to the slaves themselves for their labor, and for promoting the religious welfare of them and their descendants. Committees were appointed, and funds provided to assist the free people of color with their advice, and to secure the education and religious instruction of their children. Religious meetings were frequently appointed for them, which were held to good satisfaction; religious visits were in some places paid to their families, and many instances occurred in which the negroes were remunerated in money for the services which they or their parents had rendered whilst in a state of slavery. By Rhode Island Yearly Meeting, committees were directed to be appointed in the Quarterly Meetings, to labor for an equitable settlement for their past services, and where any persisted in refusing to comply with the advice of the committees in this respect, they were to be dealt with as "disorderly walkers." Although disownment was thus authorized, the object was gained without resorting to it in any case; so that in 1787 the effecting of a satisfactory settlement for the past services of those who had been held in slavery in that Yearly Meeting, was happily brought to a close. Something similar to this took place within the Yearly Meeting of New York, and probably also in the other parts of the Society.

It was not till all these duties were performed, and this debt of justice had been paid, that the Society felt itself called upon to plead the cause of the slave before the world at large, and to remonstrate with the rulers and the people against the iniquity of the slave-trade and the wickedness of slaveholding; the first memorial to the general government having been presented by the Yearly Meeting of Pennsylvania, about two years after the extinction of slavery within its own limits. From that period the Society has continued to labor with diligence and perseverance in this righteous cause; endeavoring to enlighten the public mind respecting the enormities of the slave-trade and slavery; to prepare the way for the extinction of these foul blots upon the Christian name, and to ameliorate the condition of the free people of color.

CHAPTER XLI.

ACCOUNT OF JOHN WOOLMAN.

WE have seen that John Woolman was one of the most useful instruments in clearing the Society of Friends from any participation in holding their fellow-men in bondage.

He was born at Northampton, Burlington county, New Jersey, in the year 1720; and before he was seven years old, he was favored with an experience of the operations of Divine love, tendering his mind, and producing a love of retirement and religious thoughtfulness beyond most children of his years. When his school-fellows were engaged in play, he delighted more in sitting in some retired spot, and there perusing the Holy Scriptures, in reading which his mind was sweetly attracted to seek after the state of purity, which he was led to believe the Almighty designed his servants to be found in.

He was from early youth remarkable for his tender feelings and sympathy for the distressed, whether of his fellowmen or the irrational animals. During his childhood, going once to a neighbor's house, he saw a robin near the road, sitting on her nest and cherishing a brood of young ones. As he drew near, she fluttered about, and betrayed her anxiety for the safety of her little flock. But John, in his childish sport, and without much thought of the consequence, threw a stone at her, which struck the poor bird, and she fell down dead. He was almost immediately seized with horror, on contemplating the effects of his wanton act. He beheld the bird lying dead, and thought of the helpless little ones for which she had been so careful, and which must now perish for want of their parent to nourish them. After some painful feelings, he climbed the tree, and taking the young ones from the nest, destroyed them all, thinking that better than to leave them to pine away and miserably die of starvation. He was reminded of the Scripture truth, "The tender mercies of the wicked are cruel;" and for some time was greatly distressed, and could think of little else than the cruelties he had committed.

As he grew towards the seventeenth year of his age, his youthful nature indulged in a love of company, which became a snare to his better feelings, and made work for bitter repentance. He was led away into some gayeties, and though he did not commit things commonly reputed reproachful, and still retained a love for pious people, particularly for his religiously concerned parents, yet he yielded to the temptations of the enemy of his happiness, in many things which afterwards produced great remorse. About the age of eighteen, the judgments of the Almighty followed him very closely, and he was, in looking over his conduct, often made sad, and longed to be delivered from those vanities in which he had become entangled. At times however, his heart, being strongly inclined towards them, turned again to folly; then sorrow and confusion renewedly seized him, and he resolved to forsake these vanities. But there remained in his heart a secret reserve—his will was not fully subjected to the Divine will—and consequently his resolutions of reformation were not effectual. At length however, through the merciful continuance of heavenly visitations, he was made to bow down in spirit before the Lord; and looking seriously at the means by which he had been drawn away from the pure truth, he learned that if he would live in the life which the faithful servants of the Most High lived in, he must not henceforth go into company as he had done, in his own will; but all the inclinations of his natural mind must be governed by the manifestations of the Divine Spirit.

Keeping to these convictions, living under the cross of Christ, and simply following the openings of His Spirit from day to day, his mind became more enlightened; his heart was often contrited before the Lord; an unspeakable change was wrought in him from the unregenerate nature; and universal love to his fellow-creatures, attending the true love and fear of his Creator, became more and more the clothing of his spirit. He still found himself often encompassed with great weakness and liability to temptation; and therefore frequently withdrawing into private places, he besought the Lord with tears, to enable him to overcome temptation; and His gracious ear was open to his cry.

After a while, his former acquaintance ceased to expect him as one of their company, and he began to be known to some whose conversation was helpful to him. The tenderness of his spirit increased, and his mind became still more strongly engaged for the good of his fellow-creatures. He went to religious meetings in an awful frame of mind, and endeavored when there to obtain an inward acquaintance with the language of the true Shepherd. One day, under a strong exercise of spirit, he ventured to stand up in a meeting and express a few words; but not keeping to the divine opening, he said more than was required of him; and soon becoming sensible of his error, it was a source of great affliction to him for several weeks. He was however at length favored with a sense of forgiveness; and some time afterwards, again feeling called upon to say a few words, in the spring of Divine love, he was faithful to the requisition, kept to his Guide, and found peace. And being now humbled and disciplined under the cross, his understanding became more enlightened to distinguish the promptings of the pure Spirit in the heart, which sometimes taught him to wait in silence for many weeks together, until he felt that to arise, which prepares the creature "to stand like a trumpet," through which the Lord speaks to his flock. He was thus taught to watch the pure opening of the spring of Gospel ministry; and also to take heed, lest, while he was standing to speak, his own will should get uppermost, and cause him to utter words from worldly wisdom, without the right authority. He was then about twenty-two years of age.

In the management of his outward affairs, he found this inward monitor a true support and source of safety; and he felt renewed solicitude that he might in all things act from an inward principle of virtue, and pursue worldly business no further than Truth opened his way therein. His employer had a negro slave; and selling her, desired John to write a bill of sale. The thing was sudden, as the man who bought her was waiting; and though the thought of it felt uneasy to him, yet considering that he was hired, and that the purchaser was also a member of the Society of Friends, through weakness he gave way, and wrote the deed. But at the executing of it, he became so much distressed, that he told the parties, he believed slave-keeping was a practice inconsistent with the Christian religion. Some time after this, another Friend asked him to write a deed of conveyance of a slave. But he now attended to his scruples, and told the person, he was not easy to write it; for though many kept slaves, he still believed the practice was not right.

From this time, his views appear to have been very clear, respecting the entire inconsistency of slaveholding with the pure religion of Christ; and he was often led, under the constraining love of the Father of all, to plead with those of his fellow-members, and of other communities also, whose attention had not at that time been sufficiently directed to the subject, to enable them to see its iniquity. And laboring as he did in great tenderness, and under true religious concern, his efforts were blessed, and many were convinced of the sin of slavery, and set their captives free.

But his mind was not so fully engrossed with this important subject as to divert his attention from his other religious duties. He was a zealous advocate for true ancient simplicity. His mind, through the power of Truth, being much weaned from the desire of outward greatness, he learned to be content with real conveniences, that were not costly; so that a way of life free from much entanglement, appeared to him to be the best, though the income might be small. He had several offers of business that appeared profitable; but did not see his way clear to accept of them, believing the business proposed would be attended with more care and cumber than it was best for him to engage in. He saw that an humble man, with the Lord's blessing, might live on little; and that where the heart was set on greatness, success in business did not satisfy the craving; but that commonly with an increase of wealth, the desire for wealth increased. He was solicitous so to pass his time, that nothing might hinder him from the most steady attention to the voice of the true Shepherd.

He was often engaged from home as a minister of the

gospel, to the edification and comfort of the churches where he travelled; and was greatly concerned to exhort his fellow professors to a self-denying life, and an inward acquaintance with the Most High. The preservation of the members of the Society of Friends in this great feature of true Christianity, was a constant subject of his solicitude, and he took care that his own life and conversation should not prove a stumbling-block in this respect to the most tender seeker after truth.

In the year 1754, as we have seen, he published the first part of his "Considerations on the Keeping of Negroes; recommended to the professors of Christianity of every denomination." In this essay he commences by stating the great position, that religion is the ground of universal brotherhood, removing that spirit which would say, in a consciousness of superior advantages, "Stand by thyself, come not near me; for I am holier than thou." He proceeds to show that the love of the Father of all is universal, and that the heart influenced thereby, becomes enlarged towards all mankind—that in humbly applying to God for wisdom, our judgment may be enabled to discern the difference between right and wrong—that the golden rule "whatsoever ye would that men should do to you, do ye even so to them," is applicable to all men—that the purchase of a man who has never forfeited his right to liberty does not by any means deprive him of this natural right—and that if we cherish motives of self-interest at variance with the general welfare of the great brotherhood of mankind, we shall be unable to answer the Almighty, when He ariseth "to make inquisition for blood." The second part was published in 1762; in which he dilates on some arguments briefly noticed in the former essay, combats the inferences deduced by some from the instances of a kind of servitude existing among the Hebrews—gives some account of the horrors of the slave-trade—and shows that if we claim any right of possession in these people as the children of slaves, we build on the foundation laid by those who made slaves of their ancestors, and thus sanction this grievous and crying wickedness. He admits that there may be difficulties met with in emancipating the negroes; but inasmuch as we are greatly indebted to them for their unrequited services, we must patiently submit to some inconvenience, and while the evil-doer might be restrained or punished, we must not forget the right of the innocent to his liberty: and he thus beautifully draws towards a conclusion, with religion the end, as it was the beginning and foundation of his argument. "There is a principle, which is pure, placed in the human mind, which hath had different names—it is however pure and proceeds from God. It is deep and inward, confined to no forms of religion, nor excluded from any, where the heart stands in perfect sincerity. In whomsoever this takes root and grows, of what nation soever, they become brethren, in the best sense of the expression."—"Whoever attains to perfect goodness and remains under the melting influence of it, finds a path unknown to many, and sees the necessity to lean upon the arm of Divine strength, and dwell alone, or with a few in the right, committing their cause to Him who is a refuge for his people in all their troubles."— "Negroes are our fellow-creatures, and their present condition amongst us demands our serious consideration. We know not when those scales in which mountains are weighed may turn. The Parent of mankind is gracious— his care is over his smallest creatures—and a multitude of men escape not his notice."—"He seeth their affliction, and looketh upon the exaltation of the oppressor. He turns the channels of power, humbles the most haughty people, and gives deliverance to the oppressed, at such periods as are consistent with his infinite justice and goodness."

For several years he was much engaged, both as an individual, and as a member of various committees appointed by the church, in exhorting his fellow-members to clear their hands of this crying evil; and his labors were blessed with much success. In company with John Churchman he visited many slaveholders in Philadelphia and its neighborhood, in 1759; which service he describes as "a time of deep exercise, *looking often to the Lord for his assistance;* who, in unspeakable kindness, favored us with the influence of that spirit, which crucifies to the greatness and splendor of this world, and enabled us to go through some heavy labors, in which we found peace—and with thankfulness to our Heavenly Father, I may say that *Divine love,* and a *true sympathizing tenderness of heart,* prevailed at times in this service." In this acknowledgment we see the true temper of mind described, in which our efforts in promoting this righteous cause should ever be carried on; not with the heated zeal of man's natural will—thinking with Saul that we may be "doing God service"—but in the peaceable and gentle spirit of the Lamb, seeking the welfare and convincement of all, and stepping forward according to the pure pointings of the heavenly finger.

His manner of proceeding in these visits may be still further elucidated by the following description of an exercise which came over him in Rhode Island. "The Yearly Meeting," says he, "being now over, there remained on my mind a secret, though heavy exercise, in regard to some leading active members about Newport, being in the practice of slave-keeping. This I mentioned to two ancient Friends who came out of the country, and proposed to them, if way opened, to have some conversation with those Friends: and thereupon, one of those country Friends and myself consulted one of the most noted elders who had slaves; and he, in a respectful manner, encouraged me to proceed to clear myself of what lay upon me. I had had, near the beginning of the Yearly Meeting, a private conference with this elder and his wife, concerning theirs; so that the way seemed clear to me, to advise with him about the manner of proceeding. I told him, I was free to have a conference with them all together in a private house; or if he thought they would take it unkind to be asked to come together, and to be spoken with in the hearing of each other, I was free to spend some time among them, and visit them all in their own houses. He expressed his liking to the first proposal, not doubting their willingness to come together; and as I proposed a visit to ministers, elders, and overseers only, he named some others, who he desired might be present also. As a careful messenger was wanted to acquaint them in a proper manner, he offered to go to all their houses to open the matter to them; and did so. About the eighth hour next morning, we met in the meeting-house chamber—when, after a short time of retirement, I acquainted them with the steps I had taken in procuring that meeting, opened the concern I was under, and we proceeded to a free conference on the subject. My exercise was heavy, and *I was deeply bowed in spirit before the Lord;* who was pleased to favor with the seasoning virtue of Truth, which wrought a tenderness amongst us; and the subject was mutually handled in a calm and peaceable spirit. At length, feeling my mind released from the burden which I had been under, I took my leave of them in a good degree of satisfaction."

In 1763, under gospel solicitude for the welfare of the Indian natives of Pennsylvania, he paid a religious visit to the Indians residing about Wyoming and Wehaloosing on the Susquehanna River, nearly two hundred miles from the city of Philadelphia; in which visit he was drawn into near sympathy with these poor people, and qualified at times by his divine Master, to impart counsel, and direct them to that unerring Guide in the secret of the heart, which would lead all men, without distinction of color, to a saving knowledge of the Lord, their Maker and their Redeemer. He often spoke to them through interpreters; but on one occasion, feeling his mind covered with the spirit of prayer, he expressed his willingness for them to omit interpreting. The meeting ended with feelings of solemnity; and before the people went away, one of the Indians who had been zealously laboring for a reformation among them, remarked to the interpreter, "I love to feel where words come from;" thus manifesting that though the language was foreign, yet there was a savor accompanying this heaven-prompted prayer, which had met a sympathetic feeling in the mind of this simple child of the forest.

Another Christian concern which came upon him this year, was occasioned by a juggler coming to Mount Holly, the place of his residence, and attracting many of the inhabitants to a certain public house to see his foolish tricks. He says, "I heard of it the next day, and understanding that the show was to be continued, and the people to meet about sunset, I felt an exercise on that account. So I went to the public house in the evening, and told the man of the house that I had an inclination to spend part of the evening there; with which he signified that he was content. Then sitting down by the door, I spoke to the people as they came together, concerning this show; and more coming and sitting down with us, the seats at the door were mostly filled; and I had conversation with them in the fear of the Lord, and labored to convince them that thus assembling to see those tricks, or sleights of hand, and bestowing their money to support men who in that capacity were of no use in the world, was contrary to the nature of the Christian religion. There was one of the company, who, for a time, endeavored by arguments to show the reasonableness of their proceedings; but after considering some texts of Scripture, and calmly debating the matter, he gave up the point. Having spent about an hour amongst them, and feeling my mind easy, I departed."

In the year 1770, John Woolman was brought very low by a severe attack of pleurisy; during which dispensation his mind was kept calm, and favored with some openings into the excellency of heavenly wisdom. One day he dictated the following instructive remarks on prayer:

"The place of prayer is a precious habitation; for I now saw that the prayers of the saints were precious incense: and a trumpet was given me, that I might sound forth this language, that the children might hear it, and be invited to gather to this precious habitation, where the prayers of the saints, as precious incense, arise up before the throne of God and the Lamb. I saw this habitation to be safe; to be inwardly quiet, when there were great stirrings and commotions in the world. Prayer at this day, in pure resignation, is a precious place: the trumpet is sounded — the call goes forth to the church — that she gather to the place of pure inward prayer; and her habitation is safe."

He had for some time had an impression on his mind that he should be called to labor in the gospel beyond the sea; and this concern ripening, he sailed with the unity of his friends for England in 1772, in company with Samuel Emlen. In travelling up and down in England, he was greatly affected in observing the splendor and delicacy in which many indulged themselves, while multitudes of their fellow-creatures were not able to obtain the necessary comforts of life; and he labored faithfully to encourage those of his own Society to simplicity and purity of life, in accordance with their self-denying profession. The last sentence in his journal on this journey is worthy of preservation.

"In this journey a labor hath attended my mind, that the ministers amongst us may be preserved in the meek, feeling life of Truth, where we may have no desire, but to follow Christ and be with him; — that when He is under suffering, we may suffer with Him — and never desire to rise up in dominion, but as He by the virtue of his own Spirit may raise us."

A few days after writing this, he came to the city of York, where he was soon taken ill of the small-pox. During his illness, he uttered many heavenly expressions; ejaculating on one occasion in the following manner: "In the depths of misery, O Lord! I remembered that thou art omnipotent, — that I had called thee Father — and I felt that I loved thee — and I was made quiet in thy will — and I waited for deliverance from thee. Thou hadst pity upon me when no man could help me. I saw that meekness under suffering was showed to us in the most affecting example of thy Son, and thou taughtest me to follow Him — and I said, thy will, O Father, be done!" On another occasion, he said, "I feel the disorder making its progress, but my mind is mercifully preserved in stillness and peace." Again, "My mind enjoys a perfect calm." In the night he exclaimed with great earnestness, "O my Father! my Father! how comfortable art thou to my soul in this trying season!" And being invited to take a little nourishment, he remarked, "I seem nearly arrived where my soul shall have rest from all its troubles."

A day or two afterwards, he broke forth in supplication in this manner: "O Lord, it was thy power that enabled me to forsake sin in my youth; and I have felt thy bruises for disobedience; but as I bowed under them thou healedst me, continuing a father and a friend. I feel thy power now; and I beg that in the approaching trying moment, thou wilt keep my heart steadfast unto thee." Perceiving a Friend to weep, he said, "I would rather thou wouldst guard against weeping for me, my sister. I sorrow not, though I have had some painful conflicts; but now they seem over, and matters well settled, and I look at the face of my dear Redeemer, for sweet is his voice and his countenance is comely." Some time after, he said to his medical attendant, " My dependence is on the Lord Jesus, who I trust will forgive my sins, which is all I hope for." Thus humbly, yet confidently, did this devoted servant of Christ look to the mercy of his Lord: who took him to Himself in sweet peace, without sigh, groan, or struggle, in the fifty-second year of his age.

CHAPTER XLII.

ACCOUNT OF JOHN CHURCHMAN.

IN the year 1775, died John Churchman, one of John Woolman's fellow-laborers in the gospel of peace, and in the cause of his afflicted brethren of the African race.

He was born in the county of Chester, Pennsylvania, in the year 1705, and was tenderly educated by his parents in the profession of the Society of Friends, and early habituated to a diligent attendance of religious meetings. He felt the reproofs of the Lord's Holy Spirit for evil words and actions at a very early period of his life; but knew not whence they came, until he was about eight years of age; when sitting one day in a small meeting, the Lord by his heavenly love and goodness overcame and tendered his heart, and by his glorious Light, discovered to him a knowledge of Himself. He was enabled to see where he was in the Divine sight, even in a state of vanity and estrangement from his Heavenly Father; and was mercifully made to feel also, that the forgiveness of his sins would follow his obedience to the discoveries of this Divine Light of Christ in his soul, reproving for sin and restraining from it; so that he might witness a dying indeed to sin, and a being raised by the power of God, into newness of life in Christ Jesus, no longer to live to himself, to fulfil the inclinations of the flesh, but to live unto Him who died to take away sin.

It was his practice, when a child, on going to rest for the night, to examine how he had spent the past day, and endeavor to feel the presence of the Lord near. This practice he found greatly helpful in enabling him to sleep with a sweet and easy mind. But notwithstanding he had been thus favored, when quite young, and enlightened to behold the beauty of true religion, yet as he advanced in years, through unwatchfulness he lost in degree this tender state of mind, and began to take pleasure in many things which he had formerly been convinced were wrong. He indulged a fondness for small musical instruments, and an aptness for jesting and witty turns in conversation, and neglected the right improvement of his mind. The condemnation which afterwards was his portion on account of his lightness and forgetfulness of God, was not to be expressed. He was followed by that merciful Hand which waited to pluck his feet out of the mire and clay into which he had fallen; and was visited by deep convictions of the sinfulness of his course. He became afraid even to be looked at in the face by virtuous persons, lest they should discern the wickedness of his heart. In this miserable condition he arrived at the nineteenth year of his age; when as he was one day walking to meeting, thinking on his forlorn condition, and remembering the heavenly bread of which he had partaken when he was a dutiful child; but of which he had now, by straying from the heavenly Father's house, been eight years in grievous want; he inwardly cried unto the Most High, "If thou art pleased again to visit me, I beseech thee, O Lord, visit my body with sickness, or pain, or whatever thou mayst please, so that the will of the 'old man' may be slain, and everything in me that thy controversy is against; that I may be made a sanctified vessel by thy power. Spare only my life, until my redemption is wrought, and my peace made with thee!" After this, he remained for several months in the same disconsolate condition; but when he had attained the age of twenty years, it pleased the Lord to remember him in judgments mixed with mercy, and make way for his deliverance. He was visited with a severe fit of sickness; which in a few days fully awakened him. His mis-spent time and all his transgressions were brought to his remembrance with heavy condemnation. In great distress he cried to the Lord for pity and deliverance from sin; his heart was made exceedingly tender under an awful sense of his condition; he wept much; and threw himself on the mercy of Him whose compassions fail not; and the Lord heard his cry, looked down from His holy habitation, and gave him a willing heart to bear those chastisements which were needful to cleanse and purify him, and create him anew in Christ Jesus unto good works. It pleased the Almighty to restore him after a while to health; and he was frequently humbled under a sense of the tender dealings of Him whose goodness and owning love he felt to be very near. From this time he loved retirement, wherein he could feel after the incomes of this love and goodness, which he felt to be his life; and was often fearful lest he should again fall away. It was soon manifested to him, that if he continued faithful, he would be called to the work of the ministry. He loved to attend religious meetings, both for divine worship and for the discipline of the church; and it was shown to him, that all those who attend these meetings for discipline should wait in great awfulness, to know the immediate presence of Christ, the Head of the church, to give them an understanding what their several services are, and for ability to answer his requirings; for none should presume to speak or act without the motion and direction of His light and Spirit. It was accordingly in great fear, that he attempted to speak in these meetings; but as he kept low, with an eye single to the honor of Truth, his peace and inward strength were increased from time to time.

This was a time of growing in the root of life. He rarely passed a day without feeling the incomes of divine life and love; though afterwards he was left for many days together without inward refreshment, and was taught not only how to abound, but also to suffer need, and to abide faithful under the withdrawings of the beloved of his soul. About the twenty-sixth year of his age, he was appointed with some other Friends to perform a religious visit to the families of the meeting where he resided. During this visit he first felt the motion of the Holy Spirit prompting to the exercise of gospel ministry; but through diffidence he put it away, and did not yield himself up to the requiring. The consequence of this unfaithfulness was a sense of desertion. After the visits were over, he kept much at home, and had work enough to watch against a lukewarm, indolent spirit, which would come over him when endeavoring to wait upon God. For though he came to meeting in a lively engagement of mind, he found the warfare against lukewarmness, sleepiness, and a roving imagination, must be steadily maintained; and that if none of these hindrances were given way to, the Lord, when he had proved his children, would arise for their help, scatter their enemies, and enable them to worship Him.

In the year 1731, he was appointed to the station of elder, though not yet twenty-seven years of age; and two years afterwards, was again united with other Friends in a family visit. He now began to think he had been under a delusion, in entertaining a belief that he should be called to the work of the ministry; but one First-day going to Kennet meeting, toward the close, something was impressed on his mind to offer to those assembled. Fearful and diffident, he had nearly forborne; but remembering what he had before suffered for disobedience, he stood up, and spoke a few sentences in fear and brokenness of spirit; and had satisfaction and peace in the dedication. On finishing the family visit, he returned home, and shortly after had again to open his mouth in the awful work of the ministry. He was gradually enabled clearly to discern between the promptings of warmth of affection for the people, which would lead to "offering strange fire" that would have no efficacy in it, and the pure motions of the Lord's Spirit, with a necessity laid upon the poor servant, and a "woe, if thou preach not the gospel." From this time he grew steadily in the gift, and was often engaged in travelling in the service of his good Master, to the comfort and edification of the churches. In 1750, he embarked for Europe, and spent four years in visiting Great Britain, Ireland, and Holland; and through the course of a long life spent in the promotion of righteousness, he proved himself "a workman that needeth not to be ashamed, rightly dividing the word of truth."

In the seventieth year of his age, it pleased his divine Master to say of all his labors in His cause, "it is enough," and to call him to his everlasting reward. During his sickness, he frequently expressed his resignation to the will of the Almighty, and especially toward the latter part of it, he frequently broke forth in heavenly melody, and aspiration of soul in praise to Him who had been pleased to shine forth in brightness, after many days of poverty and deep baptism, which had been the means of still further purifying from the dregs of nature. Being asked by a Friend, how he was, he replied, "I am yet in the body; and when I go out of it, I hope there is nothing but peace;"

and soon after added, "I have seen that all the bustles and noises that are now in the world, will end in confusion; and our young men who know not an establishment in the Truth, and the Lord's fear for a ballast, will be caught in a trying moment." At another time he said, "I feel nothing but peace, having endeavored honestly to discharge myself in public, and privately to individuals, as I apprehended was required."

With reference to the Society of which he was a member, he thus expressed himself: "I love Friends who abide in the Truth, as much as ever I did; and I feel earnest breathings to the Lord, that there may be those raised up in the church who may go forth in humility, sweetness, and life, clear of all superfluity in expressions and otherwise, standing for the testimony, that they may be useful to the church." And again, about three days before his death, several Friends being in his room, he said: "Friends in the beginning, if they had health and liberty, were not easily diverted from paying their tribute of worship to the Almighty on week-days as well as First-days. But after a while, when outward sufferings ceased, life and zeal decaying, ease and the spirit of the world took place with many, and thus it became customary for one or two out of a family to attend meetings, and to leave their children much at home. Parents also, if worldly concerns were in the way, could neglect their week-day meetings sometimes, yet be willing to hold the name, and plead excuse because of a busy time, or the like. But I believe that such a departure from primitive integrity ever did, and ever will, occasion a withering from the life of true religion."

On the 24th day of the Seventh month, he sat up for a considerable time, and appeared lively and sensible, though very weak; and thus expressed himself: "I am much refreshed with my Master's sweet air—I feel more life, more light, more love and sweetness than ever before;"—and often mentioned the Divine refreshment and comfort he felt, flowing like a pure stream to his inward man. In the evening he remarked again, "the sweetness that I feel." Soon afterwards the difficulty of breathing increased, and at his own request he was placed in a chair; in which he peacefully expired, leaving the savor on the spirits of those who knew his character, of "an Israelite indeed, in whom is no guile."

CHAPTER XLIII.

THE SUFFERINGS OF FRIENDS IN IRELAND, FOR THEIR FAITHFUL ADHERENCE TO THE PRINCIPLES OF PEACE, DURING THE REBELLION OF 1798.

IN the latter part of the eighteenth century, divers prophetic warnings had shadowed forth the coming of a storm over Ireland, not only in the political atmosphere, but also within the peaceful precincts of the Society of Friends. John Pemberton, who travelled with John Churchman in Ireland, so far back as 1752, remarks, on one occasion, that "Friends were exhorted to be more inward, and to seek to get into the valley; for the faith of some would be tried, and the church also would suffer a trial; and it seemed as though the Lord would dry up the torrents on the mountains, and would restrain the clouds, [spiritually,] and would scorch these high places, and they should be barren; therefore there was need for all to sink low, and get into the valley of true humility, that they might have something to refresh them, when the Lord is pleased to cause a famine of the word to come. It was also testified, that He would likewise prove in an outward manner, though it was not to be declared in the will of man, nor the time to be limited; for 'a thousand years with the Lord are as one day, and one day as a thousand years.' Yet if it did not happen in their time, it might in that of their offspring," &c. Whether these expressions were uttered by himself, or by John Churchman, does not appear; though most probably by the latter. And about thirty-two years afterwards, William Matthews, travelling also with John Pemberton in that island, is mentioned by the latter, as having spoken in a meeting for worship in the province of Ulster, "of a day of trial, that in some way or manner would overtake, wherein the professors of the truth would be deeply proved; and therefore Friends were exhorted to be prepared for it." John Pemberton was also present at a meeting in Dublin, at the conclusion of the National Half-year's Meeting, in 1783, wherein Mary Ridgway spoke prophetically "of a day approaching that would try the foundations of the professors of Truth." And a few days afterwards, "our dear friend Samuel Neale had to express, in a lively, feeling manner, his sense of a day approaching, which would prove the faith and try the foundations of the professors of the Truth. He had not only at that time, but at divers others, been made deeply sensible thereof—whether by pestilence, or other means, he could not tell—but he exhorted Friends to prepare for trials."

The deeds to be narrated in the few succeeding pages, developing in some degree, the scenes of insurrectionary violence and rapine which brought Ireland into anarchy and distress towards the close of that century; and the closely following deep trials which had well nigh overwhelmed the Society of Friends in Ireland, in perils from false brethren, will naturally lead to the conclusion, that the Most High still continues to favor his faithful servants with a true sense of the state and dangers of the church, and even, at times, with a prophetic insight into the counsels of his holy will.

About the year 1798, this beautiful island became the scene of all the horrors of civil war. It is not needful here to detail the causes which led to this rebellion; which was a struggle against the government, by a party incongruously composed of two classes: the one crying out for civil license, and the other for Popish superstition; under the respective names of liberty, and of religious uniformity. In their attempts to accomplish their object, the insurgents defied all order and government, and committed most dreadful ravages in various parts of the country. The Society of Friends was a numerous body, particularly in the eastern portion of the island; and as it could neither unite on the one hand with the insurgents, nor concur on the other with the warlike measures of the government to suppress them, it was not to be supposed that either party would feel very friendly towards its members. There was therefore a gloomy prospect for those who were disposed to look forward with the eye of human reason, rather than with that of faith in the protecting arm of Him who never forsakes his flock.

Friends saw the gathering storm, and endeavored to strengthen each other for the trials which might await them. Before the rebellion broke out into actual bloodshed, both parties in the struggle successively made search in private houses for arms. The Quarterly Meetings had in 1795-6 recommended to all their members, that those who had guns or other weapons in their houses, should destroy them, in order "to prevent their being made use of to the destruction of any of our fellow-creatures, and more fully and clearly to support our peaceable and Christian testimony in these perilous times." Committees had been appointed by the several Monthly Meetings, to go round to the members, and see that this recommendation was attended to; whose labors met with considerable success; so that when the government ordered all arms to be given up to the magistrates, it was a source of satisfaction, that the members generally were found without any such thing in their possession. They were also much relieved from the midnight depredations of the insurgents, to which most of their neighbors were exposed, in the lawless search for weapons; as it was now known that none were kept in their houses.

A Friend residing at Ferns, being appointed on one of these committees, and feeling the necessity of first clearing his own hands, took his fowling-piece and broke it in pieces in the street before his door, bearing a testimony to his neighbors, of his resolution that nothing of his should be made use of to the destruction of human life. Some of the magistrates, with the priest of the parish, came to his house to expostulate with him on having destroyed his gun, instead of delivering it up to the government, to assist in opposing the insurgents, and defending himself and his family; though the priest, as it were involuntarily, acknowledged that he believed the Friend put his confidence in a higher power. Shortly afterwards the town of Enniscorthy was burned, this priest was murdered, and his body, with many others, was exposed several days in the streets, until a few Friends ventured to bury what the swine had left of their remains. One of the magistrates was also murdered, and his house burned over his body.

This Friend had afterwards opportunities, by standing firmly to his principles, of alternately saving individuals of both parties from the cruelties of war. He was however subjected to much danger, on an occasion when the military were preparing to hang some suspected persons,

and fasten pitch caps on the heads of others. He foresaw
the probability of his being applied to for ropes, which he
had for sale in his way of business, and the risk which he
might incur, in a time of martial law prevailing, if he refused to sell them. But he could not be easy to sell his
goods for a purpose so repugnant to his principles; and when
the soldiers came to purchase ropes for halters, and linen for
the pitched caps, he nobly refused to sell them, or, when
they were forcibly taken from his shop, to receive any pay
for them. This took place before the general rising in that
part, and becoming known to his neighbors, he had reason
to believe that, under the direction of Divine Providence,
it contributed to the preservation of himself and his family
at that juncture. For very soon after this occurrence,
when the whole town was in consternation and tumult, and
the Protestant inhabitants in continual terror, a man supposed to be of the party called "United Irishmen," entered
his house early in the morning, declaring, "Let who may
be killed, the Quakers will be spared." That morning,
houses and grain-stacks were to be seen in flames in all
directions; the Protestants were fleeing for safety into the
towns and villages, some wounded and bringing dismal news
of others slain; and every one's concern seemed to be to
escape with his life. The next day the scene was changed.
The military and Protestant inhabitants had left the town
of Ferns, which soon became filled with an ungovernable
mob of many thousand insurgents, following the steps of
the military, and occupied in demolishing the houses and
property of the loyalists. His house was soon filled with
them; when to his astonishment and humbling admiration,
instead of the massacre which he and his family had apprehended, they were met with caresses and protestations
of friendship, and demands of nothing but something to
eat. It happened that the day before, the Friend had prepared large quantities of food for the distressed people, who

had then fled into the town in a destitute condition; but this had not been eaten, and now furnished a supply for the hungry multitude of insurgents who had crowded into his house. After this, they departed, and in a short time columns of smoke ascending into the air from a distance of six miles, gave the melancholy tidings that the whole town of Enniscorthy was in possession of the insurgents, who fixed their camp on Vinegar Hill.

The houses of Friends now became asylums for the relief of the suffering and the destitute, and often places of hospitable entertainment, without distinction of party; so that it was wonderful how their provisions and means held out. And though they often appeared in great danger from each party, on account of their houses being filled with the adherents of the opposite one, yet preservation was experienced in a marvellous manner throughout.

The above-mentioned Friend at Ferns was threatened one morning that his house would be burned that day, for his refusal to turn out some Protestant women who had sought refuge with him. He meekly replied, that he could not but keep his house open to succor the distressed; and if they burned it, he must turn out along with his guests, and share in their affliction. That day being the day on which the Monthly Meeting was to be held, about a mile from Ferns, notwithstanding this alarming denunciation, he believed it his duty to attend the meeting, and took his family with him, expecting that before the next day he should be without a habitation or the means of present support. But his faith was strong in the preserving power of the Lord; who saw the sincerity of his obedience, and caused even the hearts of his enemies to change towards him, so that they not only refrained from fulfilling their threats, but never afterwards made a like demand from him.

Soon afterwards, standing at the door of his house, while

the army was entering the town in pursuit of the flying insurgents, a soldier stepping up, presented his gun at his breast, and was on the point of drawing the trigger, when the Friend desired him to "desist from murder." The soldier was struck with amazement, and immediately let his gun fall from his shoulder. The commanding officer afterwards desired, in relation to some suspected persons made prisoners, who pleaded their innocence, that if there were any Quakers in the town, these persons would get certificates of good behavior from them; and this same Friend was applied to by several, and had the satisfaction of procuring their liberation from prison, and perhaps from death.

Friends were now subjected to great danger throughout the country, but were not willing to relinquish their duty of assembling together for the public worship of the Almighty; though it was often necessary for them to go many miles to their meetings, through parts infested with armed and violent men, and to leave their homes, in all human probability, a prey to pillage or fire during their absence. In the county of Wexford, some Friends having been observed thus to persevere in attending their place of worship, were apprised by the insurgents, that if they persisted in it, they should be dragged to the altar of a Popish chapel near which they passed, and suffer the penalty of their obstinacy. One family, in particular, received notice, that unless they gave up the attendance of meetings, and united in the papal forms of worship, they should all be put to death, and their house should be burned. The next day was meeting-day, and the heads of the family feeling the solemn responsibility of their situation, were brought under deep mental exercise, accompanied with fervent prayers that they might be enabled to come to a right determination in this awful crisis. Collecting their family together into solemn retirement, they laid the matter before their children. The noble and Christian language of the eldest son, then a very young man, was, "Father, rejoice that we are found worthy to suffer!" His parents were much affected, and their minds strengthened to conclude to attend their meeting as usual. In the morning, accordingly, they proceeded to their place of worship along the public road, not being easy to go privately through the fields; and their enemies were prevented from carrying their threats into execution, by the sudden arrival, unknown to these Friends, of the royal army in that part of the country. Thus they were preserved from harm, and had the satisfaction of not having flinched from their duty, under so great a trial of faith.

A neighboring family of Friends, containing several daughters, was similarly threatened; but the young women faithfully maintained their testimony to the duty of assembling to worship the Almighty in that way which He had pointed out; and as their parents, being advanced in years, and having had their horses taken away, were unable to go so far as the meeting-house, which was about four miles distant, they sometimes had to walk the whole distance without any male attendant, in the very height of the commotions. And though they went by the usual public road, not being easy to seek a more private way, and thus had to pass through the midst of the very people who had threatened them, yet they were preserved from injury. On one occasion, after being more than usually threatened, the protection afforded them seemed very remarkable; for they were escorted, voluntarily, for several miles, by a dog with which they were entirely unacquainted, and which left them on seeing them safe at their own home.

Friends generally of this meeting were threatened with the flames; their meeting-house was to be converted into a Popish chapel; and a blunderbuss was presented at one Friend, in order to deter him from attending the meeting;

but Friends remained firm; very few were deterred from the fulfilment of this duty; and on the very evening before the meeting-day when so many were to be devoted to destruction, and their houses to the flames, the power of the insurgents was broken by a decisive battle on Vinegar Hill; and during the meeting the next morning, many of these misguided people, instead of coming to destroy, actually sought the meeting-house as an asylum of safety to themselves.

The Friends of Cooladine and Enniscorthy were menaced in like manner with those of Forrest; but though some of them had to lament the loss of their property, and even the destruction of their houses, yet the threats of personal violence to them were found to be impotent, and their lives were providentially preserved.

At the time of the Monthly Meeting at Enniscorthy, the house was put in preparation to be fired, and some of these malicious persons were actually in the galleries at the time when Friends assembled; but after a while they went away without doing injury. At the Leinster Quarterly Meeting also, held at the same place, many Friends assembled from distant parts; though at the time it seemed almost impossible to accomplish it, and several of them had to pass through heaps of slain on the road, and were obliged to remove the dead bodies out of the way, that they might not trample upon them; a great slaughter having occurred at the battle of Vinegar Hill, a day or two before.

An aged Friend had his house entered by the insurgents, who required him to undergo the Popish ceremony of water baptism; and on his refusal, threatened him with certain death. On their afterwards returning and repeating the demand, he still firmly refused. A third time, they demanded his compliance, and he still refusing to sacrifice his peace by complying with their desires, they told him that they were now resolved to hang him before they left the house, if he did not comply. They accordingly fastened a rope around his neck, took him to an out-house on his premises, and were in the act of fastening the rope to a joist for the completion of their wicked design, when a sudden alarm of the approach of soldiery scattered them, and his life was preserved.

Friends in the county of Westmeath witnessed many heart-rending scenes, some of them living in solitary places, surrounded by the insurgents, and not feeling themselves at liberty to follow the example and persuasions of their Protestant neighbors, in fleeing from their habitations to the garrison-towns. But being favored with faith and patience to abide in their lots, and conscientiously adhering to their principles, they experienced the name of the Lord to be a strong tower, in which they found safety.

Friends residing in the county of Kildare, though they were often in danger, escaped personal injury from either party. The country people generally spoke well of them, appearing to be sensible that though they would not join them, neither would they on the other hand take part against them. When the military came to quell the insurrection, the Popish priest ran to borrow a Friend's coat, to disguise himself, and thus save his life. Many respectable persons of the county of Wexford, on the evening of the battle of Ross, apprehending themselves not secure in their own houses, flocked with their families into those of Friends; and some of these belonging to an armed association, and clad in military garb, readily acquiesced in the remonstrances of the peaceful proprietors, and assumed a dress in this time of fear, of a more peaceable appearance. Thus was protection often witnessed in a wonderful manner to the Society of Friends, as had been foretold by several of their ministers some years before, and the prediction of one in particular was literally fulfilled, who was heard to declare in gospel authority, that "in a time of trial which was approaching, if Friends kept their places, many would be glad to take shelter under the skirts of their garments."

A Protestant minister near Enniscorthy, seeing the danger approaching, requested that the clothes of a Friend might be given to him, hoping that in such a dress he might be preserved, or might effect his escape. But it was remarked, that such a disguise could be of no advantage; and he hid himself by the river-side, where he was soon afterwards found and murdered.

Some circumstances connected with the battle of Antrim are worthy of record. The regular army was not able to make a stand against their opponents; and when it was found that the latter were likely to enter the town, the inhabitants were directed to close their doors and windows, and a general dismay spread itself among them. There was a family of Friends residing in the town, consisting of a very young man and his sisters, whose father was then travelling in America in the service of the gospel. At the time of his preparing to leave Ireland for that purpose, a fellow-minister was led into public supplication, in the Quarterly Meeting, for his preservation and safe return, and expressed a belief that during his absence the sword would be near his house, and the dead bodies lying in the streets, but no harm should befall his family, for the Lord would encamp about them, and preserve them as in the hollow of His hand. This was now literally accomplished. At the time of the battle, the family designed staying in their house; but when they found that the action had commenced, and that the cannon was placed directly opposite their door, thus exposing the house to imminent danger, they thought of taking refuge in the fields. This however they found was impracticable, from the dense crowd of people around their house, as the heat of the action was in that spot. In a very short time, the insurgents became masters of the town, cutting off about one-third of the soldiery opposed to them; but their victory was of short duration; for a reinforcement arriving, they were dispersed, and the town retaken. This family during the battle had taken in a poor wounded man of the insurrectionary party, and afforded him what assistance was in their power; but when the firing had almost ceased, they urged the propriety of his endeavoring to escape, both for his own safety and theirs. He had scarcely quitted the premises, when a body of soldiers knocked furiously at the door, demanded immediate entrance, and insisted on knowing whether any strangers were in the house. Some were for going up-stairs to search; but one of the officers observed, that "the Quakers were people that would not tell a lie—that their word might be taken—and if any strangers were there, it would not be denied." The behavior of the soldiers now became civil, and they brought in a fatally wounded man of their own party, to receive their kind attentions, and promised them protection. After the battle, the town presented an awful spectacle—dead bodies of men and horses lying in the blood-stained streets—and the people here and there saluting their neighbors, as those who had survived a pestilence or an earthquake. For several days the inhabitants were kept in constant alarm, and the part of the town where this family resided, being a suspected district, was ordered by the soldiery to be burned. But while the commanding officer was riding up the street to give the orders, one of the sisters ventured through the crowd towards him, and simply asked him if their house was to share the same dismal fate. He gave her an assurance of protection to them, and without their knowledge, a yeoman was placed as a guard at their door, while the work of destruction was going on. They were afterwards also remarkably saved from the common fate of the inhabitants, of being plundered by the soldiery.

It was not known that during the whole of this gloomy

season of anarchy and destruction, the Society of Friends lost more than one of its members by the violence of war. And this was a young man who had deviated from their principles, in a faithful adherence to which, his brethren in profession were so wonderfully preserved. This youth, apprehending that he could find no safety for his life but by outward means of defence, resolved to put on a military uniform, and to associate with armed men. Telling his connections that they would all be murdered, if they remained in the country in so defenceless a state, he fled to a neighboring garrison-town. But this very place was attacked and taken; the door of the house where he had been firing from a window, was forced open by the enraged enemy; and though, in terror for his life, he sought concealment in the chimney of an upper chamber, he was discovered and put to death; furnishing an awful example of the sad result of casting away confidence in the protecting arm of the Almighty, and bartering the pure principles of Christianity for a reliance on the arm of flesh.

But the follower of a crucified Lord must not expect always to escape from suffering, nor make his allegiance depend on a hope of security in this life. He may be required at times even to offer up his natural life, as a seal to his testimony for a good conscience. At Kilbroney, in the county of Wexford, were two brothers, named John and Samuel Jones: neither of whom was ever in membership with Friends, but the latter had attended their meetings, and was attached to their principles. The following affecting circumstances will scarcely be denied to entitle them (particularly the younger) to the name of Christian martyrs.

Samuel was of a meek and gentle spirit, and remarked for the benevolence of his disposition. He had of late become increasingly serious, and expressed on different occasions an apprehension of being shortly taken away. The two brothers were taken prisoners by the insurgents, conveyed to Scullabogue, and confined in a house close to a barn, in which a few days afterwards, a large number of their fellow-creatures, men, women, and children, were horribly burnt to death. Upwards of two hundred were massacred in this way, and by shooting them in the adjacent lawn. John Jones, the elder brother, was now brought into a close searching of heart, and found cause to lament that in time past he had not sought after a preparation for death; but was encouraged by his brother to faithfulness. Samuel's wife was permitted to accompany them to their prison; and on the morning of the day when the barn was burnt, as they were reading the New Testament, she inquired of one of the guards, the cause of the peculiar smell, which she perceived, like burning animal matter. He coolly told her, it was some beefsteaks preparing for breakfast! To a further inquiry, "What was meant by the firing of guns?" he replied, "that it was some criminals they were shooting." About five minutes after this, the three were taken from the prison into the lawn, and Samuel was required to turn to the Romish religion. He replied, "Where shall I turn, but where my God is?" And being urged to have his children undergo the ceremony of water-baptism, he said, "My children are innocent; and I will leave them so." Some person now saying that these prisoners "were Quakers," it was replied that if they could make it appear that they were so, they should not be put to death. But as they were neither of them really members, this could not be done. Some of them now took Samuel aside, and offered him his life on certain conditions; but finding these to conflict with his sense of religious duty, he firmly rejected them; and when the "holy water," as they termed it, was brought to them, he turned his back upon it, in testimony against their bigotry.

He encouraged his brother John to faithfulness to the last, fearing lest his steadfastness might give way; and reminded him of the words of our blessed Saviour; "Whosoever shall deny me before men, him will I also deny before my Father which is in heaven;" and "he that findeth his life shall lose it; and he that loseth his life for my sake, shall find it." John was then shot by the insurgents. Samuel desired his love to be given to certain Friends, whom he named; but the party endeavored to work upon his feelings, by falsely asserting that they had already forfeited their lives at the camp. To this however he meekly replied, "then they died innocent." He now took an affectionate leave of his wife, who with admirable fortitude stood by him and held his hand, until he was shot by the side of his brother. His last words were those with which he had endeavored to encourage his brother, and which now afforded inexpressible support to himself; "He that loseth his life for My sake, shall find it."

CHAPTER XLIV.

THE SEPARATION IN IRELAND, IN 1799, ETC.

ALTHOUGH many were thus faithful in maintaining their testimony to the peaceable nature of the Gospel, during a season of sore trial, yet there were at this time in various parts of the nation, those under our name who had imbibed more or less of a sceptical and self-righteous spirit. These deluding themselves and others by false pretensions to spirituality, and greater light on religious subjects than their brethren in that or former ages, began to promulgate many wild and unsound notions relative to certain important doctrines of the Christian religion. In-

flated by a fond conceit of their own attainments, and by
the presumptuous idea that they possessed the plenary inspiration of the Spirit, and therefore needed not the fainter
light of external evidence, they boldly rejected a large portion of the sacred volume, renounced the epithet "Holy,"
as applied to the Scriptures, and set up in their stead the
wild vagaries of their own feverish imaginations. They
strenuously advocated the propriety of bringing every subject to the test of reason; and deciding on its credibility,
by its accordance with their ideas of what such a Being as
they chose to consider the Creator, *ought to* require of his
rational creatures. But while they were high in profession
of "rational belief," they adopted and openly professed
many absurd and extravagant notions.

Discontented and restless in themselves, and conscious
that they were professing to be what the Searcher of hearts
knew they were not, they seemed ready to catch at any
novelty, either in faith or practice, which promised to
make them conspicuous as reformers of the Society, or, by
occupying their attention, to divert them from a sense of
their own corruptions, and their great need of a change
of heart. Renouncing the faith of their fathers, and dis-
daining the pure and simple doctrines of Christianity, they
struck out for themselves a new system; a primary feature
of which was, a denial of the truths recorded in the Bible,
under the specious pretence, that the "light within," as
they irreverently termed what was nothing more than *their
own fallen reason*, or the workings of a morbid imagination, had enabled them to see beyond all outward evidence.
Hence they rejected as untrue, the doctrine of the "eternal
power and godhead" of our Lord Jesus Christ, his propitiatory sacrifice on the cross for the sins of mankind, his
mediation, and his intercession; regarding him in no
higher point of view, than as a blessed example and holy
pattern. Indeed, with the confidence which they had

in their own righteousness, it was impossible that they should believe in a necessity of His atonement for their sins. Not satisfied with the clear and sublime account written by Moses, of the creation of the world, they declared it an allegory: they mysticized the description of the garden of Eden into a mere metaphorical account of the human heart and its propensities, asserting that it was never intended to be construed literally: and by the same method they evaded the force of other parts of the Bible, which did not comport with their own notions.

Conceiving that no act connected with religion was obligatory upon them without a special and immediate impulse of duty, they declined the salutary practice of observing the First-day of the week as a day of rest and religious exercises, pursued their usual avocations, and refused to assemble at stated times for the purpose of Divine worship; only attending when they considered themselves particularly moved thereto, which would sometimes happen to be at the time the assembly were about to separate.

Against the consistent members of the Society of Friends, they inveighed with much acrimony and zeal, as formal, traditional, and lapsed professors, resting in the commandments of their fathers, and adding thereto the superstitions and corruptions of other religious societies. The excellent code of discipline which for many years had proved a means of preservation and strength to the church, they became dissatisfied with, wishing to remove all restraints, and leave every man at liberty to "do that which was right in his own eyes."

About this time, Hannah Barnard, of Hudson in the state of New York, who occupied the station of a minister, opened to her Monthly Meeting a desire to visit Great Britain and Ireland. Friends of that place, though probably in some degree influenced by affectionate feelings in her behalf, yet appear to have felt unusual hesitation on the subject; the matter being referred to a committee, in whose hands it remained about nine months, before they could report in favor of granting the usual credentials. They were however at length, partly by earnest appeals to the affections of the young and inexperienced members, induced to set her at liberty, in the latter part of the Eighth month, 1797, and she sailed for Europe.

Travelling in Ireland, her discourses public and private, though artfully disguised for a time, were calculated to foster this spirit of insubordination, and even eventually of unbelief; and she was eagerly followed by those who were already more or less under its influence.

At the next Yearly Meeting in Dublin, this sorrowful subject claimed the serious attention of the body; which directed the Monthly Meetings timely to labor in Christian love and tenderness, for the restoration of these deluded persons; and where they could not be reclaimed, they were, with the advice of the Quarterly Meetings, to be testified against, as out of the unity of Friends. The Yearly Meeting also appointed a committee to visit the Quarterly, Monthly, and other Meetings, to assist them with advice and counsel in the trying circumstances under which many of them were placed. The appointment of this committee struck dismay into the ranks of the dissentients, as they saw that it rendered their prospect of carrying their own measures entirely hopeless.

David Sands, a valuable minister from the state of New York, before mentioned, who had arrived in Great Britain in 1795, had been drawn in the love of Christ to visit Ireland; and being led into very plain dealing among them, in imparting the whole counsel of his Divine Master, he became a principal mark for their enmity. Many of them refused to acknowledge his ministry by uniting in the usual orderly practice of standing up and taking off the hat, while he was engaged in meetings for worship in the solemn act of addressing the Most High.

Richard Jordan also, of North Carolina, a fellow-laborer in the same glorious gospel, was moved at that juncture to visit the afflicted Society in Ireland; and is believed to have been eminently useful in strengthening the weak hands of those who were faithfully opposing this spirit of unbelief and disorder, and in confirming the feeble faith of some, who were ready to falter under the plausible appearances which were presented. He bore a solemn and powerful testimony against the dangerous tendency of this delusion; he labored with undaunted zeal to expose its fallacies; he warned both young and old against suffering themselves to be entangled therein; and under the influence of a prophetic spirit, he foretold the sorrowful consequences which these errors, if persisted in, would inevitably produce.

But notwithstanding the earnest labors of many deeply concerned Friends, the leaders of this secession continued their course, until many lost their membership in the Society. In the province of Ulster, all the elders were displaced from their station; and a considerable number of ministers and elders in various parts were disowned from membership. Hannah Barnard, notwithstanding the private labor which had been abundantly bestowed upon her, at length so openly avowed her unbelief in the divinity and atonement of the blessed Saviour, and the authenticity of the Holy Scriptures, that on her leaving Ireland, in the spring of 1800, she was called to account before the Yearly Meeting of Ministers and Elders in London, for her unsound doctrines, discouraged from continuing to travel as a minister, and advised to return home.

The committee of the Yearly meeting of Dublin to visit and aid the subordinate meetings, was reappointed each year until 1802, when the painful duty of separating from the body those who persisted in adhesion to this heresy, appeared to be nearly completed, and the Society clear from responsibility for their errors. The hand of Divine Providence seemed to be turned in an awful manner against these deniers of the Divinity of the Lord Jesus; so that the predictions of Richard Jordan and others were remarkably verified. Some of them who had lived in affluence, experienced a sad reverse in their condition; many not only lost their religious reputation, but even suffered in their moral character, and became an astonishment to their former acquaintances. Others, however, awakened by timely warning, abandoned their errors, and through the mercy of a gracious Redeemer, came to experience repentance and forgiveness; these embraced the Christian religion in renewed faith and sincerity, and were restored into the fellowship of the church.

Hannah Barnard, not complying with the admonitions of the Yearly Meeting of Ministers and Elders in London, her case was brought into the Monthly Meeting of Devonshire House in that city, which also, after examination, advised her to return home. She was not willing to take this advice, and finally appealed to the Yearly Meeting in 1801; which, after a patient investigation of the case, confirmed the advice of the Monthly Meeting. On her return, her own Monthly Meeting being apprised of her unsoundness, she was, after ineffectual attempts to reclaim her, at length disowned by Friends, and sunk into obscurity.

CHAPTER XLV.

THOMAS SHILLITOE'S EARLY LIFE AND CONVINCEMENT—
HIS REMARKABLE GOSPEL LABORS IN IRELAND, ETC.

ONE of the most remarkable men who joined the Society in modern days, was Thomas Shillitoe. He was born in London, in the year 1754, and educated according to the views of the Episcopal society, of which his parents were zealous members. From about the twelfth year of his age, he was exposed to many temptations. His father taking charge of a large tavern at Islington, in the suburbs of that great city, Thomas, whose disposition was naturally volatile, was exposed to the contamination of evil examples in almost every kind of vice. He was afterwards placed as apprentice with a person much given to liquor and unprofitable company; so that his situation continued to be one of great danger. But, though thus exposed, adorable mercy awakened in his mind a degree of serious thoughtfulness, which no doubt preserved him from many gross evils. Growing up towards manhood, he occasionally attended the meetings of Friends with a young relative; but this was not from a pure motive, and did not appear to be productive at that time of much effect on his mind. He generally spent the afternoon of the First-day of the week in idleness and rambling about for pleasure, giving greater latitude than ever to his natural inclinations. But the retrospect of this, in times of serious reflection, was not productive of that comfort which he had once known, when this day of the week had been differently occupied. He was, however, mercifully again visited by the reproofs of the Holy Spirit, and his attention arrested, to consider the misery into which the road he was now travelling must eventually lead him, if he continued to pursue it. He found he must now attend meetings for worship from a sense of religious obligation, and that too both morning and afternoon; and as he faithfully gave up to this duty, his desires increased after an acquaintance with the Almighty, and a knowledge of His law. Earnest were his prayers, that in this day of the Lord's powerful visitation, in mercy renewed to his soul, the Father of all grace would not leave him to become a prey to his soul's enemy—that His hand would not spare, nor his eye pity, until an entire willingness was brought about in him, to cast himself down at the Lord's holy footstool. As resignation was thus produced in him, to yield to the purifying operation of the Holy Ghost and fire, that the fan of God's Word and power should separate between the precious and the vile, corresponding fruits were brought forth, and manifested in his outward conduct.

His father showed great displeasure at his attending the meetings of Friends, and endeavored to dissuade him therefrom, representing the Society in as unfavorable and ridiculous a point of view as he could; but without effect. Thomas soon felt that it would be right for him to use the pure language of *thou* and *thee*, instead of *you*, to a single person, and to refuse to conform to the vain compliments of the world. During the mental exercises which he passed through on this account, he fell under much discouragement; especially when his father told him that he must quit his paternal abode, and go among those with whom he had associated in religious profession. But in this season of close trial, he was not deserted by Him who cares even for the sparrows. A situation was procured for him as clerk in a banking-house. Here he entertained a hope of being out of the way of much temptation; but alas! he soon found his mistake; and that no situation was safe.

without maintaining the daily, unremitted watch. Very few of his new companions were acquainted with that inward work of religion which he so greatly desired, many of them being much given up to the world and its delusive pleasures. For want of keeping steadily on the watch, he had nearly made shipwreck of faith. But the mercy of God snatched him again as a brand out of the burning, and pointed out to him the need of increasing circumspection.

The business of his employers required him at times to purchase lottery tickets for country correspondents, and to attend to some other matters which he felt a scruple against; and this brought him under fresh trial, desiring to retain a situation in which he was making a respectable livelihood, and yet not feeling easy to continue in the practice of that which was manifested to him to be wrong. But submissively seeking divine direction, he was enabled clearly to see that he must settle down to that manner of obtaining his livelihood, which Truth would point out to him. And crying unto the Lord, in earnest prayer, that He would be pleased to direct him, the Most High in mercy heard his cries, and answered his supplications, pointing out to him the humble business of a shoemaker, as the means by which he should hereafter gain a living more consistently with his religious scruples. This intimation at first involved him in great distress of mind; partly from the fear lest he should not soon be able to earn enough to supply himself with what was necessary for his sustenance, as he had saved but little from his present salary. But leaving his employers, he engaged with a person to teach him the business, and trusted to the Lord for preservation. Great were the trials to which for a time he was subjected; his little stock of money wasted fast; and his earnings over what he had to pay his instructor, were so very small as not to allow him for the first twelve months, more than bread, cheese, and water, and sometimes bread only, to keep clear of debt; and this he carefully avoided.

After he had acquired sufficient knowledge of the business, he commenced on his own account, with a capital of a few shillings. His prospects brightened; his business prospered; and in 1778 he entered into the married state, under the sanction and guidance, as he believed, of Him who had thus far mercifully cared for him.

For some time his mind had been exercised with a belief, that if he continued faithful to divine requirings, a gift in the ministry of the gospel would be committed to his charge. Earnest were his secret cries for the Lord's preservation, under the prospect of this awful work—to be kept, on the one hand, from running before he was sent, and on the other, from overstaying the right time, when the command should be distinctly heard, "Go forth."

About the 24th year of his age, he first opened his mouth as a minister of the gospel, and was favored with great peace for this act of dedication. But he soon found, to his sorrow, that Satan can transform himself into an angel of light; and when he cannot effect his evil purpose, by causing us to lag behind, he will then strive to hurry us on before our good Guide, and thus in one way or the other endeavor to mar the Lord's work. From this snare, however, he was favored to recover himself; and as he humbly followed the puttings forth of the heavenly finger, looking neither to the right hand nor to the left, he grew in his gift, and increased in understanding of the things of God; and for many years was employed by his divine Master, in strengthening and confirming the churches, in various places, at a distance from his own abode.

Before undertaking some of these religious engagements, he was at times much discouraged, from fears lest his outward concerns should suffer during his absence; as he had no experienced person under whose superintendence to leave them. On one occasion these discouragements were presented, if possible, with double force; but as he yielded to the influence of divine help, the power of the Almighty was mercifully manifested, his mind was tendered under its influence, and he heard in the secret of his soul, intelligibly addressed to his mental ear, the following language: "I will be more than bolts and bars to thy outward habitation—more than a master to thy servants—more than a husband to thy wife, and a parent to thy infant children." Thus was his faith confirmed; he no longer dared to hesitate, but proceeded on his Master's mission; and on returning home, he found his outward concerns in as good order as if he had himself had the management of them during the interim.

In the year 1793, he apprehended it to be his duty to pay a religious visit to King George the Third. The interview proved satisfactory, and that which he communicated, appeared to be well received. The king stood in a solid manner during its delivery, and was so much affected that the tears trickled down his cheeks.

About the year 1805, having been so far favored with success in trade, as to have saved an income of about one hundred pounds a year, he was not easy to go on accumulating; but under a sense of duty, relinquished his business, and devoted himself more fully to the work to which he had been called of God, for the benefit of his fellowmen. He often felt himself constrained to address those in power, on the great prevalence of vice and irreligion among the people; and some of these addresses were very close and striking. It also pleased his Divine Master to lay upon him the duty of visiting the most depraved and abandoned of the human family, and of warning and pleading with those who were either encouraging or conniving at their evil practices.

In his travels, especially in Ireland, he beheld with sorrow the great number of places where ardent spirits were sold, the crowds of persons who frequented them, and the degrading and brutalizing effects produced by this pernicious article, particularly on the lower classes; subverting every thing like a sense of religion, destroying the physical and mental powers, and involving its victims in squalid wretchedness and poverty. He had not long witnessed the misery produced by these drinking-houses, before he felt constrained to visit the keepers of them in certain parts, and to plead personally with them and their visitors against their evil practices; notwithstanding the prospect, at times realized, of meeting with insult and abuse.

The first visit of this kind was in the town of Waterford, in company with Elizabeth Ridgway, a Friend who had a similar religious concern. Their service was not confined to the keepers of the houses, but frequently extended to the company sitting in them to drink; who mostly behaved respectfully, and heard quietly what they had to offer. Yet they met with a few instances of the contrary, and some of the remarks made, as well as the crowd that followed them from house to house, were very humiliating. But as they endeavored to keep near in spirit to their Holy Helper, they were strengthened in an admirable manner, to go through the service, and to deliver "all the counsel of God" among those dark spirits, settled down apparently in gross superstition and ignorance. Even among these, they often found a door of entrance for the gospel message, and returned home at length, with hearts truly contrited, under a fresh sense that all things are possible with the Most High.

Soon afterwards he felt it his duty to visit the drinking-houses at Carrick-on-Suir, and Ross, in company with the same female friend. On entering Carrick, they became the subjects of much remark. They generally found both houses and hearts open to receive them and what they had to communicate. They were followed from house to house by crowds of people. Thomas's account states, that "although the houses would be so filled, that there did not appear to be room for another to squeeze in, yet quietness soon prevailed, and was in a remarkable manner preserved, especially whilst we were engaged in delivering our message. Truly we may say this was the Lord's doing; and that we were able to attain to any quiet in ourselves is marvellous in our eyes. By endeavoring to keep in the patience, and to have our minds clothed with that love which would have all gathered, taking quietly such insults as were offered, and any opposition to what we had to communicate, the veil of prejudice would generally give way: love would beget love, and make way for free and open communication." "Sometimes, on entering a house, we found persons in a state of intoxication. Their companions, aware of our errand, boasted they *would* have liquor, calling out for large quantities. But on our appearing not to notice them, but to take our seats quietly amongst them, others would take pains to keep them still, and in time, all has been hushed into silence, as much so as I have known in our own meetings."

In 1810, he again felt it his duty to visit Ireland. Soon after arriving there, he engaged in visiting the drinking-houses at Clonmel and several other towns. A few extracts from his own account of these visits, will furnish some idea of their trying character, as well as of the marvellous manner in which he was helped to perform them. In speaking of the visit at Clonmel, he says: "My companion used often to say, it seemed as if the Good Master went into the houses before us to prepare the way. Such were the feelings of solemnity we met with on entering the houses, and when sitting with the keepers of them, and their customers, that at times it seemed much like paying a family visit among Friends.

"At Callen, the crowd that gathered around us was very interrupting, and they behaved in an uncivilized manner; yet my mind was preserved quiet, feeling the necessity of letting them see that my dependence was placed on the Supreme All-powerful Preserver of the universe." In some of the towns, whose inhabitants were principally Papists, bigotry and superstition prevailed to a very great extent; and the priests had endeavored to prejudice the people against them. After concluding the visits to the drinking-houses, it was his practice to visit either the magistrates, or the bishops and priests; and sometimes he did not feel clear until he had faithfully spoken to all.

The following account of one of these interviews, will furnish an example of the uncompromising manner in which he spoke what he believed was required of him. "On our arrival at the house, we were ordered up stairs, where the bishop received us with great civility, ushered us into a room, brought me a chair, placing it opposite to a sofa, on which he took his seat. My companions taking seats also, we dropped into silence; which I broke by saying, a visit had been paid to the drinking-houses in Kilkenny, which I supposed he had been acquainted with: to which he replied, 'Well.' I observed, that in performing this visit, my fears, and the various reports I had heard, were fully confirmed; that the 'laity' profess to believe the 'clergy' have full power to forgive their sins; adding, the people may be so deceived as to believe the priest has this power, but I did not believe it possible the 'clergy' could believe it themselves. And therefore, as their superior, to whom the people were taught to look up for counsel, I desired he would look to the Almighty for help, and, as he valued his own precious soul, as ability was afforded him, endeavor to turn the minds of the people from man unto God and Christ Jesus, who only can forgive sins: otherwise he would incur a load of condemnation too heavy for him·

to bear in the great day of account, when the deceiver and the deceived would be all one in the sight of God, whether actively or passively deceiving the people. That at times, when considering the subject, it was my belief that if the Almighty had one vial of wrath more powerful than another, it would be poured out upon those who thus deceived the people. Here I closed for the present. He manifested great confusion, shutting his eyes, as not being able to look me in the face. A pause ensued. After a while, he began by saying, it was very indecorous and unchristian in me to come to his house, a stranger to him, and from another land, and address him in such a manner; charging him, a man of so much experience in the church of God, with being a deceiver; saying, surely I must be mistaken. I told him, it was in love to his soul, and under an apprehension of religious duty. He called upon me to produce my authority for my mission. I told him, my authority was in my own breast. I queried with him: 'Are not the people thus deceived? Do they not believe the 'clergy' have power to forgive their sins? Art thou endeavoring to undeceive them? For the 'clergy' cannot be so deceived as to believe this power is vested in them'—exhorting him to be willing to co-operate with that Divine help, which, if rightly sought after by him, would be extended; whereby ability would be received to undeceive the people; again reminding him, that the deceiver and deceived were all one in the sight of God; and that it continued my firm belief, if the Almighty had one vial of His wrath more powerful than another, it would be poured out on those who thus deceived the people, whether actively or passively engaged therein. He said he believed I meant well, and that he commended my principles, but he could not say he thanked me for my visit. I expected at times he would turn me out of the room. We rose from our seats to take our leave; when the bishop clasped my hand, and holding it, paused, saying, 'I believe I may say, I feel thankful for it' (the visit). Requesting us to take some refreshments, he kindly conducted us to the stairs again, and we parted, never more to meet on this side of eternity."

In the year 1811, Thomas Shillitoe was again engaged, still more extensively, in visiting the drinking-houses in some of those cities and towns in Ireland, which had before been omitted. In these, as at other times, he was concerned, not only to set before them the evil consequences of taking strong drink, but also to point out to them the sure way of life and salvation; with the absolute need there was of ceasing from all dependence on man, and of depending simply on the Lord alone for salvation. Many insults and reproaches were offered to him; but having an evidence in his own mind, that he was fulfilling a duty laid upon him by his Divine Master, he was carried through them all. He had indeed frequently the satisfaction of believing that the opportunities were signally owned; great seriousness and solemnity being obviously produced in minds often of the most abandoned persons.

A description of one of the six hundred visits he paid to the drinking-houses in the city of Dublin, will show the humiliating nature of the service, and the manner in which he was enabled to warn and exhort those whom he met with in those sinks of dissipation and vice. He says: "We proceeded to Barrack-street. The first house we entered made a deplorable appearance. It was very early in the morning; yet we found, on descending the steps into the drinking-room, which resembled a cellar, the window-frames and glass broken, and several young women, without shoes, stockings, or caps, dancing to the fiddle. We made towards the room set apart for the keepers of the house; where we met with the mistress. Requesting, if she had a husband, to have his company, he soon made his appearance. I endeavored to lay before them what arose, although

I found it difficult to get fairly relieved. The fiddle, and at times the screaming of the dancers, was a great interruption. The man remained quiet for a short time, and then left us, the woman appearing to have the management of the house. What I had to say brought her to tears. On inquiry, I found she had children; I therefore requested her seriously to consider what would be her conclusion respecting the conduct of any person who should harbor her children, and suffer them to go on in such wicked practices as she was now encouraging the young girls in under her roof, who might be without parents or friends to take charge of them; saying, I did not wish for a hasty reply. She confessed she should think they acted a cruel part. I therefore entreated her to attend to that Divine Monitor in her own breast, which she confessed she at times witnessed to be near; which would clearly make known to her the necessity to rid her house of such company as she now harbored; which would be one way whereby she might hope for the Divine blessing on honest endeavors for the support of herself and family; otherwise she must look for a blast following them every way. She continued tender, and at our parting, in a feeling manner expressed her desire, that what had been communicated might be profitably remembered by her. After receiving her warm expressions of gratitude, we proceeded to leave the house; but on reaching the step of the entrance, my attention was again arrested, and I found I must be willing to return into the apartment where the dancing was going forward, and quietly submit to any insults that might be the result of my being found in the way of my duty. On my companion being informed hereof, he appeared tried as well as myself; but I found it would not bring peace to our minds to hesitate. We therefore turned back; which the woman of the house observing, came and stood by us, I supposed to prevent any rude behavior that might be offered. I requested

the man who had the fiddle to cease playing and take his
seat; which he complied with; and those who were dancing
to do the like, which each one yielded to. The scene exhibited in different parts of this large room, if it were possible fully to describe, would produce a picture of as great
human depravity and misery, as well can be conceived. On
a bench near us lay young girls, overcome with their night's
revelling and drunkenness, past being roused by anything
that occurred around them; others, from the same causes,
reclining on the tables, barely able to raise their heads and
open their eyes, and altogether incapable of comprehending
what was going forward. Companies of men and women, in
boxes, were in other parts of the room drinking. Strength
was received to utter what was given me; and after I had
been some time engaged in addressing this band of human
misery, I think I shall not, whilst favored with mental
powers, wholly lose sight of the distress and horror portrayed
in the countenances of those young women who had ceased
their dancing. Feeling my mind relieved, and being about
to depart, such of the company as were equal to it, arose
from their seats, acknowledging their gratitude for the
labor that had been extended, and their desire that what
had been said might not be lost upon them, and that a
blessing might attend us. My back was towards the door,
and not hearing a footstep of those who came in while we
were engaged, when we turned to go out, I was surprised
at the addition made to our company. My companion remarked, that it appeared as if something brought an awe
over their minds on entering, and they quietly took their
seats, and when the seats were full, others sat on the
ground."

At the conclusion of these labors, he felt it required of
him to visit the mayor, sheriff, and police magistrates, as
well as the Romish and Protestant bishops, endeavoring to
lay before the Romish bishop in particular, the great re-

sponsibility that rested on him, from the implicit dependence which the people placed on the priesthood, and the sorrowful account those will have to give in a future day, who are encouraging the people in this reliance on themselves, instead of turning their attention to Christ within, the hope of glory.

In 1812, Thomas believed it required of him to unite with a female minister, in paying a religious visit to an organized company of desperate characters, who for nearly fifty years had infested the neighborhood of Kingswood, in England; who lived by plundering, robbing, horse-stealing, and other evil practices; and were so great a terror to the neighborhood, that it was considered dangerous to travel on the roads infested by them. In the prosecution of this trying service, which extended not only to "the Gang," as these robbers were called, but also to the families of miners and colliers living in that section of country, Thomas and his companion were often obliged to travel by night; but they were mercifully raised above apprehensions of danger, through faith in the protecting care of Him, who, they believed, had called them forth. They were favored from time to time, with memorable evidences of the sufficiency of His almighty power to subdue the strong wills, and soften the hard hearts of wicked men. While pleading with these abandoned characters respecting their evil practices, they were often made sensible that the Divine Witness in their hearts was reached; their hearers acknowledged the truth of what they had to say, and expressed their obligations for the counsel given.

CONCLUSION.

NO attempt has been made to embody the whole history of the Society of Friends in these few pages. Many volumes would be requisite to describe even a small portion of the gracious dealings of the Lord with his dependent children, and the wonderful instances of divine support vouchsafed to them in the hour of need. But in the view which we have briefly taken of the principal events characterizing the rise and progress of this people, the reader may have observed, that though exceedingly various were the natural dispositions and conditions of the individuals successively brought into the service of the Truth, yet the work of the Holy Spirit has been one and the same. In every instance, the operation of divine grace has been accompanied by a great abasement of self, a deep sense of the fallen and corrupt state of man, and a looking to the Lord alone for help and strength to overcome the evil propensities of the unregenerate nature. There has been a conviction that no half work would be accepted, but that the whole heart was to be cleansed and renewed, and the whole mind and will made submissive to the manifestations of the light of Christ Jesus in the soul.

We have seen the faithfulness of many of these servants of the Lord, and observed that their devoted lives furnished conclusive evidence that they knew and felt the force of the apostolic precept: "Ye are not your own, for ye are bought with a price; therefore glorify God in your bodies and in your spirits, which are God's." We have also remarked the marvellous manner in which they were preserved and supported in the hour of trial, and the futility of all attempts to suppress the growth of the plant of the Lord's planting, by the most severe and sanguinary persecution. We have likewise, on the other hand, had sorrowful evidence that this Society has not been without its troubles from false brethren, by whom, under various specious disguises, the great enemy of Truth has striven to divide and scatter the flock.

In this day of outward ease, that cunning adversary has changed his mode of attack; the spirit of the world, in its various transformations, is now the chief snare laid for the feet of the unwary; and many have fallen a prey to its entanglements. But it is surely not arrogating too much, to encourage the belief that the same Hand which brought this vine out of Egypt and planted it, will still watch over His own seed, will water it with the dew of heaven, and preserve its fruits to his own praise.

It ought to be borne in mind, that the enlightened men and women who were employed of the Lord in gathering our religious Society in the beginning, were fully persuaded that they were not collecting together a mere sect or division of the Christian church; but that the principles which they advocated, being no other than those of ancient pure Christianity, were designed by the Almighty, in a time to come, to extend over the whole earth. This was unquestionably their belief, and this belief animated them through all discouragements, to press forward in their endeavors to spread the glorious gospel in its own simplicity and purity. Several of the testimonies held forth by ancient Friends, have since their day found a remarkable place in the estimation of serious individuals of various names; and it remains to be seen, whether the faithfulness of a future generation shall not be made use of in the divine Hand, to spread the knowledge of the truth over the lands as the waters cover the sea.

Should this be happily the case through the medium of this highly favored people, it is scarcely needful to say, that it must be by an uncompromising adherence to the ancient principles of the church, and a practical exemplification of their efficacy, in life and conduct. Divine truth is the same in the present day, as it was when the apostles went forth in the power of the Spirit of their Divine Master; and as it was when George Fox and his fellow-laborers, in a measure of the same spirit, boldly testified against spiritual wickedness in high places. And the same necessity exists, as ever did, for the faithful maintenance of their testimony to pure and spiritual religion, in the face of a world lying in wickedness, or lulled in the lap of error, disguised under the plausible appearance of truth.

Let then the inheritors of these precious principles examine well their position, and see that they fall not back from that holy vocation wherewith their fathers were called. Let them not desire to dwell in their ceiled houses, while the house of God lies waste: but with holy magnanimity and true devotedness of heart, and in the pure Christian zeal of the Lord's own begetting, individually seek to know their calling, and therein abide.

THE END.

NOTICE TO THE READER.

THE author, in preparing this work for a second edition, has believed it best to close the volume with the beginning of the present century; leaving to the pen of future history the delineation of the important events connected with the two great manifestations of defection from the faith of our forefathers, which have occurred in our own day.

www.ingramcontent.com/pod-product-compliance
Lightning Source LLC
Chambersburg PA
CBHW050846300426
44111CB00010B/1142